THE MEDIEVAL NETWORKS IN EAST CENTRAL EUROPE

Medieval Networks in East Central Europe explores the economic, cultural, and religious forms of contact between East Central Europe and the surrounding world in the eight to the fifteenth century. The sixteen chapters are grouped into four thematic parts: the first deals with the problem of the region as a zone between major power centers; the second provides case studies on the economic and cultural implications of religious ties; the third addresses the problem of trade during the state formation process in the region, and the final part looks at the inter- and intraregional trade in the Late Middle Ages.

Supported by an extensive range of images, tables, and maps, *Medieval Networks in East Central Europe* demonstrates and explores the huge significance and international influence that East Central Europe held during the medieval period and is essential reading for scholars and students wishing to understand the integral role that this region played within the processes of the Global Middle Ages.

Balázs Nagy is Associate Professor of Medieval History at Eötvös Loránd University, Budapest and visiting faculty at the Department of Medieval Studies at the Central European University, Budapest. His main research interests are medieval economic and urban history.

Felicitas Schmieder is Professor of Premodern History at FernUniversität Hagen. Her main research interests are the history of cross-cultural contacts, urban history, cultural memory, and pre-modern cartography.

András Vadas is Assistant Professor of Medieval History at Eötvös Loránd University, Budapest. His research interests are the environmental, urban, and economic history of the Middle Ages and the Early Modern period.

THE MEDIEVAL NETWORKS IN EAST CENTRAL EUROPE

Commerce, Contacts, Communication

Edited by Balázs Nagy, Felicitas Schmieder, and András Vadas

Routledge
Taylor & Francis Group

LONDON AND NEW YORK

First published 2019
by Routledge
2 Park Square, Milton Park, Abingdon, Oxon OX14 4RN

and by Routledge
711 Third Avenue, New York, NY 10017

Routledge is an imprint of the Taylor & Francis Group, an informa business

© 2019 selection and editorial matter, Balázs Nagy, Felicitas Schmieder, and András Vadas; individual chapters, the contributors

British Library Cataloguing in Publication Data
A catalogue record for this book is available from the British Library

Library of Congress Cataloging in Publication Data
Names: Nagy, Balázs, editor. | Schmieder, Felicitas, editor. | Vadas, András, editor.
Title: The medieval networks in East Central Europe: commerce, contacts, communication / edited by Balázs Nagy, Felicitas Schmieder, and András Vadas.
Description: Abingdon, Oxon; New York, NY : Routledge, 2019. |
Includes bibliographical references.
Identifiers: LCCN 2018017473 | ISBN 9781138554849 (hardback: alk. paper) | ISBN 9781138554856 (paperback : alk. paper) | ISBN 9781315149219 (ebook)
Subjects: LCSH: Europe, Central–History–To 1500. |
Europe, Eastern–History–To 1500. | Civilization, Medieval. | Middle Ages.
Classification: LCC DAW1046 .M45 2019 | DDC 943.7/022–dc23
LC record available at https://lccn.loc.gov/2018017473

ISBN: 978-1-138-55484-9 (hbk)
ISBN: 978-1-138-55485-6 (pbk)
ISBN: 978-1-315-14921-9 (ebk)

Typeset in Bembo
by Out of House Publishing

CONTENTS

FIGURES

MAPS

TABLES

ACKNOWLEDGMENTS

Many of the papers published here were read at the first conference organized by the Medieval Central European Network (MECERN), held in Budapest at the Central European University in 2014. The papers read at this conference are published in two separate volumes, the first of which has been edited by Gerhard Jaritz and Katalin Szende (*Medieval East Central Europe in a Comparative Perspective: From Frontier Zones to Lands in Focus*. New York: Routledge, 2016). Their volume provided the framework for the present, second, volume. We are thankful to the editors of the first volume for helping with the proposal for this volume.

Most of the chapters were submitted by the authors in English. Wojciech Kozłowski translated the contribution of Grzegorz Myśliwski, for which the editors are grateful. András Vadas translated the contribution of Bence Péterfi. We would like to express our gratitude to Karen Stark for proofreading Bence Péterfi's and Beata Możejko's contributions. Judith Rasson provided the English proofreading for all the other contributions. Her careful reading and comments far exceeded a language proof, for which we are grateful.

We are thankful to Routledge for providing financial help for part of the proof reading as well as to our editor at the publisher, Laura Pilsworth, for her patience.

The editors

NOTES ON CONTRIBUTORS

Dariusz Adamczyk is a researcher at the German Historical Institute in Warsaw in a project about monetization and commercialization in the Middle Ages funded by the Deutsche Forschungsgemeinschaft and teaches the history of Eastern Europe at Leibniz University of Hannover. He is author of the book *Silber und Macht. Fernhandel, Tribute und die piastische Herrschaftsbildung in nordosteuropäischer Perspektive (800–1100)* (Wiesbaden, 2014) and co-editor (together with Stephan Lehnstaedt) of *Wirtschaftskrisen als Wendepunkte. Ursachen, Folgen und historische Einordnungen vom Mittelalter bis zur Gegenwart,* (Osnabrück, 2015) and with Norbert Kersken of *Fernhändler, Dynasten, Kleriker. Die piastische Herrschaft in sozialen und kontinentalen Beziehungsgeflechten vom 10. bis zum frühen 13. Jahrhundert* (Wiesbaden, 2015).

Florin Curta is professor of Medieval History and Archaeology at the University of Florida. His main research interests are the history and archaeology of the early medieval Balkans and East Central Europe, but he has published extensively on many topics of medieval history and archaeology. His books include *The Making of the Slavs: History and Archaeology of the Lower Danube, ca. 500–700* (Cambridge, 2011), which received the Herbert Baxter Adams Award of the American Historical Association; and *Southeastern Europe in the Middle Ages, 500–1250* (Cambridge, 2006). Curta is the editor of five collections of studies, and the editor-in-chief of Brill's series *East Central and Eastern Europe in the Middle Ages, 450–1450.*

Matthias Hardt is honorary professor for the early history and archaeology of Central Europe at Leipzig University. His research focuses on the trade networks and circulation of coins in early medieval Central Europe. He is the author of the monograph *Gold und Herrschaft. Die Schätze europäischer Könige und Fürsten im ersten Jahrtausend* (Berlin, 2004) and co-editor of numerous volumes on the archaeology of the early medieval period in Central Europe.

Matthew Koval is a PhD candidate at the University of Florida and received his MA from that university in 2014. He has presented his research at the International Medieval Congress at Kalamazoo and the CEU-sponsored "Forgotten Region" conference in Budapest. He is the author of an article in *Medieval and Early Modern Studies for Central and Eastern Europe* and of several entries in *Great Events in Religion: An Encyclopedia of Pivotal Events in Religious History*. His dissertation topic is childhood and growing up in the minds of medieval people.

Beata Możejko is Professor of the Medieval History of Poland and Auxilliary Sciences of History at the University of Gdańsk. Her main field of interest is the history of late medieval Gdańsk and the Hanseatic League. She also focuses on the study of medieval society and King Kazimierz Jagiellończyk of Poland. In her recent monograph, she presents *Peter von Danzig– the Story of a Great Caravel, 1462–1475* (2011). She is also co-editor of the volumes: *The Natural History of Food. Between Ancient Times and the Nineteenth Century* (2012); *Catalogue of Documents and Letters of the Kings of Poland. From the State Archive in Gdańsk (to 1492)* (2014), and *In the Era of Sailing Ships. Sea Between Ancient Times and the Eighteenth* Century (2015).

Sergiu Musteață is Professor at the History and Geography Faculty of Ion Creangă Pedagogical State University in Chisinau, Moldova. He holds a PhD in history from Alexandru Ioan Cuza University in Iași. He is a former Fulbright research fellow at the University of Maryland, OSI scholar at the University of California-Berkeley, Stanford University, and Central European University. He was DAAD and Humboldt Foundation fellow at the RGK (the German Archaeological Institute), and has been visiting professor at Bonn, Freiburg, and Braunschweig universities. He is the author of seven monographs, more than 200 scientific publications, editor of over 20 books, as well as the editor of two journals. His major academic interests are the archaeology and history of the Eastern Europe, cultural heritage preservation, and textbook analysis.

Grzegorz Myśliwski is Associate Professor at the Institute of History at Warsaw University. His research focuses on the socio-cultural and economic history of East Central Europe (especially on long-distance trade). He has written two monographs: *Człowiek średniowiecza wobec czasu i przestrzeni. Mazowsze od XII do połowy XVI wieku* [Medieval man towards time and space. The Masovia Region from the 12th to the mid-16th century] (Warsaw, 1999) and *Wrocław w przestrzeni gospodarczej Europy (XIII–XV wiek). Centrum czy peryferie?* [Wrocław in the economic space of Europe between the 13th and the 15th century. Core or periphery?] (Wrocław, 2009).

Balázs Nagy is Associate Professor of Medieval History at Eötvös Loránd University and visiting faculty member at the Department of Medieval Studies at the Central European University, Budapest. His main research interest is the medieval economic and urban history of Central Europe. He is co-editor with Frank Schaer of the Latin-English bilingual edition of the autobiography of Emperor Charles IV (Budapest, 2001), has edited with Derek Keene and Katalin Szende, *Segregation – Integration – Assimilation: Religious and Ethnic Groups in the Medieval Towns of Central and Eastern Europe* (Farnham, 2009), and with Martyn Rady, Katalin Szende, and András Vadas *Medieval Buda in Context* (Leiden and Boston, 2016).

Mária Pakucs-Willcocks is a senior researcher at the "Nicolae Iorga" Institute of History in Bucharest, Romania. She defended her PhD in 2004 at the Central European University in Budapest, and her dissertation was published as a monograph: *Sibiu-Hermannstadt. Oriental Trade in Sixteenth Century Transylvania* (Cologne, 2007). Her research interests include trade and merchants in the Ottoman Balkans and the social and economic history of Transylvanian towns in the Early Modern period.

Bence Péterfi is Research Fellow of Medieval History at the Research Centre for the Humanities, Institute of History of the Hungarian Academy of Sciences, Budapest. His main interest lies in the political and social history of Central Europe in the Late Middle Ages, especially the relations between Austria and Hungary. He has published a book on the career of a late medieval condottiere of the Hungarian king, Matthias Corvinus (*Egy székely két élete. Kövendi Székely Jakab pályafutása* [Two lives of a Szekler man: The career of Jakab Székely of Kövend], Pécs, 2014) and co-edited of three volumes of the book series *Micae mediaevales* with Judit Gál, Zsófia Kádár, Gábor Mikó, and András Vadas (Budapest, 2012–2013).

Christian Raffensperger is Associate Professor of History at Wittenberg University, as well as an Associate of the Harvard Ukrainian Research Institute. He has published multiple books, including *Reimagining Europe: Kievan Rus' in the Medieval World* (Berlin, 2012) and *Ties of Kinship: Genealogy and Dynastic Marriage in Kyivan Rus'* (Cambridge, MA, 2016). He is also the series editor for *Beyond Medieval Europe*, a book series published by ARC Humanities Press.

Sébastien Rossignol is Assistant Professor in the Department of History at Memorial University, Newfoundland and Labrador. He is the author of a monograph on early urbanization in Central Europe (*Aux origines de l'identité urbaine en Europe centrale et nordique*, Turnhout, 2013) and co-editor of several collected volumes dedicated to the interdisciplinary study of medieval Europe east of the Elbe. In addition, he is interested in the history of Slavic tribes in the Elbe area in the Carolingian age and has written articles on the Linons, the Dalemincians, and the text of the so-called Bavarian Geographer.

Felicitas Schmieder Professor of Premodern History ("Geschichte und Gegenwart Alteuropas") at FernUniversität Hagen since 2004 and recurrent Visiting Professor at the Department of Medieval Studies, Central European University (Budapest).

Her main research interests are medieval cross-cultural contacts and perceptions, prophecy as political language, medieval German urban history, pre-modern cartography, and, most recently, European cultural memory. She has authored a number of monographs, amongst others *Europa und die Fremden. Die Mongolen im Urteil des Abendlandes vom 13.–15. Jahrhundert* (Sigmaringen, 1994), *Johannes von Plano Carpini, Kunde von den Mongolen (1245–1247)* (Sigmaringen, 1997), and edited with Marianne O'Doherty *Travels and Mobilities in the Middle Ages. From the Atlantic to the Black Sea. Collected Papers of the IMC Leeds 2010, "Travel and Exploration"* (Turnhout, 2015).

Daniel Syrbe is Post-Doctoral Researcher in the NWO research project "Constraints and Tradition" at Radboud University in Nijmegen, the Netherlands. His research interests are in the field of political and cultural transitions between Late Antiquity and the Early Middle Ages. In his current project he explores how societies and politics in this period were shaped by traditions originating from a Roman imperial past and how these traditions were transformed over time. Together with Orsolya Heinrich-Tamáska, Ivan Bugarski, and Vujadin Ivanišević he co-edited a volume on the transformation of the middle Danube area between Late Antiquity and the Middle Ages (*GrenzÜbergänge*, 2016). He has also studied the interrelations between nomadic and sedentary people in late Roman and Byzantine North Africa and at the lower Danube.

András Vadas is Assistant Professor of Medieval History at Eötvös Loránd University (Budapest) from where he holds a PhD. His research interest is the environmental and economic history of the Middle Ages and the Early Modern period. His works discuss the problem of the environmental change brought about by military activities in the Carpathian Basin as well as mills and milling in medieval Hungary. His monograph *Körmend és a vizek. Egy település és környezete a kora újkorban* (Körmend and the waters. A settlement and its environment in the Early Modern period) was published in 2013; he co-edited *Medieval Buda in Context* with Balázs Nagy, Martyn Rady, and Katalin Szende (Leiden and Boston, 2016).

Mária Vargha is Research Assistant at the Institute of History at the University of Vienna and PhD candidate at the Central European University, Budapest. Her research interest is the material culture of the High Middle Ages, the archaeology of religion, and the Christianization of East Central Europe. Her work also deals with GIS analysis of archaeological data and socioeconomic and religious processes focusing mostly on the Carpathian Basin. She has published a monograph entitled: *Hoards, Grave Goods, Jewellery: Objects in Hoards and in Burial Contexts during the Mongol Invasion of Central-Eastern Europe* (Budapest, 2015).

Roman Zaoral is Senior Lecturer in Medieval History at the Faculty of Humanities, at Charles University in Prague. His research in the field of monetary and financial history concerns medieval trade and cultural exchanges between Venice and

Bohemia, the collecting of papal tithes in Central Europe, taxation of late medieval towns, the ready money of pilgrims, and the circulation of gold in Italy. He also participated in the international project entitled *Fuchsenhof hoard Der Schatzfund von Fuchsenhof* (2004). He recently edited the volume: *Money and Finance in Central Europe during the Later Middle Ages* (Basingstoke, 2016).

INTRODUCTION

History writing has always been influenced by the biases historians apply automatically – necessarily taking the perspective of their own time and place. Scholars have usually treated East Central Europe, if at all, as somewhere between three regions (the West, Byzantium, and Russia/the Central Asian steppes), a dead end, a road or, at best, a region of passage. In the second half of the twentieth century, not the least due to the influence of the Cold War, the medieval East and West were judged to be completely separate from each other. What can historically be defined as Central Europe – the regions between the Rhine (with its German urban culture) in the West and the rim of the expansion of Latin Christianity on the east – was torn apart politically and its role in historical processes was not considered. In the last quarter of the twentieth century, however, shortly before the regime changes in East Central Europe and the fall of the Iron Curtain around 1990, both historians and the general public inside and outside the region began to devote increasing attention to East Central Europe, that is, east of the cultural region of Central Europe.

This has helped the region reinforce its identity in the European context; scholarship in Western and West Central Europe has benefited from a broadening of the framework of investigations.[1] Now, half a generation later, the framework has shifted once again and European history is seeking its place within a new conceptualization of the "Global Middle Ages" that is on the agenda worldwide. One trend is that specific attention is turning towards regions that are usually considered somewhere on the margins. Researchers are using different conceptual frameworks – frontier regions, interregional, and global contacts – instead of national histories. They are focusing more and more on spaces in between and looking for regions that serve as bridges.

Among the first attempts to broaden the focus were those looking at seas: the Mediterranean Sea, the North Sea, the Atlantic Ocean, but also the Baltic Sea and the Black Sea as centers of cultural regions instead of barriers between them.[2]

Scholars began to examine vast lands such as deserts and steppes with seemingly few cultural achievements. This has led most importantly – for the topic of this volume – to utilizing the benefits of comparative Eurasian history and demonstrating contacts between (Western) Europe, the Middle East, and China, mostly through the vast network usually called the "Silk Road". Nevertheless, East Central Europe – neither a cultural center nor a typical transition zone in the sense just mentioned – continued to be ignored and global historians seldom took into account the results of research on the region.[3] It is time that the region is examined seriously as a contact zone between global regions, and at the same time as a microcosm of the contacts that enabled global contact and the resulting exchange. What kinds of persons, ideas, institutions, cultural and material goods found their way to other parts of the world from East Central Europe or through the mediation of this region? What motivated such transfers and interactions?

In the past few years, new initiatives have aimed at understanding how much historians of the Middle Ages can benefit from engaging in global history.[4] A number of research fields – climate and disease history, material culture studies, the history of communications, the history of symbols and gestures, migration history, frontier studies, and others – have benefitted from integrating the results of research on Sub-Saharan Africa, the Americas, and Australia in comparative studies.[5] In most of these works, however, East Central Europe never took on major importance, perhaps because of the variable national historiographies and regional languages. So how can considering this region contribute to or challenge a new interpretation of the Middle Ages beyond its traditional limits in space and time and beyond the established conceptual schemes?

As this volume aims at demonstrating, in the past decade, thanks to a growing number of written sources accessible to scholars as well as numerous archaeological excavations and new techniques, significant results have been achieved in better understanding the relationships between medieval East Central Europe and the rest of the world as well as the connections within the region itself. In order to communicate the research results of recent decades a new network was founded in March 2014, the Medieval Central European Research Network (MECERN).[6] The aim of the MECERN is to create a common platform for historians of medieval Central Europe to think in non-national narratives, to integrate the research results of neighboring countries. The first conference of the new initiative was held in Budapest in 2014, organized by the Central European University. The conference – *A Forgotten Region? East Central Europe in the Global Middle Ages* – demonstrated that there is considerable interest in the region and the need for a better understanding of the region in the context of the Global Middle Ages. The first step in this process was to develop a clear picture of East Central Europe as a historical region. A number of papers were dedicated to this issue at the conference, and many of them have been published recently in the volume edited by Gerhard Jaritz and Katalin Szende (*Medieval East Central Europe in a Comparative Perspective: From Frontier Zones to Lands in Focus.* New York: Routledge, 2016).

The other main problem the conference addressed was briefly noted above: the problem of East Central Europe as a region of transfer in the Middle Ages, a contact zone. The essays in this volume apply the theoretical framework provided by the studies of the volume edited by Jaritz and Szende to discuss this issue and show that the region was anything but a no man's land in the Middle Ages. It had a wide range of connections – cultural, political, economic, religious, and many others – with all the surrounding regions. These studies not only touch upon external connections, but also aim to illuminate the intraregional connections and demonstrate how close these connections were in different periods of the Middle Ages.

János M. Bak, in his short reflections written as an epilogue to the volume by Jaritz and Szende, came to the conclusion that "it is to be hoped that the alleged special character of the region will vanish and merge into an all-European (or even global) view of the past."[7] The entanglement of the polities and economies of East Central Europe with other powers of Eurasia leaves little doubt that in the long term the histories of East Central Europe will be organic parts of the histories of medieval Europe, Asia, the Mediterranean, Eurasia, and so on. The different chapters of this volume move towards understanding the nature of these economic, cultural, and religious connections.

The papers are grouped in four main thematic units. The first group deals with the problem of the region as a zone between major power centers in the Middle Ages. This group of essays can be understood as an introduction to the area as a contact zone. Based on different sources, they all argue that East Central Europe and Europe as regions have to be constantly reconsidered and re-conceptualized. In different forms and based on diverse evidence – both written and archaeological – these papers argue that what was outside and what was inside Europe has changed constantly not only in the modern scholarly and political perception but even in the perception of the medieval West.

In his paper, Christian Raffensperger re-thinks the static understanding of medieval Europe. He emphasizes the need for a more dynamic conceptualization of medieval European history with borders open to other regions, ideas, and cultures. His paper calls for looking towards the East in order to 'create a larger medieval Europe.' Expanding what medieval Europe is also means that historians have to open their eyes to areas and periods without literacy. Due to the lack of written sources, the early medieval history of the Carpathian-Danube region has to be written based solely on archaeological material and has therefore not been written in its own right at all until very recently. Sergiu Musteață has assembled a synopsis of the results of settlement archaeology and started constructing a map of a "region without history" that still shows gaps to be filled by further research. The Slavs have always been considered one of the "youngest" European peoples, not the least because they started to produce their own written sources only relatively late in the High Middle Ages, and also because they seem to have been mostly overlooked by Western contemporaries.[8] Sébastien Rossignol shows the prominent place Slavic groups had on the mental map of an early ninth-century world chronicle written in southern Gaul, demonstrating that medieval Europe was not as divided as is conceived by many modern historians. The steppes, especially the steppes "beyond" East Central Europe, have been considered a cultureless region where civilization ends and where no one wants to go anyway. By re-evaluating this bias among Western historians and showing the nomadic lifestyle of medieval Westerners as well as the cultural achievements of nomads, Felicitas Schmieder tries to enhance the meaning of Central Europe as a transmitter of modern world historical research.

The second thematic group offers case studies on the economic and cultural implications of religious ties. If East Central Europe is not only a region of passage but a region where traditions (from having been inside or outside the Roman Empire) and influences from all sides formed a distinct culture worth looking at, then it is especially interesting to look at traditional Christianity or Christianization between East and West and the cultural, social, and technological changes that came with it. Daniel Syrbe looks at the transition period between Late Antiquity and the Early Middle Ages, examining letters that Pope Gregory the Great, as bishop of Rome, sent to the region (Dalmatia and Illyricum) in order to understand the means by which Rome tried to bring its bishops under control. The role of legal arguments as well as customs and tradition can be identified as tools not necessarily effective immediately, but important for later periods that referred to Gregory's authority. Florin Curta and Matthew Koval examine radical changes in the burials of children and possibly funeral rites in two different regions of East Central Europe with different traditions and different outside influences – Hungary and Poland – in a period when Christianization took place. While it is difficult to pinpoint the influence of Christianization on social structures, the burials show that the very notion of family changed in both Poland and Hungary in the period of the appearance of Christianity. Medieval monasteries have generally been considered transmitters of civilization in the regions where they were established. András Vadas reviews material that seems to indicate that water mills came to East Central Europe together with Christianity around 1000 and shows that there is reason to doubt in principle whether the establishment of monasteries also brought water mills to the kingdoms of Hungary, Bohemia, and Poland. Mária Vargha is interested in the same period (the eleventh and twelfth centuries), the social basis of the organization of the network of parochial churches in Hungary, and looks specifically at their correlation with castle buildings. Mapping parish churches and castles shows a clear correlation that is worth comparing with what was called the *Eigenkirchen* system in the German-speaking lands of the Early and Early High Middle Ages.

The third group of essays addresses the problem of trade during the processes of state formation in the region. These studies argue that despite the relative shortage of written evidence, archaeological sources can significantly broaden the knowledge of contacts among the peoples of East Central Europe as well as between the region and outside polities in the fifth through the eleventh century. The authors of the third unit look at different ways the connections of East Central Europe with the outside world can be investigated during the period of state formation. Historians of East Central Europe, depending on the different political regimes in modern times, have emphasized different directions that seem to have had strong historical economic and political ties.

Dariusz Adamczyk looks at a direction perhaps the least emphasized in the national historiographies of the twentieth and twenty-first centuries, the link with the Islamic world. Adamczyk argues, based mostly on archaeological evidence, that a sophisticated and well-organized network was created among the tribal leaders of East Central Europe and Islamic merchants which contributed to the establishment of new elites in the states of East Central Europe. Matthias Hardt's contribution also touches on a rarely discussed area. He shows that Slavic princes and the Moravian Principality exchanged their subjects for silver through trade connections from North Africa to Central Asia. Bence Péterfi's paper also deals with the period of state formation. He looks at regional trade connections based on a rarely investigated type of evidence – pottery. Graphite pottery, a regional trade item not produced locally, has been recovered in great quantities at Óbuda (on the edge [or periphery] of present-day Budapest), one of the most important early economic and political centers of the Kingdom of Hungary. Péterfi shows that despite the lack of written sources on Hungary's trade relations at the time, archaeological data can contribute to understanding the relations of Hungary with other regions of Central Europe in the eleventh and twelfth centuries.

The last group of essays makes use of the significant amount of written evidence available on the inter- and intraregional trade of the countries of East Central Europe after the state foundation processes. This source material is somewhat different than those of the earlier periods; up to the twelfth or thirteenth century, as demonstrated by the essays in Part 3, most researchers use primarily archaeo-logical evidence when discussing inter- and intraregional trade connections. From the thirteenth century onwards, however, with literacy increasing in East Central Europe, written sources come to play a key role in the study of these connections. The essays in this section use mostly economic history sources – account books, customs registers – to provide an image of the connections Poland, Bohemia, and Hungary had with each other and the surrounding polities such as the Hanseatic towns, the Italian city-states, and the Ottoman Empire.

Roman Zaoral's paper discusses the effects of precious-metal mining and admin-istration in Bohemia and the roles Italian businessmen played in its formation. He argues that, on the one hand, Italian businessmen tried to get interests in mining and/or coinage of the precious metal extracted in the country, and, on the other hand, tried to collect taxes for the Papal Curia, which also proved to be a major source of income for some Italian families. Beata Możejko focuses on the role of one city, Gdańsk, as an intermediary between the Western, Hanseatic and East Central European areas, covering not only commercial but also political and dip-lomatic links. She argues that King Kazimierz Jagiellończyk (1446–1492) played a crucial role in the formation of these contacts. She demonstrates clearly the poten-tial of sources traditionally exploited by political history in the study of late medi-eval trade connections. Grzegorz Myśliwski also discusses the trade connections of a Polish town, Wrocław. He focuses on the town's links with Hungary in the Late

Middle Ages. Wrocław, one of the leading urban centers of the region, created a key hub of commercial contacts in the region. Myśliwski accessed a whole set of archival sources not utilized previously to reconstruct trade routes and lists of the most significant commercial goods. He shows that the town had extensive connections with Hungary and that merchants from all over the country frequented Wrocław for both buying and selling; the town's merchants entered Hungary on a regular basis to trade with different goods. In the last paper of this part Mária Pakucs-Willcocks investigates the appearance of two commercial goods, textiles, and spices, in the customs registers of Braşov and Sibiu at the turn of fifteenth century. Both towns, situated at the southeastern corner of medieval East Central Europe, played important roles in the transit trade with the Middle East. Pakucs-Willcocks demonstrates that these connections did not cease to exist later, when the Black Sea trade was controlled by the Ottomans.

In the final essay of this part, Balázs Nagy takes a historiographical approach. It is an often-repeated point in recent scholarship that the integration of this region into a wider European framework depended partly on its commercial contacts. Nagy reviews the historiography of the last decades on the trade contacts of East Central Europe with special attention to the approaches of the main handbooks that cover the economic history of this region. These perceptions vary from complete disregard through limited discussion to detailed analysis.

Balázs Nagy, Felicitas Schmieder and András Vadas

Notes

1 See most recently the excellent overview of Nora Berend on the problem: eadem, "The Mirage of East Central Europe: Historical Regions in a Comparative Perspective," in *Medieval East Central Europe in a Comparative Perspective. From Frontier Zones to Lands in Focus*, ed. Gerhard Jaritz and Katalin Szende (New York: Routledge, 2016), 9–23.

2 E.g., *Across the Mediterranean Frontiers: Trade, Politics and Religion, 650–1450* (International Medieval Research, 1), ed. Dionisius A. Agius and Ian Richard Netton (Turnhout: Brepols, 1997) and *Travels and Mobilities in the Middle Ages. From the Atlantic to the Black Sea*, ed. Marianne O'Doherty and Felicitas Schmieder (Turnhout: Brepols, 2015).

3 See, e.g., one of the pioneering attempts at a Eurasian history: Janet Abu-Lughod, *Before European Hegemony: The World System A.D. 1250–1350* (Oxford: Oxford University Press, 1989). See here 34, Fig. 1.

4 See the Defining the Global Middle Ages Research Network led by the University of Oxford (http://globalmiddleages.history.ox.ac.uk/) and the European Network in Universal and Global History organized at the Centre for Area Studies at the University of Leipzig (http://research.uni-leipzig.de/~eniugh/congress/about-eniugh/) and the workshops of both associations (both last accessed: 19 January 2017). See the thoughtful report of Catherine Holmes and Naomi Standen, "Defining the Global Middle Ages (AHRC Research Network AH/K001914/1, 2013–15)," on the Global Middle Ages Networks main research questions. Online document: www.medievalworlds.net/0xc1aa500e_0x00324b69.pdf (last accessed: 21 January 2017).

5 To name but a few important titles that indeed take a global approach in medieval studies: Bruce M. S. Campbell, *The Great Transition: Climate, Disease and Society in the*

Late-Medieval World (Cambridge: Cambridge University Press, 2016), *Universal Empire. A Comparative Approach to Imperial Culture and Representation in Eurasian History*, ed. Peter Fibiger Bang and Dariusz Kolodziejczyk (Cambridge: Cambridge University Press, 2012), *Grenzräume und Grenzüberschreitungen im Vergleich* (Europa im Mittelalter 7), ed. Klaus Herbers and Nikolas Jaspert (Berlin: Akademie, 2007), and *Migrationen im Mittelalter. Ein Handbuch*, ed. Michael Borgolte (Berlin and Boston: de Gruyter, 2014).

6 On MECERN (Medieval Central European Research Network), see http://mecern.eu (last accessed: 23 July 2017).

7 János M. Bak, "What did we learn? What is to be done? Some insights and visions after reading this book," in *Medieval East Central Europe*, 254–256, here 255.

8 See most importantly: Florin Curta, *The Making of the Slavs: History and Archaeology of the Lower Danube Region, c. 500–700 A.D.* (Cambridge Studies in Medieval Life and Thought, Fourth Series, 52) (Cambridge and New York: Cambridge University Press, 2001) and idem, *Southeastern Europe in the Middle Ages, ca. 500–1250* (Cambridge Medieval Textbooks, 39) (Cambridge and New York: Cambridge University Press, 2006).

PART ONE

East Central Europe – No Man's Land or Historical Region?

1

REIMAGINING EUROPE

An Outsider Looks at the Medieval East–West Divide

Christian Raffensperger

As the subject of this article is bias, intentional and otherwise, the best way to begin is to be open about my own identity and the perspective from which I am approaching the topic. Though it is possible to take such postmodern ideas too far, in this case, appraising one's audience of one's identity seems to be only good sense when discussing such fraught issues as those related to modern identity and the creation of historical narratives and regions. This particular framing of the article will result in often returning to a first person narrative that is rare in academic writing, but which better suits the points discussed here. First off, I am an American, though one who speaks more than one language and does care about history. This means that I am divorced in not just time but also space from the medieval past. None of the places where I lived or grew up had cathedrals built in the High Middle Ages or historic battlefields marking resistance against the Turks, Mongols, French or Russians. Second, but related, my roots as an American stretch back to the eighteenth century, thus despite my name I have no connections to Germany or Austria or any European kin. Third, I am comparatively young – I remember the Soviet Union, but it fell before I was in high school and I never visited there. I teach classes about Eastern Europe but I never experienced it, I have only read about it. By the time I got to college and then graduate school to begin my studies on medieval Europe there was no reason to think about a divided Europe and certainly no reason to project one back into the past. I offer all of this personal clarification by way of introducing my topic – an outsider (in many different ways) looking at the medieval European past and especially the medieval East–West divide.

My identity and the time in which I have lived have shaped my scholarship immensely. When I read Dimitri Obolensky's *Byzantine Commonwealth* in graduate school in the early 2000s, I found its framing completely obsolete.[1] It was clear to me then that he was using a Cold War mentality to project an East-West divide into the past. I wrote this in an article and subsequently it developed into the first chapter of my book, *Reimagining Europe*.[2] In *Reimagining Europe* I talked about a new way to envision Byzantium's influence on Europe as an ideal empire, hence the title of the chapter – "The Byzantine Ideal." Byzantine art, architecture, titulature, etc. was appropriated by people throughout medieval Europe, not just those who happened to fall to the east of Obolensky's medieval Iron Curtain. But even there I referenced, but did not pursue, the idea that it was not just medieval Europeans of East and West who appropriated from Byzantium, but others as well including the Turks, especially the sultanate of Rum.[3] Removing the idea of a divided Europe did not change the history of appropriation from Byzantium, but it did change the way I talked about it; moving from Obolensky's idea that it impacted solely Eastern Europe to seeing how Byzantium affected all of Europe. From this early engagement with the idea of projecting an East-West divide back into the past came my academic cause – to introduce to American medieval scholarship the idea that there was a kingdom of Rus' and that it (and the rest of eastern Europe) was part and parcel of the larger medieval world.

This is particularly a challenge because of the normative classroom portrayal of medieval Europe in higher education in the United States. The vast majority of medievalists are teaching survey classes that deal primarily with western Europe, and rarely (if ever) with anything to the east of the Rhine or Elbe Rivers.[4] One can examine this portrayal in a variety of ways, but here I will simply look at one textbook in some detail and then two others quite briefly to make the point. In 2012 the third edition of William Cook and Ronald Herzman's *Medieval World View* came out from Oxford University Press. This is a major university press, and is the third edition of a popular medieval history textbook for classroom use. Cook and Herzman do not deal with eastern Europe in the book in any specificity, instead continuing to perpetuate the idea of Obolensky's Byzantine Commonwealth and reading an East-West barrier back into history. For instance, in one mention they say that, "When we think of problems and misunderstandings within Europe today, we in large part think of tensions and conflicts that exist along the lines of Western and Byzantine spheres of influence, for example, the line between Poland and Russia or that between Croatia and Serbia."[5] Continuing the theme, they ascribe the violence in the Balkans to its place between Byzantium, the Latin world, and the Islamic world in the Middle Ages.[6] But even with these brief tidbits, this is virtually all there is to say about interactions with anything east of the Rhine River. Perhaps this lacuna is better illustrated in the maps that they provide in the book (included here as Maps 1.1, 1.2 and 1.3). The first map depicts that same divide between the Byzantine, Islamic, and "Western European" worlds (see Map. 1.1).

What defines "Western Europe," and what period this covers is in fact difficult to determine and is not clarified. One might guess roughly Merovingian due to the exclusion of Saxons from "Western Europe," but then the situation in the Italian peninsula is wrong, as is the situation in the Balkans. However, despite these still relatively major problems, the biggest problem is the gaping white space east of the Rhine, north and east of the Danube and north of the Black Sea. This does not improve in more detailed maps such as the one showing the Early Middle Ages (see Map 1.2).

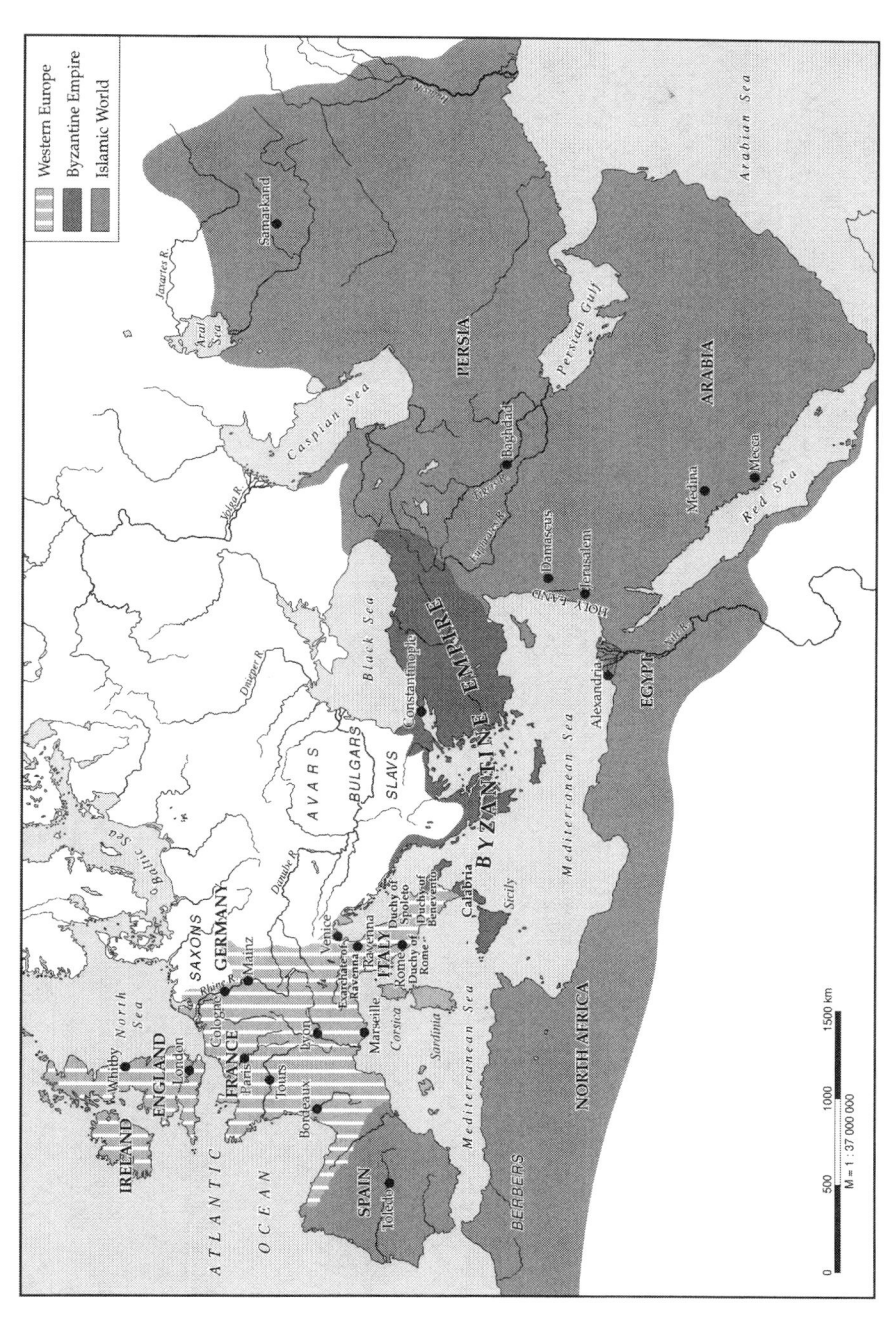

MAP 1.1　Europe, Byzantium, Islam (after Cook and Herzman, *The Medieval World View*, drawn by Béla Nagy)

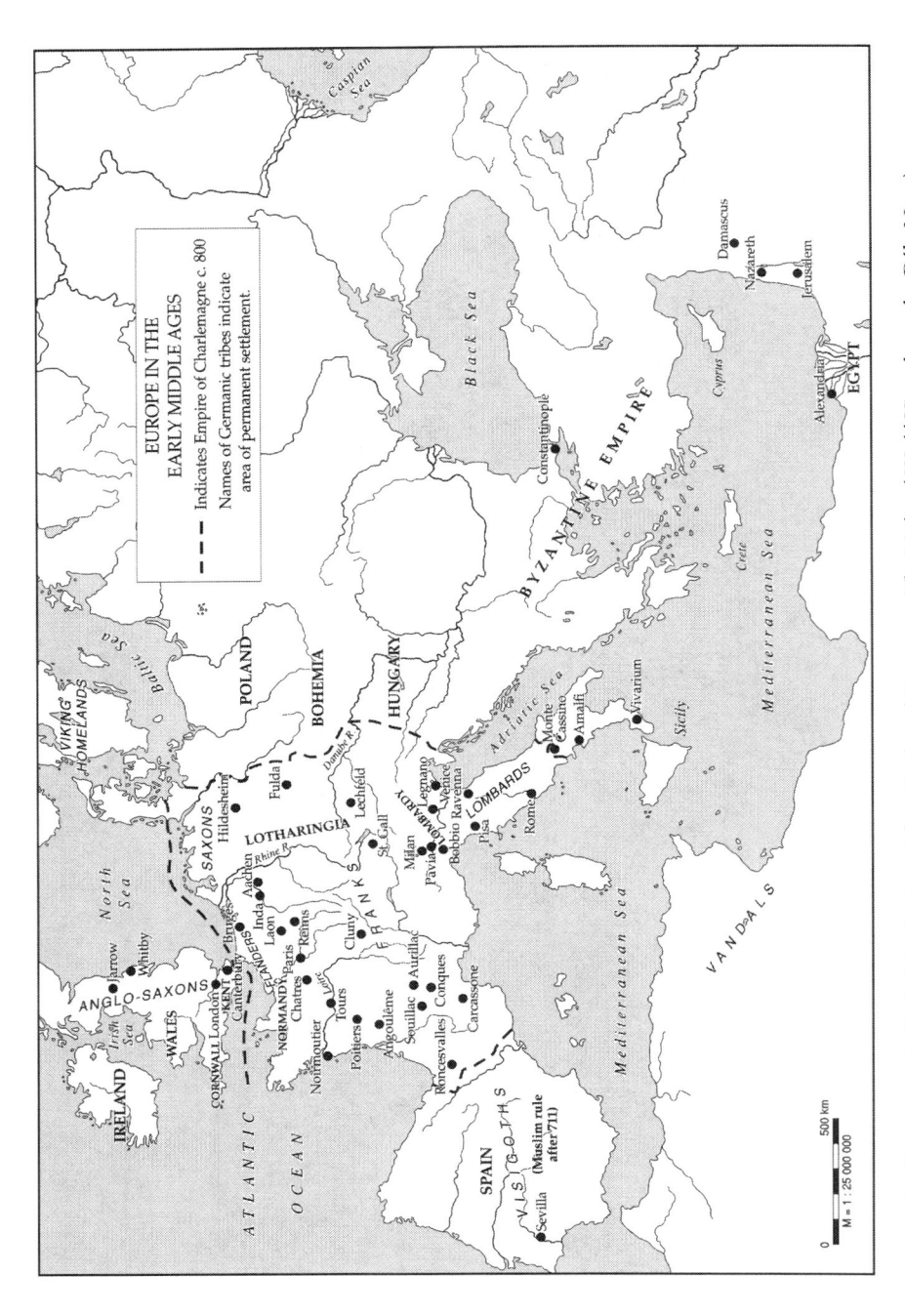

MAP 1.2 Europe in the Early Middle Ages (after Cook and Herzman, *The Medieval World View*; drawn by Béla Nagy)

In this map, the empire of Charlemagne is indicated, but so are Poland, Bohemia, and Hungary, though Rus' is left out. There is clearly a rich urban existence among the Franks, where there are two dozen cities important enough to be named, while east of the Elbe there is not a single city worthy of recognition, and in the entire Byzantine Empire, Constantinople is the only city worth putting on the map.

The entire eastern half of Europe fares no better in the High Middle Ages (see Map 1.3). The cities have multiplied in France and England, but the anachronistically named Holy Roman Empire has seen a reduction in cities and the enormous labels of Poland, Bohemia, and Hungary are gone, but at least Prague is now labeled, though it is entirely alone on the eastern half of the European portion of the map. The authors have gone to the trouble to choose a map which includes eastern Europe, and even has the full hydrography for it, in fact the eastern portion of Europe takes up a full page in the book, yet there is virtually nothing on that page barring the labels for the Adriatic Sea, the Black Sea, the Mediterranean Sea, and five cities spread out throughout Europe, Asia, and Africa.

I have chosen *The Medieval World View* to pick on here, but reviewing other popular textbooks reveals some of the same problems. Both Barbara Rosenwein and Lynette Olson in their textbooks use the framework of the Byzantine Commonwealth to talk about Rus' for instance.[7] Though they do at least talk about Rus', Byzantium, and some of the other parts of eastern Europe, they do so in such a way that emphasizes their difference rather than their similarity. They are often sectioned off and their mentions are to prove a later point, for instance Olson says, "The elevation of Slavic into a sacred and written language, subsequently spreading with the conversion of Serbia and Russia, was of immense cultural significance, for it buttressed Slavic culture in the areas most to be affected by the later Mongol and Turkish invasions."[8] While this comment is not necessarily factually incorrect, Olson does not use events in western European history to prove points about later events, but for eastern Europe, that seems to be the point of the inclusion of the information. Generally, it is not much, if any, of an exaggeration to say that this is a largely accurate portrayal of the state of medieval European textbooks in the American higher educational system.

When medieval European history classes in American academia do leave western Europe, the focus is on topics like the Crusades, but only the crusades that go to the eastern Mediterranean, thus the presence of cities like Constantinople, Jerusalem, and Damascus on the High Middle Ages map, or to Iberia, which similarly has cities included (see Map 1.3). The Baltic Crusades involving Poland, Hungary, and Rus', the last as both participant and enemy, go almost entirely unremarked.[9] This is especially odd when they might well serve the pedagogical purpose of enshrining western European exceptionalism by highlighting those crusades as moments defining what is Western, or more broadly, Latin Europe, fighting against the non-Latin East. A similar moment, the Mongol invasion of Europe is often mentioned, but only as an attack by an eastern other. Béla IV's flight from Muhi and subsequent capture and ransom by a German duke is absent,

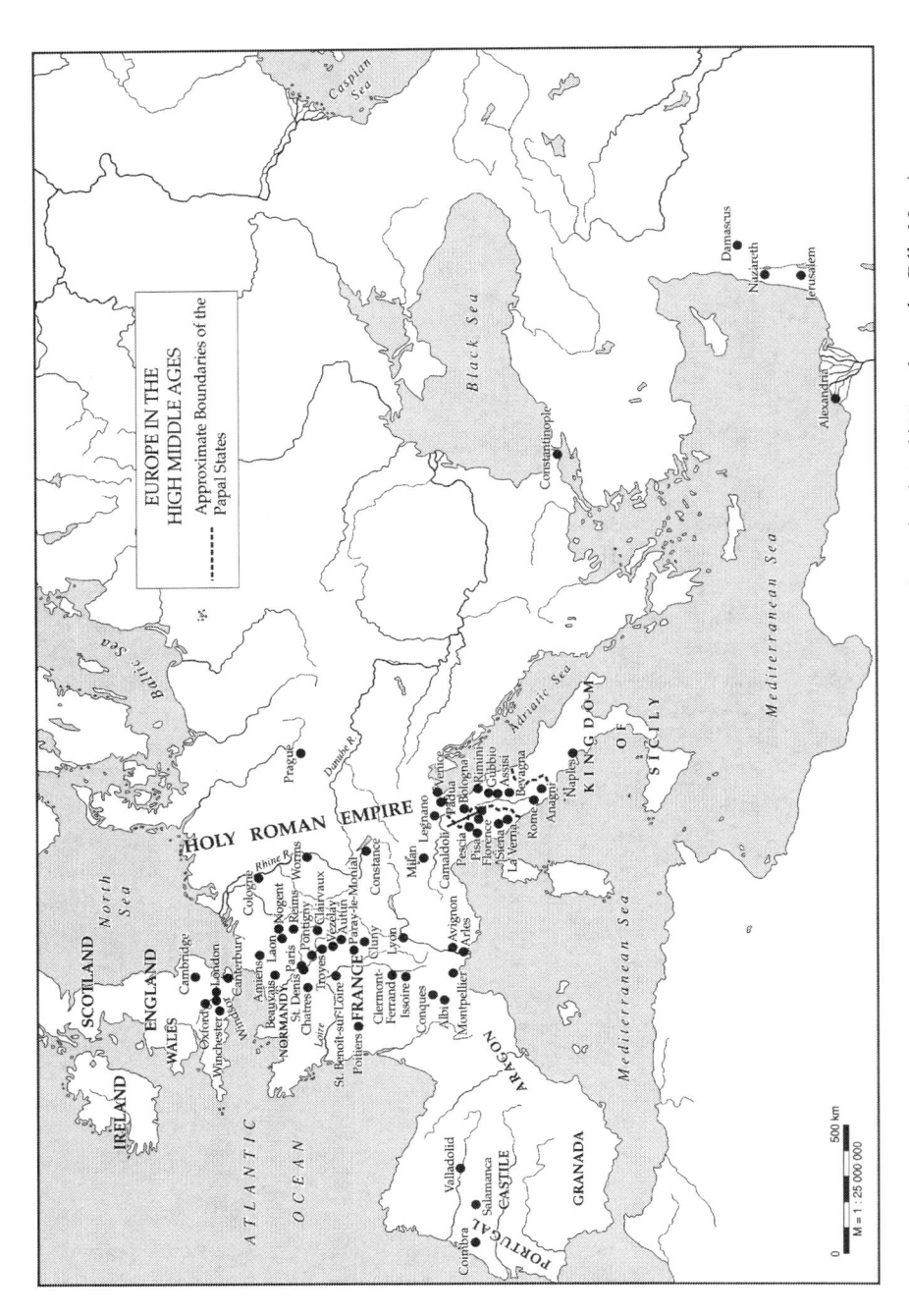

MAP 1.3 Europe in the High Middle Ages (after Cook and Herzman, *The Medieval World View*; drawn by Béla Nagy)

as is his letter defining Hungary as the Gate of Christendom which has been so well publicized in recent years by the excellent work of Nora Berend.[10] This too, the letter in particular, would work nicely to create the image of a line demarcating western medieval Europe as a distinct entity – the West; from eastern medieval Europe – the East. Of course, if those two markers were invoked (Béla's letter, and the Baltic Crusades), the boundary for western Europe would not be the Rhine but the Vistula and the steppe. Even with the traditional focus on England and France, interactions with the larger non-western European world are often left out. Just in regard to the themes already discussed, England and France work with the Mongols as part of various Crusades, including Louis IX of France and Edward I of England coordinating with the Mongol general Samaghar when planning an attack on the Mamelukes, earlier both Khan Berke and Hulegu wrote letters to Louis IX of France (each demanding or asking for very different things!), and there were even Mongol emissaries to both French and English kings seeking assistance.[11] These are fascinating, instructive, moments in medieval European history that demonstrate the breadth of that history and its interconnectivity with the rest of the world, but they are largely left out of traditional narratives in the classroom. I would suggest that this is because they do not fit a picture that has evolved little geographically (though it has evolved tremendously in areas such as theory and gender) in the last fifty years as far as the broad portrayal of the Middle Ages.

Changing that master narrative of medieval Europe as Western Europe has been the impetus for good scholarship in recent decades. Now, Iberia and the Mediterranean in general are very popular parts of the medieval European world to be studied. That work done by scholars such as Remie Constable changed Iberia from the periphery or solely part of the Islamic world to an integral part of the medieval European experience.[12] In the east, similar work has been done by Nora Berend and the incredibly productive Gábor Klaniczay, who has worked with the clear image in mind that Hungarian history was simply part of medieval history.[13] These changes have pushed the boundaries of medieval Europe in scholarly discourse, even if the trickle down to textbooks has not been achieved with any regularity. Now it is not entirely uncommon to hear discussion about Hungary, Bohemia, and even occasionally Poland at medieval history conferences.[14] However, with that piecemeal expansion of medieval Europe have come new divisions which continue to be exclusive, not inclusive. Recently, Nora Berend, Przemysław Urbańczyk, and Przemysław Wiszewski published *Central Europe in the High Middle Ages* with Cambridge University Press. This excellent book, which I have taught with myself,[15] is an incredibly welcome addition to the field and brings the medieval histories of Poland, Hungary, and Bohemia to the larger medieval studies community if they choose to read, or assign, this book.[16] Where the book has problems, and is seemingly self-conscious of those problems, is in its use of the label "Central Europe" to define these territories. Berend writes an exhaustive chapter surveying the literature on regional naming and stating several times explicitly that this label is not exclusive.[17] Yet, if the authors are correct in stretching medieval Europe to include Bohemia, Poland, and Hungary, but nothing else to the east, then what is left out is only Rus'. Drawing that firm boundary on the eastern periphery of those three medieval polities reflects modern politics, not medieval politics, in which modern Central Europe is eager to be identified as West and not East, the sole remaining occupant of which is the once-again expansionist Russia. When Berend, Urbańczyk, and Wiszewski write about the events of their High Middle Ages, they are as unable to keep Rus' out of the story as they are the German Empire. The criteria that they use to create a Central Europe apply to Rus' as well as to other medieval polities in the region. While we all have boundaries that we need to draw, as it is impossible to cover everything in our work, this one strikes me (and others such as Florin Curta) as too political.[18]

My proposal to correct this problem is not a radical solution, it is in fact quite simple – we should return to the primary sources and use them as our guide. Who do our primary sources talk about? How do they portray these various groups? What is their sense of geography and connectivity? If we just look at a couple of examples from the German Empire, which works nicely because it is near the geographic middle of medieval Europe, we can see the answers to some of these questions, as well as path toward further research. The first source is the late eleventh-century Adam of Bremen, and the second is the early eleventh-century Thietmar of Merseburg. Adam of Bremen will be discussed in more detail, though many of the same points can be made for both sources. Adam of Bremen conceived of a world in his *History of the Archbishops of Hamburg-Bremen* that included most of all of what is currently identified as medieval Europe, as well as much more.[19] Adam, who also tells us that his information comes from informants, which is a nice touch for historicity, conveys information about Iceland, Greenland, and even Vinland.[20] His concept of the world that he lives in is a broad one and to focus on his narrative helps us to see what his definitions of boundaries might be. For instance, he lends great weight to Christianity and its propagation, but that does not mean that he excludes non-Christian lands. His is the main reference for the pagan temple at Uppsala, whether we accept that information as accurate or not. He also provides geographical information to his readers, and that information includes the Slavic world. In his description of the Baltic he talks about the Slavs occupying the eastern shores of that sea, which he calls Scythian. He takes his readers on a tour of Slavia where he includes the Bohemians and Poles "because they differ neither in appearance nor in language."[21] He continues in this vein for some time narrating the various groups and says that Slavia stretches "clear to Bavaria, Hungary, and Greece."[22] He even includes Rus' in this description noting more cities than were included on the maps from the modern textbook – *Medieval World View* (see Maps 1.2 and 1.3). He says, famously, of Kiev that it was the "rival of the scepter of Constantinople, the brightest ornament of Greece."[23] Following Adam of Bremen, one gets a sense that his world is not constrained to a medieval Western Europe comprised of England, France, and the German Empire. He talks at length about Scandinavia, stretching as far as Scandinavian people have traveled, through the Baltic to Rus', down through eastern Europe to Byzantium, as well as all of the traditional western European territories. Looking at the primary source base, even just this one source, makes it clear that the picture provided in modern textbooks of medieval Europe is a false one not reliant on the picture provided by our primary sources.

Further, it is clear that Adam is not an outlier. If we look at the slightly earlier example of Thietmar of Merseburg, he too has the same broad perspective. Thietmar was writing in the early eleventh century, not the late, but he too talked about Scandinavia, eastern Europe, and Byzantium as well as the traditional territories of western Europe.[24] He in fact talked about Poland a lot because he truly did not care for Bolesław Chrobry, or his politics.[25] Thietmar's world was one in which the German Empire was as embroiled with France and the Italian peninsula as it was with the Poles and Bohemians and that comes through clearly in his narrative of people, places, and events.

Earlier I suggested that we should turn to the primary sources, but this too is a problem for many. Adam of Bremen may be well known, maybe even Thietmar of Merseburg, but not all medievalists know Cosmas of Prague or Henry of Livonia (despite the excellent translations into English by Lisa Wolverton and James Brundage, respectively),[26] not to mention the *Povest' vremennykh let* (inaccurately titled in its English translation as the "Russian Primary Chronicle"),[27] or even the array of sources for Poland and Hungary which Central European University Press has been putting out in excellent facing translations.[28] Yet this too has a relatively simple solution and that is to follow the narrative of the sources themselves. Do not exclude places that your chosen source talks about simply because they are not France and England or even because they are not in your research profile. This might seem like it could lead to a never-ending research project, but at least for familiarization purposes it is not a bad idea. Taking as a starting point the narrative of Adam of Bremen discussed above. If one starts with Adam, that could lead you to a text from Bohemia, a place which he discusses quite often, for instance, the work of Cosmas of Prague. Adam might also lead you to something on Poland, maybe Gallus Anonymus, something on Rus', Hungary, Byzantium, etc. From texts covering those areas, your research web could be extended even further. It is one thing to circumscribe a research area for a modern purpose and acknowledge it. In *Reimagining Europe*, I self-consciously noted that I was drawing a line to the east of Rus' and not pursuing topics further in that direction. I say self-conscious and I mean it in its variety of meanings.[29] I, in a good post-modern fashion, noted my shortcomings and biases as a historian for my audience. But I also mean that I felt, and feel, slightly bad about that choice. I had to stop somewhere and stopping there was part of my rhetorical point, but the story of interconnectivity does go further to the east. In a slightly earlier period than mine there is an excellent collection, published by Penguin, that has the Tale of Ibn Fadlan, but also includes excerpts from a variety of Arabic sources translated into English that also narrate events in eastern Europe involving the Khazars, Bulgars, Saqaliba, Rus', and others.[30] This wonderful collection extends the reach of medieval Europe even beyond Rus' and connects it further into Eurasia, all following the primary sources themselves and their vision of how interconnected the medieval world was.

The final step in this primary source-focused project is to rely on the primary sources to tell you what they know and not overwrite their ideas with modern ones. This is not a blanket statement that the primary sources should be trusted to the exclusion of all else, but we need to acknowledge that the sources are saying what they are saying. We can critique that material, analyze it, say it is biased, but it is better to at least try and accept it and deal with it on its own terms at the very least. To give only a couple of examples regarding titulature, a subject which I deal with in my own work,[31] Henry of Livonia narrated the Baltic crusades in Livonia from the perspective of a pro-German, if not German himself, Christian in or around Riga Bay and the Dvina River in the early thirteenth century. As part of his story he talks in some detail about not just the Germans who come to crusade, settle, and trade in the area, but the various groups of crusaders, the Danes and Swedes who come to the region, various Slavs, and the Rusians who are neighbors, occasional allies and often enemies. In his text, written in Latin, he uniformly uses the title *rex* for the Rusian rulers, all of whom are known in Rusian sources by the title *kniaz'*.[32] However, Brundage in his translation goes to some pains to point out the problem with this, adding editorial footnotes that say, "Vladimir was a Russian prince, not a king, as Henry calls him" or later, "Like the 'king' of Polozk, the 'king' of Gerzika was a Russian prince."[33] These editorial notes were, I would imagine, simply corrections in Brundage's mind, similar to when a primary source in tracing someone's descent mistakes a father's name for a grandfather's name or vice versa, and the editor of the text corrects it. However, these notes change meaning and perception and belie what Henry himself wrote. Henry, utilizing his knowledge of medieval titles, called these rulers "rex". This may not have been an informed choice based upon an in-depth study of medieval titulature, but he used it consistently, applying the same title to different individuals. The editorial lowering of the title from "king" to "prince" alters the meaning in the mind of the reader and thus reshapes the narrative that Henry created. If Henry is writing about a world where Rusian rulers are kings, this is a much different story than the one Brundage is telling where Rusian rulers are princes. Both the connotation and denotation of each word are different and affect the perception of the reader and they create in that reader's mind a different picture of the political playing field of medieval Europe.

The same thing happens at the southern end of Europe as well, with perhaps an even greater degree of bias. Don Ostrowski has gone through the sources for Rus' and pointed out that while the primary sources refer to the leaders of the nomadic steppe peoples almost uniformly as *kniaz'*, the same title by which those sources refer to the rulers of Rus'; in secondary sources, again almost uniformly, those same nomadic rulers are titled 'khan'.[34] This is not only ahistorical given the primary source base; it also lends a certain image to those rulers, invoking the Mongols at the very least. Florin Curta has done the same thing for what is often called the First Bulgar Empire in the Balkans.[35] The primary sources, he points out, have a wealth of titulature for the rulers of the Bulgars, including 'rex', 'basileus' and 'khagan'. However, in the secondary sources what appears almost without exception is khan. I have written and taught about the conversion of Khan Boris in the mid-ninth century. If we shift the focus back to the primary sources and use their language rather than our own, it would change the modern perception of these events. King Boris presents an immediately different mental picture than Khan Boris. King Boris negotiating with the king of the Franks, the emperor of Byzantium (or even king of Constantinople in Anthony Kaldellis's re-interpretation)[36] and the papacy, is on a much more equal footing than Khan Boris, who is seeking not just conversion but, implicitly, civilization from those neighbors.

Names and titles matter. Following the primary sources and what they called people is an important step in creating a more accurate picture of the medieval world or at least one that would be more familiar to the people who actually inhabited it.

In conclusion, what I have to offer here is that the image of medieval Europe is far too static in most regards. Academic scholarship has progressed by leaps and bounds in the last fifty years in developing the study of women, borderlands, interconfessional zones, and even expanding what might be included in Europe. But those changes are slow, almost glacially slow, to make their way into the common mental world of the average medievalist. I have used textbooks to illustrate this, but conversations with American medievalists could be distilled to the same purpose. They may see that there is an article on Byzantium, or more rarely medieval eastern Europe, in *Speculum*, the journal of the Medieval Academy of America, but oftentimes if the article is not on their specific area or an area they cover in teaching, they do not read it. And even if they do, they do not typically take that next step and then integrate that material into what they themselves are working on or teaching about. This point can be illustrated with an anecdote from my own experience. My first book, *Reimagining Europe*, won the Ohio Academy of History's Publication Award a few years ago and the organization assembled a panel to discuss the book as part of the award. To demonstrate the breadth of the book, they recruited a Byzantinist, a medievalist, and a Russianist, to discuss the book and its impact on their fields. For the medievalist they chose a scholar who works on medieval France. When medieval history colleagues saw the panel participants, they were shocked, "Why would a French medievalist read your book?" To truly create a new, larger, medieval Europe we need to be aware of other areas of medieval Europe beyond our particular, often narrow, subject area. Beyond that, to really make an impact, we should be writing and talking about these ideas in a variety of venues, including popular ones, and we need to be following the primary sources as closely as possible to demonstrate that this is not a new nationalist movement to expand Europe to the east, but a corrective to the old limitation of Europe to the west.

Notes

1 Dimitri Obolensky, *The Byzantine Commonwealth, Eastern Europe 500–1453* (London: Weidenfeld and Nicolson, 1971).

2 Christian Raffensperger, "Revisiting the Idea of the Byzantine Commonwealth," *Byzantinische Forschungen* 28 (2004): 159–174 and idem, "The Byzantine Ideal," *Reimagining Europe: Kievan Rus' in the Medieval World* (Cambridge, MA: Harvard University Press, 2012).

3 One might also note the Ottoman appropriation of Byzantine titles later, as conveyed in Dariusz Kołodziejczyk's study of early Ottoman imperial titles. Idem, "Khan, Caliph, Tsar and Imperator: The Multiple Identities of the Ottoman Sultan," in *Universal Empire: A Comparative Approach to Imperial Culture and Representation in Eurasian History*, ed. Peter Fibiger Bang and Dariusz Kołodziejczyk (Cambridge and New York: Cambridge University Press, 2012), 175–193, which includes such early Ottoman imperial titles as *kayser*, *basileus*, and *imperator.*

4 Admittedly there are outliers to this beyond myself such as Piotr Górecki at the University of California – Riverside, and Paul Milliman at the University of Arizona to name just two.

5 William R. Cook and Ronald B. Herzman, *The Medieval World View: An Introduction* (3rd ed. New York and Oxford: Oxford University Press, 2012), 114.

6 Ibid.

7 Barbara H. Rosenwein, *A Short History of the Middle Ages*, 3rd ed. (Toronto: University of Toronto Press, 2009), 146–147 and Lynette Olson, *The Early Middle Ages: The Birth of Europe* (New York: Palgrave Macmillan, 2007), 123–124 and 149.

8 Olson, *Early Middle Ages*, 124.

9 For excellent coverage of these crusades in English see, Eric Christiansen, *The Northern Crusades* (London: Penguin, 1997).

10 Nora Berend covers this letter and much more in her 2001 monograph, eadem, *At the Gate of Christendom: Jews, Muslims, and 'Pagans' in Medieval Hungary, c. 1000–1300* (Cambridge: Cambridge University Press, 2001).

11 Peter Jackson discusses all of these interactions, as well as many more in, *The Mongols and the West, 1221–1410* (Harlow: Pearson, 2005).

12 For just one example see, Olivia Remie Constable, *Trade and Traders in Muslim Spain: The Commercial Realignment of the Iberian Peninsula, 900–1500* (Cambridge: Cambridge University Press, 1996).

13 There are a host of works that could be mentioned here. Berend's *At the Gate of Christendom* was cited above, but in this vein she also edited *The Expansion of Central Europe in the Middle Ages* (Farnham: Ashgate, 2013). Gábor Klaniczay has written a great deal on this topic as well, including, *Holy Rulers and Blessed Princes: Dynastic Cults in Medieval Central Europe* (Cambridge: Cambridge University Press, 2002), idem, "The Birth of a New Europe about 1000 CE: Conversion, Transfer of Institutional Models, New Dynamics," in *Eurasian Transformations, Tenth to Thirteenth Centuries: Crystallizations, Divergences, Renaissances*, eds. Johann P. Arnason and Björn Wittrock (Leiden and Boston: Brill, 2004), 99–130, Gábor Klaniczay, "Von Ostmitteleuropa zu Westmitteleuropa: Eine Umwandlung im Hochmittelalter," in *Böhmen und seine Nachbarn in der Premyslidenzeit*, ed. Ivan Hlaváček and Alexander Patschovsky (Sigmaringen: Jan Thorbecke, 2011), 17–48, and *Saints of the Christianization Age of Central Europe (Tenth–Eleventh Centuries)* (Central European Medieval Texts, 6), ed. Gábor Klaniczay (Budapest: Central European University Press, 2013).

14 A brief perusal of recent programs for the International Medieval Congress held annually at the University of Leeds will demonstrate the presence of such papers, though inevitably, not many.

15 Admittedly in my "Medieval Eastern Europe" class which I teach due to university/departmental politics not because I prefer the territorial division.

16 Nora Berend, Przemysław Urbańczyk, and Przemysław Wiszewski, *Central Europe in the High Middle Ages: Bohemia, Hungary and Poland, c. 900 – c. 1300* (Cambridge: Cambridge University Press, 2013).

17 Ibid., Ch. 1.

18 See my review of the book in *Speculum* 90 (2015): 774–775; and Florin Curta's review of it in *The Medieval Review* 15.04.19. See online: http://scholarworks.iu.edu/journals/index.php/tmr/article/view/18870/24979 (last accessed: 25 October 2015).

19 Adam of Bremen, *The History of the Archbishops of Hamburg-Bremen*, trans. Francis J. Tschan (New York: Columbia University Press, 2002).

20 Ibid., Bk. 4, Chs 36–39.

21 Ibid., Bk. 2, Ch. 21.

22 Ibid.

23 Ibid.

24 *Ottonian Germany: The 'Chronicon' of Thietmar of Merseburg*, trans. David A. Warner (Manchester: Manchester University Press, 2001).

25 Ibid., Book 3, Ch. 58; Bk. 5, Ch. 9; Bk. 7, Ch. 95 and many more.

26 *The Chronicle of the Czechs by Cosmas of Prague*, trans. Lisa Wolverton (Washington, DC: The Catholic University of America Press, 2009) and Henricus Lettus, *The Chronicle of Henry of Livonia*, trans. James A. Brundage (New York: Columbia University Press, 2003).

27 *The Russian Primary Chronicle: Laurentian Text*, ed. and transl. Samuel Hazzard Cross and Olgerd P. Sherbowitz-Wetzor (Cambridge, MA: The Mediaeval Academy of America, 1953).

28 To take just one example from each polity – *Gesta Principum Polonorum / The Deeds of the Princes of the Poles* (Central European Medieval Texts, 3), ed. Paul W. Knoll and Frank Schaer (New York: Central European University Press, 2003), Simon of Kéza, *Gesta Hungarorum / The Deeds of the Hungarians* (Central European Medieval Texts, 1), ed. László Veszprémy and Frank Schaer (Budapest: Central European University Press, 1999).

29 Though I address the issue in the conclusion in regard to broader world history, Raffensperger, *Reimagining Europe*, conclusion.

30 *Ibn Fadlan and the Land of Darkness: Arab Travellers in the Far North*, ed. Paul Lunde and Caroline Stone (New York: Penguin, 2012). I teach with this work as well.

31 Christian Raffensperger, *The Kingdom of Rus'* (Kalamazoo, MI: ARC Medieval Press, 2017).

32 Henricus Lettus, *Heinrici Chronicon Lyvoniae* in *Monumenta Germaniae Historica. Scriptores. Scriptores rerum Germanicarum in usum scholarum separatim editi*, XXX, ed. Georgius Heinricus Pertz (Hannover: Impensis Bibliopolii Hahniani, 1874).

33 *The Chronicle of Henry of Livonia*, Bk. 1, note 39, Bk. 3, note 8.

34 Simon Franklin and Jonathan Shepard, *The Emergence of Rus, 750–1200* (New York: Longman, 1996), 272. Byzantine secondary sources consistently seem to refer to these rulers as "chieftains." Michael Angold, *The Byzantine Empire, 1025–1204: A Political History* (New York: Longman, 1997), 132–133, and Paul Stephenson, *Byzantium's Balkan Frontier: A Political Study of the Northern Balkans, 900–1204* (Cambridge: Cambridge University Press, 2000), 101.

35 Florin Curta, "Qagan, Khan, or King? Power in Early Medieval Bulgaria (Seventh to Ninth Centuries)," *Viator* 37 (2006): 1–31.

36 Anthony Kaldellis has written a corrective to almost all of the current historiography on Byzantium, in which he talks about it as a republic and challenges some of the ideas of empire and even the translation of *basileus* as emperor. Idem, *The Byzantine Republic: People and Power in New Rome* (Cambridge, MA: Harvard University Press, 2015).

2

THE CARPATHIAN-DANUBIAN REGION DURING THE EIGHTH AND NINTH CENTURIES

A General View Based on Archaeological Records

Sergiu Musteață

Natural landmarks define the area known in the literature as the Carpathian-Danube Region or the northern region of the Lower Danube. The Tisza, Danube, and Dniester rivers lie to the west, east, and south, the Black Sea coast to the southeast, and the Northern Bukovina region to the north. This is certainly part of the so-called forgotten or neglected Europe, areas which now lie in Moldova, Romania, and Hungary. For a better understanding of the role of such areas through the centuries when the written sources are almost non-existent we need other means to explore these hidden regions, such as archaeological data. The first step is to collate all the known data, map them, and then move to research at the macro- and micro-regional levels. The second step concerns the regional distribution of archaeological sites and artifacts. Recording, mapping, and examining the archaeological data from surface surveys and excavations (rescue or systematic) has made rich and diverse archaeological materials available about the populations north of the Lower Danube in the early medieval period.

The Carpathian-Danube Basin has undergone many environmental changes over the past two millennia; geographic and climatic conditions directly influenced the lifestyle of human societies.[1] The natural features of the landscape are also important in studying changes in the environment in relation to the human habitat. An increase or decrease in the number of archaeological sites in a region speaks of the attractiveness or insignificance of that area in the period studied. During the Holocene, the development of a temperate climate favored the expansion of complex vegetation. Beech forests came from areas west and northwest; oak forests came from the south, and steppe vegetation from the east. During the time of the Roman Empire (150 BC to AD 300) a cooling period began that lasted until about AD 900 (although the average global temperature remained relatively warm until about AD 600). The archaeological record of the Carpathian-Danube region from the end of the seventh until the late ninth century reveals significant historical developments in Central and Southeast Europe. The lower chronological limit marks the migration of the Bulgars south of the Danube (680/681) and the upper limit coincides with the movement of the Hungarians from the East European steppes to the Carpathian Basin (895/896).

After a cold period with probably higher-than-average precipitation at the end of seventh century, a dry period started that peaked at the end of eighth century and affected large areas of Asia[2] and Eastern Europe. From the temperate zone of the Volga and the Carpathians (from the mouth of the Danube to the mouth of the Volga), the steppe vegetation was largely the same.[3] A great increase in the density of settlements in the Carpathian-Danube region occurred from the eighth to the tenth century (a similar development has been noted for the period of the third to the fourth century). In some Transdanubian areas, recent pollen analyzes have highlighted a sudden drop in the water-levels around the year 800, which led to several lakes drying up and finally a change in the composition of the local vegetation, seen, for example, around Lake Balaton in Hungary.[4] The location of early medieval settlements in floodplains supports the idea of a low water-level in this period. In general, the period between 900 and 1150 was predominantly warm and dry, with some variation depending on the season and landform (mountains, hills or plains).[5] The Middle Ages in Europe fell within the period of the so-called Medieval Climatic Anomaly, which lasted from approximately AD 950 to AD 1400, when the climate in this part of the European continent enjoyed mild winters and hot summers.[6]

Settlement archaeology

Collecting data for settlement archaeology depends on several processes. Occasionally local residents discover archaeological materials on their landholdings and report them to the local museum, which records the location. Archaeologists often select an area for research and make searches by fieldwalking. This method is quite systematic, but only surface finds can be recorded. Excavation is undertaken later at some localities; the dates and details of other known sites remain in the records based only on surface finds. Large infrastructure projects (dams, for instance) generally include a pre-construction archaeological survey to record sites in the area to be affected, sometimes including excavation.

The discovery and study of archaeological remains are not exempt from cultural and political influences. Sometimes research is oriented toward establishing historical occupations connected to particular historical polities.[7] The sites noted in Maps 2.1 and 2.2 were compiled from the archaeological records in different countries where research trends may have been affected by different goals. The large number of sites, however, suggests that conclusions based on mixed discovery methods will be compensated for somewhat by sheer numbers.

Mapping the sites from the eighth and ninth centuries north of the Lower Danube reflects both the demographic situation and the degree of archaeological research in the region. Compared with the previous period (the sixth and seventh centuries), a demographic jump seems to have been characteristic throughout the Carpathian-Danubian area. In the Prut-Dniester area, the number of settlements practically doubled from the eighth to ninth century compared to the sixth and seventh centuries.[8]

The historical and social explanation for this phenomenon can be found in the process of successive resettlement from one area to another imposed by climatic factors, in addition to settlements that resulted from the migration of populations from other regions to this area. The record of an impressive number of settlements in the northern Lower Danube dated to the eighth through the ninth centuries does not presume continuous occupation at each location through two centuries.[9] The large number of settlement features identified within a single archaeological layer, such as at Alibunar (Serbia),[10] Békéscsaba (Hungary),[11] Černovka (Ukraine),[12] Costeşti (Râşcani; Moldova),[13] and elsewhere is mostly due to excavations and field surveys. Communities may have moved intermittently within a one to three-kilometer radius.[14]

Environmental problems (floods and changes in the water-level) and invasions of various groups, especially from the east, were crucial factors in settlement relocation. In this context, two pieces of stratigraphic evidence must be taken into account. Thin cultural layers in sites probably represent short occupations, and the accumulation of mounds or tells comprising many layers suggests prolonged occupation of the same area. Organized movements took place, in all likelihood, within clearly delineated geographical micro-regions.[15]

The density of archaeological sites in the eighth and ninth centuries varies (see Maps 2.1 and 2.2). The reasons for this are the geopolitical and economic conditions in this period and the fact that more research has been done in some areas than others, a problem which has been noted by Dan Gh. Teodor,[16] Victor Spinei,[17] and more recently by G. T. Rustoiu.[18]

Geomorphology helps suggest why settlements are absent or their numbers are low in some areas (swampy regions, mountains, steppe areas). Settlements were located in areas with average humidity and on mountain plateaus rather than plains, where they are less numerous. In addition to other political and economic causes, climate change and topographic conditions may explain the lack of settlements in steppe areas north of the Lower Danube in the fifth through the seventh century. Some good examples are the southern part of the hilly steppe area at Bugeac and Horincea-Elan-Prut,[19] where settlements are not attested in the fifth through the seventh century, but the ninth and tenth centuries saw a "settlement number explosion" (see Maps 2.1 and 2.2). This phenomenon may be related to climatic, demographic, and cultural changes that together facilitated the appearance of large numbers of settlements in some regions like the lakes in the southern Bessarabia area. The confrontations between the Avar Khaganate, the Carolingian Empire, the Byzantine Empire, and the Bulgarian Khanate were the most important factors in these changes. These caused population movements, with some groups settling in the regions north of the Danube River (see Map 2.1). The same situation occurred in the Banat-Crişana plains region. In the Banat, most settlements are located on

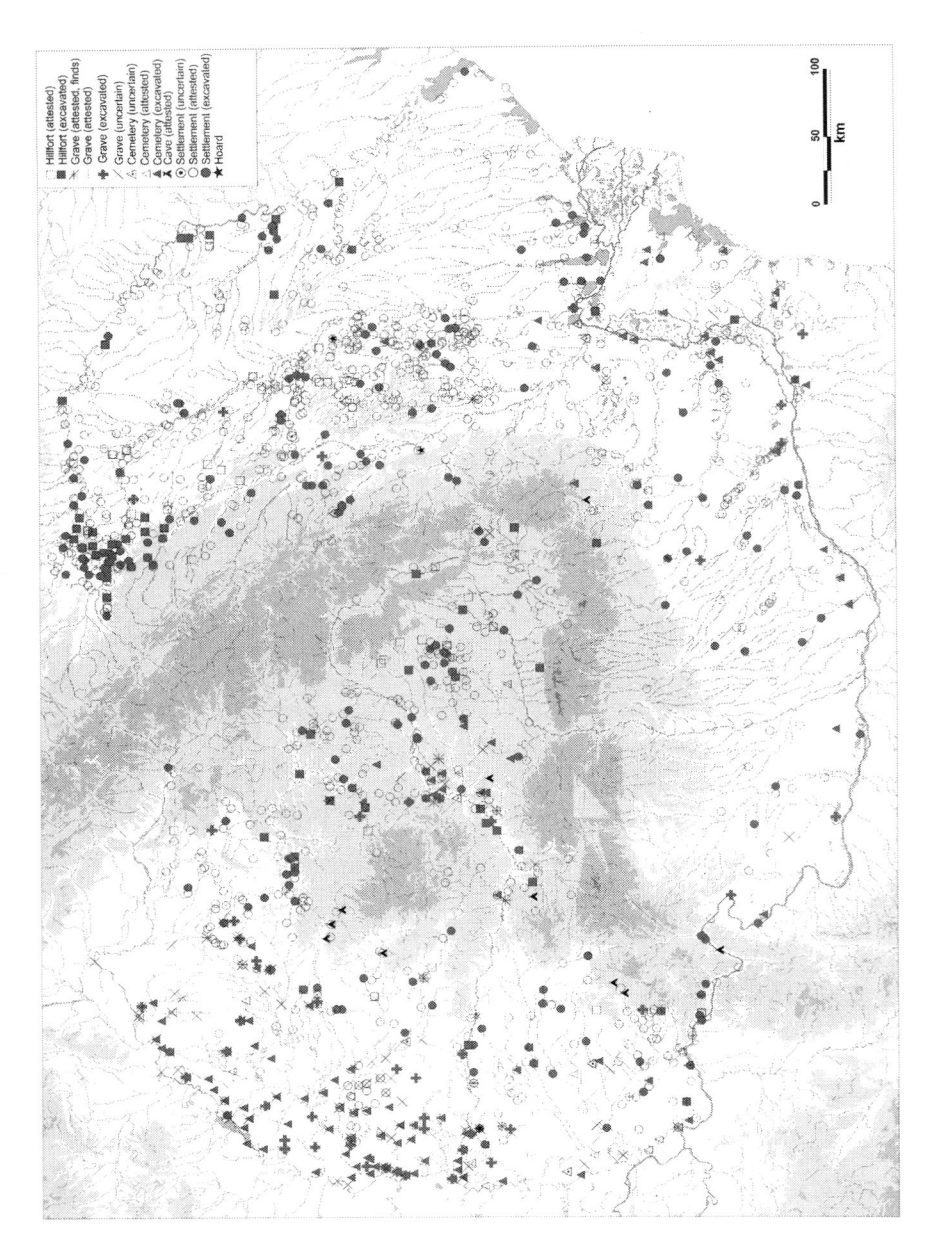

MAP 2.1 Map of sites dated to the eighth through ninth century

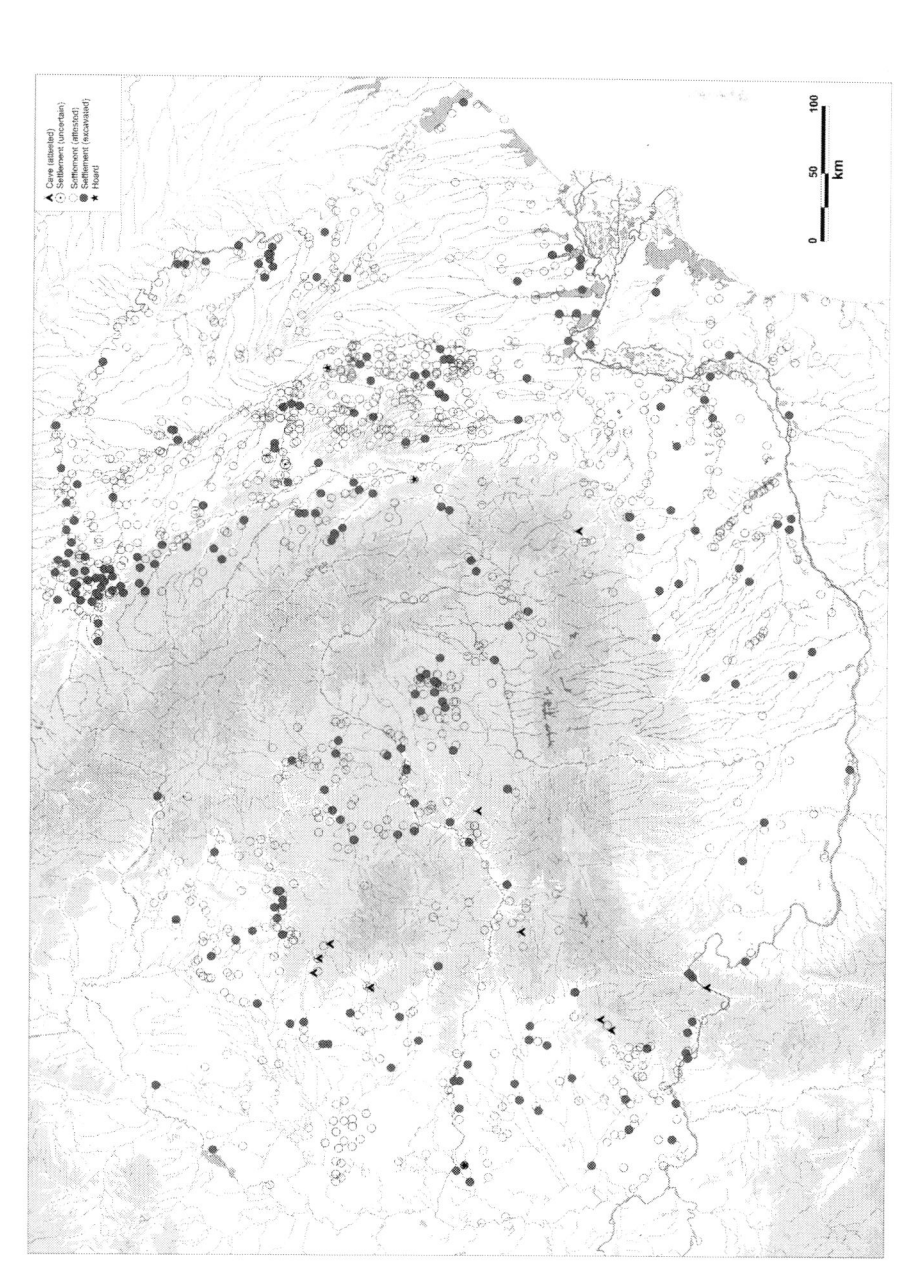

MAP 2.2 Map of settlements, dated to the eighth through ninth century

the floodplains, such as near the Danube River between Orşova and Moldova Nouă, along the Bega River, next to the town of Timişoara, along the Timiş River, and in the mining zone of Ocna de Fier (see Maps 2.1 and 2.2).[20]

In eastern Wallachia, in both northern and southern areas, sites are found in clusters in relatively high density close to Buzău and Râmnicu Vâlcea, around Brăila, in the area bounded by the Buzău, Călmăţui, and Danube rivers, on the Bărăgan plain, along the Ialomiţa river,[21] in the areas of Bucov and Slon, in the Călăraş and Mostiştei regions, between the Danube and Argeş rivers, between Colentina and Dâmboviţa, and between Vedea and Teleorman.[22] In Oltenia, the number of early medieval sites is lower (see Maps 2.1 and 2.2). The assertion of the Soviet archaeologists G.B. Fëdorov and L.L. Polevoj in the 1970s that there were no settlements in Wallachia and Oltenia dating from the eighth to the tenth century has not been confirmed.[23] In the territories east of the Carpathians settlements are concentrated in the river basins of the Bukovina, Siret, Prut, and Dniester, in the Central Moldavian Plateau region, between the Prut and Bârlad, on the Bugeac Plain, in the Danube lakes region of Bessarabia, and on the Lower Dniester Plain (see Map 2.1).[24]

In terms of geography, settlements from the eighth and ninth centuries can be predicted to be found on most landforms along the northern Lower Danube (plains, hills, and foothill areas) with the exception of mountainous regions and some sectors of the plains (Bălţi, Bugeac, northern Oltenia, and Wallachia; see Maps 2.1 and 2.2). Identifying settlements in the rugged, mountainous, often wooded areas provides limited opportunities for archaeological investigations, as Romanian archaeologists have stated.[25]

In most cases, settlements from the eighth and ninth centuries are located in areas suitable for agriculture with relatively easy defense.[26] The distribution of settlements differs from one area to another, with the largest numbers found in hilly areas, near rivers, and near the tributaries of large rivers. Concentrations of demographic groups can be observed clearly defined by geographical areas (see Map 2.1), but as noted above the geographic distribution of sites from the eighth and ninth centuries reflects the state of research and the intensity of investigations in different areas rather than the actual situation.

At some settlements, continuity of habitation in the same place can be seen for centuries, as has been attested in the excavated settlements of Biharea,[27] Brăneşti,[28] Cefa,[29] Černovka,[30] Hansca-*Limbari Căprăria,*[31] Lopatna,[32] Măşcăuţi-*Livada Boierului,* Pohorniceni,[33] and others. Some settlements in the same geographical area, especially in valleys and on river terraces, occur either because of successive movement or because of political, economic or natural factors.[34]

The demographic situation indicates continuity of habitation, especially in the hilly and plateau regions of the Carpathian-Danube area, in the Early Middle Ages (the fifth through the eighth century), which shows a sedentary population living north of the Lower Danube that had preferences for living in certain areas. The demographic growth of the population was directly influenced by the geographical environment, the rich resources of this region, and the population movements of the eighth and ninth centuries in Central and Southeastern Europe, which caused the displacement of population from one region to another.

Archaeological data can partly compensate for a lack of written sources on the population of the northern Lower Danube, but a numerical estimate of the population of the northern Lower Danube in the eighth through ninth centuries is not possible at this time. Archaeological research, however, has gathered a rich collection of material in recent decades that makes it possible to at least count the number and variety of sites. At the time of this writing, we have inventoried 2595 archaeological sites from the eighth and ninth centuries in the Carpathian-Danube region (see Table 2.1). Of the total number of sites recorded in the northern part of the Lower Danube region, there are 2101 settlements (see Map 2.2), 91 hill forts and 11 caves with cultural layers from the eighth and ninth centuries (see Maps 2.1 and 2.2). Also, 389 sites with funerary remains have been recorded, of which 221 are cemeteries, 79 are individual burials, and 89 are uncertain discoveries (archaeological items probably related to graves) (see Map 2.1 and Table 2.1).[35] Of the total number of known sites, only about 20% have been tested archaeologically by excavation; the remaining sites are described and dated based on ceramic material discovered on surface.

Compared to the sixth and seventh centuries,[36] the number of sites increased in the eighth and ninth centuries, as well as the diversity of site types. Based on site size, location, and the artifacts recovered, three types of sites were in use in the Carpathian-Danube area during the eighth and ninth centuries: settlements, hill forts and mixed sites (i.e., hill forts with satellite settlements). In the most general terms of social organization this implies social units larger than a family with some sort of sociopolitical structure (perhaps like a tribe). It further implies some supra-family organization of burials (in cemeteries rather than at individual house sites). Some tension with neighboring or outsider social groups is implied by the construction of hill forts, which required a group effort of many hours to

TABLE 2.1 Recorded archaeological sites dating to the eighth and ninth century in the Carpathian-Danube region compiled from publications from Moldova, Ukraine, Romania, Serbia, and Hungary

Sites	Total
Settlements	2101
Hill forts	91
Caves	11
Cemeteries	221
Single burials	79
Uncertain finds of burials	89
Hoards	3
Total	**2595**

construct. Analogies to the use of caves in other times and places suggests that they may have served as shelters for herders and travelers as well as refuges from social discord.

Of the recorded archaeological sites, 90% seem to have been agricultural settlements (see Table 2.1).[37] Large ceramic vessels were probably used for storing grain and other foodstuffs (see Fig. 2.3). The rural character of the early medieval settlement network was typical of most regions in Europe.[38] Certain functional areas are distinguished in settlement organization: spaces reserved for living (buildings), and space for fields, pastures, meadows, and forests belonging to the settlement. There is some archaeological data for settlement structure and internal organization, but for the economic space and activities such information is practically absent.

A specific problem is determining the size of a settlement, which is difficult to assess because of the lack of complete excavations at most sites. Based on the available data, in the eighth and ninth centuries both the number of settlements and their individual territories increased compared to previous centuries. Thus, if the surface of the settlements averaged ca. three hectares in the fifth through the seventh century, in the eighth and ninth centuries such territories exceeded three to four hectares.[39] The situation varies from one region to another, however; in some areas the site sizes are over 10 hectares (Gornea – 15 hectares, Moleşti – 30 hectares,[40] and others[41]). Some settlements are impressively large, but they are exceptions: Calfa – 120 hectares,[42] Brăneşti-*Valea Budă* – 50 hectares,[43] Hansca-*Limbari-Căprăria* – 30 hectares,[44] Logăneşti – 40 hectares, Pohorniceni-Petruha – 40 hectares, and Černovka II – *Rula* (with traces of more than 160 buildings).[45]

Partly or fully researched settlements, although limited in number, can illuminate certain aspects of internal organization. The structural elements of an early medieval settlement included the surface of the site, dwellings, manufacturing complexes, shared spaces, and in some cases a cemetery.[46] The number and location of the dwellings in one settlement can be judged by examples from Izvoare-Bahna-*La Pod la Hărmăneşti*, Neamţ County in Romania, where 23 dwellings and two fireplaces were found dating to the eighth or ninth century, which overlap buildings from the sixth or seventh century.[47] The dwellings are arranged irregularly; in some cases, they are aligned with the contours of the site. Some residential buildings are concentrated in pockets which could have belonged to groups of extended families, as in the cases of $L_1 - L_5$ or L_{27}, $L_{29} - L_{33}$.[48] Mitrea, the archaeologist who found the settlement, while noting that not all buildings were contemporary, estimated the parallel existence of approximately ten to 12 dwellings/families. Based on archaeological data, Mitrea believes that the settlement dating to the sixth and seventh centuries consisted of 28 to 32 people and that in the eighth and ninth centuries the number of inhabitants doubled, reaching 40 to 60 people.[49] Attempts to estimate the population often have a large margin of error.[50]

At the Hansca-*Limbari-Căprăria* settlement, 22 dwellings grouped in ten clusters were found from the eighth century and 17 dwellings from the ninth century, concentrated in eight groups. Eight of the housing groups from the eighth century overlap those from the fifth through the seventh century and only two were located in previously uninhabited areas. In five of the ten groups from the eighth century, dwellings were grouped by twos, in one case by threes and in another by fives, and in three cases there was only one single building. A group of five dwellings and another group of six were new appearances in the eighth century and also in the ninth century (see Map 2.1).[51]

At the Raškov-*Levada* settlement 80 dwellings from the seventh to the eighth century were investigated, of which 15 were from the seventh century, 34 from the eighth century, and 31 from the ninth century. The groups of houses from the eighth century overlap areas inhabited in the previous century (six groups) and two groups are new. Thus, two of the eight cases are concentrated into three and four dwellings and in one case into two to seven dwellings. Dwellings from the ninth century overlap surfaces from the eighth century, during which two new groups were added (see Fig. 2.1).[52] The situation attested in the settlements from *Hansca-Limbari-Căprăria*, Raškov-*Levada*, and elsewhere shows that the inhabitants of these zones used the center of the settlement for a long time, which demonstrates the continuity of occupation and the population's preference for certain geographic areas (see Fig. 2.2).

At the settlement of Ilidia, dwellings were concentrated in four to six dwelling groups,[53] with unoccupied spaces among them probably intended for agricultural activities. The dwellings in the settlement in Dodeşti–*Călugăreasca*, Vaslui County in Romania, stood in two rows arranged in a semi-circle with vaulted ovens located in the space between the dwellings.[54]

Teodor has estimated the average number of settlements for the eastern Carpathian area through the Middle Ages,[55] stating that houses in the eighth and ninth centuries were grouped in threes or fours or more, based on family criteria, and were also sometimes arranged along streets.[56] For the eighth and ninth centuries, the amount of construction varies from one case to another.[57] Assertions concerning settlement size, the number of inhabitants, and housing have to be made carefully, however, because settlements in most cases are only partially explored and dwellings recovered could belong to several phases of occupation. Typically, dwellings are near a number of auxiliary construction and production sites, which indicates the existence of centers of production.

Cemeteries were usually situated on the edge of a settlement. At Černovka, the cemetery is located near the settlement[58] and at Revno it is located on a high promontory in the early medieval settlement near the fortress Revno IB.[59] The early medieval cemetery at Hansca-*Limbari-Căprăria* is composed of two areas, one in the southeastern part of the settlement and the other in the western part. The graves of the first sector date from the ninth to the twelfth century[60] and those in the second sector from the seventh to the ninth century.[61]

In Northern Bukovina some sanctuary places have been discovered. At Revno, a sanctuary was part of the settlement[62] and at Ržavinci II – *Hrinova*[63] and Gorbova I – *Cetate*[64] the sacred complexes were integral parts of the hill fort's sanctuary.

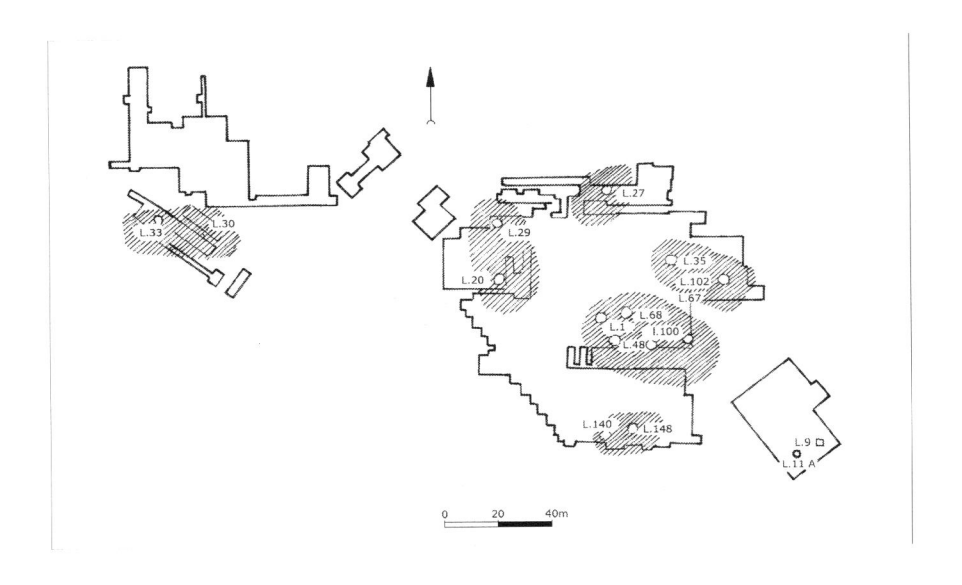

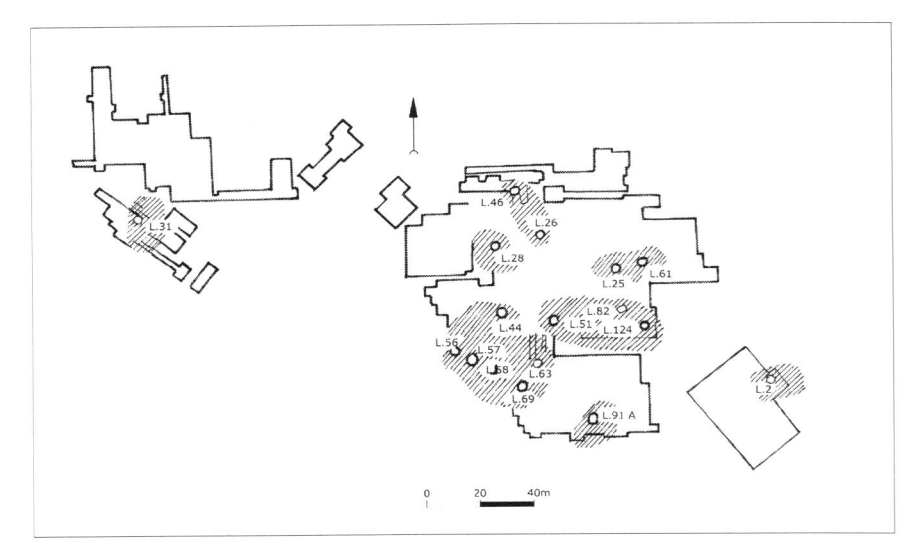

FIG. 2.1 General plan of the Hansca-*Limbari-Căprăria* site showing the groups of dwellings in the northern part of the eighth- through ninth-century settlement

Source: Gheorghe Postică, *Românii din codrii Moldovei în evul mediu timpuriu* [Romanians from the Codri Forests during the Early Middle Ages] (Chişinău: Universitas, 1994).

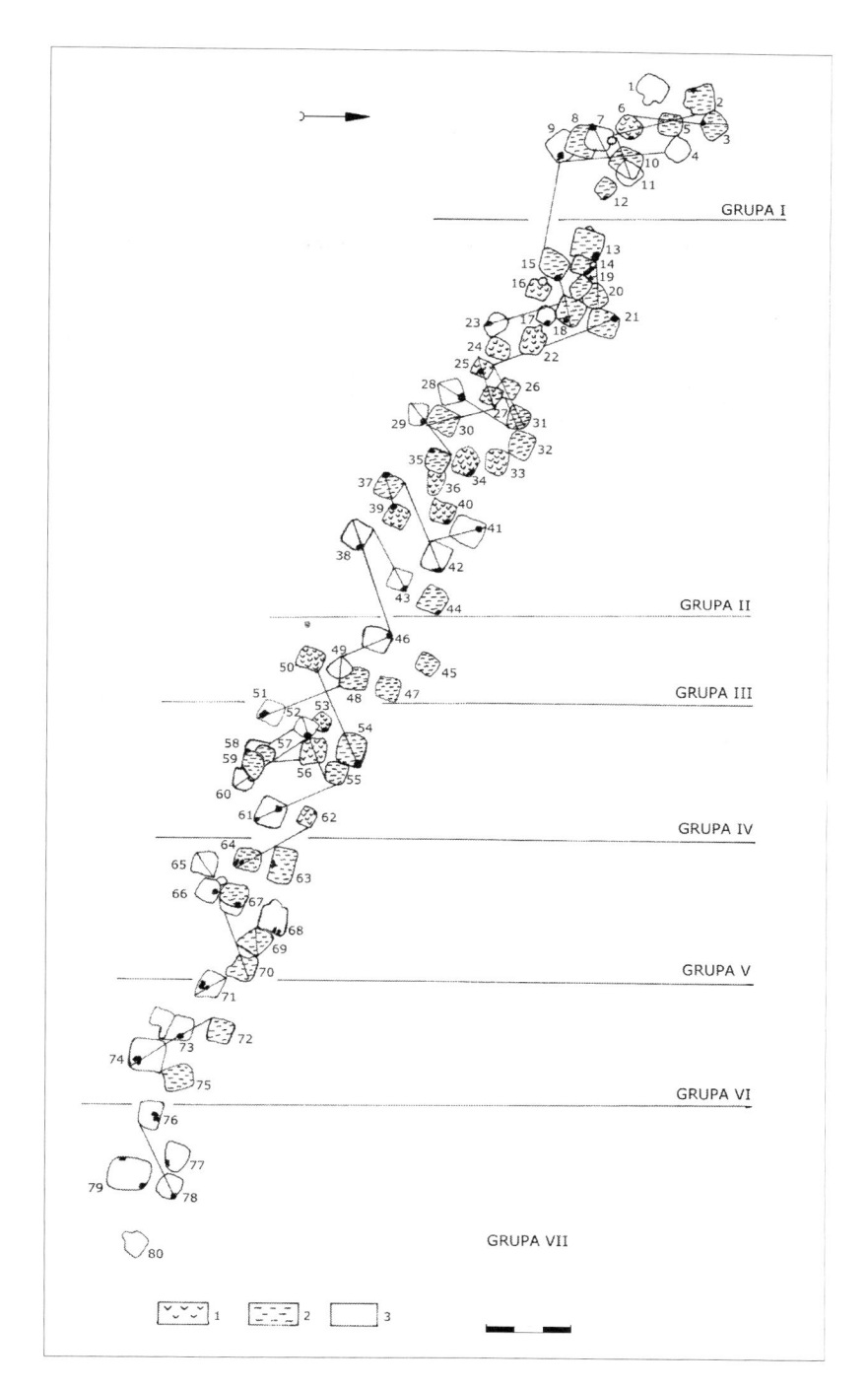

GRUPA I

GRUPA II

GRUPA III

GRUPA IV

GRUPA V

GRUPA VI

GRUPA VII

FIG. 2.2   General plan of the Raškov I settlement showing shifts in the occupation through time

Source: Jaroslav V. Baran, "Poselennja Raškiv i na Dnistri," in *Pivdennorus'ke selo IX–XIII st.* [The Dniester settlement Raškiv I, in A north Russian village, 9th to the 13th century] (Kiev: Institut archeologii NAN Ukrainy, 1997), 19–33.

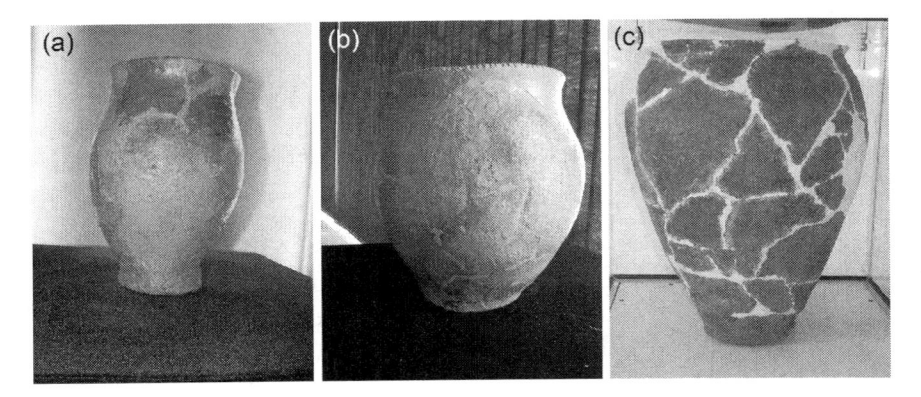

FIG. 2.3   Large ceramic storage jars, averaging about 50 centimeters in height, from the Bacău-Curtea Domnească and Izvoare-Bahna sites, (eighth to ninth century) and the Oncești site (ninth century)

Fortresses, a special type of human settlement, emerged along with residential settlements in the eighth and ninth centuries in the Carpathian-Danube area. The problem of fortresses with earthen walls and wooden palisades with adjacent external ditches has been widely debated in the historiography of the socialist bloc in Romania as well as in the Soviet Union, but a paper synthesizing the debate is still lacking.[65] Using published data, I recorded and mapped 91 hill forts (see Map 2.1), but archaeological excavations have only been conducted at a few. Analysis of such sites must be done carefully to prevent errors in understanding their chronological and cultural relations and developing typologies of defensive systems should be based only on archaeological excavations. Extensive investigations of excavated and fully researched fortresses are rare. Most of the fortresses were located to take advantage of opportunities of the land configuration that was needed for natural defense. Such opportunities depended directly on the appearance of defensive constructions, but also had to give the defenders good visibility. The chronology of fortified settlements that have not been excavated is a difficult problem to solve, as the archaeological material found on surface is insufficient for establishing a chronological framework of these sites. To clarify issues concerning peculiarities in societies from north of the Lower Danube in the eighth and ninth centuries, it will be necessary to expand archaeological excavations to as many sites as possible in the future. This research will also increase the opportunity to elucidate the most important transformations in the early medieval societies in the Carpathian-Danube area.

Conclusions

Climatic factors, along with political and military factors, directly influenced the cultural, economic and social environments of the Carpathian-Danube region in the seventh through ninth centuries. The dry climate of the eighth century led to the location of settlements close to water sources, even on the floodplains of rivers and lakes. With environmental and political changes beginning in the ninth century, the number and size of settlements increased considerably in the Carpathian-Danube region.

Mapping the sites from the eighth and ninth centuries highlights some regions as having a higher density of settlement than others. This is, on the one hand, due to the current level of research in which some areas are better researched than others, and, on the other hand, also reflects the demographic situation of this period. In most cases, settlements are located in regions favorable for agriculture, which highlights the sedentary lifestyle of these populations. The dimensions of settlements also differ from one case to another, and an estimation of the occupied surfaces is very hard to reconstruct due to the lack of complete investigations. For a better understanding of this period we need more complex and more comparative surveys on larger areas in East Central and Eastern Europe.

Notes

1 Iosif Constantin Drăgan, *Geoclimate and History* (Rome: Nagard, 1987).
2 In Asia, drought had catastrophic effects, a range of water sources dried up (rivers, lakes, and springs), many hill forts were abandoned and some towns were covered by sand.
3 Marcu Botzan, *Mediu și viețuire în spațiul carpato-dunăreano-pontic* [Environment and habitat in the Carpathian-Danubian-Pontic region] (Bucharest: Editura Academiei Române, 1996), 19.
4 Imola Juhász, "The Pollen Sequence from Baláta-tó," in *Environmental Archaeology in Transdanubia* (Varia archaeologica Hungarica, 20), ed. Csilla Zatykó, Imola Juhász, and Pál Sümegi (Budapest: Archaeological Institute of the Hungarian Academy of Sciences, 2007), 246–247. See also: Andrea Kiss, "Floods and Long-Term Water-Level Changes in Medieval Hungary," (PhD diss., Central European University, 2011). Available online: www.etd.ceu. hu/2011/mphkis22.pdf (last accessed: 23 October 2017).
5 Drăgan, *Geoclimate*, 303.
6 Ibid.
7 For more details on the history of archaeological survey in Romania, see Sergiu Musteață, "Contributions to the History of Romanian Archaeology. The History of Research on Archaeological Sites from the 8th–9th c. North of the Lower Danube," in *Studia Antiqua et Medievalia. Misellanea in honorem annos LXXV peragentis Professoris Dan Gh. Teodor oblata*, ed. Dan Aparaschivei (Bucharest: Editura Academiei Române, 2009), 331–346.
8 231 settlements have been identified from the sixth and seventh centuries and 572 settlements from the eighth and ninth centuries, see Gheorghe Postică, "Observații privind topografia și structura așezărilor medievale timpurii din spațiul pruto-nistrean" [Comments on the topography and structure of early medieval settlements in the Prut-Dniester area], *Tyragetia* 15 (2006): 60–76, here 60.
9 Some archaeologists believe that the maximum duration of a settlement may continue for two or three generations, Călin Cosma, "Considerații privind așezările rurale și tipurile de locuințe din Transilvania în secolele VIII–X" [Considerations on rural settlements and housing types in Transylvania from the 8th to 9th centuries], *Ephemeris Napocensis*

6 (1996): 261–279, here 263, idem, *Vestul şi nord-vestul României în secolele VIII–X d. Hr* [Western and northwestern Romania in the 8th to 10th centuries] (Cluj-Napoca: Editura Nereamia Napocae, 2002), 38; Ioan Stanciu, *Locuirea teritoriului nord-vestic al României între antichitatea târzie şi perioada de început a epocii medieval timpurii (mijlocul sec. V – sec. VII)* [Settling the northwestern part of Romania between Late Antiquity and the Early Middle Ages (mid-5th to the 7th century)] (Cluj-Napoca: Academia Română, 2011).

10 Around the village Alibunar, over 20 settlements from the seventh to tenth centuries have been identified, Stanko Trifunović, "Antička i srednjovekovna arheološka nalazišta opštine Alibunar, rekognosciranja terena" [Ancient and medieval archaeological sites in the Alibunar district. A field survey], *Rad Vojvođanskich Muzeja* 30 (1989–1990): 99–130, here 101.

11 19 settlements are recorded from the eighth to ninth century, *Archäologische Denkmäler der Awarenzeit in Mitteleuropa*, I–II (Varia Archaeologica Hungarica, XIII/1–2), ed. József Szentpéteri (Budapest: Magyar Tudományos Akadémia, 2002), II, 450–456.

12 In Cernovka, nine settlements and a hill fort are recorded from the eighth to tenth century. Boris Timoščuk, *Vostočnoslavjanskaja obščina VI–X vv. n.ė.* [Eastern Slavic society 6th–10th centuries] (Moscow: Nauka, 1990), 178–180.

13 Valentin Anisimovič Dergačev, *Materialy raskopok arheologičeskoj ekspedicii na Srednem Prute (1975–1976)* [The finds of the archaeological excavations on the Middle Prut (1975–1976)] (Chisinau: Štiinca, 1982), 64–77.

14 At Ilidia, four locations of habitation have been identified on a length of two kilometers, Adrian Bejan, "Economia satului bănăţean la începutul feudalismului (sec. VIII–XI)" [The economy of a Banat village at the beginning of the feudal period (8th–11th centuries)], *Analele Banatului* 12–13 (2004–2005): 265–293, here 268.

15 Settlement mobility in the early medieval period was typical for most European regions. Anne Nissen Jaubert, "Ruptures et continuités de l'habitat rural du haut Moyen Âge dans le nord-ouest de l'Europe," in *Habitat et Société. XIXe Rencontres Internationales d'Archéologie et d'Histoire d'Antibes*, ed. Frank Braemer, Serge Cleuziou, and Anick Coudart (Antibes: Association pour la promotion et la diffusion des connaissances archéologiques, 1999), 519–533, here 521.

16 Dan Gh. Teodor, *Teritoriul est-carpatic în veacurile V–XI e.n.* [The Eastern-Carpathian area in the 5th–11th centuries] (Iaşi: Junimea, 1978), 69.

17 Victor Spinei, *Realităţi etnice şi politice în Moldova Meridională în secolele X–XIII. Români şi turanici* [Ethnic and political realities in southern Moldova from the 10th to 13th century. Romania and Turanic] (Iaşi: Junimea, 1985), Fig.3. The map of the local population settlements discovered in central and southern Moldova during from the ninth to eleventh centuries (Dridu Culture), Fig. 2 – uncharted areas or with brief research.

18 Thorough investigations of some areas are directly related to the activity of Romanian archaeologists, such as: C. Gaiu – Bistriţa-Năsăud area, V. Lazăr – Mureş and Târnave, Şt. Ferenczi – Cluj area, N. Vlasa – Mureş, M. Blăjan – Cluj area, Mureş and Târnave, etc. Gabriel Tiberiu Rustoiu, "Exploatarea sarii si habitatul uman în Transilvania, în a doua jumatate a secolului V si prima jumatate a secolului VI" [Salt exploitation and human habitat in Transylvania in the first half of 5th and the beginning of the 6th century], in *Comerţ şi civilizaţie. Transilvania în contextul schimburilor comerciale şi culturale în antichitate* [Trade and civilization. Transylvania in the context of trade and cultural exchanges during antiquity], ed. Călin Cosma and Aurel Rustoiu (Cluj-Napoca: Mega, 2005), 269–294, here 275.

19 Ghenuţă Coman, "Cercetările arheologice cu privire la secolele V–XI în sudul Moldovei (stepa colinară Horincea-Elan-Prut)" [Archaeological research of the 5th through 11th

century in the southern Moldavian area (the steppe of the Horincea-Elan-Prut region)], *Arheologia Moldovei* 6 (1969): 277–315, here 277.

20 Bejan, "Economia satului," 266; Ştefan Pascu, Ştefan Olteanu, Dan Gh. Teodor and Octavian Iliescu, "Dinamica structurilor demo-economice (reţeaua demografică, structurile teritoriale, îndeletnicirile agrare, creşterea animalelor, exploatarea bogăţiilor miniere 'economia de transformare', circulaţia mărfurilor şi a banilor)" [The dynamics of demographic-economic structures, the demographic network, territorial structures, land occupation, farming, mining exploitation, "economic transformation," trade and money], in *Istoria Românilor. Genezele româneşti*, III [Romanian history. Romanian geneses], ed. Ştefan Pascu and Răzvan Theodorescu (Bucharest: Enciclopedică, 2001), 143–212, here 151 and Adrian Bejan, *Contribuţii la istoria şi arheologia Banatului în mileniul I d. Hr. şi începutul feudalismului* [Contributions to the history and archaeology of the Banat in the first millennium AD and the beginning of feudalism] (Timişoara: Excelsior Art, 2006), 74–89.

21 Anca Păunescu and Elena Renţa, "Aşezarea medieval timpurie de la Bucu, judeţul Ialomiţa" [The early medieval settlement from Bucu, Ialomiţa county], *Arheologie Medievală* 2 (1998): 51–77, here 58.

22 Pascu et al., "Dinamica structurilor," 151.

23 Gheorghi B. Fëdorov and Lazar L. Polevoj, *Arheologija Rumynii* [The Archaeology of Romania] (Moskva: Nauka, 1973), 300.

24 Pascu et al., "Dinamica structurilor," 149–150; Sergiu Musteaţă, *Populaţia spaţiului pruto-nistrean în secolele VIII–IX* [Population of the Prut-Dniestr space during the 8th and 9th centuries] (Chisinau: Editura Pontos, 2005), 33, Postică, "Observaţii privind topografia," 60–76 and Gheorghe Postică, *Civilizaţia medievală timpurie din spaţiul pruto-nistrean (secolele V–XIII)* [Early medieval civilization in the Prut and Nistru (5th to 13th century)] (Bibliotheca Archaeologica Moldoviae, 7) (Bucharest: Editura Academiei Române, 2007), 96–119.

25 Dan Gh. Teodor, *Descoperiri arheologice şi numismatice la Est de Carpaţi în secolele V–XI d.H. (Contribuţii la continuitatea daco-romană şi veche românească)* [Archaeological and numismatic discoveries east of the Carpathians in the 5th through 11th century AD (Contributions to Daco-Roman and Old Romanian continuity)] (Bucharest: Muzeul National de Istorie a României, 1997), 12.

26 Spinei, "Realităţi entice," Map 2.2. Map of the probable extent of forests in ancient Dacia and in the Middle Ages, drawn after maps of soils, vegetation, and the aridity index.

27 Sever Dumitraşcu, "Descoperiri arheologice din sec. V–VI e.n. de la Biharea" [Archaeological discoveries of the 5th through 6th century from Biharea], *Ziridava* 10 (1978): 81–100, idem, "Săpăturile arheologice de la Biharea" [Archaeological Excavations in Biharea], *Materiale şi Cercetări Arheologice* 14 (1980): 137–145, idem, "Descoperiri arheologice din anul 1979 de la Biharea, datînd din secolele VI–X" [Archaeological finds in Biharea at the excavations in 1979 dating from the 6th to the 10th century], *Sargetia* 15 (1981): 71–81, idem, "Biharea – în cadrul unitar al civilizaţiei feudale timpurii româneşti" [Biharea – the unique framework of early Romanian feudal civilization], *Muzeul Naţional* 6 (1982): 85–90; and S. Dumitraşcu, *Biharea I. Săpăturile arheologice (1973–1980)* [Biharea. Archaeological excavations] (Oradea: Editura Universităţii din Oradea, 1994).

28 Gheorghi B. Fëdorov, "Naselenie prutsko-dnestrovskogo mežđureč'ja v I tysjačeletie n.ė." [The Prut-Dniestr population during the 1st millennium AD], *Materialy i Issledovanija po Archeologii SSSR* 89 (1960): 1–380, here 378.

29 Ioan Crişan, "Descoperiri arheologice în hotarul localităţii Cefa (jud. Bihor)" [Archaeological discoveries in the border village Cefa (Bihor county)], *Crisia* 17 (1987): 19–35, idem, "O locuinţă feudală timpurie descoperită la Cefa (jud. Bihor)" [An early feudal dwelling discovered in Cefa (Bihor County)], *Crisia* 21 (1991): 297–305, and idem, "Săpăturile arheologice din anul 1993 de pe şantierul Cefa–La Pădure, judeţul Bihor" [Excavations in 1993 on the site Cefa-La Padure, Bihor county], *Crisia* 24 (1994): 23–42.

30 Timoščuk, *Vostočnoslavjanskaja obščina*, 179.

31 Gheorghe Postică, *Românii din codrii Moldovei în evul mediu timpuriu* [Romanians from the forests of Moldova during the Early Middle Ages] (Chisinau: Universitas, 1994), 10. Roman type gives the place name, italics indicate the site name in every case.

32 Gheorghi B. Fëdorov and Gheorghi F. Čebotarenko, *Pamjatniki drevnih slavjan (VI–XIII vv.)* [Settlements of old Slavs (6th to the 13th c.)] (Archeologičeskaja Karta Moldavii 6) (Chisinau: Štiinca, 1974), 28–29.

33 Gheorge Postică, *Satul medieval Petruha – argument al continuităţii românilor din Moldova. Procese etnoculturale şi etnosociale la finele mileniului I î.e.n. – prima jumătate a mileniului I e.n. în sud-estul URSS şi teritoriile limitrofe* [Medieval village of Petruha – argument for Romanian continuity in Moldova. Ethnocultural and ethnosocial processes from the end of the 1st millennium BC to the first half of the 1st millennium AD in southeastern USSR and the neighboring areas] (Chisinau: USM, 1991), 66–68.

34 Dumitraşcu, *Biharea I*, 18.

35 Within the category of doubtful funerary finds are places where archaeological funerary objects have been found occasionally which were probably part of the inventory of burials from the seventh to ninth or eighth to tenth centuries.

36 Igor Corman, *Contribuţii la istoria spaţiului pruto-nistrian în epoca evului mediu timpuriu (sec. V–VII d. Chr.)* [Contributions to the history of the Prut-Dniester area during Early Middle Ages (5th to 7th century AD)] (Chisinau: Cartdidact, 1998), 9, Musteaţă, *Populaţia spaţiului*, 32 and Postică, "Observaţii privind topografia," 64.

37 In the Prut-Dniester area 572 archaeological sites are attested (settlements, hill forts, cemeteries, and isolated graves), of which over 90% are settlements. See Musteaţă, *Populaţia spaţiului*, 32–33 and Postică, "Observaţii privind topografia," 60.

38 For more details: Nissen Jaubert, "Ruptures et continuités de l'habitat rural," 519–533.

39 In most cases, based on the survey data, the settlement areas were established very precisely. In the case of Andrid–Drumul Poştei, Satu Mare County, the area is estimated at 3.4 hectares, see: János Németi, *Repertoriul arheologic al zonei Careiului* [Archaeological Repository of the Careiu area] (Bucharest: Vavila Edinf, 1999), 28, Cosma, *Vestul şi nord-vestul*, 163; at Bârnova *II*, district Ocniţa – ca. 500x700 meters, Ivan Grigorievic Vlasenko, "Novye arheologičeskie pamjatniki v Moldavii" [New archaeological settlements from Moldova], *Archeologičeskie Issledovanija v Moldavii v 1981* [1985], 198–205, here 200; at Bogatoe *I*, reg. Odessa – 300x50 meters, Aleksandra V. Gudkova, Sergej B. Ohotnikov, Leonid V. Subbotin and Ivan T. Černjakov, *Arheologičeskie pamjatniki Odesskoj oblasti (spravočnik)* [Archaeological sites in the Odessa region (guide)] (Odessa: Ukrainskoe obščestvo ohrany pamjatnikov istorii i kultury, 1991), 62.

40 Bejan, "Economia satului," 268.

41 Cosma, *Vestul şi nord-vestul*, 27; Postică, "Observaţii privind topografia," 61, I; Tentiuc, *Contribuţii la istoria şi arheologia spaţiului pruto-nistrean. Siturile de la Durleşti şi Moleşti* [Contributions to the history and archaeology of the Prut-Dniester area. Sites from Durleşti and Moleşti] (Chisinau: Bons Offices, 2012), 128–134.

42 Gheorghi F. Čebotarenko, *Kalfa–gorodišće VIII–X vv. na Dnestre* [Kalfa – 8th–10th-century hill fort by the Dniester] (Chisinau: Štiinca, 1973), 3–4.

43 Postică, "Observații privind topografia," 61.

44 Postică, *Românii din codrii*, 10.

45 Boris O. Timoščuk, *Slov'jani Pivničnoj Bukovini V–IX st.* [The Slavs of Northern Bukovina in the 5th through 9th centuries] (Kiev: Naukova Dumka, 1976), 167; idem, *Vostočnoslavjanskaja obščina*, 179–180; Irina P. Rusanova and Boris A. Timoščuk, *Drevnerusskoe Podnestrov'e* [The Russian Upper Dniester] (Užgorod: Karpati, 1981), 42.

46 Postică, "Observații privynd topografia," 62.

47 Ioan Mitrea, *Așezarea din secolele VI–IX de la Izvoare-Bahna. Realități arheologice și concluzii istorice* [Settlement from the 6th to 9th century at Izvoare-Bahna. Archaeological results and historical conclusions] (Piatra Neamț: Nona, 1998), 46.

48 Ibid., 88, Fig. 25.

49 Ibid., 95.

50 Teodor, *Teritoriul est-carpatic*, 69; Ioan Marian Țiplic, *Contribuții la istoria spațiului românesc în perioada migrațiilor și evul mediu timpuriu (secolele IV–XIII)* [Contributions to the history of the Romanians during migrations and the Early Middle Ages (4th–13th c.)] (Iași: Institutul European, 2005), 22–31; Mugur Andronic, *Poiana o așezare din secolele VIII–IX d. Chr.* [Poiana: A settlement from the 8th to 9th centuries] (Suceava: Anuarul Muzeului Național al Bucovinei. Supliment, 8) (Suceava: Istros, 2005), 33.

51 Postică, "Observații privind topografia," 65.

52 Jaroslav V. Baran, "Poselennja Raškiv I na Dnistri" [Raškiv I, a settlement by the Dniester], in *Pivdennorus'ke selo IX–XIII st.* [A village in the northern Rus, 9th–13th centuries] (Kiev: Institut archeologii Narodowa Akademia Nauk Ukrainy, 1997), 19–33.

53 Adrian Bejan, *Banatul în secolele IV–XII* [The Banat region in the 4th–12th centuries] (Timișoara: Editura de Vest, 1995), 93.

54 Dan Gh. Teodor, *Continuitatea populației autohtone la est de Carpați în secolele VI–XI e.n.* [The continuity of the autochthonous population in the Eastern Carpathians in the 6th through the 11th century] (Iași: Junimea, 1984), 51, fig. 21.

55 Teodor, *Descoperiri arheologice*, 14, 17, 21, 23, and 25.

56 Ibid., 23.

57 Ștefan Olteanu, *Societatea românească la cumpănă de milenii (sec. VIII-XI)* [Romanian society at the turn of millennia (8th through 11th century)] (Bucharest: Editura Științifică și Enciclopedică, 1983), 153; Ștefan Olteanu, Eugenia Zaharia, Mircea Rusu, and Ștefan Pascu, "Evoluția structurilor sociale (accentuarea diferențelor sociale; stadiul raporturilor de aservire)" [The evolution of social structures (social acceptance of differences, stage servitude relations)], in *Istoria Românilor*, III, 212–220, here 214.

58 Ljubomir P. Mihajlina, *Naselennja verhn'ogo Popruttja VIII–X st.* [The population of upper Prut in the 8th to 10th century] (Černivci: Ruta, 1997), 73–74; Ol'ga Manigda, "Mogil'niki Severnoj Bukoviny (v kontekste evoljucii ot jazyčestva do hristianstva)" [The cemeteries of northern Bukovina (in context of evolution from pagan to Christianity)], *Analele ANTIM* 2 (2001): 46–52, here 47.

59 Mihajlina, *Naselennja*, 70–72 and Manigda, "Mogil'niki," 47.

60 Ivan G. Hynku, *Kapraria-pamjatnik kul'tury X–XII vv.* [Kapraria: the site of a 10th–12th-century culture] (Chisinau: Štiinca, 1973), 49.

61 Ivan G. Hynku, *Limbari – srednevekovyi mogil'nik XII–XIV vekov v Moldavii* [Limbari – medieval cemetery from 12th–14th-century Moldova] (Chisinau: Štiinca, 1970), 65–66.

62 Timoščuk, *Slov'jani Pivničnoj*, 65–72 and 162–163 and idem, *Vostočnoslavjanskaja*, 17.

63 Timoščuk, *Slov'jani*, 164 and idem, *Vostočnoslavjanskaja*, 156, fig. 21.
64 Boris O. Timoščuk, *Pivnična Bukovina – zemlja slov'jans'ka* [Northern Bukovina – Slavic land] (Užgorod: Karpati, 1969), 152–153, and idem, *Slov'jans'ki gradi Pivničnoj Bukovini* [The Slavic hill forts of Northern Bukovina] (Užgorod: Karpati, 1975), 106.
65 Musteață, *Populația spațiului*, 37–42.

3

THE ENTRY OF EARLY MEDIEVAL SLAVS INTO WORLD HISTORY

The Chronicle of Moissac

Sébastien Rossignol

Frankish sources began to make regular mentions of Slavic peoples living in the areas east of the Elbe in the early ninth century, as a number of tribes were involved in conflicts with the Franks. The evidence suggests that these conflicts had been caused by the aggressive policies of the Franks, who required the payment of tribute from these groups. These mentions are found primarily in annals and consist mostly of brief mentions of political and military events. This was long before western Slavs assumed a prominent place in a proper chronicle – for instance, as the adversaries of the Eastern Franks in the tenth-century work of the Saxon monk Widukind of Corvey[1] – and longer still before chronicles depicting the origins and early history of specific Slavic peoples would be put in writing, not until primarily the twelfth century.[2] Little attention has been given to explaining the prominent place of Slavic groups in a universal chronicle compiled in the early ninth century, the *Chronicle of Moissac*, and for good reason: an edition of the complete chronicle was only made available to the scholarly community a few years ago.

Arguably, this was the first time that western Slavs were given such a consistent place in a historical narrative that recounted more than events of regional concern and was written in a place far from areas populated by Slavs. This paper investigates the reasons that this chronicle shows interest in the Slavs and how it contributed to disseminating knowledge about groups that had only recently been noted by Frankish authors in the Elbe area. Recent scholarship has emphasized the importance of understanding the construction and intentionality of medieval historical writing.[3] What information was available to the author of this source? What was the author's intention in producing this text and how did these objectives influence the result? Answering these questions will help assess the meaning of the appearance of Slavic groups in the *Chronicle of Moissac*.

Slavs in the early Carolingian era

The first time that Slavs, or Wends, were mentioned as neighbors of the Franks was in the episode concerning Samo, a Frankish merchant who, according to the so-called Fredegar chronicle, had become a "king" (*rex*) of the "Slavs who are called Wends" (*in Sclavos coinomento Winedos*) during the reign of Dagobert in the early decades of the seventh century. Attempts to locate the "kingdom" (*regnum*) of Samo have proven futile and nothing is known about these events apart from the so-called Fredegar's narrative. Whoever Samo might have been and whatever the nature of his political construction, and in spite of the fact that he is supposed to have had twelve wives, twenty-two sons, and fifteen daughters, his reign was short-lived and had no apparent lasting consequences.[4]

Slavs began to be mentioned regularly in Frankish annals beginning in the late eighth century and mostly in the early ninth century. Tribes of Slavs with a variety of names were mentioned as living in the areas east of the Elbe and Saale and were frequently involved in military and political events with the Franks. From what can be reconstructed, it appears to have been primarily the Franks who displayed a hostile attitude, wanting to control the eastern frontier of their realm by making the Slavic tribes tribute-paying.[5] While some of these Slavic groups had had "kings" (*reges*) since the earliest mentions, others appeared in the Frankish sources as acephalic groups.[6] The social organization of these Slavs probably resulted from the disintegration of the Avar Empire as well as from the need to respond to the aggressive policies of the Franks.[7] It is improbable that the collective identities and social constructions of these Slavs corresponded to ancient traditions shared among them; they were likely the outcome of entirely new circumstances.[8]

The *Chronicle of Moissac*

The *Chronicle of Moissac* (*Chronicon Moissiacense*), preserved in an eleventh-century manuscript and a related twelfth-century text,[9] has been known in the scholarship mostly because the anonymous author apparently used lost sources, possibly including a version of the *Annals of Lorsch* (*Annales Laureshamenses*) that is otherwise unknown. The *Annals of Lorsch* are preserved in a version covering the period until 803; the compiler of the *Chronicle of Moissac* might have used a continuation reaching until 818.[10] Apart from that, the *Chronicle of Moissac* has been dismissed as a meaningless compilation of well-known sources. Study of the chronicle in its entirety was impeded by the lack of a reliable and, even more importantly, complete edition of the text. This has now been remedied by the edition and commentary of Ir. J.M.J.G. Kats, posthumously completed and revised by David Claszen.[11]

What is known as the *Chronicle of Moissac* is the text contained in the eleventh-century manuscript cataloged as Paris, Bibliothèque nationale de France (BNF), Ms. Lat. 4886; it is a universal chronicle covering a period ranging from the time of Adam until the early years of the reign of Louis the Pious. While the work is a compilation of otherwise well-known sources, the section covering the years 803–818 contains entries taken from now-lost sources, among them possibly the *Annals of Lorsch* noted above. Closely related to the text of the *Chronicle of Moissac* is that of the *Aniane Annals*, preserved in the twelfth-century manuscript Paris, BNF, Ms. Lat. 5941. It contains a series of entries covering the years 640 to 840. The scribes of the *Chronicle of Moissac* and of the *Aniane Annals* used a common text, now lost, but the two works were devised according to entirely different principles. While the Aniane text is primarily a compilation of annals, that of Moissac is a full-fledged universal chronicle, making use of a wide variety of sources with the aim of providing a comprehensive narrative of world history in the tradition of a popular medieval genre of historical writing.[12] As such, the *Chronicle of Moissac* merits analysis as more than just a compilation, rather as an original work of history designed according to a conscious pattern and, presumably, with specific intentions.

BNF, Ms. Lat. 4886 is first mentioned as belonging to the collection of the abbey of Moissac, hence the name under which the chronicle has since been known. A fifteenth-century note in the manuscript refers to the book as belonging to the priory of Rabastens, a dependency of Moissac Abbey. It appears unlikely that the *Chronicle* was composed in either of these places, however; the note only attests that the manuscript was there in the Late Middle Ages. In fact, earlier inventories of the books available in Moissac do not hint at this manuscript.[13] An excerpt discovered by Patrick Geary in a twelfth-century manuscript indicates that at least part of the text was known in Narbonne by that time.[14] Based on a series of manuscript indications, Walter Kettemann has unveiled connections between the *Chronicle* and the monastery of Psalmodi, located in the same region as Narbonne and Aniane, in present-day Languedoc-Roussillon.[15] Other manuscript texts derived from the *Chronicle* also point towards a provenance in present-day southern France.[16]

Apart from the *Chronicle of Moissac*, BNF, Ms. Lat. 4886 comprises a miscellany of edifying and moralistic texts, excerpts from biblical commentaries and papal decretals, and lists of apostles and popes. This collection of texts suggests a monastic provenance for the codex.[17] The first part of the *Chronicle of Moissac* is based on chapter 66 of Bede's *De Temporum Ratione*, entitled "De Sex Huius Saeculi Aetatibus," also known as Bede's "Chronica Maiora;" the compiler modified and expanded Bede's text to add more information.[18] Kats and Claszen infer that the *Chronicle* is the work of two authors. They refer to the author of the first part, reaching until 741, as a "composer," and to the author of the second part, completing the narrative up to 818, as a "compiler." Whereas the composer showed some creativity in dealing with the sources, the compiler mostly copied sections from available materials without altering them significantly. Nonetheless, the result was "a new book of history on the basis of his sources;" the compiler apparently had "his own purpose, his own assessment of historical values, and his own audience."[19]

The section authored by the composer was probably written between 751 and 761 and the author had access to historical works that had only recently become available. Some of these, including the *Liber Historiae Francorum*, were known primarily in Austrasia (the northeastern section of the Merovingian Kingdom). It seems likely that the composer was active in a scriptorium with an important library located in Austrasia.[20] The compiler completed his predecessor's narrative sometime after 818; a more precise *terminus ante quem* is not possible. What can be said is that the compiler, whose work is reflected in the *Chronicle of Moissac* and in the *Aniane Annals*, used sources from the southern as well as northern regions of the Frankish realm. The most likely explanation, although ultimately it cannot be proven, is that the compiler was active in the south, but had access to numerous manuscript sources from the north, which would have been made possible by monks moving between Aniane and Austrasia.[21]

Summing up, the first part of the *Chronicle of Moissac* was written in the transitional period from Merovingian to Carolingian rule, probably in Austrasia, by someone having access to a library rich in recent Austrasian sources; the second part was added sometime in the ninth century, probably not too long after 818, completing the earlier work with a narrative covering early Carolingian history, by someone probably based in southern Gaul. The first part is based on Bede's "Chronica Maiora" with several interpolations, and the second part is a continuation based on a variety of more recent sources, the most prominent of which seems to have been the *Annals of Lorsch*.[22]

A universal chronicle

The tradition of universal chronicles was largely influenced by the *Chronicon* of Eusebius of Caesarea, who, connecting biblical with ecclesiastical history, was regularly emulated by later historians. Eusebius became accessible to Latin scholars through Jerome's translation and continuation. Orosius's *Historia Adversus Paganos*, with its comprehensive narrative of imperial history, also became a major source for later chroniclers. Early medieval historians pursued this tradition, although they tended to have a stronger focus on their own region or kingdom. Bede's 'Chronica Maiora' provided an influential model and source for early medieval chroniclers following this concept of historical writing.[23]

The category of the universal chronicle, however, was actually coined by nineteenth-century scholars; ancient and medieval authors had no special phrase for this genre and designated such a narrative simply as *chronicon* or *chronica*, which was translated by Isidore of Seville as *series temporum*.[24] Universal or world chronicles nonetheless all had in common, in contrast with other chronicles usually focusing on a kingdom, region, or institution,[25] that they were narratives of world history leading to salvation, beginning with creation and ending with Judgment Day and with human history in between.[26] The history of humankind was thus part of divine revelation and the aim of studying it was to decipher the divine will. In principle, universal chronicles had to consider the history of the entire world and the entirety of its existence. Medieval chroniclers, however, often attached more attention to temporal than to spatial comprehensiveness.[27] As Anna-Dorothee von den Brincken and Hans-Werner Goetz have explained, medieval chroniclers wrote from the point of view of where they were in space and time: they aimed to explain their world to their contemporaries by outlining how world history led to where they were, demonstrating how the past was linked to the present.[28]

From a political perspective, human history was often framed around the idea of four world empires, an idea influenced by the Greek-Roman fascination with imperial history and corresponding with Daniel's prophecies in the Old Testament. Empires were divided into *regna*. The Roman Empire was the fourth and last of the world empires and was seen as an instrument of God as it had provided the framework necessary for the diffusion of Christianity.[29]

From the point of view of salvation, history was divided into the six ages of the world. The model of the six ages had been outlined by Augustine, summarized by Isidore, and popularized by Bede as a framework for the narration of world history. The sixth age begins with Christ and ends with the apocalypse.[30] For medieval writers, the first five ages were well known, based on the Old Testament, and had already been narrated by several authors. The sixth age, however, provided authors of universal chronicles with a more complicated task. As long as the end of the world had not happened, there was constantly something new to add, and consequently the diversity of world events made it difficult to conceive a unified narrative.[31] Recent periods were difficult to interpret in view of salvation; even though chroniclers often intended to provide moral lessons, historical progress was not always obvious when hindsight was lacking.[32]

The *Chronicle of Moissac* presents itself clearly in the tradition of universal chronicles and both parts present consistency in geography, time, and subject. Using Bede's "Chronica Maiora" – which Bede originally conceived as a section of his comprehensive book on time reckoning, *De Temporum Ratione*,[33] as a framework, the composer and compiler added information connecting the history of the Franks with major world events. As Kats and Claszen phrase it, "instead of writing a history of the Franks, the composer wrote the Franks into history."[34]

The intentions of the composer and compiler

The *Chronicle* begins with the preface of Bede's *De Temporum Ratione*. Because the first folio of the manuscript is lacking, the beginning of the preface is lost; however, there is no reason not to assume that the text included the entirety of Bede's preface.[35] It can arguably be presumed that Bede's preface was included consciously because it seemed meaningful to the composer or compiler to indicate what Bede's intention had been. In his preface, addressed to his abbot, Hwaetbert, Bede explains that he wants to write two books "on the nature of things, and on the reckoning of times."[36] He indicates that he used the Hebraic version of the Bible (i.e., the Vulgate) instead of the Septuagint translation,[37] but inserted additions where discrepancies in his sources appeared. He justifies his approach with a reference to Augustine, who said that it is "necessary to make several books out of several, with diverse style, but not with varying faith."[38]

Bede's preface is followed by the beginning of chapter 66 of *De Temporum Ratione*, here with the heading *De Sex Huius Seculi Etatibus: Beda Presbiter*. As in

Bede's text, the chapter begins by outlining briefly, in a factual manner, the main features of the six ages of the world.[39] This is followed by an interpolation, probably by the composer, which again discusses the six ages of the world, but from a moralistic perspective. Each age begins gleefully as human beings live in harmony with God until they start neglecting God's advice, fall into sin, and the age comes to a tragic end marked by unhappy events. The sixth age begins when Christ has been made man for the redemption of humankind and it will end at an unknown time, when the arrival of the Antichrist will signal the beginning of the decline which will lead into the Last Judgment.[40]

These outlines are followed by a definition of a chronicle, taken from Isidore's *Etymologies*,[41] and a colophon, probably penned by the compiler, indicating the objective of his or her endeavor. The chronicle is described as "the book of the chronicles of the priest Bede, servant of Christ", combined with the works of Jerome, Augustine, Ambrose, Isidore, Orosius, Josephus, Rufinus, and Count Marcellinus, based on the Hebraic and Septuagint Bibles. To this has been added "the years from the incarnation of the Lord until now."[42]

To sum up, all of this provides some indication of what the composer and the compiler must have intended. The composer seems to have intended a narrative of the six ages of the world, based on Bede's work, but with a moral perspective that was found lacking in Bede. A chronicle of salvation with moralistic undertones could possibly have been conceived as meaningful reading for the monastic *lectio*, providing matter for rumination on the mysteries of divine creation. The compiler, who may have been the one who added Bede's preface, wanted mainly to make a compilation from different books – in the same spirit as Bede and Augustine – in order to provide a comprehensive narrative of the six ages of the world that would reach to his or her own time. In view of the contents of BNF, Ms. Lat. 4886, the compilation could have been intended or used as a work of reference about world events.

Slavs in the first part of the Chronicle of Moissac

For the proposed narrative of the sixth age, the composer penned a history of the early medieval Christian world, using Bede's "Chronica Maiora", the chronicle of the so-called Fredegar, and the *Liber Historiae Francorum* as the main sources. The author paid attention not only to events taking place in the Frankish realm, but also in the kingdoms of the Lombards, Visigoths, and Anglo-Saxons, as well as in the Greek East. It did not, however, seem important to him to include events involving non-Christian peoples on the peripheries of the Frankish realm. For instance, in a section summarizing events taking place in the Frankish kingdoms and based on the narrative of the so-called Fredegar, the composer entirely left out the episode of Samo, the Frankish merchant who became "king" among the Wends.[43] The *Winidi* are only mentioned once in the first section of the *Chronicle*: King Dagobert has heard of an army of Wends invading from Thuringia and receives envoys of the Saxons. They promise to protect the frontier against the Wends if Dagobert relieves them from the tribute they pay the Franks; Dagobert accepts the offer. Thus summarized, the episode is not included to provide information on the Wends, but on the fact that since Dagobert's rule the Saxons had ceased to pay the usual tribute.[44] This episode is followed immediately by the mention of Dagobert's death through diarrhea.[45] Although the two events are not explicitly related, they are here conflated, which was not the case in the compiler's source, the chronicle of the so-called Fredegar.

Other mentions of the Avars and Slavs in the sources used by the composer are also omitted from the narrative.[46] The composer seemed generally uninterested in peoples on the peripheries of the Frankish Christian realm. When the *Liber Historiae Francorum* mentions that Pippin attacked the Frisian chieftain Radbod, described as *gentilis*, and the *Suevi* (695), it suffices for the composer to indicate that Pippin waged wars against "several *gentes*."[47] The composer does not refrain from mentioning the pagan religion of some of the barbarian groups like the Franks and Lombards although he knows that they would later convert to Christianity.[48]

The composer, in contrast, notes the arrival of the "Saracens" in the Byzantine provinces under Heraclius[49] and their conquest of the kingdom of the Goths.[50] The composer explains, following the narrative of the so-called Fredegar, that Heraclius had become a heretic, married the daughter of his sister, and shortly afterwards had died of fever.[51] As for the Visigothic king, Witiza, he was, according to the composer, "given up to women, and he instructed the priests and the people, following his example, to live voluptuously, which raised the fury of the Lord."[52] Thus, in the composer's view, the Muslim conquest was the direct result of the reprehensible behavior of Christians.

Summing up, the composer of the first part of the *Chronicle* was primarily concerned with the history of Christian peoples. When non-Christians are mentioned, it is mostly done with moralistic overtones: pagan Franks and Lombards fortunately become Christians; Dagobert dies after liberating the Saxons from their tribute; the Muslim conquest is the consequence of the sinful behavior of Christians.

Slavs in the second part of the Chronicle of Moissac

Slavs are decidedly more prominent in the second part of the *Chronicle*. For the year 789, the *Chronicle* mentions the "*Calssclavi* who are named *Vulti*" and their "kings" (*reges*), led by a king called Dragowit (here *Tranguito*), who surrender their territories to Charlemagne.[53] The information is taken from the *Annals of Lorsch*.[54] The *Chronicle* adds for that year the mention of the death of a Saxon bishop and events in Italy, although the source for this additional information is unknown.

For 795, the compiler mentions the death of Wizlaus II (here *Wizizin*), king of the Abodrites and vassal of the Frankish king, who is killed by the Saxons. This is part of a longer entry, taken from the *Annals of Lorsch*, about events on the eastern frontier concerning the Saxons and the Avars.[55] For 798, the compiler again includes an entire yearly entry from the *Annals of Lorsch* in which the Abodrites are called "our Slavs" (*Sclavi nostri*).[56] The entry for 804 mentions a king of the Abodrites,

Thrasco (here *Irosuc*), who brings gifts to Charlemagne.[57] Information about this event could be found in a variety of annals. For 805, the compiler details a series of military events involving the Franks, the Bohemians (*Beuwidines*), the Saxons, and the Dalemintians (*Demelcion*) and their "king," Semela.[58] While the *Annales Regni Francorum* do allude to these expeditions,[59] it is clear that the compiler has obtained additional details from a different source; nothing suggests direct borrowing.

In the entry for 806, the compiler mentions the death of Miliduch (here *Milito*), king of the Sorbs (*Siurbi*), during a Frankish expedition on the other side of the Saale. The Franks destroy *civitates* of the Sorbs and their "kings" surrender and send hostages; Charlemagne then orders new strongholds to be built in the just-conquered territory.[60] Again, the *Annales Regni Francorum* recounts this expedition, including a mention of the death of Miliduch, but with fewer details;[61] again, they do not seem to have been the source of the *Chronicle's* compiler.

For 808, the *Chronicle* mentions an expedition led by Charles the Younger, son of Charlemagne, against the "Slavs, who are called *Linai*" (the Linons), as well as a raid of Godfred, "king" of the Danes, against "those Slavs who are called the Abodrites."[62] Once again, the *Annales Regni Francorum* mentions these events, but apparently independently.[63]

The note for 809 includes the mention that Charlemagne has sent an army to the other side of the Elbe and that it has destroyed, "with our *Guinidini*" (*cum nostris Guinidinis*), a stronghold there which is called *Semeldinc Connoburg*.[64] "Our Wends" are presumably here the Abodrites,[65] earlier called "our Slavs," although the corrupted spelling makes it unclear if the compiler understood who the "Wends" were. According to the *Annales Regni Francorum*, the Franks and their allies had, in that same year, attacked the "greatest stronghold" (*maxima civitas*) of the *Smeldingi*.[66] While this refers to the same expedition, nothing indicates direct borrowing.

In the entry for 810, the *Chronicle* indicates that the Danish "king" Godfred has sent someone to kill Thrasco (here *Drosocus*), "king" of the Abodrites.[67] This is mentioned in the *Annales Regni Francorum* for 809.[68] The entry for 811 alludes to a Frankish expedition against "those Slavs, who are called *Linai* and *Bechelenzi*;"[69] the entry for 812, to an expedition against "those Slavs, who are called *Wilti*" involving the Abodrites.[70] The entry for 813 includes a brief mention of events involving the Danes and the Abodrites. The source for the information included in these entries is unknown.

The compiler's sources

To pen this narrative of the late eighth and early ninth century until 803, the compiler used the *Annals of Lorsch* as the main source, which is made clear by a comparison between the texts. It is unlikely that the compiler would have had access to the *Annales Regni Francorum*; although both works are about the same period and despite multiple overlaps appearing in the contents, there are no similar formulations that would suggest direct borrowings. Since, however, the putative later section of the *Annals of Lorsch* – or whatever other materials might have been used – is not preserved, it is impossible to reconstruct how faithfully the compiler copied the sources, or if, or to what extent, he or she made interpolations.

A close comparison between the narrative of the *Chronicle* and its main source is, however, possible for the section covering the late eighth century. It appears that the compiler followed the *Annals of Lorsch* "closely and consistently."[71] Nonetheless, the compiler did add some interpolations and made a few changes, adding clarifications to passages that might have seemed unclear or slightly changing the formulation. He also added a few noticeable episodes with information taken from sources other than the *Annals of Lorsch*. Several of these episodes concern events in Al-Andalus, Muslim raids in southern Gaul, and other events taking place in the south; there is also some additional information about protagonists from more northerly parts of the Frankish realm who might not have been as familiar to readers of the south.[72] In view of this, it can be presumed that for a compiler active in southern Gaul, the *Annals of Lorsch* seemed the most useful source for events in the north of the kingdom and on the eastern frontier, but that other sources were necessary to complement them. The compiler was especially interested in adding information about the south of the kingdom and the Muslim frontier.

It can arguably be suspected that the entries for the years 803 to 818 were compiled following a similar methodology, that is, that they were based on a rendering of the lost *Annals of Lorsch* to which interpolations were added. If that is the case, a few deductions are possible. It would be futile to speculate to what extent the information concerning the Frankish court and the Frankish realm generally was taken from the lost *Annals of Lorsch* or from other similar, now lost, sources. It is, however, probably safe to assume that mentions of events from other parts of Europe have been taken from sources other than the *Annals of Lorsch*, as was the case for the entries concerning the late eighth century. The entry for 812 narrates an embassy of Abd-ar-Rahman I of Córdoba (here *Abulaz*), "king of the Saracens," to the Frankish court.[73] An assembly in Paderborn is mentioned as having taken place in 815, in which the armies of the Franks, Burgundians, and Alamans had taken part, as well as Bernard, king of the Lombards.[74] The entry for 816 mentions the visit of the Lombard king, Bernard, as well as Pope Stephen, to the court of Louis the Pious. The entry finishes with a brief indication of a rebellion by the Gascons with their *princeps Garsiamuci*, a usurper who dies shortly afterwards.[75] For 818, expeditions against the Bretons and the Gascons are mentioned.[76] It can be considered likely that at least the events concerning Al-Andalus, and possibly those referring to the Gascons, were taken from sources other than the *Annals of Lorsch*; this would indicate that the compiler proceeded for the years 804 to 818 in the same manner as had been done for the late eighth century, that is, the *Annals of Lorsch*, whose focus was on the northern part of the Frankish realm and the frontier areas with the Danes, the Abodrites, and other Slavic groups, would have been used as the main source and template, and information added from southern sources that could not be found in the main source.

Why are the Slavs important?

If the compiler was active somewhere in southern Gaul in the early ninth century, it is probably safe to assume that he or she knew little about the Slavs on the Elbe frontier. Such a person would have read about them in the set of annals that was the main source for the continuation of the universal chronicle that was being undertaken. Military and political events on the Frankish-Slavic frontier played an important role in these annals and there was no reason not to include them. The compiler felt the need to add information about events and peoples closer to home, however, which were a more obvious concern for those living in his own region, and presumably for his prospective readers. These concerned mostly the Muslims of Al-Andalus, and possibly the Gascons in the Pyrenees. The result was a narrative of a world centered on the Franks, but with a strong presence of peoples neighboring the Frankish realm who were involved in conflicts and alliances with the Franks. In the north, these were the Danes, the Abodrites, and diverse Slavic groups, in the south, Muslims and other groups from the Iberian Peninsula and the Pyrenees.

The compiler and the readers of the *Chronicle* presumably knew little about these Slavic groups, who had only recently appeared on the horizon of Frankish authors; the confused spellings of the scribe suggest little familiarity with these names. Annalists from the north, who were much closer to the Elbe frontier, were often not well informed themselves.[77] It must have been even more challenging for someone from the south to find reliable information. As Thomas Lienhard has remarked, Frankish annalists never mentioned the fact that these Slavs were pagans and never alluded to cultural or linguistic characteristics of these groups;[78] for a compiler living far away from these regions, it must have been difficult to distinguish these groups from others mentioned in the same texts. But, owing to the compiler's objective, stated in the preface, to include information from as many books as possible, the Slavs made their entry into this version of world history.

Most of these Slavic groups are, in the compiler's narrative, clearly identified both as being Slavs and as having more specific ethnic names. Several of these groups were led by "kings". The image that emerges from this narrative is of a variety of small groups with specific names that, collectively, are identified as Slavs, and who are involved in a variety of conflicts and alliances with the Franks.

The composer of the first part of the *Chronicle of Moissac* was interested in providing a moral interpretation of world history. This is sometimes reflected in the composer's comments and certainly in the choices made about what to include and what to leave out. This history of salvation is focused on the Christian community. Other peoples are mentioned primarily when the events in which they are involved permit a moral interpretation of the behavior of Christians; if such an interpretation did not seem obvious to the composer, they were omitted. These choices and this approach can easily be reconstructed by comparing the *Chronicle*'s version of these events with those of the sources. This was presumably intended as meaningful reading for a monastic audience.

The compiler of the second part, however, had a different take on world history. The compiler's focus was on the events of the last eighty years and he or she probably had fewer sources to choose from, which made it more challenging to propose a coherent narrative and to suggest a moralistic interpretation of such recent history. As a result, the compiler was more inclined to write a comprehensive compilation of the information available than a selection of events based on their potential for moral instruction. Indeed, the compiler, in contrast to the composer, did not leave much out; on the contrary, he or she added information from a variety of sources to the template of the main narrative. Such a methodology can be assessed by comparing the *Chronicle*'s version of these events with those of the compiler's sources for the late eighth century; even though most of the sources for the early ninth century are now lost, everything suggests that the compiler's approach was consistent. Possibly the author intended to provide useful information for reference more than reading for meditation.

In the course of the ninth century, the Slavic tribes east of the Elbe and Saale became part of the mental map of scholars of different backgrounds in Western Europe; thus, mention of some of these Slavic groups was included in the Old English translation of Orosius's geographic description of the world in the late ninth century.[79] The place of the *Chronicle of Moissac* in the early Europe-wide diffusion of knowledge about Slavic groups from the Elbe area has not yet been properly assessed. The diffusion of Frankish knowledge across Europe contributed to making early medieval scholars from southern Gaul to England aware of the presence of these groups. That they had not been known earlier does not, however, seem to have led to speculation about their origins. It is as if they had always been there. The Slavs arrived quietly on the world stage.

Notes

1 Helmut Beumann, "Historiographische Konzeption und politische Ziele Widukinds von Corvey," in *Settimane di Studio del Centro Italiano di Studi sull'Alto Medioevo XVII: La storiografia altomedievale* (Spoleto: Presso la Sede del Centro, 1970), 857–894.

2 Norbert Kersken, *Geschichtsschreibung im Europa der "nationes": Nationalgeschichtliche Gesamtdarstellungen im Mittelalter* (Münstersche Historische Forschungen, 8) (Cologne, Weimar and Vienna: Böhlau, 1995).

3 For overviews of the scholarship of recent decades in English, French, and German, see Justin Lake, "Current Approaches to Medieval Historiography," *History Compass* 13, no. 3 (2015): 89–109 and idem, "Authorial Intention in Medieval Historiography," *History Compass* 12, no. 4 (2014): 344–360.

4 *Chronicarum quae Dicuntur Fredegarii Scholastici Libri IV cum Continuationibus* in *Monumenta Germaniae Historica. Scriptores Rerum Merovingicarum*, II, ed. Bruno Krusch (Hannover: Hahn, 1888), 144–145 (cap. 4,48) and 154–155 (cap. 4,68). See Walter Pohl, "Samo," *Neue deutsche Biographie* 22 (2005): 408, Nora Berend, Przemysław Urbańczyk, and Przemysław Wiszewski, *Central Europe in the High Middle Ages: Bohemia, Hungary and Poland, c. 900 – c. 1300* (Cambridge: Cambridge University Press, 2013), 54, and P. M. Barford, *The Early Slavs: Culture and Society in Early Medieval Eastern Europe* (Ithaca, NY: Cornell University Press, 2001), 79–80.

5 Barford, *The Early Slavs*, 104–108. The Linons have been studied in the most detail through an interdisciplinary project, the results of which have been published in two volumes: *Slawen an der unteren Mittelelbe. Untersuchungen zur ländlichen Besiedlung, zum Burgenbau, zu Besiedlungsstrukturen und zum Landschaftswandel. Beiträge zum Kolloquium vom 7. bis 9. April 2010 in Frankfurt a. M.* (Frühmittelalterliche Archäologie zwischen Ostsee und Mittelmeer, 4), ed. Karl-Heinz Willroth et al. (Wiesbaden: Reichert, 2013) and *Slawen an der Elbe* (Göttinger Forschungen zur Ur- und Frühgeschichte, 1), ed. Karl-Heinz Willroth and Jens Schneeweiß (Neumünster: Wachholtz, 2011). For an overview of the evidence from the written sources, see Sébastien Rossignol, "Die Linonen zwischen Tat und Wort. Die Schriftquellen über die Entwicklung an der unteren Mittelelbe unter Berücksichtigung der interdisziplinären Forschungsergebnisse," in *Slawen an der unteren Mittelelbe*, 135–150, and idem, "Aufstieg und Fall der Linonen. Misslungene Ethnogenese an der unteren Mittelelbe," in *Slawen an der Elbe*, 15–38. For a case study of the Daleminicians, see idem, "Les Daleminciens face aux Francs. Conflits, tribut et structures sociales," in *Pillages, tributs, captifs. Prédation et sociétés de l'Antiquité tardive au haut Moyen Âge* (Histoire ancienne et médiévale, 153), ed. Rodolphe Keller and Laury Sarti (Paris: Publications de la Sorbonne, 2018), pp. 139–160.

6 Rossignol, "Die Linonen," 138–139 and idem, "Les Daleminciens."

7 Berend, Urbańczyk and Wiszewski, *Central Europe*, 50–56, Rossignol, "Die Linonen," 136; Thomas Lienhard, "Les combattants francs et slaves face à la paix: crise et nouvelle définition d'une élite dans l'espace oriental carolingien au début du IXe siècle," in *Les élites au haut Moyen Âge. Crises et renouvellements* (Collection Haut Moyen Âge, 1), ed. François Bougard, Laurent Feller and Régine Le Jan (Turnhout: Brepols, 2006), 253–266.

8 Thomas Lienhard, "À qui profitent les guerres en Orient? Quelques observations à propos des conflits entre Slaves et Francs au IXe siècle," *Médiévales* 51 (2006): 69–83.

9 Paris, Bibliothèque nationale de France (BNF), Ms. Lat. 4886, from the eleventh century; and Paris, BNF, Ms. Lat. 5941, from the twelfth century or *Chronicle of Aniane*.

10 See Wilhelm Levison and Heinz Löwe, *Deutschlands Geschichtsquellen im Mittelalter. Vorzeit und Karolinger. II. Heft. Die Karolinger vom Anfang des 8. Jahrhunderts bis zum Tode Karls des Großen* (Weimar: Böhlau, 1953), 187–188 and 265–266.

11 "Chronicon Moissiacense Maius. A Carolingian World Chronicle from Creation until the First Years of Louis the Pious, I–II," MA thesis on the basis of the manuscript of the late Ir. J.M.J.G. Kats, prepared and revised by D. Claszen (Oegstgeest, 2012). In addition to the manuscripts of the *Chronicle of Moissac* and of the *Aniane Annals*, Kats has taken into account other manuscript sources, including the *Chronicon Universale 741* and the extant versions of the *Annales Laureshamenses*. The texts of the *Aniane Annals* and the last section of the *Chronicle of Moissac* were edited previously by Walter Kettemann, "Subsidia Anianensia: Überlieferungs- und textgeschichtliche Untersuchungen zur Geschichte Witiza-Benedikts, seines Klosters Aniane und zur sogenannten 'anianischen Reform,' I–II," (PhD–diss., Universität Duisburg-Essen, 2000).

12 *Chronicon Moissiacense*, I, Introduction, 13–14.

13 Ibid., I, 21–23.

14 Ibid., I, 23–24. See: Patrick J. Geary, "Un fragment récemment découvert du *Chronicon Moissiacense*," *Bibliothèque de l'École des Chartes* 136, no. 1 (1978): 69–73.

15 *Chronicon Moissiacense*, I, 24–25 and Kettemann, *Subsidia*, 503–520.

16 *Chronicon Moissiacense*, I, 25–27.

17 Ibid., I, 27–31.

18 Venerable Bede, *De Temporum Ratione Liber* in *Opera, Pars VI: Opera Didascalia*, II (Corpus Christianorum Series Latina, 123 B), ed. Charles William Jones (Turnhout: Brepols, 1977), 462–535. See: *Chronicon Moissiacense*, I, 18.

19 Ibid., I, 19.

20 Ibid., I, 55–56.

21 Ibid., I, 56–57.

22 Ibid., I, 85.

23 Ibid., I, 85–90. See: Karl Heinrich Krüger, *Die Universalchroniken* (Typologie des sources du Moyen Âge occidental, 16) (Turnhout: Brepols, 1976), 34–49 and Anna-Dorothee von den Brincken, *Studien zur lateinischen Weltchronistik bis in das Zeitalter Ottos von Freising* (Düsseldorf: Triltsch, 1957), 43–95 and 233–234.

24 Isidore of Seville, *Etymologiarum sive Originum Libri XX* (Scriptorum Classicorum Bibliotheca Oxoniensis), ed. W.M. Lindsay (Oxford: Clarendon, 1911), cap. 5,28; Krüger, *Universalchroniken*, 13–16, von den Brincken, *Studien*, 39; and Hervé Inglebert, "The Universal Chronicle in Antiquity and in the Middle Ages," in *Vehicles of Transmission, Translation, and Transformation in Medieval Textual Culture* (Cursor Mundi, 4), ed. Robert Wisnovsky et al. (Turnhout: Brepols, 2011), 75–101, here 76–78.

25 Hans-Werner Goetz, "Die Gegenwart der Vergangenheit im früh- und hochmittelalterlichen Geschichtsbewußtsein," *Historische Zeitschrift* 255, no. 1 (1992): 61–97 and idem, *Geschichtsschreibung und Geschichtsbewußtsein im hohen Mittelalter* (Orbis mediaevalis. Vorstellungswelten des Mittelalters, 1) (Berlin: Akademie, 1999).

26 Von den Brincken, *Studien*, 38. Hans-Werner Goetz, "On the Universality of Universal History," in *L'historiographie médiévale en Europe. Actes du colloque organisé par la Fondation européenne de la science au Centre de recherches historiques et juridiques de l'Université Paris I du 29 mars au 1er avril 1989*, ed. Jean-Philippe Genet (Paris: Éditions du Centre national de la recherche scientifique, 1991), 247–261, here 247–248, and Isabelle Heullant-Donat, "Les prologues des chroniques universelles à la fin du Moyen Âge," in *Les prologues médiévaux. Actes du colloque international organisé par l'Academia Belgica et l'École française de Rome avec le concours de la F.I.D.E.M., Rome, 26–28 mars 1998*, ed. Jacqueline Hamesse (Turnhout: Brepols, 2000), 573–591.

27 Wolfram Drews, "Transkulturelle Perspektiven in der mittelalterlichen Historiographie. Zur Diskussion welt- und globalgeschichtlicher Entwürfe in der aktuellen Geschichtswissenschaft," *Historische Zeitschrift* 292, no. 1 (2011): 31–59, here 42, and Patrick Gautier Dalché, "L'espace de l'histoire: le rôle de la géographie dans les chroniques universelles," in *L'historiographie médiévale*, 287–300.

28 Goetz, "On the Universality," 260 and von den Brincken, *Studien*, 38.

29 Ernst Breisach, "World History Sacred and Profane: The Case of the Medieval Christian and Islamic World Chronicles," *Historical Reflections / Réflexions historiques* 20, no. 3 (1994): 337–356, here 346–347; Inglebert, "The Universal Chronicle," 237–238; Krüger, *Universalchroniken*, 24–25; and von den Brincken, *Studien*, 235–236.

30 Augustine of Hippo, *Sur la Genèse contre les Manichéens / De Genesi contra Manichaeos* (Bibliothèque Augustinienne), ed. Pierre Monat et al. (Paris: Institut d'études augustiniennes, 2004), 1–35–41; Augustine, *De Civitate Dei*, ed. Bernhard Dombart (Leipzig: Teubner, 1863), 22 and 30; Isidore, *Etymologiarum sive Originum Libri XX*, cap. 5, 38–39. See also Drews, "Transkulturelle Perspektiven," 44–45 and Krüger, *Universalchroniken*, 26–27, von den Brincken, *Studien*, 108–109 and 235.

31 Breisach, "World History," 348.

32 Brezzi, "Chroniques," 237.

33 Von den Brincken, *Studien*, 110–113.

34 *Chronicon Moissiacense*, I, 93.

35 Bede, *De Temporum Ratione*, preface, 263.

36 Ibid., 265. See Augustine of Hippo, *De Trinitate Libri XV*, I (Corpus Christianorum Series Latina, 50–50 A) (Turnhout: Brepols, 1968), iii, 25–28.

37 Probably the older Latin translation made from the Greek. See Peter Hunter Blair, *The World of Bede* (Cambridge: Cambridge University Press, 1990), 234.

38 *Chronicon Moissiacense*, II, text edition, preface, 1.

39 Ibid., II, preface, 1–2.

40 Ibid., II, preface, 2–4

41 Isidore of Seville, *Etymologiarum sive Originum Libri XX*, cap. 5,28.

42 *In Christi nomine incipit LIBER CRONICORUM BEDANE PRESBYTERI FAMULI CHRISTI, collectum breviter ab auctoribus ceterisque storiografis, Iheronimo, Augustino, Ambrosio, Ysidoro, Orosio nec non Iosepho, qui multa de temporum seriem scripsit Rufino vel Marcellino comite, de totis summatim incipiens ab Adam numerum annorum et aetates temporum. Secundum Hebreos vel secundum LXX interpretes, iuculente scripsit. Addens ad huc annos ab incarnatione domini* – Chronicon Moissiacense, II, preface, 5.

43 *Chronicon Moissiacense*, II, *anno 35 regni Clotarii*, 98. See *Chronicarum quae Dicuntur Fredegarii*, 144–145 (cap. 4,48) and 154–155 (cap. 4,68).

44 *Chronicon Moissiacense*, II, *anno 10 regni Dagoberti*, 100; *Chronicarum quae Dicuntur Fredegarii*, 158 (cap. 4,74).

45 *Chronicon Moissiacense*, II, *anno 16 regni sui*, 100; *Chronicarum quae Dicuntur Fredegarii*, 161 (cap. 4,79).

46 Ibid., 150 (cap. 4,58).

47 *Chronicon Moissiacense*, II, 109, and *Liber Historiae Francorum* in *Monumenta Germaniae Historica. Scriptores rerum Merovingicarum,* II (Hannover: Hahn, 1888), 323–324 (cap. 49).

48 The Franks plundered churches until Clovis was baptized: *Chronicon Moissiacense*, II, 90; the Lombards were given their name by Wotan: ibid., II, 93.

49 *Chronicon Moissiacense*, II, *anno Heraclii 16, indicione 15*, 99; cf. *Chronicarum quae Dicuntur Fredegarii*, 153–154 (cap. 4,66).

50 *Chronicon Moissiacense*, II, 111.

51 Ibid., II, *anno Heraclii 16, indicione 15*, 99.

52 *Iste deditus in faeminis, exemplo suo sacerdotes ac populum luxuriosae vivere docuit, irritans furorem Domini. Chronicon Moissiacense*, II, 111. The source for this passage is unknown.

53 Ibid., II, *a.* 789, 127.

54 *Annales Laureshamenses* in *Monumenta Germaniae Historica. Scriptores*, I, ed. Georg Heinrich Pertz (Hannover: Hahn, 1876), *a.* 789, 34.

55 *Chronicon Moissiacense*, II, *a.* 795, 134; *Annales Laureshamenses, a.* 795, 36.

56 *Chronicon Moissiacense*, II, *a.* 798, 136; *Annales Laureshamenses, a.* 798, 37.

57 *Chronicon Moissiacense*, II, *a.* 804, 142.

58 Ibid., II, *a.* 805, 142.

59 *Annales Regni Francorum* in *Monumenta Germaniae Historica. Scriptores rerum Germanicarum in usum scholarum separatim editi*, VI, eds. Georg Heinrich Pertz and Friedrich Kurze (Hannover: Hahn, 1895), *a.* 805, 120.

60 *Chronicon Moissiacense*, II, *a.* 806, 143.

61 *Annales Regni Francorum, a.* 806, 121–122.

62 *Chronicon Moissiacense*, II, *a.* 808, 143.

63 *Annales Regni Francorum, a.* 808, 125.

64 *Chronicon Moissiacense*, II, *a.* 809, 144.

65 Kettemann, *Subsidia*, II, 112 note 1.

66 *Annales Regni Francorum, a.* 809, 129.
67 *Chronicon Moissiacense,* II, *a.* 810, 144.
68 *Annales Regni Francorum, a.* 809, 129.
69 *Chronicon Moissiacense Maius,* II, *a.* 811, 145.
70 Ibid., II, *a.* 812, 145.
71 Ibid., I, 120.
72 Ibid., I, 119–123.
73 Ibid., II, *a.* 812, 145.
74 Ibid., II, *a.* 815, 147.
75 Ibid., II, *a.* 816, 148.
76 Ibid., II, *a.* 818, 150.
77 Lienhard, "À qui profitent les guerres," and idem, "Les combattants," 259–260.
78 Lienhard, "À qui profitent les guerres."
79 Janet Bately, "Ohthere and Wulfstan in the Old English *Orosius,*" in *Ohthere's Voyages. A Late 9th-century Account of Voyages along the Coasts of Norway and Denmark and its Cultural Context* (Maritime Culture of the North, 1), ed. eadem and Anton Englert (Roskilde: Viking Ship Museum, 2007), 18–39, here 24–26.

4

MEDIEVAL LATIN EUROPE CONNECTING WITH THE REST OF THE WORLD

The East Central European Link

Felicitas Schmieder

Is East Central Europe a forgotten region in medieval history? Why, and what can be done about it? These questions were posed at "A Forgotten Region? East Central Europe in the Global Middle Ages," a conference held at the CEU Department of Medieval Studies in Budapest in March, 2014, in honor of János Bak, who has done so much for Medieval Studies in the region. The easy answer to the question "why?" is that for at least half of the twentieth century East Central Europe, mostly positioned behind the Iron Curtain, was seen from the point of view of Western-dominated international Medieval Studies. Historians, including medievalists, are aware today how much of what we see in history is formed by our own present, in the questions we ask, in the answers we get, and, not least, in the places we look for them.

This is true from any perspective, so it is not helpful to count East Central Europe as either part of the East or of the West, even though one or the other view may be politically correct in certain epochs. It may be more productive to look into the idea of an East Central Europe with internal similarities that distinguish it from both West and East. (This insight is guided by present-day ideals of basic individuality and a world free of political-military blocks.) This problem of perspective is true not only for time but also for space: We are dependent on the place where we live, grew up, and were educated. For a German such as me, born in the middle of the Cold War, from the old Bundesrepublik Deutschland, without German roots in the East, the eastern parts of Europe were quite out of focus. They were even more distant, maybe forgotten, when Western historians turned to approaches on global history. German medievalists still seem to have no problem comparing, for example, German urban historical features and developments with the quite different ones in Italy or Flanders while ignoring Romania, Croatia, Slovenia, Hungary, Slovakia, Bohemia, Poland, Western Ukraine, the Baltic States, even Belarus or the west of Russia where much greater similarities would be found.

And this was more prevalent even before the Cold War that blocked Western European views from "remembering" this region properly. Looking back into the Middle Ages, East Central Europe seems to have lain at the rim. Beyond it there was Russia, which seems to have always been blocked by basically insuperable cultural borders. Russia is usually seen as a region that has always been far away, foreign, and with only scarce relations that were finally mostly severed by Christianization because shortly after the "baptism of the Rus'" ("Taufe Rußlands") the "Great Schism" abruptly and effectively cut off any real connection. More recent research has made it seem plausible that not only did the schism not pervade the Christian societies too deeply and too quickly, but that – as Christian Raffensperger points out in this volume – we were also prevented from seeing the rich (martial and economic) ongoing exchanges between East and West that were strong before the Mongol conquest due to this conquest that really cut Russia off and, again, to the twentieth-century Iron Curtain that seemed to prolong the centuries-old border most naturally.[1]

Also, a fascination with Byzantium did not help the region much. It lay beyond East Central Europe from the Western point of view and was certainly a source of the latter's culture and traditions. But we usually consider the transmission as having happened only via the Mediterranean Sea (probably based on the idea of European history running mostly along the lines of the Roman Empire long after this empire had ceased to exist and therefore the light of civilization was shining from the south and the west into the barbaric eastern parts of the continent). Byzantium itself is often considered a bit strange, not really "European", and it was also estranged by the schism. When the Muslim Ottomans gradually took over the former Byzantine Empire, the impression of East Central Europe as a specific type of border region was only strengthened. In the later Middle Ages and the Early Modern period, East Central Europeans used to consider themselves the *antemurale Christianitatis*,[2] a metaphor that at first glance speaks of defense, by which they claimed – and reminded their Latin Christian partners further west – that in their lands they defended true Christianity against the Ottomans and also against Orthodox Christianity. This image of a wall further strengthened, in the West, the idea that East Central Europe always lay somewhere on the margin, less able to develop civilization due to a permanent struggle for defense.

Furthermore, it would not even have been worthwhile (in the minds of modern historians) to climb the wall, for beyond it and the schismatic Christians lay something even less desirable: the steppes. This brings us to what we may call the nomadic bias in historiography. East Central Europe was considered (and still is by historians) not only the edge of Christianity (or true Christianity by the measure of the Latin West), but also as far too close to the edge of civilization in an even more atavistic sense. Although a modern ideal is to have open borders, they should ideally be open between societies that live in a similar way and respect the same moral, social, and legal rules, which is *a priori* not perceived as possible between sedentary and nomadic societies. Even if historians learn, following in the footsteps of Christian Raffensperger and others, to accept Russia as a part of Europe, this would probably still end from the time when it was cut off by the Mongol onslaught in the 1230s.

This onslaught interfered deeply in the structures of the Rus' principalities and made them "Asian" or part of the foreign peoples who created the "true" nomadic dead end of East Central Europe's roads and of historians' thoughts about civilization.

One of the main challenges of a global history of culture based on cultural encounters is to reach a clear perspective on the entanglement of the historic parties involved. All sides have to be taken seriously in themselves; they have to be considered active and productive partners in the encounter; and they have to be expected to change (to accept, more or less willingly and consciously, learning from the example of the other). Thus, when looking at encounters between, for instance, Islamic and Byzantine civilization, we can easily apply the concept. We consider encounters between Islam and Latin Europe an exchange in both directions in the long run (first "our" Greek and Roman ancestors exported "European" civilization to them, then they "gave it back" to us[3]). But what about the nomads – who may or may not be able to learn from the sedentary civilizations? Can we[4] learn anything from them? As Florin Curta has stressed it has even been difficult for a long time to imagine, for example, the nomadic Avars not as a threat to but as transmitters of Byzantine culture (not so much at the gate of Byzantium, but themselves the gate into Byzantium).[5]

We are all members of sedentary cultures, and as such we are still not used to considering a nomadic society as culturally developed, as able to have a civilization of its own, in the first place. Mostly, we consider our own "ancestors" sedentary, thus civilized to a certain and important degree – while we usually do not give the same credit to nomadic peoples. According to widespread ideas about them, they did not live in houses, they did not cultivate land, had no literary culture, and thus were not civilized. They depended fully on the neighboring sedentary cultures (whom they raided frequently to acquire of the finer things in life), depending on them to teach them how to become civilized.

The images of nomads that are still present in popular European culture and elsewhere are exactly of this type: they were trotting after their cattle, now and then raiding some helpless sedentary peasants, during these raids stupidly laying waste to the fields, killing domestic animals and skilled farmers in the most brutal way possible. Or they were fierce, in uncountable numbers, and seemingly invincible fighters who mercilessly slaughtered those who dared to defend themselves (which actually happened at times, just as more "civilized" fighters did if it seemed useful), who reigned through terror, exploited the land they conquered by taking its goods and skilled craftsmen and other specialists. Any of their empires broke apart only three or four generations after it began because they basically only lived off the skills and achievements of others. They even (to mention just some of the more basic barbarian stereotypic traits) drank blood, or at least excessive alcohol, and ate anything from worms or mice up to human flesh.[6]

Against these barely human humans, logically the borders had to be closed – thus stranding East Central Europe on a dead-end road. The *antemurale* metaphor, however, not only alluded to the defending wall, but also to the bridgehead of Christian mission among the pagans beyond. It also defined a border region full of knowledge and experience of the world beyond this border, especially but not only in the vast Kingdom of Hungary – experience people in the region were well aware of and put to use for Christianity. In the 1230s, Hungarian Dominicans noted:

> In the deeds of the Christian Hungarians it was found that there is another, greater, Hungary from where seven leaders with their followings [*populis suis*] had emigrated in order to find a place to live [*habitandi*] because their land could no longer feed [*sustinere*] the mass of inhabitants. After wandering through and laying waste to many realms [*regna*] they finally reached the land that today bears the name of Hungary but was then called the pastures of the Romans ... Here they were finally brought to the right faith by Saint Stephen, their first king, while the earlier Hungarians from whom they descended remained infidels and remain infidels up to today. The Dominican friars who found this in the old writings felt pity for the Hungarians, from whom they knew they were descended and who were still in the error of infidelity. They sent four brethren out to search for them, to see whether they could find them with the help of God. They knew from the writings of the Ancients that it [the land] was located towards the East, but where exactly was completely unknown ... In a pagan land they found some people speaking their language, from whom could be learned with certainty where they [the nomads] lived.[7]

This story, extraordinary in our sources, whether it is true or invented and whether it stems from the very time or has been written and stylized in hindsight,[8] tells a medieval story of a civilizing mission to bring the steppes closer. According to it, the Dominicans remembered that the Hungarians had lived in the steppes as pagans and had come to be part of Christianity only after leaving it. They also intentionally revived the link to the steppes in order to bring their relatives into their own world. They had the knowledge and they felt close to these people, not assuming in principle that the border with the steppes was something that should be kept closed tightly.

This was quite different from the Flemish Franciscan William of Rubruck, who, in 1253, shortly after the Hungarian Dominican endeavors, described his way into the steppes as passing through the "gates of hell" (*unam portam inferni*).[9] He was not visiting distant ancestors, but the Mongols who had only recently successfully attacked Central European lands. Part of his feeling may also have arisen from him stemming from an urban environment in the far west of Europe. We simply cannot tell how much of this kind of comparison is connected to personality, personal experience or just the literary genre in which it is presented. What we should consider is that the degree of sedentism differed greatly in medieval Europe and this also means that many of the societies in the Latin European sphere were much less sedentary than is usually believed. One of the ideas of the mendicant orders was to be on the move and to change places often, one of the reasons why they took up far-reaching missionary work so easily. Merchants in thirteenth-century Latin

Europe, in the highly urbanized south and west and even further north and east, were still quite used to traveling personally along with their goods to go out and find new markets. Neither group may have found towns as they knew them in the steppes, but quite a few of their members found a way of traveling that they must have been quite used to.[10] They knew how to adapt to conditions much less different than we may think they were.

In the nineteenth century, when scholars like E.G. Ravenstein[11] started to research migration and tried to describe its rules, they were impressed by the recent huge movement and even displacement of millions of people as a result of the Industrial Revolution. This is also when the image of a largely immobile pre-modern society arose – and the clear dichotomy between nomadic and sedentary peoples was derived from this modern perspective. Today it is known that in wide regions of medieval Latin Western (as well as Eastern) Europe, the elites, the lords and their followings were bound together in family-like structures and were highly mobile. They covered huge areas rapidly and had to be personally visible practically everywhere as frequently as possible in order to fulfill military necessities and be accepted as rulers in face-to-face communities. They did "not yet" (as it is usually described in hindsight) have permanent residences – one could also say they were still living a nomadic life in which they were hunting for fighting practice and for food while sedentary peasants partly supplied their needs on a regular basis.[12]

Nomads, however, did not just follow their cattle but had permanent pastures which changed through the seasons of the year.[13] They were bound together in clans, normally constituted in an agnatic way and organized by military aristocracy – not much different from the Latin European elites. They lived in an economic-ecological system dependent on nature and they needed additional products from their sedentary neighbors. Due to the fragility of their subsistence they often had to move away from their usual pastures. Conflict among clans or between a clan and the sedentary peoples created further movement since a clan could be pushed back or displaced. These conflicts could also result in rule over others or submission to others. If larger communities were formed in this way they remained soft entities, easily experiencing periods of disintegration. As a soft entity any nomadic community or "empire" is kept together by loyalties derived from the clan structures or feudal relations. Led by charismatic leaders, these loyalties could stretch far beyond the normal reach of pastoral clans grazing their herds on their own pastures. Clans were grouped around one nuclear clan, creating relatively loose clan confederations. Once created, this kind of dominion could last over several generations (though rarely with a stable structure), if and as long as the kin heirs of the founder could claim succession, especially in the area of booty, which provided the additional subsidies that a nomadic society needed. Certainly there are differences compared with medieval Western conditions – but are they really that great? Wouldn't it help to understand medieval nobility if we thought about it for once from a nomadic angle instead of the not-yet-completely-modern one?

I would claim, firstly, that the life of the medieval Latin Europeans who actually encountered nomads was, for a very long time, not really far from the nomadic way of life – and thus the border may not have been considered and experienced as sharp and closed as modern historians more or less automatically expect. Secondly, the nomads were far less primitive than we use to think; neither were they just shepherds, driven by their herds, nor were they unable to create their own cultural achievements. Thus, we should start to see them as peoples who not only enabled cultural transmission across wide distances, but who actively entangled cultures by creating their own cultural skills – who, therefore, were anything but a dead end for neighboring cultures.[14]

Let us now paint an image of cultivated nomadic Mongols bringing their very own cultural experiences into the encounter with their sedentary neighbors. This cultural experience was probably based on the wide linguistic difference any traveler encounters when crossing a continent like Asia. It was probably also present in the mixed units in the military *tümen* system that Činggis Khan seems to have introduced:[15] an army of ten thousand men composed of groups of a thousand that were composed of groups of a hundred that were composed of groups of ten men. These ten were absolutely loyal to each other and, more importantly, were from different tribes; old loyalties were broken up in order to strengthen the new one. The Mongol regime in China preferred barbarians, as members of the old Chinese Mandarin elite complained, because they spoke more than one language.[16] Marco Polo mirrors this impression of necessary skills when he tells how the Great Khan was impressed by him mastering several languages and several alphabets.[17] In China as well as in other places of the vast Mongol empire the Mongol linguistic experience met very different literary cultures, resulting in a vast lexicon culture – a lexicon culture that went far beyond the usual bilingualism.

The most impressive output of this culture stems from mid-fourteenth-century Yemen, never part of the Mongol Empire but touched by it in manifold ways (as can be seen in Marco Polo's report on his travels from China to Persia with a Mongol embassy). Like nearly every other realm in the old Eurasian world of the thirteenth and fourteenth centuries, Yemen had its own "Mongol experience."[18] The Rasûlid Hexaglot (named after the then-ruling Yemenite dynasty) combines six different languages, putting them side by side in six columns: Arabic, Persian, Turkic, Mongol, Armenian, and Greek.[19] The Hexaglot is written in the Arabic alphabet, a fact that may, at first glance, seem unusual, but which is typical for the Mongol lexicon culture. The Mongol imperial language and alphabet (Mongol is written in a version of the Uighur alphabet) was not dominant; the main important languages and writing systems were Chinese in the East and Persian in the Arabic alphabet in the West.

Beyond this, the language and alphabet of the cultural group influenced by the Mongol lexicon culture were important, showing the influence and its transfer at the same time. This can be seen in the example of the *Codex Cumanicus* (today kept in Venice, Biblioteca Marciana, Lat. Z. 549 = 1597). The codex is an Italian collective manuscript written around 1330, probably compiled in one of the Italian merchants' colonies on the Crimea. They were one of the most stable intersections of Latin European and Mongol nomadic steppe cultures north of the Black and

Caspian seas, the Qiptchak or Cumans. At the very same time missionaries, some from East Central Europe, were also present in the area.[20] The codex includes a trilingual dictionary with Latin words in alphabetical order in the left column, their Persian translation in the right column, and in the middle a Cuman translation (a Turkic language probably spoken by members of the tribes inhabiting the Mongol territories north of the Black Sea – an unwritten language at the time of the Codex). Since Persian was the most important lingua franca in the west of the Mongol Empire, only the Cuman may hint at the specific region of origin. Similarly important, the dictionary is written in the Latin alphabet and thus the Mongol technique of a multilingual dictionary was adapted by the Latin Europeans, who thus learnt from the nomads.[21]

The steppe region beyond East Central Europe can therefore be considered fertile ground for cross-cultural learning.[22] The Latin Europeans went onto the steppes knowing how to learn from the nomads, something we, in our modern societies, tend to overlook completely. If the Mongol Empire is seen as one of several global empires creating a world system before Europeans started to dominate the world, while they were still living on a marginal periphery,[23] then the East Central European link to the steppes was certainly one of the main important bridges by which Latin Europe could appear on the world stage and come into contact with the rest of the world. The time of the Mongols was, for Latin Europe, the moment to begin its long road to global cultural dominance, a road that was filled with learning from others in order to improve their own abilities to conquer and rule. With the help of the Mongol Empire Latin Europeans reached China and India, and although the Eastern European link to the Asian steppes was not the only one possible way (there was also the option of going through the Middle East and across the Indian Ocean[24]), it was the first and the one that lasted much longer than the others. The Franciscans John of Plano Carpini and William of Rubruck as well as the Venetian merchants Niccolò and Maffeo Polo (father and uncle of the much more famous Marco) and thus the first European diplomats, missionaries, and merchants we know by name who reached Eastern Asia, did so by way of the steppes.[25] The Italian merchant colonies in the Black Sea area – Genoese Caffa on the Crimea and Venetian Tana at the mouth of the Don River – were the last to remain links for Latin Europeans to trans-Asian trade routes long after the Middle East had been closed again; they fell to the Ottomans in 1475 and 1463, respectively.

The discrepancy to the fact that East Central Europe was literally a blank spot on the mental map of Western European historiography for a long time is clear. My main point is to raise questions by presenting the steppes beyond the *antemurale Christianitatis* not as a no-go zone for the sedentary Western Europeans, but as a space used by Latin Europeans as soon as it became possible. The East Central European border region was full of knowledge about the world beyond this border and willing to connect with it – and thus it is worthwhile for us to look at it. Some of the seemingly most distinctive differences between the steppes and the West have been created by modern biased historians. We should actively strive to rethink, to actually define, where the Eastern borders of "Europe" lie, even if today it still makes us relatively uneasy and if, wherever they are, they blur into the dangerous unknown of something between the Russian forests and the Mongol steppe.

Transitional regions are too easily overlooked in world history; everything passes through them and nothing seems to leave traces in the region and on the people, objects, and ideas passing through. Even if this were correct, the transit would still be of immense importance for the civilizations at both ends – the transit changes the regions it touches and the regions deeply influence what passes through. Medieval Europe was relatively unimportant when measured on the contemporary global level. By the means and experiences of East Central Europe, however, it profited from the Mongol empire-building and was culturally developed enough to include in its achievements core nomadic elements that the empire of the Mongols brought from Eurasia. In the words of Michal Biran, the Mongols "bolstered Eurasian integration and broadened the horizons of their subjects and neighbors. Mongol nomadic culture had an enormous impact on Eurasian exchange under their auspices."[26] By building an important, lasting bridge to Eurasia, East Central Europe connected the West to the rest of the world.

Notes

1 Christian Raffensperger in this volume and more broadly in his book *Reimagining Europe. Kievan Rus' in the Medieval World* (Harvard Historical Studies, 177) (Cambridge, MA: Harvard University Press, 2012).

2 Paul Srodecki, *Antemurale Christianitatis. Zur Genese der Bollwerksrhetorik im östlichen Mitteleuropa an der Schwelle vom Mittelalter zur Frühen Neuzeit* (Historische Studien, 508) (Husum: Matthiesen, 2014); Małgorzata Morawiec, "*Antemurale christianitatis*. Polen als Vormauer des christlichen Europa," *Jahrbuch der europäischen Geschichte* 2 (2001): 249–260; Paul W. Knoll, "Poland as *Antemurale Christianitatis* in the Late Middle Ages," *The Catholic Historical Review* 60 (1974): 381–401; and Renzo U. Montini, "Polonia, *Antemurale Christianitatis*," *L'Europa orientale: politica, economia, cultura, bibliografia a cura dell'Istituto per l'Europa Orientale* 22 (1942): 14–31. The journal *Antemurale* was published by the Polish Institute in Rome between 1954 and 1985.

3 This also seems to be a considerable distortion of what is and has always been European, but that is a different topic that has to be left aside here.

4 "We" in this case means the Latin Europeans, but it could easily be replaced with members of Islamic or Chinese civilizations.

5 Florin Curta, "East Central Europe: the Gate to Byzantium," *Byzantinische Zeitschrift* 108 (2015): 1–41, here 35–36, cf. *The Other Europe in the Middle Ages. Avars, Bulgars, Khazars, and Cumans* (East Central and Eastern Europe in the Middle Ages, 450–1450, 2), ed. idem (Leiden and Boston: Brill, 2008).

6 Felicitas Schmieder, "Nomaden in Europa und Europäer unter Nomaden. Lateinisch–mittelalterliche Verarbeitungen einer fremdartigen Lebensform," in *Der imaginierte Nomade. Formel und Realitätsbezug bei antiken, mittelalterlichen und arabischen Autoren*, ed. Alexander Weiß (Wiesbaden: Reichert, 2007), 137–154 (where I contrasted the lifeways of nomads and sedentary people). For similar images in the Islamic world, only a few examples: David Cook, "The Image of the Turk in Classical and Modern Muslim Apocalyptic Literature," in *Peoples of the Apocalypse. Eschatological Beliefs and Political Scenarios*, ed. Wolfram Brandes, Felicitas Schmieder, and Rebekka Voß (Berlin: de Gruyter, 2016), 225–236; Yehoshua

Frenkel, "The Turks of the Eurasian Steppes in Medieval Arabic Writing," in *Mongols, Turks, and Others. Eurasian Nomads and the Sedentary World* (Brill's Inner Asian Library, 11), ed. Reuven Amitai and Michal Biran (Leiden: Brill, 2005), 201–241; David O. Morgan, "Persian Perceptions of Mongols and Europeans," in *Implicit Understandings: Observing, Reporting, and Reflecting on the Encounters Between Europeans and Other Peoples in the Early Modern Era*, ed. Stuart B. Schwartz (Cambridge: Cambridge University Press, 1994), 201–217.

7 Julian von Ungarn, *Itinera* in *Drei Texte zur Geschichte der Ungarn und Mongolen: Die Missionsreisen des fr. Julian OP ins Uralgebiet (1234/5) und nach Rußland (1237) und der Bericht des Erzbischofs Peter über die Tartaren*, ed. Heinrich Dörrie (Göttingen: Vandenhoeck & Ruprecht, 1956), 151–152.

8 Nora Berend, Przemysław Urbańczyk, and Przemysław Wiszewski, *Central Europe in the High Middle Ages. Bohemia, Hungary and Poland, c. 900–c. 1300* (Cambridge: Cambridge University Press, 2013), 69–70.

9 Willem van Ruysbroeck [William of Rubruck], *Itinerarium* xii, 3 in *Itinera et Relationes Fratrum Minorum saeculi XIII et XIV* (Sinica Franciscana, 1), ed. P. Anastasius van den Wyngaert OFM (Quaracchi: Collegium S. Bonaventurae, 1929), 147–332, here 193, translated and commented on: *The Mission of Friar William of Rubruck. His Journey to the Court of the Great Khan Möngke 1253–1255*, trans. and notes by Peter Jackson and David Morgan (London: Hakluyt Society, 1990), 104. William did not enter the steppes via East Central Europe. About a decade earlier John of Plano Carpini – cf. note 25 – from the same order chose to travel by ship via Byzantium to the Crimea rather than via the road through Poland and Kiev. When William had left behind the first group of Tatars, he felt like he had escaped the clutches of demons: IX, 3, 189, transl. 98).

10 Jean Richard, *La papauté et les missions d'orient au Moyen Age (XIIIᵉ–XVᵉ siècles)* (Rome: École française de Rome, 1977).

11 Ernest G. Ravenstein, "The Laws of Migration," *Journal of the Statistical Society* 48, no. 2 (1885): 167–235.

12 Felicitas Schmieder, "Von der 'Christianitasnach' 'Europa' – Europa," in *Die Welt 1000–1250* (Globalgeschichte. Die Welt 1000–2000, 1), ed. Peter Feldbauer and Angela Schottenhammer (Vienna: Mandelbaum, 2011), 213–238, here 219–220. The image of nomadic life used to describe the movements of even Western European nobility in the fifteenth century is explicitly addressed by Zita Rohr, "On the Road Again. The Semi-Nomadic Career of Yolande of Aragon (1400–1439)," in *Travels and Mobilities in the Middle Ages. From the Atlantic to the Black Sea* (International Medieval Research, 21), ed. Marianne O'Doherty and Felicitas Schmieder (Turnhout: Brepols, 2015), 215–244, but is today described as such on a regular basis.

13 *Mongols, Turks, and Others*, here see especially Naomi Standen, "What Nomads Want: Raids, Invasions and the Liao Conquest of 947," 129–174, and Elizabeth Endicott, "The Mongols and China: Cultural Contacts and the Changing Nature of Pastoral Nomadism (Twelfth to Early Twentieth Centuries)," 461–481. See also: Felicitas Schmieder, "Steppe, People of (Hungarians, Huns, Avars, Mongols)," in *Encyclopedia of Global Human Migrations*, vol. 5, ed. Immanuel Ness (Malden, MA: Wiley-Blackwell, 2013), 2876–2886.

14 Nicola Di Cosmo, "State Formation and Periodization in Inner Asian History," *Journal of World History* 10 (1999): 1–40. This has been stressed more frequently recently: Michal Biran, "The Mongols and the Inter-Civilizational Exchange," in *The Cambridge World History V: Expanding webs of exchange and conflict, 500 CE – 1500 CE*, ed. Benjamin Z. Kedar and Merry E. Wiesner-Hanks (Cambridge: Cambridge University Press, 2015), 534–558; *Nomads as Agents of Cultural Change: The Mongols and Their Eurasian*

Predecessors (Perspectives on the Global Past), ed. Reuven Amitai and Michal Biran (Honolulu, HI: University of Hawai'i Press, 2014).

15 Michael Weiers, *Erbe aus der Steppe: Beiträge zur Sprache und Geschichte der Mongolen* (Tunguso-Sibirica, 28) (Wiesbaden: Harrassowitz, 2010), 131–132; and David O. Morgan, *The Mongols* (Oxford: Blackwell, 1986), 84–96 ("The Mongol Army").

16 Thomas T. Allsen, "The Rasûlid Hexaglot in Its Eurasian Cultural Context," in *The King's Dictionary. The Rasûlid Hexaglot: Fourteenth Century Vocabularies in Arabic, Persian, Turkic, Greek, Armenian and Mongol,* ed. Peter B. Golden (Leiden: Brill, 2000), 25–49, here 35–36.

17 Marco Polo, *Milione, c.* XVI, ed. Luigi Foscolo Benedetto (Florence: Olschki, 1928), 10. Whether we believe Marco's (who was in China) high-level career or not, he clearly knew what was needed for one.

18 Allsen, "The Rasûlid Hexaglot," 42: "In many instances such interests were directly connected with a given society's 'Mongol experience,' an experience that often provided both reason and opportunities to pursue studies of the languages of others."

19 *The King's Dictionary.*

20 Michael Bihl and Arthur Christopher Moule, eds., "*De duabus Epistolis Fratrum Minorum Tatariae Aquilonaris an. 1323,*" *Archivum Franciscanum Historicum* 16 (1923): 89–112, idem, eds. "Tria nova documenta de missionibus Fr. Minorum Tatariae aquilonaris annorum 1314–22," *Archivum Franciscanum Historicum* 17 (1924): 55–71.

21 Felicitas Schmieder, "Die Welt des *Codex Cumanicus.* Außereuropäische Kontexte lateinisch-christlicher Sprachgrenzüberwindungen," in *Grenzen und Grenzüberschreitung im Mittelalter. 11. Symposium des Mediaevistenverbandes vom 14. bis 17. März 2005 in Frankfurt an der Oder,* ed. Ulrich Knefelkamp and Kristian Bosselmann-Cyran (Berlin: Akademie, 2007), 285–294.

22 This may even go further, if the one music sheet in the Codex is actually from the 1330s, it displays a type of notation that was only just about to emerge in the writing of medieval Western music and that may, therefore, have come from these semi-nomadic peripheries into European music: Jason Stoessel, "Voice and Song in Early Encounters between Latins, Mongols, and Persians, c.1250–c.1350," in *Towards a Global History of Music,* ed. Reinhard Strohm and Martin Stokes (Abingdon: Routledge, 2018, forthcoming). Perceiving this has to do with a shift in music history where people are looking more frequently at the peripheries instead of claiming every invention for the center – and maybe with the fact that the music historian in question is Australian and thus from the peripheries of research on the Western Middle Ages himself).

23 Janet L. Abu-Lughod, *Before European Hegemony. The World System A.D. 1250–1350* (New York and Oxford: Oxford University Press, 1989).

24 The learned doctor Pietro d'Abano (died 1315/1318), for example, criticized the Genoese Vivaldi brothers, who tried to sail around Africa to get to India, which was in his eyes superfluous due to easy access through the Mongol Empire: (*Liber) Conciliator differentiarum philosophorum et praecipue medicorum* (Venedig, 1504), Diff. LXVII. fol.98ᵛ.

25 Johannes de Plano Carpini [John of Plano Carpini], *Storia dei Mongoli,* ed. Paolo Daffinà et al. (Spoleto: Centro italiano di studi sull'alto medioevo, 1989), trans. and commented on by Felicitas Schmieder, *Kunde von den Mongolen (1245–1247)* (Fremde Kulturen in alten Berichten, 3) (Sigmaringen: Thorbecke, 1997, repr. Wiesbaden, 2015), on Rubruck see note 9, on the Polos see note 17.

26 Biran, *Mongol Empire,* 554–555.

PART TWO

Christianization and the East–West Link

5

GREGORY THE GREAT AND THE BISHOPS

Papal Letters and the Ecclesiastical Integration and Disintegration of East Central Europe

Daniel Syrbe

Integration into the Christian community was one of the main factors that connected East Central Europe to the world surrounding it and, in Roman antiquity, especially to the Mediterranean. In addition, Christianity, with its ecclesiastical structure, was a key factor for religious, social, and cultural continuity in the transition from Late Antiquity to the Middle Ages.[1] In contrast to the central regions of the late Roman Mediterranean, the development of theological thought and ecclesiastical structure in the Christian communities in East Central Europe is often only poorly documented in written sources. One of the most important groups of literary texts reflecting the integration of East Central Europe into the ecclesiastical community of the late Roman and early medieval world are collections of the letters written by ecclesiastical authorities, among them the bishops of Rome.[2]

Modern historical research on late antique and early medieval papal letters faces two main methodological problems. Firstly, these letter collections provide only a one-sided perspective, especially on controversial questions, because only the view of the letter writer is presented in a direct and often elaborate way. In contrast, any conflicting opinion of the addressee must be deduced almost entirely indirectly from the letter writer's response and it is necessary to keep in mind that the original argument of the addressee may have been distorted and contradicted by the writer. The second methodological problem lies in the complex process of collecting letters. In contrast to the later Middle Ages, late antique and early medieval papal letters were not handed down as systematic and (more or less) complete registers, but mostly survived in collections from Carolingian times.[3] This means that late antique and early medieval papal letters were subject to a selection process that depended on specific interests of – at least in case of papal letter collections – the recipients of the letters.[4] As a consequence, late antique and the early medieval papal letters often reflect the development of Christianity and ecclesiastical structures only incompletely and, therefore, cannot be used simply as a quarry for historical information without contextualizing their content and selection.

Nevertheless, papal letters are a significant source for understanding Christianity, especially in East Central Europe, because they reflect different trajectories of the development of Christian communities, which in the long run resulted in a certain diversity of ecclesiastical practices and traditions. Even more interestingly, papal letters provide insights into the complex interrelation between the bishop of Rome and his fellow bishops in East Central Europe and, although presenting exclusively a Roman perspective, the various efforts of the popes to integrate East Central Europe into an ecclesiastical hierarchy centered on Rome.[5] Such trials of centralizing ecclesiastical authority are also of particular interest in the context of the shift of the centers of political gravity in and the slow drifting apart of the Western and the Eastern parts of the Roman Empire from the late fourth century onwards.[6] Both processes especially affected the geographical area of East Central Europe.[7]

For questions of the ecclesiastical integration and interrelation of East Central Europe at the turn of Late Antiquity and the Middle Ages the letters of Gregory the Great, bishop of Rome from 590 to 604,[8] to addressees based in the ecclesiastical provinces of Dalmatia and Illyricum provide an instructive example. With its more than 850 letters the register of Gregory not only is the most extensive collection of late antique and early medieval papal letters in general, offering the opportunity to compare Gregory's communication with East Central Europe to other parts of the former Roman world, but it is also one of the few detailed literary sources for the ecclesiastical history of East Central Europe at the end of the sixth and beginning of the seventh century.

From the point of view of the episcopal See of Rome, both regions, Dalmatia and Illyricum, were of great importance and integral parts of the area of Roman supra-metropolitan authority. Dalmatia was connected to Italy – politically, culturally, and economically – for centuries and the Church of Rome held extensive properties in the province, especially in the area of the metropolitan see Salona and around Scodra in southern Dalmatia.[9] In contrast, in terms of ecclesiastical affiliation, the metropolitan diocese of Illyricum was a contested area at the end of the sixth century. Illyricum fell under the supra-metropolitan authority of the See of Rome, although in many ways oriented to the Greek East and Greek-speaking in large parts because in Late Antiquity the development of ecclesiastical administration *grosso modo* followed the example set by the civil administration of the Roman Empire with its elaborated hierarchy of provinces, civil dioceses as mid-level administration instances, and praetorian prefectures. The ecclesiastical metropolitan province of Illyricum was attached to the supra-metropolitan authority of the See of Rome because in early fourth century the civil diocese of Illyricum was part of the Western Roman Empire, but also for practical reasons because without Constantinople being an important bishopric at that time, Rome then was the nearest bishopric for the bishops of Illyricum with supra-metropolitan authority. Later in the in fourth century the civil administrative affiliation of Illyricum shifted from the west to the Eastern Roman Empire and Constantinople gained more importance as a metropolitan see; as a result, recurrent conflicts between Rome and Constantinople over the ecclesiastical integration of Illyricum came up and remained important until the ninth century in the context of missionary activities among the Bulgarians.[10]

In Gregory's letters to Dalmatia and Illyricum questions of ecclesiastical administration, observance of canon law, and the moral standards of office-holding are the most prominent topics, while the political and military developments in the late sixth- and early seventh-century East Central Europe only play a very minor role.[11] Nevertheless, Gregory's letters to East Central Europe have been referred to in research mostly for the bits and pieces of historical information they contain. The present study tries a different approach. In discussing various issues, Gregory's letters – as is the case for other letter collections – primarily present the writer's Roman point of view. Gregory reveals insights into Roman strategies for the See of Rome to claim and exercise superior authority. Gregory's letters to East Central Europe therefore provide interesting material for a case study which addresses the question of how Gregory communicated the authority of Rome in Dalmatia and the Illyricum. The intention of the following study is to test this approach to the letters of Gregory rather than a complete exegesis. First I will focus on the geographical and social dimension of Gregory's correspondence to Dalmatia and Illyricum and then on two of Gregory's lines of argumentation, namely, his efforts to enforce legal concepts on the bishops of Dalmatia and Illyricum and his use of "customs" and "traditions" as an argument for creating an ecclesiastical community.

Gregory's world in East Central Europe

The letters of Gregory the Great did not survive as a systematically collected, more or less complete, register but in a variety of manuscripts which can be grouped into three manuscript classes according to the number and selection of letters they contain.[12] In its form used in historical research today, as edited by Ewald and Hartmann in the *Monumenta Germaniae Historica* (MGH) and Norberg in the *Corpus Christianorum Series Latina*, Gregory's register is the result of complex medieval manuscript traditions and modern editing procedures.[13] The MGH edition contains 872 documents in total; 866 of them comprise the register of Gregory's letters in a stricter sense. Another six letters, most of them written by Gregory's predecessor, Pelagius II, were added by the editors of the MGH as appendices I to IV.[14] Of the 866 documents of the register ten were not written by Gregory[15] and nine are not letters in a strict sense or at least it can be doubted that these texts were composed as letters.[16] The register definitely did not survive completely and the chronological sequence of the letters is quite uneven. It has been repeatedly discussed whether it is possible or not to calculate the approximate number of letters that Gregory wrote during his bishopric, but any such attempt faces methodological problems. For example, it is difficult if not impossible to identify what criteria were used to select letters at the various stages of the transmission process. As a consequence, it is also impossible to say if the surviving letters reflect a representative profile of Gregory's communications;[17] for the surviving letters to addressees in East Central Europe it is likely that they do not.

An evaluation of Gregory's letters to what we call today East Central Europe necessarily starts with the problem of framing the area under consideration. In total, Gregory's register contains 53 letters written to addressees in the ecclesiastical provinces of Dalmatia, Illyricum, Epirus, and Greece. Besides these, a number of letters to various office holders in Italy and Constantinople, including the Empress Constantina, refer to issues in one way or another related to the same geographical area. In some cases it is difficult to identify addressees and regions with sufficient probability.[18] Although strictly speaking, Epirus and Greece are not part of what the studies in this volume understand as East Central Europe, from a historical point of view it makes sense to include letters directed to addressees in both regions because, on the level of metropolitan hierarchy, Epirus and Greece in Late Antiquity were part of the Roman archdiocesan organization and therefore under the direct supervision of the bishop of Rome.[19] Consequently, on a regional level, Gregory's letters show that in terms of ecclesiastical politics and administration the bishops of Illyricum and Greece were closely interrelated.[20]

A closer examination of the geographical range and the social status of the addressees of Gregory's letters to East Central Europe can contribute to understanding selection processes behind the transmission of the letters. Most (83%) of Gregory's surviving letters to the area under consideration (see Tables 5.1 and 5.2) were addressed to one person or a group of up to 12 explicitly named individuals. A total of 18 addressees received more than one letter from Gregory. In nine cases (out of 53) Gregory directed his advice to one or more social groups of a city or a province without mentioning any individuals. When Gregory, for example, wrote "to the clergy of the church of Salona,"[21] "to the entirety of the bishops based in the province of Helladia,"[22] or "to the presbyters, deacons, and the clergy, the nobles as well as the people based in Iadera and the soldiers,"[23] it can be assumed that he expected his letter to be circulated within the addressed social groups or to be read and displayed in public.[24] This last aspect means that Gregory's letters were intended to reach a much broader and more diverse audience than is indicated by the number of letters surviving in the register alone.

The geographical range of Gregory's communications with Dalmatia and the Balkans seems to be limited at first sight. In Dalmatia (see Table 5.3), 19 of Gregory's 29 surviving letters were sent to addressees in Salona, the metropolitan see and center of the imperial civil administration in Dalmatia; another four letters were sent to Iadera (Zadar).[25] Other cities on the Dalmatian coast and in its hinterland remain a *terra incognita* from Gregory's letters. Gregory sent another six letters either to all the bishops of Dalmatia or to office holders who were not connected to a specific place of residence, as for example, Bishop Malchus, who was responsible for the property of the See of Rome in Dalmatia, and the subdeacon Antoninus, who acted as the representative of the Roman see in the same region (and therefore was possibly based in Salona). For the Balkan provinces the picture is less clear, but here too most of the surviving letters to this region were sent to cities of metropolitan

TABLE 5.1 Numbers and addressees of Gregory the Great's letters to Dalmatia and the Balkans

	Dalmatia	Illyricum	Greece and Macedonia	Epirus	Multiple regions	Total
Number of letters	29	10	9	3	2	53
Letters addressed to:						
A single named person	24	8	6	2	-	44
A group of named persons (number)	-	-	1 (= 5 addressees)	1 (= 5 addressees)	2 (= 16 addressees in the Balkans only[27])	
Social groups	5	2	2	-	-	9
Addressees in total	29	10	13	7	16 (in the Balkans only)	75
Other or unclear	1 addressee lost[28] 1 doublet[29]					2

TABLE 5.2 Addressees of Gregory the Great's letters in Dalmatia and the Balkans

	Dalmatia	Illyricum	Greece and Macedonia	Epirus	Total
Different addressees named in salutation	12	7	11	7	37
Addressees receiving more than one letter	7	4	4	3	18

status such as Iustiniana Prima in Illyricum or Thessalonica or Corinth in Greece (see Table 5.4).[26] These numbers indicate that especially letters to addressees based in the centers of ecclesiastical and civil administration in Dalmatia and Illyricum dominate the scene, but it is difficult to decide whether this depended on the political importance of these places or possible selections made by later recipients.

A closer look at the content of the surviving letters indicates that the register does not reflect the chronological frequency and geographical range of Gregory's communication in a representative way. In July 595, in a letter to John, bishop of

TABLE 5.3 Cities in Dalmatia as destinations of Gregory's letters

	Number of letters
Salona	19
Iadera	4
Dalmatia in general/ without specific place	6
Total	29

TABLE 5.4 Cities in the Balkans that were destinations of Gregory's letters

	Number of letters
Illyricum in total	10
Iustiniana Prima	3
Serdica	1
Resinum	2
Scodra	1
Illyricum in general/ place not specified	3
Greece in total	9
Thessalonica	2
Corinth	4
Larissa	1
Greece in general/ place not specified	3
Epirus in total	3
Corcyra	2
Epirus in general/ place not specified	1
Total number	22

Corinth, Gregory praised the careful investigation that a certain Secundinus, bishop of a place not specified by Gregory, had carried out in the obscure case of Anastasius, the predecessor of John as bishop of Corinth.[30] From the content of this letter it is likely that Gregory, Secundinus, and probably also John had discussed the case earlier, in all likelihood by exchanging letters. In another letter to John from August of the same year, Gregory explicitly mentions that "from a reply" (*renuntiante*) of Secundinus he had learned about the details of an occurrence in which the bishop of Larissa in Greece was involved.[31] In October 592 Gregory wrote to Natalis, bishop of Salona, that it had been reported to him (*nuntiatum siquidem nobis est*) that a certain Florentius had been deposed from his office as bishop of Epidauros in southern Dalmatia without a trial according to canon law.[32] Five years later, this conflict was still relevant and in a letter from December 597, Gregory asks Sebastianus, bishop of Iadera, for more detailed information because the inhabitants of Epidauros had requested (*poposcerunt*) that Florentius be reinstated as their legitimate bishop.[33] In 591, Gregory informed the Dalmatian bishop, Malchus, about a request of John, the *consiliarius* of the prefect of Italy, to settle a conflict with Stephen, the bishop of Scodra in southern Dalmatia.[34] The outcomes of these conflicts remain mostly unclear, but these examples from Gregory's correspondence indicate that conflicts resulted in more communication that involved more people in various places than is evident from the surviving letters of the register alone. The East Central European addresses of Gregory's letters were part of a much wider and at the same time much denser communication network. This also means that in terms of communication close ties existed between Rome and East Central Europe.

A brief examination of the social status of the addressees Gregory communicated with in Dalmatia and Illyricum reveals similar questions and answers. For Dalmatia, the surviving letters of Gregory were addressed to a variety of ecclesiastical and secular office holders – among them the *proconsul Dalmatiae*, a high-ranking representative of the Byzantine civil administration, the bishops of Salona and Iadera, a local deacon of the church of Salona, and also to the clergy and city populations of Salona and Iadera. On a general level, the Dalmatian addressees were of different social statuses, but a clear majority of the surviving letters – at least 15 out of 29 (52%) – was sent to bishops or archbishops (taking into account the three letters Gregory sent to Maximus, the bishop-elect of Salona, in the mid-590s, a time when Gregory did not accept him as the legitimate bishop, the number rises from 15 to 18). For the Balkans the situation is much simpler; except for one letter to Iovinus, the *praefectus praetorio Illyrici*,[35] all of the addressees of Gregory's surviving letters were bishops or archbishops. For Greece and Epirus likewise, only bishops or archbishops were addressed in the letters included in the register. Against this background it is interesting to come back to the situation in Dalmatia; except for one letter to Bishop Malchus[36] all of Gregory's other letters are in one way or another connected to his intense conflicts with Natalis and Maximus, the two bishops of Salona at the time Gregory held the See of Rome. In addition, at least five more letters – four to ecclesiastical office holders in Italy and Constantinople and one to the Empress Constantina[37] – refer to both conflicts in more or less detail.[38] These letters have in common that they are specifically significant for the question of the supra-metropolitan authority of the bishop of Rome, especially for a later, "post-Gregorian" recipient of Gregory's writings. These letters discuss matters which were of high importance for the question of papal authority, regarding the observance of canon law and the good practice of office holding, not only in the time of Gregory, but also later in the Middle Ages. Therefore, especially when the medieval perception of Gregory was based on his moral writings, his conflict-ridden correspondence with the Dalmatians could be seen as valuable proof of his theological theory in practice.[39]

The Dalmatian letters also indicate that other questions, for example, the administration of the Church of Rome's property in Dalmatia, originally were much more important and probably entailed further communication than can be seen from the surviving letters. That Gregory had a firm interest in financial matters is indicated by his detailed instructions to his subdeacon, Antoninus, to make a detailed inventory of church properties to prevent any misappropriation after rumors of the death of Bishop Natalis spread to Rome.[40] Gregory's letters concerning the investigations against Malchus, "bishop in Dalmatia" and being responsible for the administration of properties of the Roman church in this region point in the same direction. Malchus was summoned to Rome, apparently because of irregularities in his accounts, where unfortunately he died, which required Gregory to explain that there was no conspiracy, as Gregory's Dalmatian opponents insinuated.[41] In letters to his subdeacon, Antoninus, and John, bishop of Ravenna, Gregory gave order that Malchus should submit evidence of his activity in financial administration (*actionum suarum expositis ratiociniis*) before coming to Rome.[42] The reason for and the details of the investigation remain unclear; Gregory's interest in the details of Malchus' financial administration suggests, however, that Rome's close economic ties to Dalmatia resulted in regular communication between the bishop of Rome and his office holders. Because Gregory takes for granted that especially his subdeacon knew what he expected when demanding detailed accounts of Malchus' activities, it seems plausible to assume that this communication was related to a much broader correspondence about economic and financial issues, especially with subdeacons like Antoninus. All in all, both aspects examined here indicate, that in the surviving letters of Gregory high-ranking ecclesiastical office holders like archbishops and bishops are overrepresented and that the social spectrum of the addressees of Gregory's letters to Dalmatia, therefore, was probably different from what the register shows.

Dalmatia, Illyricum and the authority of Rome

The dominant theme of Gregory's correspondence with East Central Europe is the complex relation between Gregory as bishop of Rome and his fellow bishops in Dalmatia and Illyricum (see Tables 5.5 and 5.6). Gregory made use of a set of instruments of power to exercise supra-metropolitan authority. For the question of integrating East Central Europe into the wider context of a changing post-Roman world in the late sixth and early seventh century, two of these instruments are of particular interest: first, legal concepts aiming at creating a common sphere of law among Rome, Dalmatia, and Illyricum and the limits of enforcing these concepts. While this is primarily a matter of governance in practice, the second instrument, the integration of East Central Europe in a common ecclesiastical tradition, is tied to the mentalities of Gregory's times.

Enforcing law

Canon law is one of the standard arguments in Gregory's letters and observing the rules set by canon law was an instrument of central importance for Gregory in exercising the authority of Rome. This becomes clear from his letters confirming episcopal elections and formally introducing a new bishop. Gregory uses different lines of argumentation and varies his language depending on the person and context, but, as a kind of standard admonition, he reminds newly elected bishops that observing the rules set by law is one of the main duties of an office holder.[43] After a

TABLE 5.5 Addressees of Gregory's letters in Dalmatia

	Total (29 letters)	Salona (20 letters)	Iadera (4 letters)	Dalmatia in general (5 letters)
Archiepiscopus	1	1	–	–
Episcopus/episcopi	14	8	3	3
"praesumptor"	3	3	–	–
Diaconus/ Archidiaconus	2	2	–	–
Clerus ecclesiae (only)	1	–	–	–
Clerus, nobilitas et populous	2	1	1	–
Subdiaconus (of Rome)	3	–	–	3
Proconsul Dalmatiae	1	–	–	1
Scholasticus	1	1(?)	–	–
Scribo	1	1(?)	–	–

TABLE 5.6 Addressees of Gregory's letters in the Balkans

	Total (22 letters)	Illyricum (10 letters)	Greece (9 letters)	Epirus (3 letters)
Archiepiscopus	2	–	2	–
Episcopus/episcopi	19	9	7	3
Praefectus Praetorio	1	1	–	–

long-lasting conflict, when he finally accepted Maximus as bishop of the Dalmatian metropolis Salona, Gregory reminds him in his letter of confirmation that not only should he leave aside all resentment against former opponents, but also that now the time has come to return to the principles of law.[44] In various other conflicts with bishops, in nearly all cases Gregory focused his arguments on legal aspects, as for example in the complicated case of Adrianus, bishop of Thebae in Thessalia in Greece.[45] Gregory's interrelations with the bishops of Salona are quite instructive in this context. Gregory criticizes Natalis for having deprived Bishop Florentius and Archdeacon Honoratus of their offices without trials according to canon law and he never tires of attacking Maximus, Natalis' successor, for being ordained illegally and in violation of the law. Regarding the accusation of simony and misappropriation of ecclesiastical properties launched against Natalis, it is possible to say that Gregory's arguments not only followed the rules of canon law as interpreted from a Roman point of view, but were also in line with the restrictions defined by the regional church council of Salona in 533.[46] This interrelation between canon law and ecclesiastical communication would be an interesting field for further study. Regarding the integration of East Central Europe, canon law in theory had the potential to focus and centralize power structures on the episcopal See of Rome. In practice, the options of enforcing law on the regional level turned out to be limited. Natalis simply ignored Gregory's threat of legal action, especially his summons to face trial in Rome, one of Gregory's standard instruments of exercising his authority in legal conflicts that therefore appears regularly in Gregory's letters. In doing this the bishop of Salona made it very clear that the bishop of Rome lacked an effective instrument for exercising the legal authority he claimed to have. The case of Maximus is even more telling because he was strongly supported by the local clerics of Salona and also by a number of bishops in the province of Dalmatia. In addition, Maximus gained the support of the exarch Romanus, the highest ranking office holder of the Byzantine civil administration in Italy and one of his contemporaries Gregory most disliked because of conflicting political opinions,[47] successfully established good relations with the imperial court in Constantinople,[48] and was able to block Gregory's attempts to enforce his legal position. The tide only began to turn when Callinicus, a close friend of Gregory, took the office of exarch of Italy and evidently increased pressure for a solution of this conflict, which had been going on for almost six years. The final compromise saw a trial investigating the accusations and a formal act of repentance by Maximus, not in Rome but in Ravenna.[49] Peter Eich interprets the result of the conflict as a success for Gregory because he managed to uphold the legal position of Rome,[50] but a closer look at Gregory's claims at the beginning and the results he achieved at the end of this conflict suggests that Gregory suffered a shattering defeat. His position had shifted remarkably from strictly refusing to accept Maximus as bishop to confirming his ordination. Even the trial investigating the case, one of Gregory's central demands in addition to the act of repentance, did not take place in Gregory's direct presence. Gregory's conflicts with the bishops of Salona show clearly that, on the one hand, Roman claims of authority had clear limits when it came to enforcing law and that, on the other hand, the bishops of Salona were in a position that enabled them to act independently and to resist Rome.

"Tradition" as an argument

Besides legal concepts, Gregory also used a more or less "soft power" approach.[51] For claiming and exercising the authority of the See of Rome, he refers to a set of common "customs" and "traditions" which connected and brought together Christian communities in different areas of the post-Roman world under the aegis of the Catholic Church. One specific form of using the "tradition" of the Roman church is Gregory's frequent reference to the authority of St. Peter, "the prince of the apostles," although often as an argumentative *ultima ratio*, as George E. Demacopoulos has pointed out in his detailed studies.[52] But Gregory also refers to other "traditions" which, according to him, operate as guidelines for the right behavior in moral as well as legal terms. In a letter to the bishops of Illyricum on the occasion of the ordination of John as bishop of Justiniana Prima, Gregory interestingly does not refer to legal constraints, but instead explains that following "ancient custom" (*antique consuetudinis*) makes ordination safe.[53] A similar thought is behind his demand to hold episcopal elections in Salona "as in ancient times" (*sicut priscis fuit temporibus*) after the death of Bishop Natalis.[54] Sending the pallium as an act of confirming the position of a newly ordained bishop also resulted from "custom" (*morem* or *ex more*)[55] or "ancient custom" (*antique consuetudinis*),[56] set a new bishop in the tradition of his predecessors,[57] and at the same time justified his obligations to obey.[58] Together with the rules of ecclesiastical administration, the "ancient custom" (*antique consuetudinis*) could also prevent faults and unlawful presumption, as Gregory explains to Sebastianus, the bishop of Iadera, who at one point had changed sides in the conflict resulting from the (in Gregory's point of view) illegal ordination of Maximus in Salona and was seeking Gregory's support.[59] These examples have in common that Gregory, at least in his East Central European letters, uses references to "customs" and "traditions" in very abstract forms. A striking contrast to this pattern is provided by a letter Gregory wrote to the Empress Constantia in 594. Responding to the empress's request to send relics of St. Paul from Rome to Constantinople, Gregory explains in detail that it is absolutely against the Roman tradition to touch any part of the body of a saint (not to mention removing parts of it).[60] The example of this letter illustrates that, if necessary, Gregory also used the argument of "traditions" in a very different and explicit way. Considering the superior social (and political) status of the empress, Gregory may have felt the need to discuss the different concepts of saints' veneration in Rome and Constantinople and to explain in detail why he is refusing the empress's wish. In other contexts, when writing to fellow bishops or ecclesiastical office holders of lower rank, there was no urgent need for Gregory to elaborate exactly what he understands as a "custom" or "tradition" of the church or to what "custom" or "tradition" he refers in a strict sense. In these contexts Gregory used "customs" and "traditions" as a set of shared knowledge which does not necessarily need to be defined exactly and is bolstered by Gregory's own authority as bishop of Rome. Such a non-specific use leaves the possibility of minor shifts and variations when trying to fill "custom" and "tradition" with specific content. The inherent ambiguity is exactly what made "custom" and "tradition" such valuable arguments, because both suggest a common sphere of accepted ecclesiastical rules and practices while at the same time being beyond question.

Conclusion

This brief examination of the letters of the Roman Bishop Gregory the Great tries to show the potential of papal letters for studying the ecclesiastical integration of East Central Europe into the wider horizon of the Church of Rome. In this context the letters of Gregory themselves are proof of the close connections between Rome and the bishops of Dalmatia and Illyricum. An examination of the content of the letters indicates that the ties between Rome and East Central Europe in the transition period from Late Antiquity to the Middle Ages were much closer than has been thought and that communication among Rome, Dalmatia, and Illyricum occurred much more frequently than is indicated just by the number of the letters that were integrated into the register of Gregory. From the letters it also becomes clear that developments in the area under consideration at the end of the sixth and beginning of the seventh century are mostly visible only through the lens of Rome. For most issues discussed in the letters it is impossible to say what consequences Gregory's authoritative statements had on the regional or local level; in fact, the intensive and long-lasting conflicts between Gregory and the deliberately independent bishops of Salona rather point to the opposite: Gregory's authority in East Central Europe was clearly limited and the bishop of Rome depended on local cooperation to assert his authority. Especially the bishops of Dalmatia managed to reach a position relatively independent from Roman claims by establishing good relations with and gaining the backup of Constantinople, the alternative center of political gravity at the time. Although Gregory often based his authority on legal arguments, it was hardly possible to enforce his positions in conflicts seriously, mostly because he lacked effective tools to exercise his legal position on the local level. The interrelations between Rome and the bishops of East Central Europe appear to be asymmetric. While Gregory tried to strengthen his authority by integrating the area of today's East Central Europe into a common ecclesiastical sphere centered on Rome, the bishops of Dalmatia and Illyricum more or less aimed at keeping the ties to Rome as loose as possible. In addition (and maybe to compensate) Gregory repeatedly referred to the common "customs" and "traditions" of the Roman church. This line of argumentation seems to have been important for Gregory because on the level of mentalities of his time he aimed at creating a common cultural sphere of accepted values to integrate East Central Europe into a wider Christian community centered on Rome.

Notes

1 Cf. Peter Sarris, *Empires of Faith. The Fall of Rome to the Rise of Islam, 500–700* (Oxford: Oxford University Press, 2011), 208–210; Arnold Angenendt, *Das Frühmittelalter. Die abendländische Christenheit von 400 bis 900* (2nd ed. Stuttgart, Berlin and Cologne: W. Kohlhammer, 1995), 35–36.
2 The bishops of Rome will be referred to as popes and their letters as papal letters, bearing in mind that the formation of papal authority is the result of a complex long-term process which came to an end in the eleventh century; cf. Sabine Panzram, "*ille ecclesiae fundamentum et hic sapiens architectus* - Die Erschaffung des Papsttums," *Historia* 65 (2016): 73–107; Bernhard Schimmelpfennig, *Das Papsttum. Von der Antike bis zur Renaissance* (WB Forum, 16) (3rd ed. Darmstadt: Wissenschaftliche Buchgesellschaft, 1988), 1–58; Angenendt, *Das Frühmittelalter*, 64–67.
3 See also Bronwen Neil, "Continuities and Changes in the Practice of Letter-collecting from Cicero to Late Antiquity," in *Collecting Early Christian Letters From the Apostle Paul to Late Antiquity*, ed. idem and Pauline Allen (Cambridge: Cambridge University Press, 2015), 3–17, esp. 10–11.
4 For a general discussion of selection processes underlying late antique letter collections see Pauline Allen, "Rationales for Episcopal Letter-collections in Late Antiquity," in *Collecting Early Christian Letters*, 18–34.
5 In the wider context of early medieval missionary activity in Central and Northern Europe, Julia M. H. Smith, *Europe after Rome. A New Cultural History, 500–1000*

(Oxford: Oxford University Press, 2005), 220–230, stresses the heterogeneity of early medieval Christianity and argues that "early medieval Christianity was neither centralized nor systematized" (ibid., 223). For large areas this might be true for the practice of the daily life of Christian communities, but nevertheless the bishops of Rome claimed a central authority in the church.

6   The problem of unity and dissociation of the Roman world is at the center of two recent conference volumes: *Osten und Westen 400–600 n. Chr. Kommunikation, Kooperation und Konflikt* (Roma Aeterna, 4), ed. Carola Föller and Fabian Schulz (Stuttgart: Franz Steiner, 2016) (see here esp. the concluding remarks of Uwe Walter, "Kommentar und Nachfragen," ibid., 301–305) and *East and West in the Roman Empire of the Fourth Century. An End to Unity?* (Radboud Studies in Humanities, 5), ed. Roald Dijkstra, Sanne van Poppel, and Daniëlle Slootjes (Leiden and Boston: Brill, 2015), here esp. Joseph Rist, "Die Synode von Serdica 343: Das Scheitern eines ökumenischen Konzils und seine Folgen für die Einheit der Reichskirche," 63–81 on the council of Serdica, which was intended to create unity but resulted in serious and long-lasting rifts in the ecclesiastical community.

7   See Frank E. Wozniak, "East Rome, Ravenna and Western Illyricum: 454–536 A.D.," *Historia* 30 (1981): 351–382.

8   For life and career of Gregory see the two major biographical works by Robert A. Markus, *Gregory the Great and his World* (Cambridge: Cambridge University Press, 1997) and Peter Eich, *Gregor der Große. Bischof von Rom zwischen Antike und Mittelalter* (Paderborn: Ferdinand Schöningh, 2016); for the broader context, see John Moorhead, *The Popes and the Church of Rome in Late Antiquity* (Routledge Studies in Ancient History) (London and New York: Routledge, 2015), 100–146.

9   For the political connection of Dalmatia and Italy see Frank E. Wozniak, "East Rome, Ravenna and Western Illyricum: 454–536 AD," esp. 354–369; for possessions of the See of Rome in Dalmatia, see Ante Škegro, "Papal Possessions in the Eastern Adriatic," *Arheološki vestnik* 55 (2004): 429–438.

10 Schimmelpfennig, *Das Papsttum*, 46–47; Jan-Markus Kötter, "Autonomie der illyrischen Kirche? Die Sixtus-Briefe der Collectio Thessalonicensis und der Streit um das kirchliche Illyricum," *Millennium* 9 (2012): 163–186; for long-term consequences of the conflict about ecclesiastical authority over Illyricum, see Axel Bayer, *Spaltung der Christenheit. Das sogenannte Morgenländische Schisma von 1054* (Beihefte zum Archiv für Kulturgeschichte, 53) (Cologne, Weimar, and Vienna: Böhlau, 2002), 18–20.

11 Political instability and military insecurity are reflected in ep. II 37 to John, bishop of Squillacium in Calabria in Southern Italy (from July 592); John was the former bishop of Lissus (Lezha in Albania) but had to leave his city after it was conquered by an enemy (*ab hostibus captivatae*). Gregory's unwillingness to accept gifts "from brethren who have been robbed and afflicted" (*a praedatis atque afflictis fratribus*), expressed in ep. V 16 written to John, the bishop of Iustiniana Prima, in November 594 can be interpreted as reflecting military insecurity, although Gregory does not give further details. In ep. IX 154 from May 599 Gregory congratulates Callinicus, the exarch of Italy, for a victory against the Slavs; in ep. X 15 from July 600 to Maximus, the bishop of the Dalmatian Metropolis Salona, he expresses his concerns and sorrow over the Slavs (*de Sclavorum gente*) threatening the region (maybe referring to Dalmatia in a general sense). Ewald Kislinger, "Dyrrhachion und die Küsten von Epirus und Dalmatien im frühen Mittelalter – Beobachtungen zur Entwicklung der byzantinischen Oberhoheit," Millennium 8 (2011): 313–352, here 321 sees ep. VI 4 as hinting at a crisis in Epirus, but it is not clear (and impossible to prove) that the Bishop Zenon mentioned in this letter is the same person as the Zenon named among the bishops of Epirus in ep. VI 7. For political and military developments in the late sixth and early seventh century Balkans, see Florin Curta, *Southeastern Europe in the Middle Ages, 500–1250*

(Cambridge: Cambridge University Press, 2006), 39–110; Kislinger, "Dyrrhachion und die Küsten von Epirus und Dalmatien," 313–352; Hrvoje Gračanin, "History of the Eastern Adriatic Region from the Vth to the VIIth Centuries AD: Historical Processes and Historiographic Problems," in *AdriAtlas et l'histoire de l'espace adriatique du VIe s. a.C. au VIIIe s. p.C. Actes du colloque international de Rome. (4–6 novembre 2013)* (Ausonius Éditions – Scripta Antiqua, 79), ed. Yolande Marion and Francis Tassaux (Bordeaux: Ausonius, 2015), 67–97; for the sixth century, see Alexander Sarantis, *Justinian's Balkan Wars. Campaigning, Diplomacy and Development in Illyricum, Thrace and the Northern World, A.D. 527–65* (ARCA Classical and Medieval Texts, Papers and Monographs, 53) (Prenton: Francis Cairns, 2016).

12 For manuscript traditions of the letters of Gregory, cf. Detlev Jasper and Fuhrmann Horst, *Papal Letters in the Early Middle Ages* (Washington, DC: The Catholic University of America Press, 2001), 70–81.

13 *Gregori I Papae Registrum Epistularum Tomus I, Libri I–VIII* in *Monumenta Germaniae Historica. Epistularum*, I, ed. Paulus Ewald and Ludovicus M. Hartmann (Berlin: Weidmann, 1891), *Gregori I Papae Registrum Epistularum Tomus II, Libri VIII–XIV* in *Monumenta Germaniae Historica. Epistularum*, II, ed. Ludovicus M. Hartmann (Berlin: Weidmann, 1899), and Gregor der Große, *Registrum epistolarum libri I–XIV* (Corpus Christianorum Series Latina, 140–140A), ed. Dag Norberg (Turnhout: Brepolis, 1982).

14 Only the letter edited as App. I was written by Gregory in 587, when he was still a deacon in Rome. App. II is a letter of Pelagius II to Gregory, dating to 584; App. III contains three letters of Pelagius to bishops of the province of Histria. App. IV is a letter attributed to Gregory, but probably dating to the early eighth century.

15 Epp. I 16a, 16b, 41a; II 1; III 66; IX 227a; XI 15; XII 7; the authors of VIII 36 (a report about the settlement of the conflict between Gregory and Maximus, bishop of Salona in Dalmatia) and XIII 1 (announcement of the death of the emperor Maurice and his family and the subsequent accession to the throne of the Phocas in Constantinople) cannot be identified with absolute certainty.

16 Epp. I 39a; II 1 and 2; V 57a; XI 15; XII 7; XIII 1 and 2. In case of ep. VIII 36 it is uncertain whether this text is to be interpreted as letter or a narrative report.

17 Eich, *Gregor der Große*, 73–77.

18 As, for example, for the deacon Cyprian and the bishop Zenon in ep. VI 4, see above, note 11.

19 For the ecclesiastical organization of Dalmatia and Western Illyricum see Rajko Bratož, "Die kirchliche Organisation in Westillyricum (vom späten 4. Jh. bis um 600) – Ausgewählte Fragen," in *Keszthely-Fenékpuszta im Kontext spätantiker Kontinuitätsforschung zwischen Noricum und Moesia* (Castellum Pannonicum Pelsonense, 2), ed. Orsolya Heinrich-Tamáska (Budapest, Leipzig, Keszthely and Rahden: Marie Leidorf, 2011), 211–248; for Thessalonica and Rome, see James Skedros, "Civic and Ecclesisastical Identity in Christian Thessalonikē," in *From Roman to Early Christian Thessalonikē. Studies in Religion and Archaeology* (Harvard Theological Studies, 64), ed. Laura Nasrallah, Charalambos Bakirtzis, and Steven J. Friesen (Cambridge, MA: Harvard University Press, 2010), 245–259, here 248–255. For the ecclesiastical development of the Adriatic region the see of Aquileia was also of some importance, see Rajko Bratož, "Der Metropolitansprengel von Aquileia vom 5. bis zum 7. Jahrhundert," in *Die Ausgrabungen im spätantik-frühmittelalterlichen Bischofssitz Sabiona-Säben in Südtirol I. Frühchristliche Kirche und Gräberfeld* (Münchner Beiträge zur Vor- und Frühgeschichte, 58), ed. Volker Bierbrauer and Hans Nothdurfter (Munich: C.H.Beck, 2015), 665–700.

20 See for example epp. III 6 and III 7, VIII 10 and IX 156.

21 Ep. III 46: *Clero ecclesiae Salonitanae.*

22 Ep. V 63: *Universis episcopis per Helladam constitutes provinciam*; other examples are ep. I 43 and V 10 (*Universis episcopis per Illyricum*), ep. II 21 (*Universis episcopis Delmatias* [sic!] *constitutes*), ep. III 38 (*Universis episcopis de Corinthiis*), and ep. IV 16 (*Universis episcopis per Dalmatias*).

23 Ep. VI 46: *Presbyteris, diaconibus et clero, nobilibus ac populo Iaderae consistentibus et Militibus*; another example is ep. VI 26 (*Dilectissimis filiis, clero, nobilibus Salonis consistentibus*).

24 In ep. V 6, written to the deacon Sabinianus in Constantinople in September / October 594, Gregory complains that Maximus, the illegally ordained bishop of Salona, had torn up Gregory's letters (*scripta*), which were "read out and displayed in public" (*publice relecta vel in civitate posita publice*).

25 For the political organization of Dalmatia and the role of Salona see Craig H. Caldwell, "The Balkans," in *The Oxford Handbook of Late Antiquity*, ed. Scott Fitzgerald Johnson (Oxford: Oxford University Press, 2012), 92–114, here 102–106.

26 For Iustiniana Prima see Stanisław Turlej, "Justinian's novella XI – A Historical Analysis," in *Within the Circle of Ancient Ideas and Virtues. Studies in Honour of Professor Maria Dzielska*, ed. Kamilla Twardowska, et al. (Cracow: Jagiellonian University, 2014), 341–359, Alexander Sarantis, *Justinian's Balkan Wars*, 149–161.

27 Ep. VIII 10 was also sent to four more addressees in Italy.

28 Ep. VIII 36.

29 Ep. IX 231.

30 Ep. V 57.

31 Ep. V 62.

32 Ep. III 8; Gregory also discusses the case of Florentius with his subdeacon Antoninus in III 9 (saying "it has reached us" – *pervenit ad nos* – that Florentius was deprived of his office).

33 Ep. VIII 11.

34 Ep. I 36.

35 John Robert Martindale, *The Prosopography of the Later Roman Empire, Volume IIIA/ B: A.D. 395–527* (Cambridge: Cambridge University Press, 1980), IIIA, 716 (Iovinus 2).

36 Ep. I 36.

37 Martindale, *The Prosopography*, IIIA, 337–339 (Constantina 1).

38 Connected to Natalis: epp. I 10, 19, 20; II 20, 21, 22, 50; III 8, 9, 22; in addition also ep. II 45 to John, bishop of Ravenna. Connected to Maximus: epp. IV 16, 20, 38; V 29; VI 3, 25, 26, 46; VII 17; VIII 11, 24; IX 158, 176, 234; X 15; XIII 10; in addition also epp. VIII 36; V 6, 39; IX 149, 177, 178.

39 Cf. Markus, *Gregory the Great*, 17–50.

40 Ep. III 22.

41 In ep. V 6 from September 594, Gregory explained in detail to the deacon Sabinianus, his representative in Constantinople, that Malchus died of natural causes and that neither he, Gregory, nor any other person betrayed by the investigation was present at the moment of Malchus's death.

42 Ep. II 22 to the subdeacon Antoninus from March 592 and ep. II 45 to John, bishop of Ravenna from July 592.

43 See, for example, ep. V 16 to John, bishop of the metropolitan see of Iustiniana Prima from November 594; ep. V 63 to John, bishop of Corinth, from August 595; but also II

37 to John, who before being ordained bishop of Squillacium in Calabria was bishop of Lissus.

44 Ep. IX 234 from August 599.

45 Ep. III 6 and III 7.

46 For the second council of Salona in 533 see Vadim Prozorov, "The Sixth Century Councils of Salona," [unpublished original Scientific Paper, 2011] (www.academia.edu/638090/The_Sixth_Century_Councils_ of_Salona, last accessed: 7 September 2017).

47 Ep.V 6.

48 Epp. IV 20 and V 39.

49 Epp. IX 149, 177, 178.

50 Eich, *Gregor der Große*, 129.

51 For the political concept of "soft power" in modern international politics, see Joseph S. Nye, *Soft Power. The Means to Success in World Politics* (New York: Public Affairs, 2004), esp. 1–32 and idem, "Soft Power," *Foreign Policy* 80 (1990): 153–171.

52 George E. Demacopoulos, "Gregory the Great and the Appeal to Petrine Authority," *Studia Patristica* 48 (2010): 333–346 and idem, *The Invention of Peter. Apostolic Discourse and Papal Authority in Late Antiquity* (Philadelphia: University of Pennsylvania Press, 2013).

53 Ep.V 10.

54 Ep. III 22.

55 Ep. V 10 to the bishops of Illyricum from October 594; ep. V 16 to John, bishop of Iustiniana Prima from November 594.

56 Ep.V 63 to the bishops of Helladia, i.e. Greece, from August 595.

57 Ep.V 62 to John, bishop of Corinth, dated to 15 August 595.

58 Ep.V 63.

59 Ep.VII 17 from April 597.

60 Ep. IV 30.

6

CHILDREN IN ELEVENTH- AND TWELFTH-CENTURY HUNGARY AND POLAND

An Archaeological Comparison

Florin Curta and Matthew Koval

Children have received much more attention from archaeologists in East Central than in Western Europe. It was not before Grete Lillehammer's 1989 article that a self-conscious approach to the archaeology of childhood appeared in the West.[1] Sally Crawford was among the first to call attention to age categories and rites of passage, and to emphasize the impact of Christianity on the development of new attitudes towards children.[2] In contrast, the special treatment of child burials in medieval cemeteries in Poland had already been recognized in the early 1980s.[3] In Hungary, however, medieval cemeteries were analyzed only in terms of chronology and the interpretation of artifacts regarded as typical (e.g., lock rings with S-shaped ends). Before 1990, very few church graveyards had been completely published.[4] Until recently, child burials received no attention whatsoever. Only recently, has the problem of children in medieval cemeteries been approached through the lens of bioarchaeology.[5] No comparison exists between child burials in various parts of East Central Europe. Several questions would nonetheless invite such an approach. Was there a radical change in the status of children, presumably visible in funerary rites, following the conversion to Christianity? Were child burials different in cemeteries with and without churches? Can any age categories be distinguished in terms of funerary rites and/or grave goods among the child burials in post-conversion cemeteries?

Our paper is the first attempt to offer plausible answers to some of these questions on the basis of a comparison between two almost contemporary cemeteries, excavated in Kérpuszta (western Hungary) and Lubień (central Poland), respectively. The choice of those two sites relies on two main factors. First, the distance between the sites has to be sufficiently large to exclude the possibility of mutual influence or any form of contact between the communities burying their dead in these two locations. Second, and more importantly, the results of the excavations are among the better, if not the best, published in East Central Europe, complete with anthropological analysis of the skeletal remains (which allows for sexing and aging), numismatic analysis of the accompanying coins, and the paleo-botanical analysis of the timber remains (in the case of Lubień). We have framed the analysis of the two cemeteries within an examination of child burials in both earlier and later cemeteries in western Hungary and central-southern Poland over a span of some 500 years between ca. 800 and ca. 1300. Our goal is to identify possibly concomitant developments, which in turn could form the basis for a discussion of the respective impact of Christianization on the medieval societies of Hungary and Poland. The role of comparison, in other words, is twofold: to reveal broader trends in funerary practice, and to raise questions regarding the local implementation of regional (possibly even pan-European) Church policies.

Childhood and age categories in the Middle Ages

While historians of the Middle Ages in Western Europe have devoted a great deal of attention to childhood over the last half-century or so, those with an interest in East Central and Eastern Europe have only recently turned their attention to this historical problem.[6] There are several regional studies, but still no monograph dedicated to medieval children in East Central Europe.[7] This is surprising, given that a strong connection has recently been discovered in narrative (particularly hagiographic) texts between children (viewed as weak and of low social status, but also innocent) and the conversion to Christianity.[8] This seems to be confirmed by the story of the Piast beginnings to be found in the chronicle of Gallus Anonymus, especially by the episode of Mieszko's miraculous healing on his seventh birthday. Since historians of early medieval Poland have not tackled the issue so far, we need to turn briefly to this episode.[9]

> In the city of Gniezno … lived a duke named Popiel, who had two sons. Now when the time had come for the cutting of their hair – a custom among the pagans – he prepared a great banquet and invited large numbers of his nobles and friends.[10]

Thus begins the story of the Piast beginnings in the chronicle written in the early twelfth century by an unknown author to whom historians refer as Gallus Anonymus.[11] The story involves two mysterious wanderers who arrive at the time of the banquet, but are turned away from the entrance to the ducal residence "in an injurious manner." Horrified by such a bad reception and the rude behavior of the duke, they then end up in the hut of a plowman of the duke, "who was about to make a banquet for his sons. Although just a poor man, he was kind. He invited the strangers into his cottage and most warmly offered them his modest means." They in turn accepted the poor man's invitation.

The plowman said:

> 'I have a jar of fermented ale, which I brewed for the cutting of my only son's hair. But what use is such a small amount? Drink it if you will.' For

this peasant had decided earlier to make ready a few dishes to celebrate his own boy's hair-cutting ... he had been planning to invite some friends of his and poor people to dinner, or rather to share a breakfast. He has also been fattening a piglet and keeping it for the same occasion.[12]

There is an evident symmetry in this story between the rude duke and the kind plowman and much has been written on the interpretation of this fictional episode.[13] However, comparatively little attention has been devoted to the very occasion for the two wanderers' visit to Gniezno – the ceremony of cutting the children's hair. Polish scholars insist that this is a genuinely Polish custom, the *postrzyżyny*, but with its overtly Biblical and spiritual meaning, the ritual of the first haircut is well documented for boys in medieval Europe from Ireland to Poland.[14] Gallus insists that such a ceremony was a pagan custom (*qui more gentilitatis*), but judging from his story, it was celebrated both by the rich and by the poor, albeit with different means. The exact age at which Popiel and Piast's sons had their hair cut is not mentioned, but the implication is that they were all of the same age. The age appears, however, in a third episode. Siemomysł, Piast's grandson and the third ruler of the dynasty, "called the gathering of his counts and other princes to celebrate a grand and lavish banquet."[15] The occasion was the seventh birthday of his son, Mieszko. There is no mention of Mieszko's hair being cut, but one can hardly escape the impression that Gallus intended those three episodes to be parallel to each other.[16] In other words, his intention was to highlight a rite of passage, the celebration of which was linked to key moments in the early history of the dynasty. That he viewed the cutting of the boys' hair at age seven as a pagan custom may simply be a narrative strategy meant to suggest to Gallus' audience the existence in pre-Christian Poland of a ritual similar to confirmation.[17] Irrespective of its role in the narrative, however, the episode implies that Gallus' audience took it for granted that special rites of passage were linked to certain age categories, at least for boys. This is in sharp contrast to the Middle High German literature, in which a girl (*maget*) became a woman (*wîp*) through marriage, and a boy (*kint, knabe*) became a man (*wirt man*) through knighting, with no intermediate stage.[18] St. Augustine, Isidore, Bede, and Hrabanus Maurus have all conceptualized *infantia* as the age from birth to seven, *pueritia* as the age from seven to 14, and *adolescentia* as the age of 14 to 28.[19] Whether Gallus' story is a distant echo of such bookish classifications remains unclear. But in the late twelfth century, and in the context of the major transformation of the geography of the Otherworld through the inclusion of Purgatory, a new place came into being in Catholic Europe: the limbo of children (*limbus puerorum*), meant for children who died without baptism.[20] In other words, there was an increased interest in the High Middle Ages in the role of children in both society and the Church. What makes Poland, in particular, and East Central Europe, in general, an interesting case in this respect is the relatively recent conversion of the region to Christianity, a process that was supposedly accompanied by great social transformations. Particularly useful in this respect are the rites of passage, such as the cutting of hair mentioned by Gallus, because rites of passage provide an excellent opportunity to see how, outside regular sacramental activities, the authority of the official church intersected with crucial decisions made by non-clerical agents, such as parents or godparents.[21] Was there a material cultural correlate to rites of passage? Did age categories influence the treatment of children in burial?

Child burial in medieval Poland: Lubień

The archaeological site in Lubień (Piotrków County, Łódź voivodeship, Poland) is located on a sand dune in the middle of a still densely forested area in the southern part of central Poland (during the Middle Ages a borderland between Greater Poland and Mazovia). The site is less than two miles away from the village, to the southwest, and nine miles south of the city of Piotrków Trybunalski. The medieval cemetery was uncovered between 1971 and 1974 as the result of salvage excavations prompted by the building of a new road between Lubień and Straszów, the neighboring village to the west. The intervention of the Polish archaeologists from the regional museum in Piotrków Trybunalski (Ewa and Andrzej Wójcik) led to the opening of a large area of some 660 square yards (550 square meters) and the discovery of 126 graves.[22] However, by the time the excavations started, between 40 and 50 graves (primarily in the central area of the cemetery) had already been destroyed through the road construction. This is regrettable, since the location of the destroyed graves strongly suggests that they belonged to the earliest phase(s) of the cemetery, which later expanded first to the north, then to the south, east, and west.

Graves with the largest number of grave goods cluster in the older parts of the cemetery and may be dated to the late tenth or early eleventh century. Rich graves are rare in the eleventh and twelfth centuries. The most recent graves in Lubień are dated to the second or third quarter of the twelfth century.[23] The sequencing of the cemetery was facilitated by the discovery of numerous coins. As a consequence, and because of the relative proximity to the Piast stronghold at Rozprza (less than four miles to the northwest), it is possible that those who buried their dead at Lubień came from that *castellum*, which is first mentioned in the written sources in 1136.[24] All the graves in the cemetery are pit inhumations loosely arranged in rows.[25] Gender differences are visible in the orientation of graves; with mild deviations and a few exceptions, most male burials have an east–west orientation and all female graves an opposite (west–east) orientation.[26] Most skeletons were in a supine position, with arms laid alongside the body. Due to the poor preservation of the bone material, only a few skeletons could be aged and sexed by means of a proper anthropological analysis.[27] Most burials had no timber or stone structures, but evidence of shrouds exists in a few instances.[28] A number of graves had no bones at all. Those are perhaps cenotaphs marking off family plots, or simply graves (some, perhaps, of children) in which the bones disintegrated completely.[29]

Graves of children represent a surprisingly high percentage of the total number of burials in Lubień. Indeed, 37 children and teenagers were found, which is about a third of the total number of burials.[30] While child graves are similar in many respects to the graves of adults, they are also different in others. For example, child graves generally follow the west-east orientation of female or the east-west orientation of male graves, but with much more pronounced deviations to the north or to the south. Likewise, child graves are significantly shallower and shorter than those of adults. Similar to contemporary cemeteries in Poland (e.g., Dziekanowice), grave goods are found in the graves of children older than three years, and a considerable number of grave goods appear in Lubień in graves of children around that age.[31] However, the proportion of burials with grave goods within the total number of child graves is higher in Lubień than on any of the contemporary sites that have been published so far: 26 out of 37 children (over 70%) were buried with some goods.[32] There were no grave goods in some graves of children, but also of five adults (three men and two women). Similarly in Dziekanowice, the cemetery located near the great Piast power center at Ostrów Lednicki, some child graves were just as well furnished, if not better than, those of adults.[33]

Despite the unusually high percentage of furnished child graves in Lubień, there are nevertheless noticeable differences between adults and children. For example, certain types of goods are present in both adult and child graves, while some were reserved for adults. Spears, flint steels, buckles, and whetstones appear only with adult men, perhaps signaling members of the ducal retinue.[34] However, such weapons as battle-axes and arrowheads have also been found in child graves. This strongly suggests the social construction of warrior status or, at the very least, some symbolic association with hunting.[35] Similarly, only adult women were buried together with spindle whorls and earrings. To be sure, there are also artifacts exclusively associated with child graves, e.g., the rattle in grave 2.[36] Pendants, beads, lock (temple) rings, ceramic pots, wooden buckets, knives, arrowheads, and axes appear in both adult and child graves.[37] At the very least, such distinctions in terms of grave goods suggest that although (some) children could receive just as many and just as rich grave goods as (some) adults, there were nevertheless artifacts considered inappropriate for child graves.

It is important to note that the age of seven is clearly marked in two child graves (12 and 31) through the deposition of axes. The estimated age of the two skeletons is six–seven and five–six years, respectively. A third axe was found in grave 83 with the skeleton of a teenager, whose age at death was estimated to be 12–15 years. The axe seems therefore to be the material culture correlate of a rite of passage for an age considered crucial for boys, even though the exact age of the individuals may have been established only approximately in the Middle Ages. The excavators have also noted that graves of children with "female" attributes contain only beads if the skeletons are under seven years of age, but often many lock rings if the age at death is more than seven years.[38] With males, there seems to be no other cut-off point before adulthood: only adult men were buried with spears, buckles, or whetstones. In other words, the analysis of the child and male graves in Lubień strongly suggests only three age categories. Whether the same was true for child and female burials is not clear from examining only the main categories of grave goods. Moreover, only a few child graves in the cemetery can be dated with any degree of certainty.

In their social and cultural analysis of the Lubień cemetery, Tomasz Kurasiński and Kalina Skóra relied primarily on an approach limited to the co-variation of no more than two variables, such as age and grave goods. Given the richness of detail in the excellent publication of this cemetery, as well as the variability within the group of child burials, we have opted instead for a multivariate analysis in an attempt to pull out something in common from a number of different variables characterizing all or most of the analyzed graves. Our goal is to detect patterns at a higher resolution that could reveal which relations were more important than others. Correspondence analysis is a technique allowing the concomitant study of relations between graves, between grave goods (or grave-good types), and between graves and grave goods. Are there any age-related patterns within the group of child burials? If so, do they reflect burial customs associated with graves of adults? Can "childhood" be identified as a social category in the material culture associated with the graves of individuals who died at a very young age? The premise for our approach is that the selection of artifacts to be deposited in child graves has something to do with the conceptual categories in existence in society at that time.

One of the first observations to emerge from this analysis is that child graves can clearly be divided into two groups – one resembling graves of men, the other resembling graves of women (see Fig. 6.1). The "male" subgroup is characterized by such features as the east–west orientation, while the deposition of buckets, weapons, buckles, and whetstones is primarily restricted to adult graves (see Fig. 6.2). Within the "female" subgroup, the west-east orientation and the deposition of beads, lock (temple) rings, finger- and earrings brings together graves of adults and children (see Fig. 6.3) This strongly suggests that from a very early stage, the children of the community burying their dead in Lubień were assigned gender roles marked in material cultural terms with the same categories of artifacts as those employed for adult men and women. Indeed, all the age markers appear in the central part of the scattergram, between the "male" and the "female" subgroups, and not too far from the adult markers (see Fig. 6.1).

This suggests that there is no significant difference in the degree of separation between males and females in early childhood. Despite two clear gender clusters, there is a lack of certain distinguishing grave goods in children's and teenager's graves, represented by a continuum of burials located in the middle of the scattergram between the two subgroups ("male" and "female"). These "in-between" burials were sometimes of older children (*infans* II, who are often furnished with fewer goods than burials of *infans* I children[39]), but more often of very young children, who were given either no grave goods or only gender-neutral attributes, such as knives. Graves of younger children were also more likely to have skewed orientations, making them less similar to adult graves. A number of adult female graves also appear in this middle section, often because of irregular grave orientation or the ambiguity of the grave goods (knives). There are comparatively fewer adult male graves in the middle section of the scattergram. In short, despite the presence of weapons in some graves of boys who died around the age of seven,

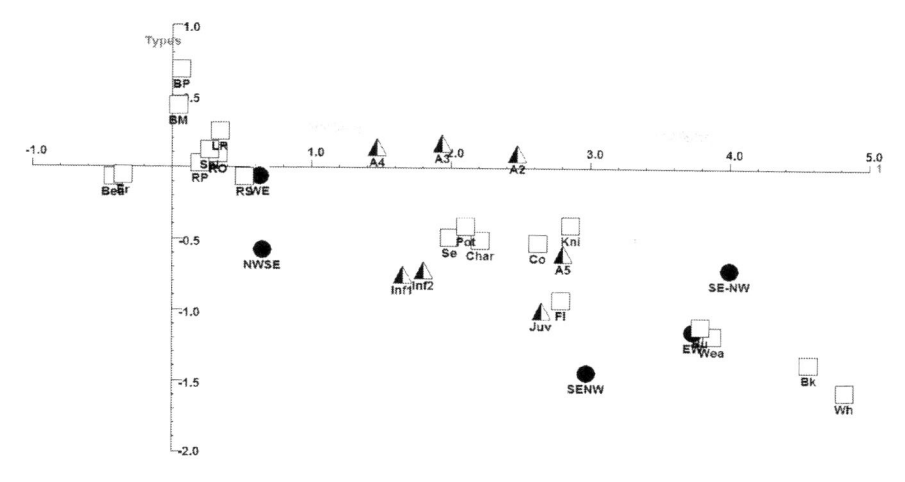

FIG. 6.1 Correspondence analysis plot of features associated with 93 burial assemblages in the Lubień cemetery

A2 – Age: 20–30 years old; A3 – Age: 30–40 years old; A4 – Age: 40–50 years old; A5 – Age: 50–60 years old; Bea–beads; Bk – buckle; BM – metal beads; BP – semi-precious stone beads; Bu – bucket; Char – charcoal in the grave pit; Co – coins; COF – coffin; Er – earrings; EW – E-W grave orientation; Fl – flint steel; Inf1 – Age: 0–6 years old; Inf2 – Age: 7–14 years old; Juv – Age: 15–20 years old; Kni – knife; LR – lock ring; NE-SW – NE-SW grave orientation; NW-SE – NW-SE grave orientation; Pot – ceramic pot; RO – ornate ring; RP – precious-metal ring; RS – simple ring; Se – plant seeds; SENW – SE-NW grave orientation; Spi –spindle whorl; SW-NE – SW-NE grave orientation; WE – W-E grave orientation; Wea – weapons; Wh – whetstone.

many *infans* I burials had few, if any, gender-specific attributes. Graves of many children thus looked more like poorly furnished graves of females with few or non-gendering grave goods, and the only hint of gender is the orientation, hence the slight slew of *infans* I and II towards the female side. In comparison, the *iuvenis* category skews slightly towards the male side, potentially the result of clearer orientation and the presence of more clearly male goods. Neither of these skews should be over-emphasized – all three age categories appear in a significant number of graves around the two gender clusters.

Correspondence analysis reveals ritual similarities between graves, which can then be checked for spatial associations on the ground. For example, when plotting the correlations revealed by the correspondence analysis on the cemetery plan, it becomes clear that three graves with lock rings (45, 46, and 56) appear within the same restricted area of the cemetery – the northwestern corner (see Fig. 6.4).[40] Graves 41 and 56 in that area are of children, both aged *infans* I. In addition to lock rings, which typically appear in the graves of females over the age of seven,[41] all three graves (41, 45, and 56) produced unusually large numbers of beads. Grave 44, next to 45, contains the skeleton of an infant (three–four years old) with the

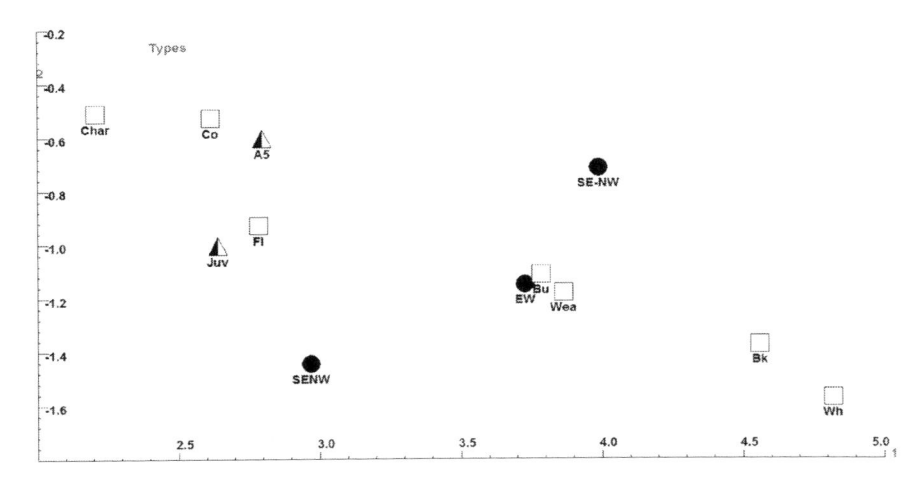

FIG. 6.2 Zoomed detail of the correspondence analysis of features associated with 93 burial assemblages in the Lubień cemetery

For abbreviations, see Fig. 6.1.

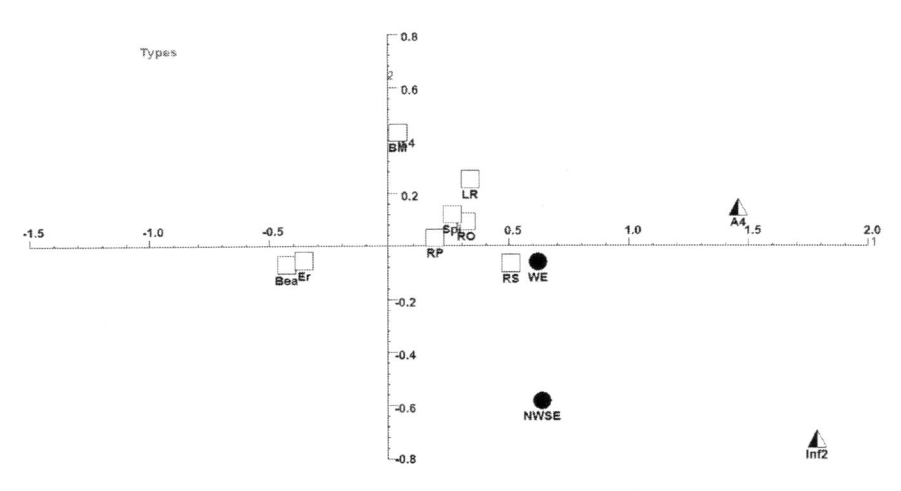

FIG. 6.3 Zoomed detail of the correspondence analysis of features associated with 93 burial assemblages in the Lubień cemetery

For abbreviations, see Fig. 6.1.

same, west–east, orientation (most typical for female burials) as graves 45 and 56 within one and the same row. Whatever the reason for this cluster of graves of young children, it is important to note that two out of three graves of adults in this region of the cemetery produced fewer and poorer goods than those found in the neighboring graves of children. Almost all the double burials recorded in Lubień appear in this region of the cemetery, and one of them contained the skeleton of

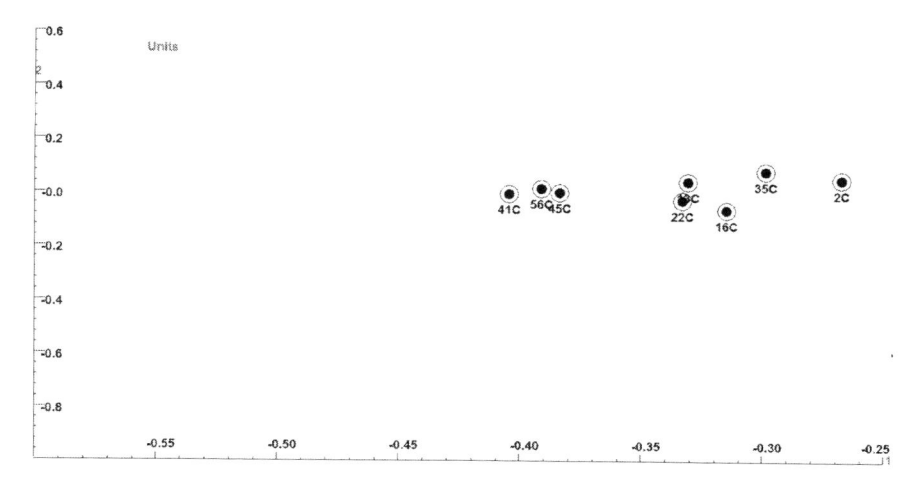

FIG. 6.4 Zoomed detail of the correspondence analysis of burial assemblages in the Lubień cemetery associated with child (C) skeletons

Numbers refer to the graves.

another child less than seven years old (grave 23). Judging from the denier found in another double grave (grave 26) and struck in Cracow no later than 1152 for the duke of Mazovia, Bolesław the Curly (1146–1173),[42] burials in the northwestern region are among the most recent of the entire cemetery. One is left with the impression that the young adults and children buried so close to each other (or even within one and the same grave) were members of the same family.

Another cluster revealed by the correspondence analysis is a group of unfurnished graves with a west–east orientation, all of them in the southeastern part of the cemetery. Graves 63 (*infans* I), 66 (*infans* II, 71 (*infans* I) and 74 (fetus) are grouped together on the scattergram (see Fig. 6.5) and are relatively close to each other on the southeastern edge of the cemetery. Next to grave 71 is 72, which although devoid of any bone remains (a cenotaph?), has a pit of the same size and may have been designed for a child as well. The most interesting aspect of this group in the southwest is that it appears to be almost the opposite of the cluster in the northwest. Those are graves of children with no grave goods whatsoever, and with a grave orientation following that of female graves. The surrounding adult graves feature fewer grave goods than in the northwest. The reason for the difference between the northwestern and the southeastern clusters cannot be chronology. The coin found with a child buried in grave 78, right next to the *infans* I in grave 71, is a denier struck in Cracow between 1076 and 1079 for the king of Poland, Bolesław the Bold (1058–1079, king between 1076 and 1079).[43] The coin is pierced, which suggests a much later date for the burial than for the coin, perhaps around 1100. But there is evidence of a later date from neighboring burials. Three graves of children (85, 87, and 90) in close proximity to 78 were buried with knives. A grave pit with no bone remains (grave 84) may also have been dug for a child. One of them (85)

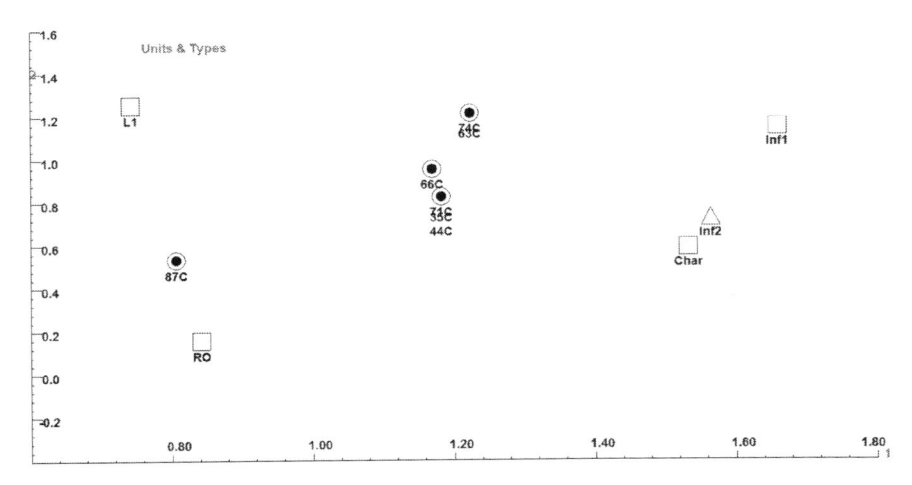

FIG. 6.5 Zoomed detail of the correspondence analysis of burial assemblages in the Lubień cemetery with child (C) skeletons, in association with the most typical features

Char – charcoal; Inf1 – Age: 0–6 years; Inf2 – Age: 7–14 years; L1 – lock ring, type 1; RO – oval grave pit. Numbers refer to graves.

had an axe as well as a fragmentary coin struck in Cracow between 1140 and 1142 for the duke of Silesia, Władysław the Exile (1138–1142).[44] Grave 87 produced lock rings; for all the three graves under discussion, this was the only one with the west–east orientation most typical for female graves. Despite the presence of such artifacts as glass beads, finger-rings, and lock rings, none of the neighboring adult graves had particularly rich furnishings. One is left with the impression that in the southwest, pairs of child graves buried next to each other follow the characteristics of the adult grave closest to them. For example, two adjacent graves of children (83 and 90) have the same orientation (east–west) as the neighboring male grave 86. In addition, all three burials produced knives. Two other graves of children located next to each other (71 and 78) have the same west–east orientation as that of the neighboring female grave 81. While no grave goods whatsoever were found in grave 71, both 78 and 81 produced lock rings and coins. Such a distinctive pattern in the southwestern region of the cemetery may be better illustrated by means of a group of five graves – three children, a cenotaph, and a young female (grave 123). The latter had no grave goods, but both 124 and 127 – both young children – have the same orientation, and they have also produced beads, a typically female attribute. Two other graves, 125 and 126 stand out in this group, the former because of having no grave goods, but an opposite orientation, the latter because of being empty (a cenotaph?). One is tempted to see this group as a children's quarter, but the presence of the young woman suggests otherwise. Hers was most likely the first grave to be dug on the southern periphery of the cemetery, as the burial is flanked by graves of children. It is quite possible that much like in the rest of the cemetery,

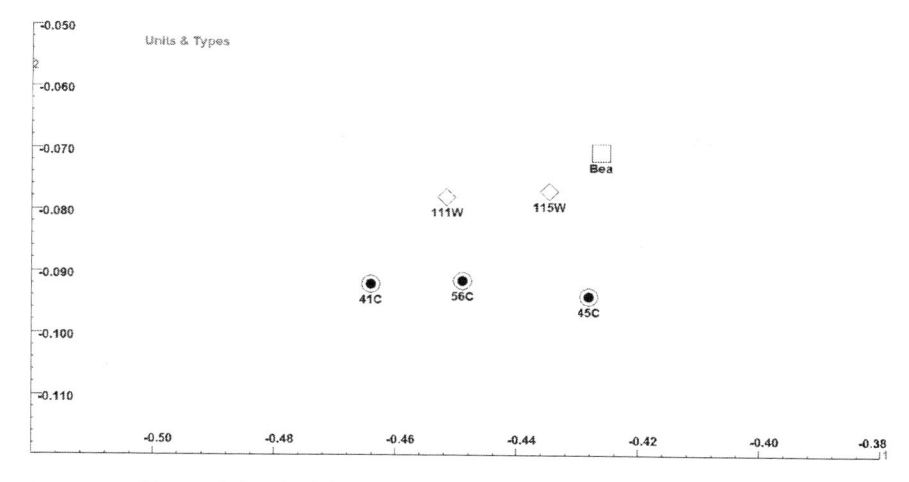

FIG. 6.6 Zoomed detail of the correspondence analysis of burial assemblages in the Lubień cemetery with female (W) and child (C) skeletons in association with the most typical features

Bea – beads. Numbers refer to the graves.

children were buried here next to members of their kin group or family and in a manner imitating their burials.

An even more interesting case is that of a group of child graves associated with two very similar female graves in the western part of the cemetery – 111 and 115 – that are very close to each other on the scattergram (see Fig. 6.6) because of their spectacular grave goods – great numbers of glass beads and lock rings. As a matter of fact, two other neighboring graves (102 and 121) produced lock rings of the same type as those in graves 111 and 115 (Kočka-Krenz's type III c[45]). This particular type of lock ring is not otherwise found in any other grave of the Lubień cemetery. Besides graves of children such as 98 (12–16 years old), 100 (under seven years old), 109 (six–seven years old), 112 (three–four years old), 116 (seven–eight years old), 120 (five–six years old), and 122 (nine–ten years old), most other graves in this part of the cemetery are of young adults.[46] The only grave of a mature individual associated with this group is 113, dated by the *terminus post quem* of the coin found therein – 1070–1076.[47] All the graves of young individuals produced large numbers of beads and lock rings, while knives, flint steels, and even a bucket (all "male" attributes) have been found in some of the child graves. Given that the only male grave in this area is 107, the combination of child and young adult graves (all of which seem to be of females) bespeaks the special character of the western group – perhaps a family plot.

The detailed analysis of the northwestern, southeastern, and western clusters of child graves reveals the existence of different sections of the cemetery in which child burials tended to follow patterns specific for each one of them. In general, however, child graves seem to imitate the nearby adult graves in terms both of orientation and grave goods. An important feature of child burials in Lubień is the relatively large number of double burials. Out of five double burials, four had children. Only one of those four burials, grave 23/25, contained the skeletons of a female (20–30 years old) and a child (*infans* I), and could thus be interpreted as the grave of a mother who died in childbirth or very early in her child's life. A woman may have also been buried with a three- to four-year old child in grave 111. However, no bones have survived in sufficient quantity in that grave to allow for proper sexing of the skeleton, which is otherwise believed to have been of a 20 to 25 year-old individual. Significantly, judging from the stratigraphic evidence, it seems that the bones of the older individual were placed in the grave later than those of the child. If so, it is remarkable that the grave chosen for this supposed woman buried with a relatively large number of dress accessories of very good quality was that of an infant. A similarly abnormal situation is that of the double grave 43, in which an adult male (20 to 30 years old) was buried with a knife and an arrowhead next to a young female (16 to 22 years old). Unlike all other females in the Lubień cemetery, the young woman in grave 43 was laid in the grave with the same orientation as that of the male skeleton, namely east-south-east to west-north-west.

The special position of children in Lubień is directly comparable to that in other contemporary cemeteries in Poland. The recently discovered grave of a ten-year-old child from Czermno-Kolonia (near Tomaszów, only a few miles southeast of Lubień) produced the remains of extraordinarily luxurious clothes.[48] Children appear in less than a quarter of all graves in the cemetery excavated in 1970 in Masłowice (Wieluń County, Łódź voivodeship), about 50 miles west of Lubień.[49] Much like in Lubień, females were buried with a west–east and men with an opposite (east–west) orientation. Eleven out of 20 graves of children follow the orientation of female graves. There is an obvious cluster of four child graves around a double burial on the southern side, which includes a female and a child skeleton.[50] At least one child was buried in a coffin (grave 21), much like a number of adults elsewhere in the cemetery (graves 55 and 58).[51] Half of all child graves had no grave goods whatsoever. However, the highest numbers of beads were found in two child graves (48 and 85).[52] One of them (48) also produced the largest number of lock rings (10) in any grave of the Masłowice cemetery.[53] The other (85) contained the oldest of seven coins found in that cemetery – a denier struck in Saxony after 983 in the name of Otto III and his grandmother, Adelaide.[54]

Among 45 medieval graves found during a two-year salvage excavation on the northern side of the village of Psary-Lechawa, on the northern outskirts of Piotrków Trybunalski (about 14 miles north of Lubień), only five are of children. In one of them (grave 33), an arrowhead was deposited on the right side of the skull. Both the arrow and its position in the grave have good analogies in Lubień.[55] This grave had an east–northeast orientation, exactly the opposite of that of the neighboring grave (37) with the skeleton of a woman buried in a coffin with a silver beads and lock rings.[56] Much farther afield to the northwest, the excavations carried out until 1997 in Dziekanowice (near Gniezno, Greater Poland) unearthed

495 graves with 572 skeletons. Of these, only 113 (22%) were of little children.[57] The largest number within that group is children who died before reaching one year of age, followed by the category of five to six years old. No graves of children under three years of age contained grave goods. The largest variety of artifacts has been noted for the age category of three to four years old.[58]

To the east-north-east of Lubień, the cemetery excavated in 1969 in Czekanów (near Siedlce, Mazovia) had 145 graves, 60 of which are of children (42%). Child graves appear all over the area of the cemetery, with a cluster of 20 graves in the southern part which has been interpreted as a special quarter for children.[59] As in Dziekanowice, the largest number is of children who died before reaching one year of age, followed by the age categories of one to two and two to four years old, respectively. Only children older than four years of age were buried together with adults, but there are also double burials of children. As in all three cemeteries in the environs of Piotrków Trybunalski (Lubień, Masłowiec, and Psary), some children were buried with a west–east, others with an east–west orientation, most likely in imitation of the orientation reserved for female and male graves, respectively. Some of the child graves were very well furnished, with no parallels either in Czekanów or elsewhere in Poland. For example, there were 267 glass beads in grave 10, while grave 56 produced a bronze cross with enamel decoration, glass and silver beads, and cowrie shells, as well as amber and rock crystal beads.[60]

A number of conclusions can be drawn from this discussion of Lubień and other Polish row-grave cemeteries. First, despite their young age and supposed insignificance in the world of the adults at the time, numerous children of all ages and sexes received spectacular treatments in death. However, not all children were treated in the same way; variations existed for age, gender, and family custom. While broadly divided into two gender groups parallel to those of adults, all children lacked certain "adult" features, and some had so few furnishings as to be gender-visible only by means of grave orientation. Differences in the treatment of children, at least in some instances, ultimately seem to reflect family plots within a cemetery. In these plots, children were buried according to rituals typical for the adults in their group or to some special rule for children in the family. Finally, children feature heavily in multiple burials, and their presence next to adults seems to have been desired, as indicated by unusual collections of grave goods or grave orientations.

Child burials in medieval Hungary: Kérpuszta

The cemetery of Kérpuszta (Somogy County, Hungary) was found accidentally in 1949 and then systematically excavated between 1950 and 1951 by a team of archaeologists from the Hungarian National Museum in Budapest led by János Nemeskéri. The site is located about a mile away from the village of Fiad to the northwest, and less than 11 miles from the southern shore of Lake Balaton. The cemetery was completely excavated, even though four or five skeletons may have been destroyed during construction work on the site prior to the archaeological excavations.[61] Out of the 388 graves discovered, only 122 had grave goods. On the basis of these grave goods, the excavators divided the cemetery into an older and a newer part. The newer, northern, part of the cemetery has richer grave goods, many silver lock (temple) rings, and coins. The cemetery began in the late tenth century on the south and was extended to the north and east, with the last graves dug on the outer limits of the cemetery in the early twelfth century.[62] Much as with Lubień, the sequencing of the Kérpuszta cemetery is based on numerous finds of coins. Since all graves with coins were found in the north, the southern part of the cemetery has been dated to the first half of the eleventh century and the northern part to the second half.[63] Because of the absence of any open settlements in the immediate vicinity of the cemetery, the excavators have advanced the idea that this was the burial ground for a number of small groups living in communities scattered around Kérpuszta, which coalesced into a village only during the second half of the twelfth or in the thirteenth century.[64]

With one exception (grave 361), all the graves in Kérpuszta are oriented west–east. Adults were buried in pits twice to four times deeper than those of child graves. All skeletons – adults and sub-adults – were found in the supine position, with a great variation of the position of the arms – sometimes folded on the chest, other times laid along the body.[65] In a few cases, the fact that both arms and legs were tightly close to each other suggests the use of shrouds, but there are no traces of coffins.[66] The relatively good state of preservation of the bones has allowed the aging and sexing of almost all the skeletons found at Kérpuszta. Out of 395 individuals identified by anthropological analysis, 187 (over 47%) are children and teenagers (ages 0–19).[67] Only 27 of the child graves (less than 15% of all of them) had any grave goods at all. The vast majority of child graves without goods were of young children (age categories *infans* I and II), with a southwest–northeast orientation (see Fig. 6.7). However, most graves without any grave goods were of males. A relatively large number of them also had a southwest-northeast orientation. A few child graves (24, 98, 117, 139, 154, 172, and 246) are grouped together because of the amorphous glass beads found in relatively large numbers in each one of them. The presence of such beads also sets apart a group of six female graves (41, 59, 83, 153, 365, and 368), some of which produced very large numbers of such beads (145 in grave 365, 126 in grave 83, and 120 in grave 59; see Fig. 6.8).[68] Not surprisingly, most of the graves of young children with grave goods appear similar to graves of adult women (over 30 years old). Females who died as teenagers (age 14–19, the *iuvenis* category) are a separate category, which is characterized by such dress accessories as heart-shaped pendants, bronze buttons, and simple finger-rings. In contrast, combining male and child graves, the *iuvenis* category is as closely associated with the graves of adult males (see Fig. 6.8). Given that the majority of the latter have no grave goods, the conclusion can only be that a few female teenagers were buried with distinctive dress accessories, different from those of both young children and adult females. Conversely, teenager males tended to be buried like most other men, namely, without any grave goods. That only two male graves (260 and 305) had the same grave orientation (southwest–northeast) as most graves of children (*infans* I and II categories), and produced lock (temple) rings strongly suggests

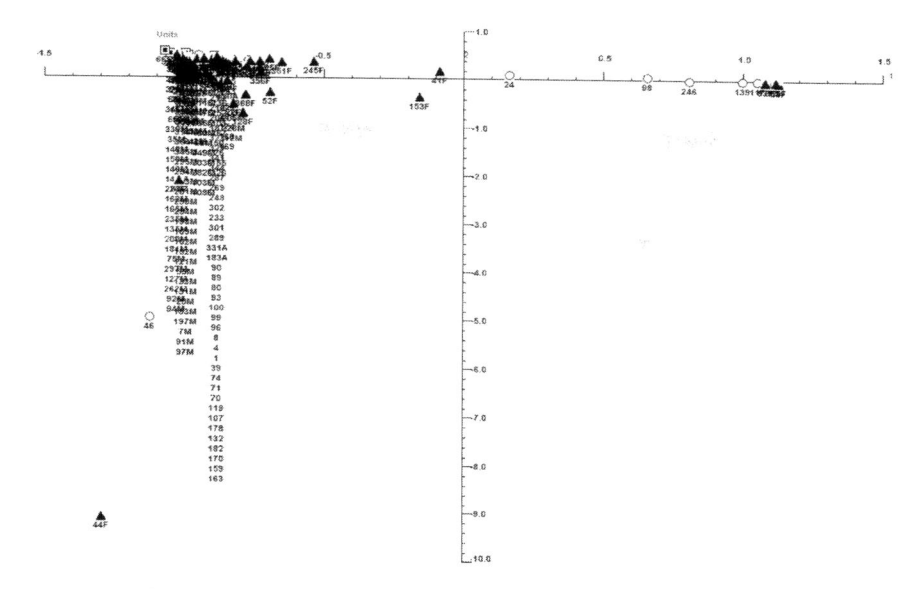

FIG. 6.7 Correspondence analysis plot of 301 burial assemblages from the Kérpuszta cemetery in relation to 32 typical features

A1 – Age: 15–20 years; A2 – Age: 20–30 years; A3 – Age: 30–40 years; A4 – Age: 40–50 years; A5 – Age: 50–60 years; A6 – Age: 60–70 years; AB – animal bones; BB – belt buckle; BCS – silver-plated, cylindrical glass beads; BG3 – corn-shaped glass beads; BG6 – amorphous glass beads; BGB – barrel-shaped glass beads; BSP – semi-precious stone beads; BU – bronze button; CO – coin; CP – ceramic pot; ES – simple earring; FL – flint; FLS – flint steel; FO – ornate finger-ring; FS – simple finger-ring; FT – finger-ring of intertwined wires; INF1 – Age: 0–6 years; INF2 – Age: 7–14 years; KN – knife; LR1 – lock ring, type 1; LR3 – lock ring, type 3; LRD – lock ring, double loop; PH – heart-shaped pendant; SW-NE – SW-NE grave orientation; TB – burnt timber inside the grave; W-E – W-E grave orientation.

that in Kérpuszta most children who died at a young age (under 14) were given a burial treatment not unlike that reserved for adult females. How many of those children were actually girls is of course impossible to tell, but the fact that the *iuvenis* category stands apart so clearly from both graves of women and graves of children seems to indicate that no gender differentiation existed within the latter group.

The only double grave in the cemetery (368) contains two skeletons of females. One of them was a 60-year old woman, the other a young individual (18 years of age). The latter was buried with a necklace of silver-foil beads and two heart-shaped pendants, while the old woman had no grave accessories at all. The reasons for this double burial remain unknown, but the contrast between the old woman and the girl suggests that the latter was the focus of attention. The old woman may have been buried together with the girl in order to partake in that attention.

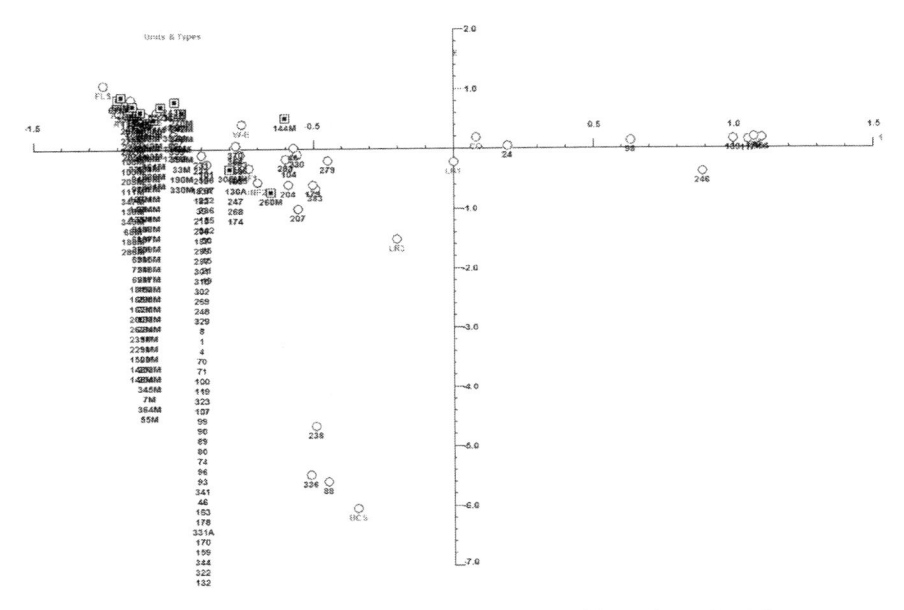

FIG. 6.8 Correspondence analysis plot of burial assemblages from the Kérpuszta cemetery associated with male (M) and child (C) skeletons, in relation to 32 typical features

For abbreviations, see Fig. 6.7.

The earlier part of the cemetery is characterized by the presence of bronze lock (temple) rings, while later graves produced lock rings made of silver. Small rings belong to the latest phase, even though large rings continued to be used, in at least two cases (grave 372 and 383), the two categories were found together.[69] The later phase of the cemetery is also characterized by finger-rings of twisted wire, conical, amethyst, and especially fluorite beads.[70]

It has long been noted that there are various clusters of child graves within the Kérpuszta cemetery.[71] There are many graves of children along the eastern side of the cemetery, which thus appears to have been reserved for such burials. However, a group of eight graves in the middle of the cemetery, between three male (18, 33, and 35), and two female graves (14, 34), included six babies (under one year of age, graves 26–30 and 32) and two young children (grave 15, ages seven–eight; grave 36, ages two–three).[72] With the exception of one of the female burials (34), none of these graves had any grave goods. The age and sex structure of this group, as well as the specific arrangement of the male and female graves around the child graves – female graves on the northern side, and male burials on the southern and western sides of the cluster – strongly suggests the existence of a family plot. A similar arrangement appears on the northeastern side of the cemetery, where a cluster of eight child graves (183a, 186, 187, 189, 192, 193, 204, and 206) – one who died at the age of two, another at five years of age, and six newborns – was flanked by the grave of a young individual (18–20 years of age) on the southern side and that of a man (40–45 years of age) on the western side. Another interesting case appears on the northern side of the cemetery. No less than five child graves (168–171 and 174), one who died at six or seven years of age, and three very young children (*infans* I), were flanked by the grave (173) of a woman (35 to 40 years old) with a lock ring made of silver, on the northern side, and that of a man (40 to 45 years old) with no grave goods, on the southern side (grave 162). Three other male graves (161, 242, and 243) were found on the western side of the cluster of child graves, all without grave goods. Two female graves were on the eastern side of the cluster, both with lock rings made of silver. Another cluster of four child graves – three babies (274–276) and a child who died at four or five years of age – was also surrounded by female graves on the northern and eastern sides (273, 277, and 309), with male graves on the southern and western sides (68, 69 and 278). On the northern side there was a female grave with a silver lock ring and a finger-ring of twisted wire (191). On the opposite, western, side of the cemetery, a cluster of four child graves (86 and 88–90) – a 10- to 12-year old and three three- to four-year-old children – is flanked by a female grave to the north, and a male grave to the south (64 and 87). A cluster of three graves (230, 232, and 233) of children who died between four and nine years of age is surrounded by no less than seven male graves on the western and southern sides (103, 226, 228, 229, 237, 253, and 254), with three female graves (227, 234, and 241) on the northeastern side. Another cluster of three child graves in the southern part of the cemetery (299, 301, and 302) includes a newborn, a four-year old, and a seven-year old child. The cluster was "guarded" on the northern and eastern sides by two graves (306 and 338) of females and a male burial (284) on the western side, all without any grave goods. The same is not true for child graves that appear alone and not in clusters. For example, to the north of the grave of a newborn found in the middle of the cemetery (16), the closest graves were of females (12 and 18). In contrast, the closest graves to the southeast, south, and west were of males (17, 37, and 41). Similarly, on the western side of grave 129 (the burial of a four- to five-year old child), there were two male and one female graves (128, 130, and 135), with only male graves on the eastern side (127, 143, and 150). Grave 82, with a skeleton aged *infans* I, was surrounded by female graves (59, 76, 85, and 89), with only one male grave (84) on the eastern side.

The excavators have suggested that clusters of child graves inside the cemetery signal the young victims of an epidemic that struck all the communities burying their dead at Kérpuszta. If so, it is remarkable that instead of being buried on the eastern side, these children were buried inside areas delimited by graves of adults. Only children were buried in such clusters, and only a few of them were found alone and not in close proximity to other graves of children. The arrangement of adult graves around clusters of child graves suggests that such clusters represented focal points for groups of burials, perhaps family plots. Judging from the distribution of graves within the cemetery, the significance of an adult grave derived from its position in relation to a cluster of child graves, and not the other way around.[73]

Conversely, no gender-related arrangement of adult graves existed in cases of child graves found alone, not in clusters. Out of 29 child graves on the eastern side of the cemetery, which the excavators believed to be the "children's quarter," 16 are of children who died under one year of age. While elsewhere in the cemetery a few babies were buried separately (e.g., graves 16 and 272), most of them appear in clusters of child graves. While some clusters had no graves of very young children, most large clusters consisted of graves of newborns, with only a few children of older age. The general impression one gets from the analysis of the Kérpuszta cemetery is that graves of newborns, when found in clusters, operated as foci of burial for both adults and sub-adults, perhaps members of the same kin group (nuclear family).

The special treatment of children in death is also apparent in other contemporary cemeteries in Hungary. Half of all graves with fluorite beads and cowrie shells, as well as seven out of 11 graves with silver-foil beads, from the cemetery excavated in Pusztaszentlászló (Zala County in Western Hungary) are of children.[74] The cemetery began in the late eleventh century and ended shortly after 1100, with new burials in the early 1130s. The cemetery is organized in three areas (north, center, and south), each with several groups, perhaps representing extended families. One of the two groups of the northern part has 35 graves, including eight child graves. The largest number of children is in the second group of the central part (15 out of 52 graves).[75] In the eleventh-century cemetery partially excavated in Szakony (near Szombathely, in Western Hungary), children were buried amongst adults, but not in clusters.[76] That children were given special treatment in eleventh- and twelfth-century Hungary is clear from the examination of other contemporary cemeteries. In Transylvania, most of the grave goods from eleventh-century cemeteries have been found in child graves, either in cemeteries associated with strongholds (Alba Iulia-Stația de salvare, Alba Iulia-St. Vânătorilor, Cluj Mănăştur-Bustul lui Gheorghe Rákoczi II, Hunedoara, and Moldoveneşti) or in rural cemeteries (Alba Iulia-Brânduşei II, Alba Iulia-Pâclişa, Deva, and Noşlac).[77] In the recently excavated cemetery in Sighişoara-Dealul Viilor, almost 30% of all graves were of little children (*infans* I). Out of six burials with coins in that cemetery, three are of children.[78] An even more interesting case of grave superposition involves three graves. Grave 28 had two skeletons – an adult and a child, both in a supine position. This grave was superposed on two other graves, 32 and 34. On the left side of the child in grave 28 was a hoard of 37 silver coins, 35 deniers struck for King Béla III (1172–1196) and two anonymous deniers.[79]

While children were clearly treated in a special way in eleventh- and twelfth-century cemeteries in Hungary, Kérpuszta stands out because of its conspicuous arrangement of graves. Child graves were foci of burial, with graves of adults specifically arranged by gender around clusters of child graves. No direct parallel to any other cemetery is known so far, but the situation in Pusztaszentlászló suggests the existence of extended families. If such an interpretation could be applied to Kérpuszta, then clusters of child graves with adult graves around them may signal family plots. It is remarkable that no clear-cut age categories seem to have existed in the communities burying their dead in Kérpuszta, even though graves of young children with grave goods appear to imitate female rather than male graves. A clear age distinction appears only for teenagers (14 to 19 years old). Teenager females were buried with dress accessories different from those of both younger children and adult females. Teenager males were buried like most other men, namely, without grave goods.

Before Lubień and Kérpuszta

Burial in both Lubień and Kérpuszta seems to have begun shortly before the year 1000. In order to understand the position of children in those two cemeteries, it is necessary to examine briefly the earlier situation in the surrounding regions of these two sites, as well as in Poland and Hungary at large. Helena Zoll-Adamikowa has noted a number of common features in early cemeteries, irrespective of regional differences otherwise clearly documented throughout Poland. Most significantly, cremation (as opposed to inhumation) was used for the disposal of bodies, and burials were organized around barrows. Ostentatious numbers of grave goods of different kinds appear in these graves much more often than in the later row-grave or churchyard cemeteries.[80] No cremation cemetery is known so far from the southern region of central Poland in the vicinity of Lubień.[81] However, the region has been included in the so-called zone C2, which, according to Helena Zoll-Adamikowa, is characterized by cremation under mounds (barrows).[82] Most barrow cemeteries dated between the eighth and the mid-tenth century are in southeastern Poland (Lesser Poland).[83] Each barrow had two or more burials, some pit, others urn cremations – most certainly not contemporary.[84] The only anthropological analyzes of cremated remains are also from that region of Poland. For example, in Kornatka (near Myślenice, Lesser Poland), two individuals were buried under barrow 4, dated between the eighth and the ninth centuries. One of them was apparently a young child (*infans* I). Two children, aged 0 to six months and *infans* I, respectively, were buried together with an adult in barrow 7 of that same cemetery.[85] This is too small of a sample to draw any firm conclusions, but the anthropological identification of burials in barrows 4 and 7 in Kornatka strongly suggests the absence of child graves not associated with graves of adults or of clusters of child graves. In other words, nothing indicates any conceptual distinction of childhood or of any age categories.

The situation in western Hungary between the eighth and the mid-tenth century was radically different. In the region of the southern shore of Lake Balaton, around Kérpuszta, inhumation was the predominant burial rite throughout the entire period. During the ninth century, this region was included in the Carolingian Empire, with Zalavár (Mosapurc) as the main power center. A number of churches were built in Zalavár and the influence of Christianity is visible in the organization of the neighboring cemeteries.[86] Children were buried in family crypts attached to the Church of St. Hadrian, such as, for example, grave 120/89 north of the northern chapel.[87] Others were buried immediately close to the southern wall of the church, such as the young child in grave 1/

2000.[88] In that respect, the church graveyards in Zalavár are no different from those associated with contemporary churches in Moravia. Out of 2,993 skeletons from Great Moravian cemeteries that have been analyzed anthropologically, only 26.2% are of children. Most are from rural cemeteries, but those that appear in church graveyards stand out in terms of their special positioning. For example, one of the 17 Carolingian-period burials discovered to the west of the rotunda in Ducové belonged to a child. This was the burial located closest to the wall of the rotunda.[89] In the cemetery around the rotunda in Mikulčice (church VI), 190 graves have been found, 97 of which are of children and adolescents. Only seven of them were located immediately next to the church, in contrast to nine graves of men and eight of women. In Pohansko, there were 300 burials in the cemetery around the Manor Church (church I). Of those graves, more than half were of children (154 graves). All male and child graves were placed immediately close to the church, some even in the narthex or in an annex built later on the south side of the church. The graves of many children buried next to the church produced very rich gold adornments, which suggests elevated social status. This is in sharp contrast to the large cemetery around the church in Staré Město-Na válach, with no less than 1,634 graves. The narrow strip around the walls of the church ("under the rain gutter") was occupied exclusively by child burials, while large graves in burial chambers ("family crypts") with rich grave goods are farther away from the building. The contrast has been explained in terms of the character of churches around which cemeteries developed in the ninth century. Unlike the rotundas in Ducové and Mikulčice and the Manor Church in Pohansko, the church in Staré Město-Na válach was not proprietary, but most likely an episcopal church.[90] Most of the children buried in church graveyards are older than the age category *infans* I. It is children older than three years that received more attention, both in terms of the layout of the pit and the number and quality of the grave goods. Children of different ages were even buried in separate clusters in various parts of the cemetery in Nitra-Zobora-Lupka.[91]

There is no evidence of continuity in terms of burial customs between the ninth- and early tenth-century church graveyards in western Hungary and the large, rural cemeteries of the tenth to the early twelfth centuries, such as Kérpuszta. In ninth-century Moravia, some children were buried in special locations closest to the church building, although there are notable differences between cemeteries associated with episcopal (Staré Město-Na válach) and proprietary churches (Pohansko). Despite remarkable similarities, such as the existence of clusters of child graves in both Nitra-Zobora-Lupka and Kérpuszta, the interment treatment of children that is so clearly associated with church graveyards in Moravia had to be re-invented in Hungary in the twelfth century.

After Lubień and Kérpuszta

During the eleventh and twelfth century, the large cemetery around the Church of St. Hadrian in Zalavár was again in use.[92] Out of the 334 identified skeletons from 350 graves that could be dated to that period, 152 (45.5%) were of individuals under 19 years of age. The largest group is that of children between one and three years old, followed by the age category of four to seven years.[93] Among twenty graves located immediately next to the walls on the southern and southeastern side of the church, eight are of children, most of them *infans* I.[94] A similar situation is documented in Gellértegyháza (a suburb of Orosháza, Békés County) in southeastern Hungary, where a small church was surrounded by a large cemetery with 680 graves. Children were a little over a quarter of the population buried there (175 graves). To judge from the chronology of the cemetery, it appears that the church was built after the first burials – some of which produced horse bones and riding gear – possibly in an attempt to "Christianize" a formerly pagan cemetery.[95] Although child graves appear in clusters across the entire area of the church graveyard, there is an evident concentration around the apse of the church.[96] Most child graves in Gellértegyháza had no grave goods at all, and that also applies to those closest to the church walls (graves 10, 51, 97, 105, 117, and 121). Because of the absence of grave goods, it is difficult to gauge the difference in the treatment of children in burial before and after the building of the church. However, it is likely that the graves around the church are in fact from the later phase of the cemetery, and that is not contradicted by finds of later coins.[97] The graves of children near the walls of the church must therefore date to the twelfth or thirteenth century.

No church graveyard is known from the region of Lubień. However, a situation very similar to that documented in Hungary is apparent from a small salvage excavation of a tetraconch church in Zawichost, near Sandomierz (Świętokrzyskie voivodeship, southeastern Poland).[98] The church graveyard contains 220 identified graves, mostly on the southern side of the tetraconch. Indeed, all but one of the child burials, probably from the twelfth century, cluster close to the southern apse of the tetraconch. This includes some single burials such as graves 111, 156, 216, 295, 309, and 327. The excavator goes so far as to call this area a "children's quarter." Grave 111 is a good example of the treatment of children in twelfth-century church graveyards in Poland. This was the burial of a three to four-year old child, buried with lock (temple) rings with S-shaped ends dated to the late eleventh or early twelfth century and a necklace of glass beads. Next to the "children's quarter," there were three triple burials. Much like the cases in row–grave cemeteries discussed above, it seems that children were buried there first, with the bodies of adults added at a later date. In grave 11, two children aged two to four years, respectively, were found alongside a very old adult of unknown sex. Similarly, grave 13 contained the skeleton of an adult male with a bronze finger ring, an individual of age *iuvenis*, and the scattered remains of a very young child.[99] Children were not only given a prized place in Zawichost, but being buried next to a child was a positive event for adults. One is led to believe that children were not just placed near the church for their own "protection," but also because their bodies (and possibly souls) had some sort of value of their own, thus attracting adult burial inside or next to child graves.

Conclusion

Archaeological evidence from ninth-century church graveyards in western Hungary and Moravia is very similar to that from other parts of Carolingian Europe. Before the Carolingian period, the right of burial in community cemeteries was rarely, if ever, extended to children.[100] In the sixth century, some children under six years of age were buried next to the apse of the church in Dassargues (on the eastern outskirts of present-day Montpellier), but many more lay on the fringes of the cemetery. This has been interpreted as a distinction drawn between baptized and unbaptized children.[101] Beginning in the ninth century, however, community cemeteries were "invaded" by child graves. In some cemeteries that start without them, child graves appear immediately after the building of a church on the site. For example, in Portejoie (near Rouen), there is a surge in child graves following the building of a church at some point in the ninth century. Moreover, they are all along the southern wall of the building.[102] Similarly, a large number of young children were buried after 800 near the south wall of the chancel of the Church of St. Bartholomew, and also at the basilica of Saint-Denis near Paris. New cemeteries opened after the ninth century typically have a special area for the burial of children. The church graveyard around the cathedral in Rouen began in the tenth or early eleventh century. About 43% of all 150 graves are of children, and of those two thirds are of children who died under four years of age, and a quarter under one year of age. A large number of sub-adults are buried along the south wall of the Church of St. Stephen, always under the rain gutter (*sub stillicidio*). About a third of all children buried in that area died before reaching one year of age.[103] Newborn babies began to be buried in community cemeteries in Zurich only during the second half of the ninth century, together with older children and young people. By the tenth century, all children were commonly buried in cemeteries.[104]

In the ninth and early tenth century, western Hungary and Moravia were certainly part of the process of change that brought children into community cemeteries and next to the church walls. However, when the same phenomenon re-appeared in twelfth-century (or later) church graveyards in Hungary and Poland, it is not a sign of continuity with the ninth-century developments, except in very general, pan-European terms. It seems that the idea of burying children in the community cemetery and next to the church had to be (re)introduced to East Central Europe from the western parts of the Continent as part and parcel of the Christianization process. Moreover, one is even tempted to link such changes taking place on the fringes of Western Christendom with the new attitudes towards children that become apparent in the late eleventh and twelfth centuries. The image of the child valued for his or her own sake began to take shape only after 1100. This coincided in time with the revival of the hagiographical model of the *puer senex* in order to create the idea of a saintly child (of which St. Elizabeth of Hungary was an early example), the parallel growth of the cult of the infant Jesus, primarily under Cistercian influence, and the cult of the Holy Innocents promoted by Peter Abelard and Bernard of Clairvaux.[105] There is even evidence of increasing awareness of age categories. Didier Lett has demonstrated that 40% of all twelfth- to thirteenth-century miracle stories involving resurrection are about children under two years of age, while resurrection miracles become less frequent as the child grows to seven or more years. The greater number of resurrections among newborn and babies has been associated with the idea that those children were in a state of *demi-monde*: "they had to undergo an exorcism upon baptism, while the innocent infant was between the mortal state and that of the angels."[106] The evolving definition of *adolescentia* in contemporary writings may also point to an evolving conceptualization of teenagers from the early twelfth century onwards.[107] Children appear in the miracles of Polish saints as well.[108] The pattern identified by Didier Lett is verified by an examination of the numerous miracles of St. Stanisław that are associated with children. Out of 18 children helped by that saint, only one – a newborn – is resurrected only to be baptized (after which the child dies again).[109]

Therefore, was childhood discovered in Poland and Hungary in the context of Christianization? Were age categories concepts "imported" from Western Europe in the course of the twelfth or even thirteenth century? To be sure, the burial of children *sub stillicidio* in the church graveyards excavated in Gellértegyháza and Zawichost is a phenomenon with good parallels in other parts of Europe. For example, in one of the last phases of the cemetery in Raunds-Furnell (East Northamptonshire), active from the mid-tenth through the late eleventh centuries, there was a cluster of children under the eaves of the church. Of all the burials located at a distance of no more than 1.5 meters from the church, 77.6% were of infants and 20% were of children.[110] Children received special treatment in other ways as well, even when their graves were not *sub stillicidio*. Some graves are in fact stone cists encasing the bodies. The excavators have identified a cluster of child graves around what is believed to be the "founder's grave," all dated before the introduction of child graves *sub stillicidio*. The placement of children around the eaves of churches also appeared in Sweden. For example, between 1050 and 1100 dozens of children were buried near the apse of the cathedral in Lund (at that time part of Denmark), along with some seemingly prestigious adult burials.[111] This was in no way abnormal for Sweden, for Kristina Jonsson points out that burial to the east of the church near the apse was typical for all Scandinavian countries following the introduction of churchyards. In some of them, much like in Portjoie in Normandy, children were placed near the baptismal font on the western side of the church, in clear association with the sacred character of baptismal water.[112]

This phenomenon points to a conceptual distinction between adulthood and childhood, which is in turn connected with the notion of sacred space. Did any such distinction exist in cemeteries not associated with churches? Unlike Western Europe, the Christianization process in East Central Europe implied the full adoption of already existing patterns. The question of whether rural cemeteries in Poland or in Hungary were Christian is a vexed one. The presence in some graves of objects with such overtly Christian symbols as pectoral crosses has rightly been rejected as a definite criterion for labeling these graves as "Christian."[113] Given that the synod of Szabolcs (1092) and the laws that King Coloman issued in the early twelfth century insist upon the burial of Christians in churchyards,[114] some historians have explained the end of rural cemeteries shortly before or after 1100 as a result of such drastic measures to impose religious uniformity across the kingdom.[115] But there is no one-to-one correlation between the legislation adopted shortly before and after the year 1100 and the end of rural cemeteries, some of which continued well into the early thirteenth century.[116] There is also some chronological overlap between cemeteries with and without churches, as in the case of Kérpuszta and Zalavár-Kapolna. Moreover, there is no serious reason to reject the idea that at least some of those buried in rural cemeteries such as Kérpuszta were Christian.[117] In Poland, rural cemeteries have generally been seen as an intermediary phase between "pagan" cemeteries and church graveyards.[118] According to such an interpretation, those buried in Lubień must have been "Christians cultivating venerable traditions" going back to pre-Christian times. The current interpretation of eleventh- to twelfth-century cemeteries without churches is therefore predicated upon the idea that the (only) archaeological correlate of a thoroughly Christianized community is the church graveyard. As a consequence, one would expect to see a sharp contrast between the treatment of children in rural cemeteries and church graveyards, respectively. But the detailed examination of child graves in the Lubień and Kérpuszta cemeteries shows a different picture.

To be sure, there are significant differences between the two communities burying their dead in those cemeteries. Kérpuszta features a much higher percentage of child graves than Lubień. While many child graves in Lubień were furnished, only a few in Kérpuszta had any grave goods. The nature, number, and kind of grave goods, when present, also varied between sites. Likewise, while family plots seem to be present in both cases, the details are quite different. In Kérpuszta, the location of children in clusters between adult graves indicates that there was a spatial component to the burial of clusters of infants. In Lubień, on the other hand, the exact location of a child within a larger family cluster was less important than the presence of a ritual pattern of grave goods. Likewise, multiple burials involving children were much more prominent in Lubień than in Kérpuszta.

Despite those differences, the similarities between the two cemeteries are striking. In both instances, the existence of what appear to be family plots is essential to the burial patterns of many children. Likewise, in both cemeteries there are multiple examples that suggest that being buried next to a child was desirable for adults. Furthermore, in both cemeteries many similar factors marked the difference between the graves of children and those of adults – variation in grave orientation and depth, as well as unique patterns of grave goods, such as the occasional mass of amorphous beads found with infants in both cemeteries. While age categories operated differently, both cemeteries provide good evidence that "childhood" was not a monolithic category. Interestingly, in both cemeteries graves of *infans* I and II resembled graves of adult females, primarily through the lack of "adult" male goods and a treatment that did not appear in what may have been male child graves. Conversely, in both cemeteries the *iuvenis* category was distinct from that of younger children, and more closely resembled graves of adult males, probably reflecting the appearance of markers of adult masculinity.

The analysis of the two cemeteries thus shows that children were already separated conceptually from adults in communities using rural cemeteries, the traditional interpretation of which is that they were "not quite Christian." In cemeteries such as Kérpuszta and Lubień, children were assigned specific places, and at least in the former case the location of their burials influenced the location of graves of adults (and not the other way around). In fact, this comes very close to the notion that children should be buried within one and the same cemetery as adults, but in a special location, next to the church. Whether or not that conceptual distinction was the result of Christianization remains to be established by future research. But it seems that no such separation existed in pre-Christian Hungary and Poland, as suggested by barrow cemeteries such as Kornatka. How, then, are rural cemeteries different from church graveyards in terms of the treatment of children? The most likely explanation of the treatment of children, especially newborns, in large rural cemeteries such as Kérpuszta, but also in comparatively smaller cemeteries as Lubień, is based on the idea of the family plot: children tended to be buried next to the graves of adult members of their kin group, and often in very similar ways. In church graveyards, the very notion of "family" changes: that children are accepted into the community graveyard is the direct result of the Christian idea that they belong to the same, larger "family" – the Christian community. While in Kérpuszta, children were "used" to mark the location of adult graves, in church graveyards in both Hungary (Zalavár-Kapolna, Gellértegyháza) and Poland (Zawichost) they were most likely believed to intercede on behalf of or in some way benefit the adult members of their larger "family." This is most likely why some of them were buried together with old adults.[119]

Notes

1 Grete Lillehammer, "A Child is Born: the Child's World in an Archaeological Perspective," *Norwegian Archaeological Review* 22, no. 2 (1989): 89–105. This article is regarded as foundational in Jane Eva Baxter, "The Archaeology of Childhood," *Annual Review of Anthropology* 37 (2008): 169–175.

2 Sally Crawford, *Childhood in Anglo-Saxon England* (Stroud: Sutton, 1999). See also her *Daily Life in Anglo-Saxon England* (Oxford: Greenwood, 2009).

3 Barabara Zawadzka-Antosik, "Z problematyki pochówków dziecięcych odkrytych na cmentarzysku w Czekanowie, woj. Siedleckie" [The issue of children's burials in the cemetery discovered in Czekanowie, voivodship of Siedlce], *Wiadomości Archeologiczne* 47 (1982): 25–57.

4 Ágnes Ritoók, "A templom körüli temetők régészeti kutatása" [Archaeological research into churchyards], in *A középkor és a kora újkor régészete Magyarországon*, II [Archaeology of the Middle Ages and the Early Modern Times in Hungary], ed. Elek Benkő and Gyöngyi Kovács (Budapest: MTA Régészeti Intézet, 2010), 473–494, here 474–475 and

477; Mária Vargha, *Hoards, Grave Goods, Jewellery. Objects in Hoards and in Burial Contexts during the Mongol Invasion of Central-Eastern Europe* (Oxford: Archaeopress, 2015), 24 and 27. The first complete publication of a church graveyard from the lands of the medieval Kingdom of Hungary is (Czecho-) Slovak, not Hungarian: Hana Hanáková, Anna Sekáčová, and Milan Stloukal, *Pohřebiště v Ducovém* [The Ducové cemetery] (Prague: Národní muzeum v Praze, 1984). For the history of research in Transylvania, see Erwin Gáll, "Churchyards in the Transylvanian Basin from the 11th to the First Half of the 13th Centuries. On the beginning of institutionalized Christianity," *Marisia* 33 (2013): 135–250, here 144–145.

5 Orsolya László, "Study of Influence of Stress on Skeletal Growth in Non-adults. Comparative Analysis of a Subadult Population from a Medieval Hungarian Cemetery, Kána," (MSc-thesis, Durham University, 2008); eadem, "'Régmúlt gyermekkor.' Középkori temetők gyermeknépességeinek összehasonlító elemzése" [Ancient childhood. The comparative analysis of the children in medieval cemeteries], in *Környezet–ember–kultúra. A természettudományok és a régészet párbeszéde* [Environment – man – culture. The dialogue of natural sciences and arcaheology], ed. Attila Kreiter, Ákos Pető, and Beáta Tugya (Budapest: Magyar Nemzeti Múzeum and Nemzei Örökségvédelmi Központ, 2012), 241–250.

6 Dorota Żołądź-Strzelczyk, *Dziecko w dawnej Polsce* [Childhood in ancient Poland] (Poznań: Wydawnictwo Poznańskie, 2003); Małgorzata Delimata, *Dziecko w Polsce średniowiecznej* [Childhood in medieval Poland] (Poznań: Wydawnictwo Poznańskie, 2004). For Bohemia, see Petr Sommer, "Dítě ve středověkých pramenech" [Children in the Middle Ages], in *Děti ve velkoměstech od středověku až na práh industriální doby. Stati a rozšířené příspěvky z 29. vědecké conference Archivu hlavního města Prahy, uspořádané ve spolupráci s Institutem mezinárodních studií Fakulty sociálních věd Univerzity Karlovy v dnech 12. a 13. říjina 2010 v Clam-Gallasové palace v Praze* [Children in cities from the Middle Ages to the beginning of the industrial age. Acts and augmented contributions to the 29th scientific conference of the City Archive in Prague, organized in cooperation with the Institute of International Studies of the Faculty of Social Sciences at the Charles University, October 12–13, 2010, Clam-Gallas Palace in Prague] (Documenta Pragensia, 31), ed. Olga Fejtová, Václav Ledvinka and Jiří Pešek (Prague: Scriptorium, 2012), 73–79 and Josef Žemlička, "Dítě v starším středověku" [Children in the Early Middle Ages], ibid., 81–88. There is no such study for medieval Hungary, and so far nothing that can be compared to Katalin Péter, *Beloved Children. History of Aristocratic Childhood in Hungary in the Early Modern Age* (Budapest and New York: Central European University Press, 2001).

7 There is absolutely no mention of children in Nora Berend, Przemysław Urbańczyk, and Przemysław Wiszewski, *Central Europe in the High Middle Ages. Bohemia, Hungary and Poland, c. 900–c. 1300* (Cambridge and New York: Cambridge University Press, 2013).

8 E.g., Cornelia B. Horn, "The Lives and Literary Roles of Children in Advancing Conversion of Christianity: Hagiography from the Caucasus in Late Antiquity and the Middle Ages," *Church History* 76, no. 2 (2007): 262–297.

9 Despite the lack of interest in the history of medieval children in Hungary and Bohemia, see the pertinent remarks of Martin Čechura, "Christian, Non-Christian or Pagan? The Burials of Newborns as the Source to Understanding of Medieval and Postmedieval Mentality," in *Kim jesteś, człowieku* [Who are you, man?], ed. Wojciech Dzieduszycki and Jacek Wrzesiński (Poznań: Stowarzyszenie Naukowe Archeologów Polskich, 2011), 289–297.

10 Gallus Anonymus, *The Deeds of the Princes of the Poles* (Central European Medieval Texts, 3), ed. Paul W. Knoll and Frank Schaer (Budapest and New York: Central European University Press, 2003), 17.

11 The scholarly literature on Gallus, his chronicle and his identity, is enormous. For an excellent survey of the most recent studies, see Eduard Mühle, "Cronicae et gesta ducum sive principum Polonorum. Neue Forschungen zum so genannten Gallus Anonymus," *Deutsches Archiv für Erforschung des Mittelalters* 66 (2009): 459–496.

12 Gallus Anonymus, *Deeds of the Princes of the Poles*, 21.

13 Jacek Banaszkiewicz, *Podanie o Piaście i Popielu. Studium porównawcze nad wczesnośredniowiecznymi tradycjami dynastycznymi* [The story of the Piast and of Popiel. A study of the early medieval dynastic traditions] (Warsaw: Panstwowe Wydawnictwo Naukowe, 1986), Przemysław Wiszewski, *Domus Bolezlai. Values and Social Identity in Dynastic Traditions of Medieval Poland (c. 966–1138)* (East Central and Eastern Europe in the Middle Ages, 450–1450, 9) (Leiden and Boston: Brill, 2010), 157–168.

14 Dorota Żołądź-Strzelczyk, "The Child in the Polish Medieval Family," *Quaestiones medii aevi novae* 9 (2004): 27–64, here 40: "Originally this was a pagan and a secular rite, which at the onset of Christianity gradually changed into a Church ceremony." See also Wiszewski, *Domus Bolezlai*, 158. For the ritual of the haircut in medieval Europe, see Robert Bartlett, "Symbolic Meanings of Hair in the Middle Ages," *Transactions of the Royal Historical Society* 4 (1994): 43–60, here 47–49. For haircutting as a rite of passage, see Arnold Van Gennep, *The Rites of Passage* (Chicago: Chicago University Press, 1960), 166. For beard cutting as a rite of passage in Byzantium, see Jane Baun, "Coming of Age in Byzantium: Agency and Authority in Rites of Passage from Infancy to Adulthood," in *Authority in Byzantium*, ed. Pamela Armstrong (Farnham: Ashgate, 2013), 113–135, here 130–131.

15 Gallus Anonymus, *Deeds of the Princes of the Poles*, 27.

16 Wiszewski, *Domus Bolezlai*, 178.

17 For the ceremony of confirmation as associated with the age of reason (seven years) in the twelfth and thirteenth centuries, see Danièle Alexandre-Bidon and Didier Lett, *Children in the Middle Ages. Fifth–Fifteenth Century* (Notre Dame, IN: University of Notre Dame Press, 1999), 29.

18 James A. Schultz, "Medieval Adolescence: The Claims of History and the Silence of the German Narrative," *Speculum* 66 (1991): 519–539, here 534. For a similar argument, see Edward James, "Childhood and Youth in the Early Middle Ages," in *Youth in the Early Middle Ages*, ed. P. J. P. Goldberg and Felicity Riddy (York: York Medieval Press, 2004), 11–23, here 23.

19 Pierre Riché, "L'enfant dans la société chrétienne aux XIᵉ–XIIᵉ siècles," in *La cristianità dei secoli XI e XII in Occidente: coscienza e strutture di una società. Atti della ottava Settimana internazionale di studio (Mendola, 30 giugno–5 luglio 1980)* (Milan: Vita e Pensiero, 1983), 281–302, here 282–283, and Schultz, "Medieval Adolescence," 531.

20 David Herlihy, "Medieval Children," in *Essays on Medieval Civilization. The Walter Prescott Webb Memorial Lectures*, ed. Bede Karl Lackner (Austin, TX: University of Texas Press, 1978), 109–141, reprinted in *Women, Family, and Society in Medieval Europe. Historical Essays, 1978–1991* (Providence, RI and Oxford: Berghahn Books, 1995), 237–238. For the limbo of children, see Didier Lett, "De l'errance au deuil. Les enfants morts sans baptême et la naissance du 'limbus puerorum' aux XIIᵉ–XIIIᵉ siècles," in *La petite enfance dans l'Europe médiévale. Actes des XVIᵉˢ Journées Internationales d'Histoire de l'Abbaye de Flaran, Septembre 1994 organisés avec le concours du Conseil Général du Gers*, ed. Robert Fossier (Toulouse: Presses universitaires du Mirail, 1997), 93–107.

21 The twelfth and thirteenth centuries witnessed an increasing role of non-clerical agents in religious rituals. See André Vauchez, "L'accession des laïcs à la vie réligieuse," in *Apogée de la papauté et expansion de la chrétienté* (Histoire du christianisme des origines à nos jours, 5), ed.idem (Paris: Desclée, 1993), 845–870. For the role of non-clerical agents in the burial of children, see Didier Lett, *L'enfant dans les miracles. Enfance et société au Moyen Age (XIIᵉ–XIIIᵉ siècle)* (Paris: Aubier, 1997), 203–205 and 215–216. For similar observations pertaining to Poland, see Małgorzata Delimata, "Choroby dzieci na podstawie średniowiecznych polskich katalogów cudów świętych" [Child diseases according to medieval Polish catalogues of saintly miracles], *Nasza przeszłość* 101 (2004): 437–449.

22 Tomasz Kurasiński and Kalina Skóra, *Wczesnośredniowieczne cmentarzysko szkieletowe w Lubieniu, pow. Piotrkowski* [The early medieval inhumation cemetery in Lubień, Piotrków Trybunalski district] (Łódź: Instytut Archeologii i Etnologii PAN, 2012), 7–9. The village of Lubień is first attested in the written sources in 1298, while the first mention of Straszów is dated to 1178.

23 Kurasiński and Skóra, *Wczesnośredniowieczne cmentarzysko*, 101.

24 Ibid., 11–12.

25 Polish archaeologists employ the phrase "row grave cemeteries" for sites dated to the eleventh or twelfth century even though the phrase (the English translation and adaptation of the German phrase *Reihengräberkreis*) refers to a much earlier and very different archaeological phenomenon in Western Europe. See Michał Kara, "Description of the Cemetery, Organization of the Burial Space, the Burial Rites in the Light of the Cultural and Historical Determinants," in *Bodzia. A Late Viking-Age Elite Cemetery in Central Poland* (East Central and Eastern Europe in the Middle Ages, 450–1450, 27), ed. Andrzej Buko (Leiden and Boston: Brill, 2015), 343–411, here 357–358.

26 Kurasiński and Skóra, *Wczesnośredniowieczne cmentarzysko*, 26–30.

27 Ibid., 24–26 and 315–332.

28 Ibid., 20–23, 339–42, and 345–350.

29 Ibid., 41.

30 Among the contemporary cemeteries that have been published, only Czekanów (near Jabłonna Lacka in Mazovia) has a higher percentage of child graves: out of 145 graves, 60 (42%) are of children. See Zawadzka-Antosik, "Z problematyki pochówków," 25.

31 Tomasz Kurasiński, "Pochówki dzieci z wczesnośredniowiecznego cmentarzyska szkieletowego w Lubieniu (charakterystyka wstępna)" [Child graves from the early medieval cemetery in Lubień (preliminary characteristics)], in *Tak więc po owocach poznacie ich* [So then you will know them by their fruits], ed. Wojciech Dzieduszycki and Jacek Wrzesiński (Poznań: Stowarzyszenie Naukowe Archeologów Polskich, 2010), 321–332, here 323–324; Kurasiński and Skóra, *Wczesnośredniowieczne cmentarzysko*, 109. For Dziekanowice, see Anna Wrzesińska and Jacek Wrzesiński, "Pochówki dzieci we wczesnym średniowieczu na przykładzie cmentarzyska w Dziekanowicach" [Child burials in the Early Middle Ages on the example of a cemetery in Dziekanowice], *Studia lednickie* 6 (2000): 41–60; Anna Wrzesińska and Jacek Wrzesiński, "Pochówki dzieci najmłodszych infans I na wczesnośredniowiecznych cmentarzyskach w Dziekanowicach" [Child burials in the Early Middle Ages: the example of the burial ground in Dziekanowice], in *Od narodzin do wieku dojrzałego: dzieci i młodzież w Polsce, V/1. Od średniowiecza do wieku XVIII* [From birth to adulthood: children and young people in Poland, V/1. From the Middle Ages to the 18th century], ed. Maria Dąbrowska and Andrzej Klonder (Warsaw: Instytut Archeologii i Etnologii Polskiej Akademii Nauk, 2002), 269–283, here 282. A similar situation is illustrated by grave 19 in the cemetery excavated in Masłowiec, near Sieradz, some 40 miles northwest of Lubień.

A two-year old child was buried in that grave without any goods: Bogusław Abramek, "Wczesnośredniowieczne cmentarzysko szkieletowe w Mąslowicach, woj. Sierądz" [An early medieval inhumation cemetery in Maslowice, province of Sieradz], *Sprawozdania Archeologiczne* 32 (1980): 227–246, here 232. For a general discussion of child graves in Poland, see Tomasz Kurasiński and Kalina Skóra, "Children's Burials from the Early Medieval Inhumation Cemetery in Radom, site 4," *Fasciculi archaeologiae historicae* 28 (2015): 41–52, here 46–47.

32 By comparison, although the percentage of children within the total number of burials is higher at Czekanów, only 25 out of 60 burials (42%) of children on that site had grave goods. See Zawadzka-Antosik, "Z problematyki pochówków," 41, who notes the absence of any significant correlation between the presence or absence of grave goods, on the one hand, and the age at death, on the other hand. On a number of contemporary sites in northern Mazovia (Pokrzywnica Wielka, Łączyno Stare, and Tańsk-Przedbory), the proportion of child graves varies between half and two thirds of all burials in any given cemetery; See Tomasz Kordala, *Wczesnośredniowieczne cmentarzyska szkieletow na północnym Mazowszu* [Early medieval inhumation cemeteries from northern Mazovia] (Łódź: Wydawnictwo Inicjał 3, 2006), 126 with table 21.

33 For example, the five- to six-year-old child buried in grave 64/94 together with a diadem with no less than nine lock rings attached to it (Wrzesińska and Wrzesiński, "Pochówki dzieci najmłodszych infans I," 276 and 282, Fig. 15).

34 For the material culture correlates of princely retinues, see Kazimierz Skalski, "Problem wykorzystania źródeł archeologicznych do badań nad składem drużyny pierwszych Piastów" [The problem of using archaeological data for research on the composition of early Piast retinues], *Kwartalnik historyczny* 102, no 2 (1995): 85–96.

35 Tomasz Kurasiński, "Dziecko i strzała. Z problematyki wyposażania grobów w militaria na terenie Polski wczesnopiastowskiej (XI–XII wiek)" [Child and arrow. On the problem of furnishing graves with militaria in early Piast Poland (11th–12th cc.)], in *Dusza maluczka, a strata ogromna* [The little soul, but a great loss], ed. Wojciech Dzieduszycki and Jacek Wrzesiński (Poznań: Stowarzyszenie Naukowe Archeologów Polskich, 2004), 131–141, here 135 and 137; Tomasz Kurasiński, "Militaria jako element wyposażenia wczesnośredniowiecznych pochówków dziecięcych – próba interpretacji na przykładzie znalezisk z ziem polskich" [Militaria as grave goods in early medieval child burials: provisional interpretation based on finds from Poland], *Archeologia Polski* 54, no. 2 (2009): 209–248, here 211, 226, 215–216 with table I, 220 Fig. 4b and 224, Fig. 8e (for another example of an axe deposited, together with an arrow head, in child grave 39 in Czekanów). Kurasiński believes, however, that the presence of arrowheads in child graves may also be an indication of protection against vampires.

36 For a similar, clay rattle, see Eleonora Wiatrolik, "Gliniana grzechotka z XII wieku z Kołobrzegu" [A 12th-century clay rattle from Kołobrzeg], *Wiadomości Archeologiczne* 22 (1955): 268–269; see also Ewelina Siemianowska, "Wczesnośredniowieczne grzechotki i pisanki w strefie przebiegu szlaku lądowego z Rusi na Pomorze" [Early medieval jingle bells and ceramic eggs on the trade route between Rus' and Pomerania], in *Kultura materialna średniowiecza w Polsce. Materiały ze studenckiej konferencji naukowej, Toruń, 24–25 kwietnia 2008 roku* [Material culture in medieval Poland. Materials from the scientific conference for students, Toruń, April 24–25, 2008], ed. Paweł Kucypera and Sławomir Wadyl (Toruń: Wydawnictwo naukowe Uniwersytetu Mikołaja Kopernika, 2008), 67–84. A metal rattle appears in another child burial (grave 100; Kurasiński and Skóra, *Wczesnośredniowieczne cmentarzysko*, 196). For metal

rattles in medieval Poland, see Tadeusz Malinowski, "O wczesnośredniowiecznych dzwonkach s ziem Polskich" [Early medieval jingle bells in Poland], *Archeologia Polski* 38 (1993): 95–122.

37 For buckets and ceramic pots as attributes of warrior graves, see Andrzej Janowski and Tomasz Kurasiński, "(Nie)militarne naczynia. Fakty i mity" [(Non)military vessels. Facts and myths], in *Nie tylko broń. Niemilitarne wyposażenie wojowników w starożytności i średniowieczu* [Not only weapons. Non-military warrior equipment in Antiquity and the Middle Ages], ed. Witold Świętosławski (Łódź: Łódzkie Towarzystwo Naukowe, 2008), 61–88, here 71–72 and 77.

38 Kurasiński and Skóra, *Wczesnośredniowieczne cmentarzysko*, 107.

39 The age categories have been labeled conventionally following the practice of physical anthropology and do not refer to the categories in use in the Middle Ages.

40 The following observations are based on the plan of the cemetery published in Kurasiński and Skóra, *Wczesnośredniowieczne cmentarzysko*, 16 Fig. 6.4.

41 Ibid., 107.

42 Ibid., 170, 352, and 354. That is the most recent coin of the entire cemetery.

43 Kurasiński and Skóra, *Wczesnośredniowieczne cmentarzysko*, 189, 351, and 354–355. Another coin struck for Bolesław the Bold between 1058 and 1076 (thus while he was duke, before his coronation as king) was found in grave 89, in the immediate vicinity of 78 (ibid., 355).

44 Ibid., 191 and 355. A denier for the Hungarian King Béla II (1131–1141) was found in grave 81, immediately to the north of grave 78 (ibid., 355).

45 The classification of lock rings found in the Lubień cemetery is based on Krystyna Musianowicz, "Kabłączki skroniowe – próba typologii i chronologii" [Temporal rings – an attempt at classification and chronology], *Światowit* 20 (1948): 115–232 and Hanna Kóćka-Krenz, *Biżuteria północno-zachodnio-słowiańska we wczesnym średniowieczu* [Jewelry of the northwestern Slavs in the Early Middle Ages] (Poznań: Uniwersytet Adam Mickiewiczu, 1993).

46 Two 20- to 25-year-old adults in graves 111 and 114, and three others, each 20 to 30 years of age, in graves 115, 118, and 121.

47 This is a fragment of a denier struck in Cracow for Bolesław the Bold, duke of Poland, in the years before his coronation as king. See Kurasiński and Skóra, *Wczesnośredniowieczne cmentarzysko*, 201 and 355.

48 Wanda Kozak-Zychman and Jan Gurba, "Pochówek dziecka ze szczątkami stroju z cmentarzyska przy podgrodziu w Czermnie Kolonii, pow. Tomaszowski" [A child burial with remains of clothes in the cemetery found in the suburb of Czermno Kolonii, district of Tomaszów], in *Słowianie i ich sąsiedzi we wczesnym średniowieczu* [The Slavs and their neighbors in the Early Middle Ages], ed. Marek Dulinicz (Lublin and Warsaw: Wydawnictwo Uniwersytetu Marii Curie-Skłodowskiej, 2003), 245–248. Similarly, the richest burial in the cemetery excavated in 2004, 2006, and 2007 in Wawrzeńczyce, near Cracow is that of a 6-year old child. See Anna Mazur and Krzysztof Mazur, "Des tombes à inhumation du Haut Moyen Age en Petite-Pologne: le cas de la nécropole de Wawrzeńczyce," in *Rome, Constantinople and Newly-Converted Europe. Archaeological and Historical Evidence*, I, ed. Maciej Salamon et al. (Cracow, Leipzig, Rzeszów and Warsaw: Instytut Archeologii i Etnologii PAN and Leipziger Universitätsverlag, 2012), 525–534, here 529 Fig. 4 and 530.

49 Bogusław Abramek, "Wczesnośredniowieczne cmentarzysko szkieletowe w Maslowicach, woj. Sieradz" [An early medieval inhumation cemetery in Maslowice, province of Sieradz], *Sprawozdania Archeologiczne* 32 (1980): 227–246, here 229.

50 Ibid., 229 Fig. 2 and 230–231.

51 Ibid., 228 and 230 Fig. 3a–b, d.

52 Ibid., 237.

53 Ibid., 235 Fig. 5a–u.

54 Ibid., 241.

55 Teresa Trębaczkiewicz, "Cmentarzysko wczesnośredniowieczne w wsi Psary, pow. Piotrków Trybunalski" [An early medieval cemetery in the village of Psary, distr. Piotrków Trybunalski], *Prace i materiały Muzeum Archeologicznego i Etnograficznego w Łódźi. Seria archeologiczna* 9 (1963): 131–166, here 138–139.

56 Trębaczkiewicz, "Cmentarzysko wczesnośredniowieczne," 139 and 141; pls IIh, VIII. 8–10 and XI.

57 Wrzesińska and Wrzesiński, "Pochówki dzieci najmłodszych infans I," 269–270 and 270, Fig. 2. 7% of all graves are of children in the *infans* II category, and an additional 10% are graves of the age category *iuvenis*. Altogether, child graves represent 39% of all graves in Dziekanowice.

58 Wrzesińska and Wrzesiński, "Pochówki dzieci najmłodszych infans I," 282.

59 Zawadzka-Antosik, "Z problematyki pochówków," 29 and 31.

60 Ibid., 33, 37, and 44–45.

61 Pál Lipták, János Nemeskéri, and Béla Szőke, "Le cimetière du XI-e siècle de Kérpuszta," *Acta Archaeologica Academiae Scientiarum Hungaricae* 3 (1953): 205–370, here 205 and 207–208. A village in the area is only mentioned in 1333–1335, its name is derived from a certain George "of Keer" (ibid., 209).

62 Ibid., 297, Jochen Giesler, "Untersuchungen zur Bijelo-Brdo-Kultur. Ein Beitrag zur Archäologie des 10. und 11. Jahrhunderts im Karpatenbecken," *Prähistorische Zeitschrift* 56 (1981): 3–167, here 57.

63 Ibid., 62.

64 Lipták, Nemeskéri, and Szőke, "Le cimetière," 210.

65 Ibid., 293–294 and 295.

66 Ibid., 295.

67 János Nemeskéri and György Acsádi, "Történeti demográfiai vizsgálatok a kérpusztai XI sz.-i temető anyagából" [Studies of historical demography on the basis of the material in the 11th-century cemetery of Kérpuszta], *Archaeologiai Értesítő* 79 (1952): 134–147, here 136, György Acsádi, János Nemeskéri and Lajos Harsányi, "Analyse des trouvailles anthropologiques du cimetière de Kérpuszta (XIᵉ siècle) sous l'aspect de l'âge," *Acta Archaeologica Academiae Scientiarum Hungaricae* 11 (1959): 419–456, here 430–431.

68 Amorphous beads appear in similarly large numbers in child graves: 120 specimens in grave 154, 80 in grave 172, 40 in grave 139.

69 Giesler, "Untersuchungen zur Bijelo-Brdo-Kultur," 63–64 and 105. There is no correlation between the size of the lock rings and the age of the individual with whom they were associated. In other words, large rings have been found with both adults and sub-adults, and small rings are not always found in child graves.

70 Ibid., 64.

71 Lipták, Nemeskéri, and Szőke, "Le cimetière," 296. The following remarks are based on the cemetery plan published in ibid. and Giesler, "Untersuchungen zur Bijelo-Brdo-Kultur" used a simplified version of that plan, without grave numbers.

72 Lipták, Nemeskéri and Szőke, "Le cimetière," 296.

73 Graves of adults must have been dug after those of the children found in clusters, for it is unlikely that the former would have been arranged in a circle around an empty area reserved for future child graves.

74 Béla Miklós Szőke and László Vándor, *Pusztaszentlászló Árpád-kori temetője* [The Árpádian-age cemetery of Pusztaszentlászló] (Budapest: Akadémiai, 1987), 59–60. In eleventh-century Hungary, fluorite beads appear in relatively rich graves. Fluorite crystals or beads may have been brought from the German lands or from Bohemia, see Miloš

Gregor, Ľubomír Vančo and Magdaléna Kadlečiková. "Mineralogické štúdium korálikov z cintorína z 11.–12. storočia z hradu Devín" [Mineralogical studies on the beads from the 11th- to 12th-century cemetery of Devín stronghold], *Slovenská Archeológia* 60, no. 1 (2012): 157–168, here 163 and 165.

75 Szőke and Vándor, *Pusztaszentlászló*, 78–80.

76 János Gömöri, "XI. szazadi temető Szakonyban" [An 11th-century cemetery in Szakony], *Communicationes Archaeologicae Hungariae* (1984): 81–108, here 88.

77 Gáll, "Churchyards," 140–141.

78 Radu Harhoiu and Erwin Gáll, "Necropola din secolul XII de la Sighişoara-Dealul Viilor, punctul 'Necropolă'. Contribuţii privind habitatul epocii medievale timpurii în Transilvania estică" [The 12th-century cemetery in Sighişoara-Dealul Viilor, place "Necropolă". A contribution to the study of the early medieval habitat in eastern Transylvania], *Analele Banatului* 22 (2014): 195–260, here 208 and 217. Two burials containing skeletons of adults and children (graves 133 and 135) were superposed two other burials of children (grave 135A and 136). This has been interpreted as a family group (Harhoiu and Gáll, "Necropola," 215–216).

79 Radu Harhoiu and Adrian Ioniţă, "Cercetări arheologice la Sighişoara 'Dealul Viilor', punctul 'Necropolă'. Un tezaur monetar din secolul al XII-lea" [Archaeological excavations in Sighişoara-Dealul Viilor, the "Necropolă" site. A 12th-century coin hoard], in *Românii în Europa medievală (între orientul bizantin şi occidentul latin). Studii în onoarea profesorului Victor Spinei* [Romanians in medieval Europe (between the Byzantine East and the Latin West). Studies in Honor of Professor Victor Spinei], ed. Dumitru Ţeicu and Ionel Cândea (Brăila: Istros, 2008), 199–223, here 203 and 221 Fig. 12. The coins were most likely deposited in the grave within a purse.

80 Helena Zoll-Adamikowa, "Zur Frage der großmährischen bzw. böhmischen Christianisierung Südpolens im Lichte der Grabfunde," in *Ethnische und kulturelle Verhältnisse an der mittleren Donau vom 6. bis zum 11. Jahrhundert. Symposium Nitra 6. bis 10. November 1994*, ed. Darina Bialeková and Jozef Zábojník (Bratislava: VEDA, 1996), 305–312.

81 The closest, according to Helena Zoll-Adamikowa, "Zu der Brandbestattungsbräuchen der Slawen im 6. bis 10. Jahrhundert in Polen," *Ethnographisch-archäologische Zeitschrift* 13 (1972): 497–542, here 499 (map) is Mętów near Lublin, some 70 miles to the east.

82 Helena Zoll-Adamikowa, *Wczesnośredniowieczne cmentarzyska ciałopalne Słowian na terenie Polski. Analiza. Wnioski* [Early medieval Slavic cremation cemeteries in Poland. Analysis. Conclusions] (Wrocław, Warsaw, Cracow and Gdańsk: Ossolineum, 1979), 205–235.

83 However, cremation cemeteries with flat graves (the so-called Alt-Käbelich type) have also been found recently in Lesser Poland. See Bartłomiej Szymon Szmoniewski and Anna Tyniec-Kępińska, "Zum Besttatungsbrauchtum in Kleinpolen im Lichte der neuen Forschungsergbnisse," in *Świat Słowian wczesnego średniowiecza* [The world of the Slavs in the Early Middle Ages], ed. Marek Dworaczyk et al. (Szczecin and Wrocław: Wydawnictwo Instytutu Archeologii i Etnologii Polskiej Akademii Nauk, 2006), 499–504.

84 Zoll-Adamikowa, "Zu der Brandbestattungsbräuchen," 511.

85 Krzysztof Kaczanowski, "Analiza antropologiczna wczesnośredniowiecznych pochówków ciałopalnych z kurhanów 1, 4 i 7 w Kornatce, pow. Myślenice" [Anthropological analysis of the cremations under barrows 1, 4 and 7 of the Kornatka cemetery], *Sprawozdania Archeologiczne* 26 (1974): 187–195, here 193.

86 For Zalavár/Mosapurc as the main power center in the region during the Carolingian age, see Thomas von Bogyay, "Mosapurc und Zalavár," *Südost-Forschungen* 14 (1955): 52–70; Ágnes Cs. Sós, "Zalavár-Mosaburg, das befestigte Herrschafts- und Kulturzentrum des

9. Jahrhunderts in Pannonien," *Kirilo-metodievski studii* 4 (1987): 148–159; Béla Miklós Szőke, "The Carolingian civitas Mosapurc (Zalavár)," in *Europe's Centre Around A.D. 1000*, ed. Alfried Wieczorek and Hans-Martin Hinz (Stuttgart: Theiss, 2000), 140–142; Béla Miklós Szőke, "Mosaburg/Zalavár und Pannonien in der Karolingerzeit," *Antaeus* 31–32 (2010): 9–52, and idem, "Mosaburg/Zalavár," in *Great Moravia and the Beginnings of Christianity*, ed. Pavel Kouřil (Brno: Institute of Archaeology of the Academy of Sciences of the Czech Republic, 2015), 262–267. For churches discovered in Zalavár, see Aladár Radnóti, "Une église du haut moyen âge à Zalavár," *Etudes slaves et roumaines* 1 (1948): 21–30; Ágnes Cs. Sós, "Über die Fragen des frühmittelalterlichen Kirchenbaues in Mosapurc-Zalavár," in *Das östliche Mitteleuropa in Geschichte und Gegenwart. Acta Congressus historiae Slavicae Salisburgensis in memoriam SS. Cyrilli et Methodii anno 1963 celebrati*, ed. Franz Zagiba (Wiesbaden: Otto Harrassowitz, 1966), 69–86; Maxim Mordovin, "The Building History of Zalavár-Récéskút Church," *Annual of Medieval Studies at the CEU* 12 (2006): 9–32; and Béla Miklós Szőke, "Eine Kirchenfamilie von Mosapurc/Zalavár (Ungarn). Neue Ergebnisse zur Kirchenarchäologie in Pannonien," in *Kirchenarchäologie heute. Fragestellungen, Methoden, Ergebnisse*, ed. Niklot Kroh (Darmstadt: Wissenschaftliche Buchgesellschaft, 2010), 561–85.

87 Szőke, "Eine Kirchenfamilie," 578–579 and 579 Fig. 7.

88 Ibid., 580.

89 Mechthild Schulze-Dörrlamm, "Bestattungen in den Kirchen Grossmährens und Böhmens während des 9. und 10. Jahrhunderts," *Jahrbuch des Römisch-Germanischen Zentralmuseums* 40 (1993): 557–620, here 563.

90 Ibid., 579, 584, and 597, 578 Fig. 22a and c, 588 Fig. 31c and 598 Fig. 42c.

91 Milan Hanuliak, "Sociálna pozícia detských jedincov petrifikovaná v pohrebiskom materiáli z 9.–10. storočia" [The social position of children as 'frozen' in the cemetery material of the 9th and 10th centuries]. *Archaeologia historica* 35 (2010): 169–181, here 176–177, 177 Fig. 6 and 178 Fig. 7.

92 For the medieval cemetery, see Agnes Ritoók, "Zalavár-Kápolna: egy temető lehetőségei és eredményei," [Zalavár-Kápolna: possibilities and results of a cemetery analysis)], in *"… a halál árnyékának völgyében járok." A középkori templom körüli temetők kutatása* ["I am walking through the valley of the shadow of death …" Archaeological research on churchyards], ed. Ágnes Ritoók and Erika Simonyi (Budapest: Magyar Nemzeti Múzeum, 2005), 173–183.

93 Balázs Gusztáv Mende, "Adatok Zalavár-Kápolna Árpád-kori népességének antropológiájához" [Data on the anthropology of the Arpadian-era population of Zalavár-Kápolna], in *"… a halál árnyékának,"* 185–196, here 186 and 193.

94 Ágnes Cs. Sós, *Die Ausgrabungen Géza Fehérs in Zalavár* (Budapest: Akademiai, 1963), 174–175 with plan 16.

95 Ritoók, "A templom körüli," 478. For a possibly similar situation in Cluj-Mănăştur, see Erwin Gáll, "Krisztianizació és régészet. A Erdélyi-medencei 11–13. századi templomkörüli temetők kutatásának stádiuma" [Christianization and archaeology. The research on 11th–13th-century churchyard cemeteries in the Transylvanian basin], in *Hadak útján XX. Népvándorláskor Fiatal Kutatóinak XX. összejövetelének konferenciakötete* [On the road of armies. XX. Proceedings of the 20th meeting of young archaeologists working on the Migration period], ed. Zsolt Petkes (Budapest: Magyar Nemzeti Múzeum, 2012), 287–313, here 292 and 295 Fig. 3.

96 Elemér Zalotay, *Gellértegyházai Árpádkori temető* [The Árpadian-age cemetery in Gellértegyháza] (Budapest: Magyar Nemzeti Múzeum, 1957). For the aging and sexing of the skeletons, see Pál Lipták and Gyula Farkas, "Anthropological analysis of

the Arpadian Age population of Orosháza-Rákóczitelep," *Acta biologica Szegediensis* 8 (1962): 221–236.

97 Ritoók, "A templom körüli," 479 Fig. 1. With the exception of graves 111 and 321 (Zalotay, *Gellértegyházai Árpádkori temető*, 13 and 29), there are no coins in child burials.

98 Dariusz Wyczółkowski, "Pochowki dziecęce związane z najstarszą fazą cmentarzyska przy kościele świętego Maurycego w Zawichoście" [Child burials associated with the earliest phase of the cemetery next to the Church of St. Maurice in Zawichost], in *Dusza maluczka, a strata ogromna* [A small soul, but a great loss], ed. Wojciech Dzieduszycki and Jacek Wrzesiński (Poznań: Stowarzyszenie Naukowe Archeologów Polskich, 2004), 16–165, here 163.

99 Wyczółkowski, "Pochowki dziecęce związane." See also the site report in *Szkice Zawichojskie* [Sketches from Zawichost], ed. Teresa Dunin-Wąsowicz and Stanisław Tabaczyński (Zawichost: Instytut Archeologii i Etnologii Polskiej Akademii Nauk/ Fundacja "Antiquitas", 1999).

100 Hansueli F. Etter and Jürg E. Schneider, "Zur Stellung von Kind und Frau im Frühmittelalter: eine archäologisch-anthropologische Synthese," *Zeitschrift für schweizerische Archäologie und Kunstgeschichte* 39, no. 1 (1982): 48–57, here 53, Alexandre-Bidon and Didier Lett, *Children*, 30. For an early example of very young children buried in a community cemetery, specifically outside the southern wall of the apse or inside it, see Bruno Bizot and Joël Serralongue, "Un edifice funéraire du haut Moyen Age à Seyssel-Albigny (Haute-Savoie)," *Archéologie du Midi medieval* 6 (1988): 25–49. The sixth- to seventh-century cemetery around the central chapel of Saint Germain in Ambérieu-en-Bugey (near Lyon) also included a relatively large number of children buried either immediately next to or inside the church.

101 Alexandrine Garnotel and Véronique Fabre, "La place de l'enfant médiéval dans l'espace des morts. Apport des fouilles du Lunellois," in *L'enfant, son corps, son histoire. Actes des Septièmes Journées Anthropologiques de Valbonne, 1–3 juin 1994*, ed. Luc Buchet (Valbonne: Editions APDCA-Sophia Antipolis, 1997), 9–24, here 19, 21 and 20 Fig. 7.

102 Cécile Treffort, "Archéologie funéraire et histoire de la petite enfance. Quelques remarques à propos du Haut Moyen Age," in *La petite enfance dans l'Europe*, 93–107, here 99.

103 Cécile Niel, "Les inhumations d'enfants au sein de la cour d'Albane, groupe épiscopal de Rouen," in *L'enfant, son corps, son histoire*, 45–61, here 46, 49–50 and 52 Fig. 4, Treffort, "Archéologie funéraire," 100, Alexandre-Bidon and Didier Lett, *Children*, 31. Children were also buried inside the Church of St. Stephen, most notably near the entrance, a location that has been associated with the presence of baptismal fonts, which were often positioned in the northwestern part of the church.

104 Etter and Schneider, "Zur Stellung von Kind und Frau," 53.

105 Patricia Healy Wasyliw, "The Pious Infant: Developments in Popular Piety during the High Middle Ages," in *Lay Sanctity, Medieval and Modern. A Search for Models*, ed. Ann W. Astell (Notre Dame, IN: University of Notre Dame, 2000), 105–115, here 106–107. See also István Bejczy, "The *sacra infantia* in Medieval Hagiography," in *The Church and Childhood. Papers Read at the 1993 Summer Meeting and the 1994 Winter Meeting of the Ecclesiastical History Society*, ed. Diana Wood (Oxford and Cambridge, MA: Blackwell, 1994), 143–151, here 147. However, a special service for the burial of children did not appear in the Western Church before 1400. The only exceptions (the so-called Visigothic liturgy and the Ambrosian liturgy) offer a specific formulary for children who died before the age of reason (7 years). See Treffort, "Archéologie funéraire," 104.

106 Barbara A. Hanawalt, "Medievalists and the Study of Childhood," *Speculum* 77 (2002): 440–460, here 448 and Didier Lett, *L'enfant des miracles. Enfance et société au Moyen Âge (XIe–XIIe s.)* (Paris: Aubier, 1997).

107 Isabelle Cochelin, "Adolescence Uncloistered (Cluny, Early Twelfth Century)," in *The Medieval Life Cycles. Continuity and Change*, ed. Isabelle Cochelin and Karen Smyth (Turnhout: Brepols, 2013), 147–182, here 167 and 170. Adolescence (as now conceived) does not appear in medieval definitions of the life cycle before the twelfth century. For 7 and 12 as particularly pivotal times in the early life-cycle of a child, according to Irish law, see Bronagh Ní Chonaill, "Flying a Kite with the Children of Hiberno-Norse Dublin: A Tentative Social Explanation," in *Dublin in the Medieval World. Studies in Honour of Howard B. Clarke*, ed. John Bradley, Alan J. Fletcher, and Anngret Simms (Dublin: Four Courts Press, 2009), 98–118, here 104–105.

108 Delimata, "Choroby dzieci."

109 Żóládź-Strzelczyk, "The Child," 32 and 63. A similar miracle is attributed to St. Hyacinth. The oldest record concerning the funeral of a child to be found in the Polish lands comes from the year 1432 (the statute of Wojciech Jastrzębiec).

110 A[ndy] Boddington, Graham Cadman, and John Evans, *Raunds Furnells: The Anglo-Saxon Church and Churchyard* (London: English Heritage, 1996), 55.

111 Maria Cinthio, *De första stadsborna. Medeltida gravar och människor i Lund* [The first townspeople. Medieval graves and people in Lund] (Stehag: Symposion, 2002), 129.

112 Kristina Jonsson, *Practices for the Living and the Dead: Medieval and Post-Reformation Burials in Scandinavia* (Stockholm: Stockholm University, 2009), 51–53.

113 Éva Révész, "Zarándokkeresztek a X–XI. századi sírokban" [Pectoral crosses in 11th–12th-century burials], in *Középkortörténeti tanulmányok 6. A VI. Medievisztikai PhD-konferencia (Szeged, 2009. június 4–5.) előadásai* [Studies in medieval history, 6. Papers presented at the VIth PhD conference in medieval studies, Szeged, 4–5 June 2009], ed. Péter G. Tóth and Pál Szabó (Szeged: Szegedi Középkorász Műhely, 2010), 189–201.

114 *The Laws of the Medieval Kingdom of Hungary, 1000–1301* (Decreta Regni Mediaevalis Hungariae, 1), ed. János M. Bak, György Bónis, and James Ross Sweeney (Bakersfield, CA: Charles Schlacks, 1989), 31 and 59.

115 Florin Curta, *Southeastern Europe in the Middle Ages, 500–1250* (Cambridge and New York: Cambridge University Press, 2006), 250, and Berend, Urbańczyk, and Wiszewski, *Central Europe*, 328. For Transylvania, this point of view was first expressed by Kurt Horedt, *Contribuții la istoria Transilvaniei în secolele IV–XIII* [Contributions to the history of Transylvania between the 4th and the 13th centuries] (Bucharest: Editura Academiei Republicii Populare Romîne, 1958), 145. For a critique of that interpretation, see Gáll, "Krisztianizáció és régészet," 288.

116 Marianna Bálint, József Laszlovszky, Beatrix Romhányi, and Miklós Takács, "Medieval Villages and Their Fields," in *Hungarian Archaeology at the Turn of the Millennium*, ed. Zsolt Visy (Budapest: Ministry of National Cultural Heritage and Teleki László Foundation, 2003), 383–388, here 386; Silviu Oța, "The Relations Between the Settlements and the Necropolises of the Banat Territory in the 11th to 13th Centuries," in *The Society of the Living, the Community of the Dead (from Neolithic to the Christian Era)*, eds. Sabin Adrian Luca and Valeriu Sîrbu (Sibiu: Universitatea "Lucian Blaga", 2006), 240–248, here 240–242.

117 See the pertinent remarks of Silviu Oța, *The Mortuary Archaeology of the Medieval Banat (10th–14th Centuries)* (East Central and Eastern Europe in the Middle Ages, 450–1450, 26) (Leiden and Boston: Brill, 2014), 74–75 and 178–179.

118 The interpretation goes back to Helena Zoll-Adamikowa, "Zum Beginn der Körperbestattung bei den Westslawen," in *Rom und Byzanz im Norden. Mission und Glaubenswechsel im Ostseeraum während des 8.–14. Jahrhunderts*, II, ed. Michael Müller-Wille (Stuttgart: Franz Steiner, 1998), 227–238. It is best illustrated in the recent literature by Jacek Wrzesiński, "The Dziekanowice cemetery – Christians Cultivating Venerable Traditions," in *Rome, Constantinople and Newly-Converted Europe*, I, 535–552. See also Arkadiusz Koperkiewicz, "Wczesnośredniowieczne dary grobowe w kontekście symboliki chrześcijańskiej" [Early medieval grave goods in the context of Christian symbolism], in *Do, ut des – dar, pochówek, tradycja* [*Do, ut des*: gift, burial, and tradition], ed. Wojciech Dzieduszycki and Jacek Wrzesiński (Poznań: Stowarzyszenie Naukowe Archeologów Polskich, 2005), 269–291.

119 In grave 11 in Zawichost, a decrepit old adult male was buried with two children of *infans* I age.

7

TECHNOLOGIES ON THE ROAD BETWEEN WEST AND EAST

The Spread of Water Mills and the Christianization of East Central Europe

*András Vadas**

It is a century-long commonplace in historiography that Christianization played a significant role in spreading technological innovations during the Middle Ages. More effective use of non-human power must rank among the most important of these innovations. Making more use of animal power was facilitated by the spread of the breast harness for draft animals and water mills proved a more effective way of grinding grain than the usual hand mills of the time. Research dating back to the basic handbook by Richard Bennett and John Elton from the turn of the twentieth century attributes the spread of mills in the high medieval period to the activity of monastic orders, primarily the Benedictines, in various regions of Europe.[1] This thesis was partly supported by the results of two essential studies published in the mid-1930s by Lewis Mumford and Marc Bloch.[2] They both believed that after the Roman period in most parts of Europe the re-introduction of water mills was primarily connected to monastic orders. Adam Lucas, however, recently drew attention to the different narratives of the two historians. Mumford believed that the spread of new technologies was intended to create better time management for the peasantry, but Bloch thought that it rather served to increase incomes from peasantry belonging to ecclesiastical domains.[3]

Bloch attempted an overview of the spread of mills in different regions of Europe. Limited opportunity to access secondary literature only allowed him to sketch out a very approximate chronological sequence. In spite of the fact that his chronology ultimately proved inaccurate, for example, for Ireland or Iberia – his main conclusion, that the areas that had been subject to Roman authority for longer used water mills earlier compared to other places – is still accepted by historians.[4] Since Bloch wrote his article, however, archaeological research has demonstrated that the use of water mills in Ancient times was much more widespread in the Roman Empire than had been assumed.[5] Despite Bloch's effort to be comprehensive, he almost completely omitted some areas, especially East Central Europe, that lacked secondary literature at the time. He, as well as other scholars aiming at providing an overview of the spread of mills in Europe, with few exceptions, did not touch the scholarship of the region even though a number of questions arose about when water mills spread as well as the role of Benedictines in the process.

This paper does not aim at providing a comprehensive survey of the entire process of technological advancement in East Central Europe, but draws attention to some of the problems noted in recent scholarship with regard to the rather over-simplified notion that water mills spread through East Central Europe with the Benedictine abbeys' support very soon after the monastic orders of Western Christianity arrived in the region. In this survey, sources and scholarship for the Kingdom of Hungary lie at the center of the analysis with reference to the sometimes strikingly similar problems in Polish, Czech, and to some extent Croatian, Serbian, and Romanian scholarship.[6]

Mills and Benedictines – some preliminary considerations

Why are early monastic communities usually associated with the spread of the water wheel in East Central Europe? Anywhere grain production was present it had to be ground. Most of this work was carried out on a variety of rather small hand mills found all over Europe at excavated sites from the Neolithic well up to Modern times. These hand mills, even a rotary hand mill, were most effective only for domestic family use and the quality of the flour it provided was in no way comparable to the product of a water mill. The energy needed to grind larger quantities of grain could not be marshaled with a hand mill. A water mill's efficiency differed considerably from that of rotary hand mills, but water mills could not be built everywhere. The location of the early Benedictine and other religious houses on hilltops did not always provide an opportunity to use water as a source of energy. Nevertheless, when Saint Benedict of Nursia wrote his *Rule* for the community he founded at Monte Cassino, he listed mills as essential elements of the monastery. According to the *Rule*, mills had to be located on the inner side of the walls of the monastery, although it is not evident whether he referred to human-muscle-driven hand mills or water mills.[7] Fresh running water may have been scarce for many of the earlier foundations of the order, but water for producing energy and for other purposes was usually considered an essential element in the later Middle Ages. This policy is reflected in the famous St. Gall monastery plan prepared at Reichenau in the ninth century. Although the rather stereotypical representation of the mills makes it difficult to decide which kinds were represented, based on a fairly detailed study it is more or less certain that by the early ninth century water mills were regarded as a defining element of Benedictine abbeys.[8] However, at the abbey of Reichenau – situated on an island in the Bodensee – there may have been a different perception of the water lying close to the abbey compared to many other monastic sites. In this one case, at least, the arguments presented primarily by Horn and Born, stand that during the Carolingian Period monastic complexes were imagined as having their own water mills. It has recently been demonstrated that water mills were spread in the wider surroundings of Reichenau in the Carolingian Period. For example, archaeological research revealed a water mill complex in Bavaria that operated from as early as the late seventh century. This very early example may indicate that mills were used in present-day southern Germany from the early medieval period onwards.[9]

Christianity came to East Central Europe from two directions. Following the Roman influence in some areas, Christian ideas spread from the Byzantine Empire and later from Western Christian areas through missionary activity. In Hungary, Poland, and Bohemia, Western missionaries were of primary importance. In Wallachia and Moldavia, however, as well as other parts of the Balkan Peninsula, Byzantine missionary activity was certainly more influential.[10] Although in recent years the use of water mills has been demonstrated in the later Byzantine areas of the Roman Empire, there is no evidence that this technology spread into the Balkans from this direction as a consequence of Roman influence in the region.[11] The question is rather difficult to discuss in this context as hardly any written evidence survives on this issue before the thirteenth century. In addition, it has recently been noted that no archaeological excavations have been carried out in Bulgaria, Serbia or Macedonia to test the validity of this suggestion.[12] However, the roughly one hundred water mills known to have functioned in early medieval Bavaria leave no doubt that water mills were used by local societies in the region where most of the monasteries in East Central Europe recruited their members from around the year 1000. The earliest monasteries founded in Bohemia – Břevnov and Ostrov – were both connected with Regensburg and Niederaltaich, although the first monks arrived at the former from Rome – another place where water mills were clearly present in that period.[13] The first monasteries in Poland may have also been built around 1000, but until the mid-eleventh century their history is unclear and the permanent presence of monks there may not predate the 1040s. In Bohemia and Silesia the Bavarian influence was clearly the most important.[14] The same is also true for the Kingdom of Hungary. The first missionaries are known to have come to the Carpathian Basin in the second half of the tenth century. Saints Wolfgang and Bruno (Prunward) were both from southern German areas, the former having been raised at the abbey of Reichenau. The first monasteries, Pannonhalma (996), Pécsvárad, Zalavár, and Bakonybél all came into existence during the rule of Grand Prince Géza and, moreover, under the reign of St. Stephen, his son. Bohemian influence besides Bavarian can certainly be detected in Hungary, just as in Silesia.[15] Thus, the monks of the first monastic foundations in East Central Europe were recruited from areas where water mills were, if not widespread, at least well known.

The first water mills in the region – historical evidence, linguistics, and (the lack of) archaeological data

As concluded above, the appearance of the Benedictine abbeys shows strong variation in the region. In light of these temporal disparities, it becomes even more interesting to look at how similar time gaps in the appearance of water mills in the region can be demonstrated. Data from Hungary is considered first, followed by comparison with the data available for Bohemia, Poland, and the Balkan states.

In Hungary, the opinions of a number of scholars vary considerably on the spread of water mills in the Carpathian Basin. The search for early written evidence – in both pragmatic and narrative sources – for the first reference to mills prevails in the existing literature, trying to determine whether these mills were driven by water-power or by human muscle. Many prominent Hungarian historians have expressed their opinions on these questions including Péter Váczy, László Makkai, Gyula Kristó, and György Györffy. Besides historians of the Árpádian period, another group of scholars, historians of technology, have also presented their arguments supporting one date or another.[16] Apart from the written evidence, this question was and can be studied by integrating other sources as well. At least two possible research directions should be considered when addressing this issue: linguistics and archaeology.

Linguistics was first integrated into the study of the spread of mills in the scholarly literature almost a century ago. Between the 1950s and the 1970s a debate unfolded amongst linguists around the origin of some words related to milling, including the term *malom* (or *molna*, the Hungarian term for mill).[17] Elemér Moór argued that the Slavic origin of the word shows the early use of water mills amongst the Slavic population living in the Carpathian Basin. Moór concluded that the term was adopted by the Hungarians from "Slovak," and based on that he believed that the term may have been adopted in the Western area of the Slovak-Hungarian language contact zone, the area of Little Hungarian Plain (the western, lowland part of the border area between present-day Slovakia and Hungary). It is even more important for this paper that based on acoustic changes in the form of the Slovak word for mill (*mlýn*) and the adoption of other water-management related terms, Moór, following in the footsteps of István Kniezsa, dated this adoption to the tenth century – although they both neglected the issue of whether water mills were used in western Slavic areas at that time. The other problem that they did not discuss was why they thought that *mlýn* (and *molna*) referred only to water mills and not hand-driven mills.

In historical scholarship, László Makkai seems to have been the first to refer to this linguistic debate in an important article published in German, although he never mentions which works he was referring to; he accepted the ninth-century adoption of the term (and, of course, of mills).[18] Walter Endrei, a historian of technology, accepted the Makkai's view without explaining why he dated the appearance of mills in the Carolingian-ruled Transdanubian area to the eighth [sic] or ninth century.[19] Dating the adoption of water mills among West Slavic peoples and Hungarians well before the year 1000 is unique in the historiography of the whole region. It is symptomatic of the uncertainty in the dating that Endrei never mentions the spread of water mills in the Carpathian Basin in the eighth or ninth century in his later works.[20] Recently, in the light of archaeological evidence, Tamás Vajda has challenged the validity of the idea of the spread of mills in the tenth century (or even in the Carolingian period).[21]

Because literacy in East Central Europe was still limited in this period, archaeological data also have to be taken into consideration. Although no archaeological excavation in the Carpathian Basin has yet uncovered any trace of a water mill predating written evidence mentioning such constructions, this area has strong research potential. In recent years, archaeological dating methods such as dendrochronology have broadened the opportunities for studying the history of various structures. In the last 50 to 60 years archaeologists in Hungary have excavated or examined a number of medieval mills, although the dating has usually proved to be problematic. This is important here as earlier scholars had dated some of these mills to post-Carolingian times.[22]

Hand-mill fragments may be useful indicators of the spread of mills in addition to actual archaeological finds of water mills themselves. The grinding stones from hand mills, indicating household flour production, have been recovered from many sites on the Great Hungarian Plain. The presence of these hand mills resulted in the idea, dominant for many years, that the western parts of the Carpathian Basin, i.e., those that were under Carolingian authority, had water mills and thus were more advanced technologically than the plains areas of the basin. This view has been strongly challenged in recent years as more and more small grinding stones have also been found in Transdanubia.[23] The archaeological village site of Kána (on the edge of present-day Budapest), where numerous hand mill fragments were discovered, is important in this context. The exact dates when these hand mills were used there are unknown, but the village seems to have been occupied in roughly the same period as the Benedictine abbey of Kána, to which the village belonged. The abbey was founded in the mid-twelfth century and functioned until the mid-thirteenth century (up to the Mongol invasion). The large number of hand mills in a village owned by Benedictines from the mid-twelfth to mid-thirteenth century shows clearly that water mills were not the only tools for grinding grain in the mid-Árpádian period, not even in monastic environments in the so-called *medium regni*, the power center of the Kingdom of Hungary, a region that is usually believed to have been the most developed at the time.[24]

Although linguistic and archaeological evidence are useful, written evidence is still of primary importance for determining the dates when mills were introduced into the Kingdom of Hungary. The early foundation charters and donations where the first references to water mills come from present some problems. In the most recent scholarly opinion, the first undoubtedly authentic document which mentions water mills in the Kingdom of Hungary dates to 1009. The document is a donation charter endowing the newly founded bishopric of Veszprém. Although the document did not survive in the original, the transcription of the document is now accepted as an authentic example of early eleventh-century literacy. Thus, most scholars accept the document as the first solid proof of the existence of water mills in Hungary.[25] In the charter, King Stephen, besides listing counties under the authority of the diocese of Veszprém, bestowed land on the bishops in three counties, Fejér, Veszprém, and Visegrád, and in the district of the castle of Kolon, all in western Hungary (Transdanubia). The lands, according to the charter, were donated with: *omnibus utensibus iugiterque pertinentiis, scilicet famulis familiabusque, pratis, vineis, areis, edificiis, campis, terris, agris cultis et incultis,* piscacionibus, aquis aquarumque decursibus, molendinis, *viis, inviis tam exitibus quam inexitibus.*[26] Looking at the order of utilities listed, there is little doubt that the mills referred to, coming as they do immediately after other water-related utilities in the text, were not hand-driven but water powered.

I argue, however, that in itself this reference does not necessarily mean that water mills indeed functioned on some of the Transdanubian estates transferred to the bishopric by King Stephen at the time of the donation. Three possibilities should be considered. The first is that water mills were indeed functioning at that time in these areas; in this case, the Benedictines might not have had as much impact as was first thought on the spread of water mills in the counties mentioned in the document. The impact of Benedictine technical know-how may not yet have been all that strong in the first decade of the eleventh century.[27] The lands in question were clearly in royal hands at the time of this donation and had no connection with monastic domains, although it can be presumed that the Church had a great impact on the early organization of royal estates. György Györffy, following in the footsteps of German diplomatic research as well as those of Imre Szentpétery, drew attention to the fact that this charter displays clear parallels with charters issued by the Holy Roman emperors, most importantly Henry II. Philological analysis usually points to the endowment charter issued in favor of the St. Michael monastery at Bamberg (Michelsberg) as the closest parallel to the donation charter of Veszprém. Although this charter does not list the utilities comprising the donation, another charter dating to the same year and connected to the same notary does list the utilities donated in exactly the same order as the one mentioned above.[28] Without going into the vexing question who was the notary in the case of the Veszprém charter, there is no doubt that he came from the lands of the empire, from either Northern Italy or Southern Germany. In this period, in both Northern Italy and in areas north of the Alps, water mills were frequent constituents of estates.[29] The notary, who is likely to have written a number of similar donations to different institutions in the empire issued under the name of Henry II, may not have been particularly aware of the physical realities of the estates affected by the donation. In donations of this kind, one finds lists of all the various utilities found on estates, independent of the fact that they may not have existed in reality. One even finds mountains – in the sense of forest-related utilities – and their income donated to landlords endowed with probably treeless lowlands. Nevertheless, the inclusion of such elements in these utilities' lists aimed at providing the new owners with the entirety of all possible forms of income related to the piece of land they had acquired, including income from water mills.[30] Thus, the second possibility is that this element was included because of the presence of this utility in the empire at the time the Veszprém bishopric was endowed and because mentioning mills was a formulaic element in donation charters there.

The third scenario is that this element is an interpolation into the charter. This is unlikely based on the close parallels of the utilities' list to the imperial charters mentioned above and other donations of Henry II. Furthermore, earlier research has already identified a number of other philological reasons. In my opinion, the second option is the most likely, i.e., that mills were mentioned in the utilities list as a possible future source of income. This focuses attention on the scholarly opinion that puts the *terminus ante quem* of the appearance of water mills in the Carpathian Basin at 1009 and should be taken into account with regard to the Veszprém charter. These arguments, however, in no way represent absolute proof that water mills did not exist in the Kingdom of Hungary by 1009.

Research usually attributes the spread of mills to the Benedictines, but, as noted above, the first reference can hardly be associated with their activity. Nevertheless, a number of references make it quite clear that water mills were introduced on monastic estates at a certain point in the eleventh century. The foundation charter of the Benedictine abbey of Tihany from 1055 – the earliest charter from the Kingdom of Hungary preserved in the original – mentions mills as well as millers. King Andrew I (1046–1060) endowed the monastery with a number of estates from his own holdings. Thus, again nothing supports the idea that these mills were built by Benedictines.[31] This charter leaves little doubt, however, that water mills existed in Hungary by the middle of the eleventh century at the latest. However, when they first began to be used and the extent of their spread remain open questions.

Based on sometimes controversial data, the spread of mills in the Kingdom of Hungary can be dated to before 1055 with a number of uncertainties and discrepancies among the different kinds of source materials. Written evidence from the Czech lands has been discussed in contexts similar to the early charters referring to mills in Hungary. Apart from the unreliable sixteenth-century vernacular *Czech Chronicle* of Wenceslaus Hájek referring to water mills in the eighth century,[32] the earliest data on mills is preserved in a charter no less controversial than most of the early written documents from Hungary. This document is the endowment charter of the Benedictine monastery of Břevnov.[33] The reference to mills in the charter is much more descriptive than in the endowment charter of Veszprém. It mentions mills and weirs not only as general pertinences of estates but in a concrete context and at fairly well-defined locations:

> *cum omni familia et terra sufficienti ac montem ad meridiem, tendentem a bivio quodam, in quo preciduntur molares, Schirnovnice dicto … Duo molendina sub ipso castro Praga et de ipso flumine Wltaue ad tria obstacula molendinorum in eodem loco. … Decimam quoque de omni agricultura in Porecze … et mansum in litore fluminis Wltaue ad horreum construendum et obstaculum in eodem loco ad molendina edificanda.*

The document has long been considered a highly interpolated charter, although Jiří Pražák has recently argued that most of it indeed dates to the tenth century.[34] Following the direction of his work, some scholars have accepted that mills and places for mills mentioned in the charter show that by then water was being used to produce power.[35] Recently, however, an important study by Oldřich Kotyza identified several important points which led him to consider this part of the charter as an interpolation dating at the earliest to the late twelfth century.[36] One clearly problematic point is the location of these mills. The Vltava River is not among the most significant rivers of East Central Europe, but its discharge was still too great to allow for suitable sites for mills. The first medieval mills were usually constructed on minor streams because building mills along major rivers, with their many obstacles, channels, and so on, required greater technological expertise.[37] Despite the number of convincing arguments he presents, Kotyza does not dispute absolutely the existence of mills in the area surrounding Prague around the year 1000. But, he believes, if there were mills they must have been located on smaller streams surrounding the town and certainly not on the banks of the Vltava.

Apart from this controversial charter from 993, the first document that clearly refers to water mills comes from more than a century later; it is dated between 1125 and 1140. Jan Klápšte drew attention to this charter and emphasized that the document notes a not-particularly-rich canon who had inherited a mill on a minor estate, suggesting that by that time a fair number of mills existed in the Czech lands. Though Klápšte did not refer to it, Únětice – the village in which the water mill is mentioned – is located close to Prague, by then a center of ecclesiastical and political matters, which would have assisted in a more rapid development than more remote areas.[38] Another source from 1130, again similar to the first Hungarian reference dating to 1009, mentions water mills in the utilities list connected to an estate.[39]

Not only legal evidence but literary sources may also be important in discussing the spread of water mills in the Czech lands. The first book (completed in 1119) of the early-twelfth-century chronicle of Cosmas of Prague refers to millers (*molendinarius*), which is more likely to be associated with a specialized group of people working in water mills than to those grinding grain on hand mills, which were generally household equipments.[40]

In Poland the scarcity of legal evidence from the period of early statehood and the lack of reference to water mills in the earliest pieces of Polish historiography – such as the chronicle of Gallus Anonymus – does not provide sufficient data to argue for or against the existence of mills in the eleventh or early twelfth century.[41] The first written record dates to roughly the same period as in the Czech lands, the middle of the twelfth century (1149), however, compared to research on Bohemia and the Kingdom of Hungary, systematic analysis of written records has only been partially conducted.[42] Research concentrates more on the late medieval period, for which promising results have been published in recent years on the spread and commercialization of the milling industry. Despite the scarcity of data on the eleventh- and twelfth-century spread of water mills in the Polish areas one well-regarded source clearly reflects the way grain was usually ground around the end of the twelfth century in Poland. The so-called Book of Henryków has made the Cistercian abbey of the same name one of the best-known ecclesiastical institutions in medieval Poland. This codex contains a detailed summary of the early history of the monastery, including a number of references to mills and milling.

One noteworthy reference was written by Peter, abbot of the abbey and the author of the first narrative part of the Book of Henryków. He recalled: "Let it be known that in those days here in the circuit, water mills were extremely rare, so the wife of the said Boguchwał the Czech very often stood at the quern to grind."[43] The short story in this chapter of the narrative part written by Peter comes from around 1200. The note of the scarcity of water mills shows clearly that even in the region of Henryków in Silesia milling was predominantly carried out on hand mills around 1200. This may also have been the situation further north and east.[44] Archaeological excavation results to date have not shown the existence of water mills predating the written sources noting their presence on rivers in either Bohemia or Poland.[45] Thus, no direct evidence exists for the use of water mills in these areas before the mid-twelfth century. However, just as in the case of Hungary, a number of hand mill fragments have been unearthed in both the Czech lands and different parts of Poland. Because they do not appear to support the early presence of water mills they may affect the linguistic debate in Hungarian scholarship on the adoption of the Hungarian term for mills from a West Slavic language sometime before the tenth century. Although scholarship has dealt less systematically with the spread of water mills in Croatia, Serbia, and Moldavia-Wallachia, what has been published reflects the technological changes taking place in the broader region. In the territory of present-day Croatia, scholars suppose the widespread use of water mills in Roman times; most of the research covers Dalmatia, however, which may have had weaker contacts with East Central Europe than the inland areas in the eleventh century. Archaeological data confirms the existence of water mills by the Jadro River by the town of Salona in Ancient times. In the early eleventh century this river was again used for milling, but there are no data on mills operating there between the Roman Period and the turn of the eleventh century. Although reference to mills was made as early as the tenth century, the document was later shown to be a late medieval forgery. Royal donations to ecclesiastical institutions demonstrate that in the eleventh century water mills were in use in the Dalmatian coastal area on both the mainland and the islands, but no written source has survived for the Kingdom of Croatia before the late eleventh-century occupation by the Hungarians.[46] In the inland areas of the Balkans, however, sources only mention water mills from the late thirteenth century onwards.[47] Roman influence on medieval milling has not only been raised in Croatia but also in Romania. Some scholars have argued for the continuous use of water mills in the former territory of the Roman province of Dacia. The arguments raised in the 1970s have been criticized in many ways since then and nowadays most scholars date the appearance of mills in this region to the twelfth or thirteenth century, the period when mills start to be mentioned in the written evidence connected to the Banat and Transylvania.[48]

Conclusions

Historical scholarship usually associates the spread of different medieval technological innovations such as water mills with the appearance of monasticism in particular regions traditionally considered the peripheries of Christianity.[49] East Central Europe is one of the regions where Christianization and the spread of monasticism took place within a relatively narrow time frame. Although Christianization started some decades earlier in the Czech lands and Poland than in the Principality (later Kingdom) of Hungary, by the middle of the eleventh century the monastic network was denser in Hungary than on the lands of its northern neighbors. In Dalmatia, a strong Christian ecclesiastical organization already existed in the Roman period and some of the bishoprics and monasteries were functioning again by the tenth century.[50] The aim of this paper was to assess how much the spread of mills can be associated with the chronological framework summarized here and the degree to which the first written references or archaeological data on mills can be connected directly with monastic orders.

The connection has proven to be far less evident than usually suggested by historians. The first references to water mills in the region do not mention that these buildings belonged to Benedictines, but consist of charters endowing new monastic foundations with these according to the *Rule of St. Benedict* essential and, no less importantly, expensive constructions. The fact that the sources that usually come down to us are royal donations favoring different church bodies, however, should mostly be attributed to the character of the early products of literacy in the countries of East Central Europe. Namely, most eleventh- or early-twelfth-century legal documents were issued in connection with royal matters – primarily donations. In Hungary, by the middle of the eleventh century not only kings but also other laymen donated to or founded monasteries and endowed them with water mills.[51]

I do not claim here that the spread of monasticism did not impact the appearance of water mills in East Central Europe, as certainly it did. The relationship between the two, however, may be more complex than previously thought. There is very little written evidence available from the eleventh and twelfth centuries suggesting the widespread use of water mills even on ecclesiastical properties, and certainly there is insufficient evidence to suggest that cereal grains were processed in water mills soon after the Benedictine monasteries spread into East Central Europe. The economy of ecclesiastical properties was undoubtedly one of the best organized in that period and thus, supposedly, the spread of mills on these estates would have been more rapid than elsewhere. There are, however, no grounds to suggest that water mills were a dominant force in agrarian production from the early eleventh century in the Kingdom of Hungary and from the twelfth century in the Czech lands and Poland.

Notes

* The author is thankful for the corrections of Katalin Szende and Alice M. Choyke (both of the CEU Department of Medieval Studies) made on an earlier version of this article. The research was supported by the Hungarian ÚNKP-17-4 New National Excellence Program of the Ministry of Human Capacities and by the Eötvös Loránd University

Higher Education Institutional Excellence Program of the Ministry of Human Capacities (1783-3/2018/FEKUTSTRAT).

1 Richard Bennett and John Elton, *History of Corn Milling*, vols. I–IV (London: Simpkin, Marshall and Co., 1898–1904).

2 Lewis Mumford, *Technics and Civilization* (New York: Harcourt, Brace and Co., 1934) and Marc Bloch, "Avènement et conquêtes du moulin à eau," *Annales d'histoire économique et sociale* 7 (1935): 538–563, also published in English: idem, "The Advent and Triumph of the Watermill," in *Land and Work in Mediaeval Europe: Selected Papers by Marc Bloch* (London: Routledge, 1967), 136–168. I used the former when writing this paper.

3 Adam Lucas, "The Role of the Monasteries in the Development of Medieval Milling," in *Wind & Water in the Middle Ages. Fluid Technologies from Antiquity to the Renaissance* (Medieval and Renaissance Texts and Studies, 322 = Penn State Medieval Studies, 2), ed. Steven A. Walton (Tempe, AZ: Arizona Center for Medieval and Renaissance Studies, 2006), 89–128, here 89–91.

4 E.g., Finbar McCormick, Thom Kerr, Meriel McClatchie, and Aidan O'Sullivan, *The Archaeology of Livestock and Cereal Production in Early Medieval Ireland, AD 400–1100* (Reconstructing the Early Medieval Irish Economy EMAP Report, 5.1) (Belfast: [N. p.], 2011), 39–42.

5 Örjan Wikander, *Exploitation of Water-Power or Technological Stagnation? A Reappraisal of the Productive Forces in the Roman Empire* (Scripta Minora 1983–84, 3) (Lund: Gleerup, 1984) and *Handbook of Ancient Water Technology*, ed. idem (Boston and Leiden: Brill, 2000), esp. his contribution in the volume. See also: Adam Robert Lucas, "Narratives of Technological Revolution in the Middle Ages," in *Handbook of Medieval Studies: Terms – Methods – Trends*, ed. Albrecht Classen (Berlin: De Gruyter, 2010), 967–990, here 979–980.

6 For a partial survey of the question with reference to Poland, Bohemia, and Hungary, see Grzegorz Myśliwski, "Utilisation of Water in Central Europe (12th–16th Cents.)," in *Economia e energia secc. XIII–XVIII*, ed. Simonetta Cavaciocchi (Florence: La Monnier, 2003), 321–333.

7 *Monasterium autem, si possit fieri, ita debet constitui ut omnia necessaria, id est aqua, molendinum, hortum, vel artes diversas intra monasterium exerceantur, ut non sit necessitas monachis vagandi foris, quia omnino non expedit animabus eorum.* – Sant Benet de Núrsia [Saint Benedict of Nursia], *Regula monachorum* (Subsidia Monastica, 21), ed. Ignasi M. Fossas (Barcelona: Publicacions de l'Abadia de Montserrat, 1997), cap. 66.

8 St. Gallen, Stiftsbibliothek, Codex Sangallensis 1092. For a comprehensive analysis of the plan, see the project: Carolingian Culture at Reichenau and St. Gall. See online: www.stgallplan.org/ (last accessed: 16 March 2016). For the problem of the mill on the plan, see Walter Horn and Ernest Born, "Water Power and the Plan of St. Gall," *Journal of Medieval History* 1 (1975): 219–258. Adam Lucas accepts the main conclusions of Horn and Born, although with some caution, Adam Lucas, *Wind, Water, Work: Ancient And Medieval Milling Technology* (Leiden and Boston: Brill, 2006), 208–209.

9 Carl I. Hammer, "'A Suitable Place for Putting up a Mill.' Water Power Landscapes and Structures in Carolingian Bavaria," *Vierteljahrschrift für Sozial- und Wirtschaftsgeschichte* 95 (2008): 319–334. For the earliest excavated mill in the region north of the Danube, see Wolfgang Czysz, *Die ältesten Wassermühlen. Archäologische Entdeckungen im Paartal bei Dasing* (Thierhaupten: Klostermühlenmuseum, 1998).

10 See a number of studies by the late László Koszta on the topic. See also Marvin Kantor, *The Origins of Christianity in Bohemia. Sources and Commentary* (Evanston, IL: Northwestern University Press, 1990) and Ian Wood, *The Missionary Life. Saints and the Evangelisation of Europe, 400–1050* (London: Longman, 2001), esp. Part 3.

11 For mills in the Byzantine Empire, see: K[onstantinos] Th. Raptis, "Water as Power: Early Christian and Byzantine Watermills in Greece: Typology and Distribution," in *1st IWA International Symposium on Water and Wastewater Technologies in Ancient Civilizations: Symposium Preprint Book*, ed. A. N. Angelakis and D. Koutsoyiannis (Iraklio: National Agricultural Research Foundation, 2006), 109–117, and Sophia Germanidou, "Watermills in Byzantine Greece (5th–12th cents.). A Preliminary Approach to the Archaeology of Byzantine Hydraulic Milling Technology," *Byzantion* 84 (2014): 185–201 (I am grateful to the author for kindly providing me with her article before it was printed). For the possible impact in the north Balkans, see, e.g., Dumitru Țeicu, *Watermill in the Banat* (Brăila: Museum of Brăila and "Istros" Publishing House, 2012), 384.

12 Biljana Arandjelović and Ana Momčilović-Petronijević, "The Water Mills Architecture in the South of Serbia," *AR-Architecture, Research* no. 2 (2010): 59–62. See online: www.fa.uni-lj.si/filelib/9_ar/ 2010/ar2010_2_07. pdf (last accessed: 13 March 2016).

13 Petr Sommer, "The Monastery of Brevnov," and "The Monastery of Ostrov u Davle," in *Europe's Centre around AD 1000*, ed. Alfried Wieczorek and Hans-Martin Hinz (Stuttgart: Theiss, 2000), 266 and 267 respectively. See also David Kalhous, *Anatomy of a Duchy. The Political and Ecclesiastical Structures of Early Přemyslid Bohemia* (East Central and Eastern Europe in the Middle Ages, 450–1450, 19) (Leiden and Boston: Brill, 2012), esp. 143–169. For the mills in Italy at the time, see Roberta Magnusson and Paolo Squatriti, "The Technologies of Water in Medieval Italy," in *Working with Water in Medieval Europe: Technology and Resource-Use*, ed. Paolo Squatriti (Leiden and Boston: Brill, 2000), 217–266, here 258–266.

14 Marek Derwich, "The Earliest Monasteries in Poland," in *Europe's Centre*, I, 332–334, esp. 334.

15 See Kornél Szovák, "A bencés szerzetesség korai századai Magyarországon" [The early centuries of the Benedictines in Hungary], and Szilveszter Sólymos, "Az első bencés szerzetesek hazánkban" [The first Benedictine monks in Hungary], in *Paradisum plantavit. Bencés monostorok a középkori Magyarországon / Benedictine Monasteries in Medieval Hungary*, ed. Imre Takács (Pannonhalma: Pannonhalmi Bencés Főapátság, 2001), 35–47 and 48–60.

16 Péter Váczy, "A korai magyar történet néhány kérdéséről" [On some questions of early Hungarian history], *Századok* 92 (1958): 265–345, here 278, László Makkai, "Östliches Erbe und westliche Leihe in der ungarischen Landwirtschaft der frühfeudalen Zeit," *Agrártörténeti Szemle* 16 [Supplementum] (1974): 1–53, here 46; idem, "A malom mint a középkori Európa erő- és munkagépe" [The mill as the power machine of medieval Europe], in *Műszaki innovációk sorsa Magyarországon: malomipar, vaskohászat, textilipar* [The fate of technological innovations in Hungary: milling industry, iron smelting, textile industra], ed. Walter Endrei (Budapest: Akadémiai, 1995), 29–35, here 33; Gyula Kristó, "A korai feudalizmus (1116–1231)" [The age of early feudalism (1116–1231)], in *Magyarország története I/1. Előzmények és magyar történet 1242-ig.* [A History of Hungary, i/1. Prehistory and Hungarian history until 1242] (Magyarország története tíz kötetben), ed. György Székely (Budapest: Akadémiai, 1978), 1007–1415, here 1025. For an overview of the historiography of the earliest mention of water mills in a Hungarian context, see Tamás Vajda, "Okleveles adatok Árpád-kori vízimalmainkról" [Charter evidence on Árpádian-age water mills], in *Medievisztikai tanulmányok. A IV. Medievisztikai PhD-konferencia (Szeged, 2005. június 9–10.) előadásai* [Studies in medieval history. Papers read at the 4th conference of medievalists, Szeged, 9–10 June 2005], ed. Szabolcs Marton and Éva Teiszler (Szeged: Szegedi Középkorász Műhely, 2005), 193–220, here 193–197, and more recently, see also Tamás Vajda, "Korai bencés apátságaink vízimalmai: a szerzetesek

szerepe a technikai fejlődésben," [Water mills of the early Benedictine abbey of Hungary and their role in technological development], in *Episcopus, Archiabbas Benedictinus, Historicus Ecclesiae. Tanulmányok Várszegi Asztrik 70. születésnapjára* [Studies in honor of Asztrik Várszegi on the occasion of his 70th birthday] (METEM Könyvek, 85), ed. Ádám Somorjai OSB and István Zombori (Budapest: Magyar Egyháztörténeti Enciklopédia Munkaközösség and Historia Ecclesiastica Hungarica Alapítvány, 2016), 25–45.

17 János Melich, "Malom" [Mill], *Magyar Nyelv* 16 (1920): 61–66 and in his footsteps in the 1950s and 1960s: István Kniezsa, *A magyar nyelv szláv jövevényszavai*, I [Slavic loanwords in Hungarian] (Budapest: Akadémiai, 1955), 325–327 and 342; Elemér Moór "Malom és molnár," [Mill and miller], *Nyelvtudományi Közlemények* 67 (1965): 130–138; Dezső Pais, "Pamlény: malom? – és az mn > ml hangváltozás" [Pamlény – mill? – and the mn > ml sonant changes], *Magyar Nyelv* 61(1965): 455–458; Antal Bartha, "Gazdaságtörténet és szavak" [Economic history and the words], *Magyar Nyelv* 65 (1969): 14–25, and again Elemér Moór, "A szóegyüttesek és a csoportos szóhiányok: művelődéstörténeti tények" [Joint words and joint word omissions: intellectual historical facts], *Magyar Nyelv* 70 (1974): 173–181. See also the reflections of Egon Maróti on the debate: idem, "A vízimalom európai elterjedésének történetéhez"[To the history of the spread of water mills in Europe], *Antik Tanulmányok* 22 (1975): 55–74.

18 Makkai, "Östliches Erbe," 44–45.

19 Walter Endrei, "Malom," [Mill], in *Korai magyar történeti lexikon (9–14. század)* [Early Hungarian historical dictionary, 9th to 14th centuries], ed. Gyula Kristó (Budapest: Akadémiai, 1994), 441.

20 See, for instance, the entry: Walter Endrei, "Malom," [Mill], and idem and György Balázs, "Vízimalom" [Water mill], in *Magyar művelődéstörténeti lexikon* [Lexicon of cultural history in Hungary], ed. Péter Kőszeghy (Budapest: Balassi, 2003–2014). Available online: http://mamul.btk.mta.hu/ (last accessed: 1 April 2016).

21 Tamás Vajda, "Régészeti adatok középkori malmainkról" [Archaeological data on medieval mills in Hungary], in *Középkortörténeti tanulmányok 6. A VI. Medievisztikai PhD-konferencia (Szeged, 2009. június 4–5.) előadásai* [Studies in medieval history, 6. Papers presented at the VIth PhD conference in medieval studies, Szeged, 4–5 June 2009], ed. Péter G. Tóth and Pál Szabó (Szeged: Szegedi Középkorász Műhely, 2010), 307–318.

22 For a critique of some of these archaeological finds, see Tamás Vajda, "Árpád- és Anjoukori vízimalmaink tájalakító hatása" [Water mills as driving forces of landscape change in the Árpádian and Angevin periods], in *Micae mediaevales II. Fiatal történészek dolgozatai a középkori Magyarországról és Európáról* [Studies of young historians on medieval Hungary and Europe], ed. Péter Jakab et al. (Budapest: ELTE BTK Történelemtudományok Doktori Iskola, 2012), 59–75, here 60–63.

23 Tamás Vajda, "Régészeti adatok."

24 For the hand mills, see Szilvia Földesi, "Remarks on the Medieval Millstones at Kána," in *Archaeological Investigations in Hungary in 2004*, ed. Júlia Kisfaludi (Budapest: Kulturális Örökségvédelmi Hivatal and Magyar Nemzeti Múzeum, 2005), 54–55. For an overview of the results of the research on the village of Kána, see: György Terei, "Az Árpádkori Kána falu" [The Árpád-age village of Kána], in *A középkor és a kora újkor régészete Mgyarországon*, I [Archaeology of the Middle Ages and the Early Modern Period in Hungary], ed. Elek Benkő and Gyöngyi Kovács (Budapest: MTA Régészeti Intézet, 2010), 81–111.

25 György Györffy, *István király és műve* [King Stephen and his legacy] (Budapest: Akadémiai, 1977), 419.

26 *Diplomata Hungariae antiquissima: accedunt epistolae et acta ad historiam Hungariae pertinentia [ab anno 1000 usque ad annum 1196]*, I, ed. Georgius Györffy (Budapest: Akadémiai, 1992), 52 (emphasis mine, AV).

27 For their role in early farming practices, see László Erdélyi, "Szent István-kori bencések hatása a föld- és kertmívelésre meg az iparra" [The role of the Benedictines in the age of St. Stephen on agriculture, gardening and industry], in *Emlékkönyv Szent István király halálának kilencszázadik évfordulóján*, I [Memorial volume on the 900th anniversary of Saint Stephen's death], ed. Jusztinián Serédi (Budapest: Szent István Társulat, 1938), 479–491.

28 *Monumenta Germaniae Historica. Diplomata regum et imperatorum Germaniae* [MGH Dipl.], III, [Henrici II et Arduini diplomata], ed. Harry Bresslau, Hermann Bloch and Robert Holtzmann (Hannover: Hahn, 1900–1903), 488–489 (no. 384).

29 For German areas, see above the works on Bavarian mills, for Italian mills, see Squatriti, *Water and Society*.

30 Berent Schwineköper, "'*Cum aquis aquarumve decursibus*' Zu den Pertinenzformeln der Herrscherurkunden bis sur Zeit Ottos I.," in *Festschrift für Helmut Beumann zum 65. Geburtstag*, ed. Kurt-Ulrich Jäschke (Sigmaringen: Thorbecke, 1977), 22–56 and Anikó Kiss, "A gyulai várbirtok malmainak története" [History of the mills in the castle domain of Gyula], *A Békés Megyei Múzeumok Közleményei* 5 (1978): 269–291, here 270.

31 *Diplomata Hungariae antiquissima*, I, 145–152; the latest edition of the charter: István Hoffmann, *A Tihanyi alapítólevél mint helynévtörténeti forrás* [The foundation charter of Tihany as a source of onomastics] (A Magyar Névarchívum Kiadványai, 16) (Debrecen: Debreceni Egyetemi Kiadó, 2010), 23–29. For the relevant part, see ibid., 28: *Sunt igitur aratra XX cum LX mansionibus, vinitores cum vineis XX, equites XX, piscatores X, agasones V, bubulci III, pastores ovium III, subulci II, apinarii II, coquinarii II, sutores II, fabri II, aurifex I, dolatores II,* molendinarii cum molendinis II, *tornator I, vestimentorum ablutor I, cerdo I, ancille X, preter hec sunt emissarii XXXIIII cum subditis equabus, vacce C, oves septingente, porci C, apium vasa L. Preter hec ad necessaria fratrum per singulos annos constituimus de armento regali L poletros. Inter omnes namque sunt servorum ecclesie mansiones CXL* (emphasis mine, AV).

32 While writing this paper I could only access an older edition of the chronicle: *Kronika česká: Podle originálu z r. 1541*, I [Czech Chronicle. From the beginnings to 1541], ed. Václav Flajšhans (Prague: Česká Akademie věd a umění, 1918), 97–98, 106 and 176. See also Bennett and Elton, *History of Corn Milling*, II, 77–78.

33 For the early history of the monastery, see Dana Koutná-Karg, "Die Anfange des Klosters Brevnov," in *Tausend Jahre Benediktiner in den Klöstern Brevnov, Braunau und Rohr*, ed. Johannes Hofmann OSB (St. Ottilien: EOS, 1993), 219–230 and also Sommer, "The Monastery of Brevnov."

34 Jiří Pražák, "Privilegium pervetustum Boleslai," in *Milénium břevnovského kláštera (993– 1993). Sborník statí o jeho významu a postavení v českých dějinách* [A millennium of the history of the Břevnov monastery (993–1993). Collection of studies on its significance and role in Czech history], ed. Ivan Hlaváček and Marie Bláhová (Prague: Karolinum, 1993), 13–24, and Kalhous, *Anatomy of a Duchy*, 140–143. For the edition of the charter, see *Codex diplomaticus et epistolaris regni Bohemiae*, I, ed. Gustavus Friedrich et al. (Prague: Sumptibus Comitiorum Regni Bohemiae, 1904/1907), 347–350 (no. 375).

35 Martina Maříková, "Středověké mlýny v českých zemích (Archeologické a písemné prameny)" [Medieval mills in Czech lands (archaeological data and written sources)], *Mediaevalia Historica Bohemica* 10 (2005): 89–148, and Tomáš Petráček, "K otázce datace počátků vodních mlýnů v českých zemích v kontextu změny vnímání dynamiky vývoje českých zemích 10.–12. století" [On the issue of dating the beginning of water mills in

the Czech lands in the context of changes in the perception of the dynamics of the Czech lands in the 10th–12th centuries], in *Sborník k poctě Jiřího Kalfersta* [Studies in honor of Jiří Kalferst] (Hradec Králové: Muzeum východních Čeché Hradci Králové, 2014), 249–252. The view that since the authenticity of the foundation charter water mills were indeed functioning in Bohemia by 993 is shared in the fairly recent work of Tomáš Petráček, *Power and Exploitation in the Czech Lands in the 10th–12th Centuries* (East Central and Eastern Europe in the Middle Ages, 450–1450, 40) (Leiden and Boston: Brill, 2017), 174–178.

36 Oldřich Kotyza, "K počátkům vodních mlýnů v českých zemích aneb o existenci vltavských jezů a hydraulických mlýnů v Praze 10. století. Poznámky k břevnovskému aktu ze 14. ledna 993" [On the origin of water mills in the Czech lands or on the existence of the weirs on the Vltava and water mills in Prague in the 10th century. Notes on the Břevnov act of 14 January 993], in *Středověká Evropa v pohybu k poctě Jana Klápště / Medieval Europe in Motion in Honour of Jan Klápště*, eds. Ivana Boháčová and Petr Sommer (Prague: Archeologický ústav AV ČR, Praha, v. v. i., 2014), 461–499; Petráček, *Power and Exploitation* does not refer to this article.

37 Hammer, "A Suitable Place for Putting," passim; András Vadas, "Terminológiai és tartalmi kérdések a középkori malomhelyek körül" [Questions of the terminology and meaning of the term *locus molendini* in the Middle Ages], *Történelmi Szemle* 57 (2015): 619–648 and idem, "Some Remarks on the Legal Regulations and Practice of Mill Construction in Medieval Hungary," in *Wasser in der mittelalterlichen Kultur / Water in Medieval Culture. Gebrauch – Wahrnehmung – Symbolik / Uses, Perceptions, and Symbolism* (Das Mittelalter. Perspektiven mediävistischer Forschung, 4), ed. Gerlinde Huber-Rebenich, Christian Rohr and Michael Stolz (Berlin: De Gruyter, 2017), 291–304.

38 Jan Klápště, *The Czech Lands in Medieval Transformation* (East Central and Eastern Europe in the Middle Ages, 450–1450, 17) (Leiden and Boston: Brill, 2012), 320–321. For the original donation, see *Codex diplomaticus et epistolaris regni Bohemiae*, I, 129–131 (no. 124).

39 *Codex diplomaticus et epistolaris regni Bohemiae*, I, 111 (no. 114).

40 Cosmas Pragensis, *Chronicon Boemorum* in *Monumenta Germaniae Historica. Scriptores rerum Germanicarum Nova Series*, II, ed. Bertold Bretholz (Berlin: Wedimann, 1923), 14 (cap. i/ 5). For the English translation of the chronicle, see Cosmas of Prague, *Chronicle of the Czechs* (Washington, DC: The Catholic University of America Press, 2009), 44. On the problem of millers, see: Vajda, "Korai bencés," 34.

41 For this see, in the case of Poland, Anna Adamska, "'From Memory to Written Record' in the Periphery of Medieval *Latinitas*: The Case of Poland in the Eleventh and Twelfth Centuries," and Ivan Hlaváček, "The Use of Charters and Other Documents in Přemyslide Bohemia," in *Charters and the Use of the Written Word in Medieval Society* (Utrecht Studies in Medieval Literacy, 5), ed. Karl Heidecker (Turnhout: Brepols Publishers, 2000), 83–100 and 133–144.

42 Grzegorz Myśliwski, "Utilisation of Water," 324. The 1149 charter referred to by Myśliwski was not at my disposal when writing this paper. For earlier, see Maria Dembińska, *Przetwórstwo zbożowe w Polsce Średniowiecznej (X–XIV wiek)* [Processing cereal in medieval Poland 10th–14th centuries] (Wrocław: Zakł. Narod. im. Ossolińskich, 1973), esp. 63–72.

43 *Sed sciendum, quia in diebus illis erant hic in circuitu aquatica molendina valde rarissima, unde dicti Bogwali Boemi uxor stabat sepissime ad molam molendo – Liber fundationis claustri Sancte Marie Virginis in Heinrichau (Księga henrykowska)*, ed. Roman Grodecki (Wrocław: Muzeum Archidiecezjalne we Wrocławiu, 1991), 47 (cap. 113). An English edition of the text can be found in Piotr Górecki, *A Local Society in*

Transition. the Henryków Book and Related Documents (PIMS Studies and Texts, 155) (Toronto: Pontifical Institute of Mediaeval Studies, 2007), 139. See also on mills ibid., 40–43.

44 On the spread of mills in the later medieval period, see Dembińska, *Przetwórstwo zbożowe w Polsce*. For the Teutonic areas, see Rafał Kubicki, *Młynarstwo w państwie zakonu krzyżackiego w Prusach w XIII–XV w. (do 1454 r.)* [The milling industry in the state of the Teutonic Order in Prussia in the 13th–15th century (to 1454)] (Gdańsk: Uniwersytetu Gdańskiego, 2012).

45 Lucie Galusová, "Vodní mlýn jako objekt archeologického výzkumu" [Water mills as subjects of archaeological research], *Archaeologia historica* 40 (2015): 267–293.

46 *Codex diplomaticus Regni Croatiae, Dalmatiae et Slavoniae*, I, ed. Ivan Kukuljević Sakcinski (Zagreb: Ex officina societatis typographicae, 1874), 121–122 (no. 138), 154–155 (no. 189), 170–176 (no. 209), and 181–182 (no. 220). On the mills of Salona, see Lovre Katić, "Solinski mlinovi u prošlosti" [The ancient mills of Salona], *Starohrvatska prosvjeta*, [Serija III.] 2 (1952): 201–219. On mills in Croatia in the medieval period, see Marin Knezović, "Voda u hrvatskim ranosrednjovjekovnim ispravama" [Water in Croatian early medieval documents], *Ekonomska i ekohistorija* 3, no. 1 (2007): 35–50, here 42–46.

47 Ranko Findrik, "Uvod u proucavanje starih vodenica" [Introduction to the study of ancient mills], *Saopstenje* 15 (1983): 95–117, and Biljana Arandjelović and Ana Momčilović-Petronijević, "Arhitektura vodnih mlinov v južni Srbiji" [The architecture of water mills in Southern Serbia], *AR Arhitektura, raziskave* 2 (2010): 59–62.

48 Ţeicu, *Watermill*, passim.

49 On the concept, see *Christianization and the Rise of Christian Monarchy Scandinavia, Central Europe and Rus' c. 900–1200*, ed. Nora Berend (Cambridge: Cambridge University Press, 2010) and more recently the studies in the volume: *Medieval East Central Europe in a Comparative Perspective: from Frontier Zones to Lands in Focus*, ed. Gerhard Jaritz and Katalin Szende (New York: Routledge, 2016).

50 On this matter see Joan Dusa, *The Medieval Dalmatian Episcopal Cities. Development and Transformation* (American University Studies, Series IX., History, 94) (New York: Peter Lang, 1991).

51 See, for instance, from 1061: *Diplomata Hungariae antiquissima*, I, 170–174. On the criticism of the heavily interpolated charter, see Bernát Kumorovitz L., "A zselicszentjakabi alapítólevél 1061-ből, 'Pest' legkorábbi említése" [The foundation charter of Zelicsszentjakab from 1061 and the earliest reference to 'Pest'], *Tanulmányok Budapest múltjából* 16 (1964): 43-83.

8

THE IMPACT OF CASTLES ON THE DEVELOPMENT OF THE LOCAL CHURCH SYSTEM IN HUNGARY IN THE ELEVENTH AND TWELFTH CENTURIES

Mária Vargha

Introduction

Pagan Hungarian tribes occupied the Carpathian Basin gradually towards the end of the ninth century, the so-called conquest period. A major change occurred in the year 1000 when Stephen I, the first king of Hungary, was crowned and with his reign the Christian state came into being. Clearly, the actual process was not so quick and simple, but it marks a crucial point for investigating the development of state power. This went hand in hand with the process of Christianization, which was accompanied by the expansion of a local church system. Although the beginnings of both the reorganization of power structures and the first steps towards Christianity were rooted in the previous century,[1] the formal steps and the organized development ment started with the foundation of the kingdom. Tracing this, however, is rather challenging. Even though the eleventh and twelfth centuries in Hungary were of major importance for the foundation of the state, and with it the formation of (secular and ecclesiastic) power structures, sources about this period are scarce, especially written evidence. Archaeology, however, can provide large amounts of data through material remains.

The construction of castles marked the development of state power. The realm was divided into counties, an important step in administration, and castles were built as military strongholds and markers of power. Although scholars have long addressed the relationship between the county castles and the ecclesiastical system, they have mostly concentrated on archbishoprics and bishoprics or deaneries, paying scant attention to local churches, mostly owing to a lack of relevant sources[2] and in accordance with the top-down direction of Christianization and thus church organization in the region. In this paper, I focus on the role and impact of castles and the castle system – the major elements of secular power – on the development of the local church system – the smallest but most numerous and least documented elements of the ecclesiastical system. The pattern of the association of local churches with the castle system has yet to be explored fully.

The process of Christianization as seen from written evidence

The Christianization process in Hungary shows similarities with that in neighboring countries of the region. By the turn of the tenth century, the states of Hungary, Bohemia, and Poland had emerged as Christian monarchies as part of the process of state formation accompanied by Christianization. The Moravian prince, Moimir, and several chieftains were baptized in the first half of the ninth century and in 873 the first Přemysl ruler, Bořivoj, also converted to Christianity. Mieszko I, a Polish prince, the first ruler of the Piast dynasty, and Géza from the Árpádian dynasty, the prince of Hungary, were baptized one hundred years later, in the last third of the tenth century. Not surprisingly, a political agenda lay behind these conversions. Although the Hungarians were first influenced by Byzantine Christianity (as early as the mid-tenth century), in order to oppose his competitor, Gyula, Géza decided to be baptized according to the Latin Christian rite together with his son, Stephen. According to written sources, Latin Christian missionaries came to the country as early as the last third of the tenth century, with varied outcomes. Sources tend to accent the missions of Adalbert, who, in the later *Legenda maior* of Stephen, was claimed to have baptized both Géza and Stephen. With the exception of his activity, no other missions are mentioned in eleventh century sources, and so probably their impact and memory had disappeared.[3]

In 1000, the third year of his reign, Stephen was crowned, together with his wife, the Bavarian princess Gisela. Their marriage (996/7), negotiated by Géza, is considered a tactical move towards the Christianization of the country, as Western military forces and missionaries both arrived from Bavaria along with Gisela. The first steps towards institutionalized Christianity preceded the coronation ceremony; the Benedictine abbey of Saint Martin at Pannonhalma was founded in 996, at the very end of Géza's rule, and the first Hungarian bishopric was founded in Veszprém, probably under the authority of the archbishopric of Salzburg. The coronation, which was a crucial precondition for establishing an independent Hungarian church, was soon followed by the foundation of the archbishopric of Esztergom and the dioceses of Veszprém, Győr, and Transylvania (the last probably only in the form of a missionary-like bishopric) by 1003, and by 1009, the bishoprics of Pécs and Eger and the archbishopric of Kalocsa were organized. This more or less completed the system, as during his reign King Stephen only founded one more bishopric, Cenad, in 1030.[4] Soon after Stephen's reign, the bishoprics of Vác and Biharia were established, the latter following a pagan revolt in 1045–46 in the area; the bishopric of Zagreb was founded in the last third of the century, and another was in Nitra around 1100.[5] According to László Koszta, the last foundations meant that the church organization that developed in the first half of the eleventh century was further corrected during the reign of King Saint Ladislas in the last third of the century by targeting the peripheries. He also notes the differences between the western and eastern half of the country – according to his analysis, in the eastern half of the country the diocesan level of church organization was only established towards the end of the eleventh century, about 80 years later than in the Transdanubian region.[6]

The castle system and church organization in Hungary

Both of these topics have been researched for a long time and some common points and differences have already been noted. The most important common point is that until very recently the castle system and the problem of church organization were discussed separately. As for the differences, while castles were considered mostly from an archaeological point of view – with the exception of their relation to the county system[7] – church organization was mostly discussed from the historian's perspective. Many archaeological reports on the excavation of individual sites have been published; here I will only mention the synthesizing works. The first comprehensive work on castles was an article by József Dénes in 1993, enumerating the castles and briefly summarizing the related research problems.[8] This was soon followed by the first large comprehensive work on castles by István Bóna, where besides addressing the related historical problems, he contextualized the castles in the region and discussed their archaeological structure, focusing mostly on the dating.[9] After a significant period, the debate continued with a contribution by Gergely Buzás, who summarized the problems of one particular structural type of castle that predominated in the eleventh century.[10] Two recent studies are Katalin Szende's article summarizing the relationship between castles and their later development as royal cities,[11] and Maxim Mordovin's monograph discussing county castles and the castle systems in Hungary, Bohemia, and Poland. This volume is so far the most complex and most detailed research on castles, with a critical overview of the existing literature, a discussion of terminology, dating, typology, and fortification structures, their roles as settlements, and, last but not least, the relationship of castles and graveyards to Christianization and church organization. The latter chapter is especially important because it is also the first comprehensive work on the problem, reviewing the legislation (both domestic and general church law), the status of churches, and cemeteries as archaeological material.[12] Besides this study, church organization has mainly been the focus of historical studies, which are dominated by topics other than parishes, although the works of László Koszta on parishes are of particular interest.[13] From an archaeological point of view, ecclesiastical topographies[14] mostly focus on the buildings themselves, collecting both historical and archaeological records, which results in huge, valuable, and informative volumes on the development of the church organization in certain regions. In consequence of the often limited archaeological information, however, the topographies cannot contribute much on questions concerning the beginnings of church organization.

Regulations on Christianization and the parish system

Written evidence on the organization of the local church system probably followed the expansion of Christianity and the organization of the dioceses with a significant delay. Regarding the Christianization of the masses, the most important element of the church was the parish and the establishment of the parochial system. There is no way to set an exact date for the legislation on parishes, however, as it developed gradually, and has other, more important components that were not necessarily recorded in the same law collections.

The question is: is it possible to speak in general of parishes in the tenth century or not? To be able to decide, it is probably best to investigate the legislation on parish rights, particularly three major points; tithes, burial rights, and church appellation, which can shed light on the hierarchy and diverse functions of early churches. Of these, legislation concerning burials has been discussed the most widely, summarized recently by Maxim Mordovin, together with the legislation on the status of churches in connection with the investigation of the churches associated with county castles.[15] According to Mordovin's investigation of general canon law, the earliest mandates regulating that burials should be situated around churches is found in the capitularies of Charlemagne, dated to 768 and 810/813, referring only to the pagan Saxon areas. In 836, the synod of Aachen stated that a priest should bury the members of his congregation according to Christian customs, and following that, in 895, the synod of Tribur enumerated the possible places of Christian burial: cathedrals, monasteries, and churches that receive the tithe.[16] This legislation is also important because it mentions the income from tithes. Next, the so-called Decretum of Burchard, compiled around 1000, and the works of Ivo of Chartres (*Decretum* and *Panormia*, created between 1040 and 1115) emphasized the importance of excluding pagans from sacred spaces, and thus their burials from inside the church.[17] Sources attest that the general use of churchyard cemeteries for the Christian population cannot be seen at the end of the eleventh century, not even in Western Europe. Even according to the twelfth-century theologian, Honorius of Autun, "since the whole world is the temple of God, consecrated by the blood of Christ, it is not indispensable for the just to be buried in the churchyard."[18] The first detailed regulation on burials can be found in the *Decretum Gratiani* (1139–1142), finalized by Guillaume Durant (1235–1296).[19]

Tithes, a second crucial element of parish rights, have been less researched. Studying a Thuringian tithe dispute, John Eldevik suggested that the power of the bishop was a crucial point in the collection of tithes. Although from the early ninth century onwards the collection and distribution of tithes was the duty of the priest, it was still the bishop who had to administer it properly and take the share of the cathedral church. From the pontificate of Pope Gelasius I onwards, the so-called quadripartition was used, which continued to be the main principle of distributing church income in the period of the Carolingian Empire; the tithe was divided into four parts: one for charity to the poor, one for the support of the priest, one for the church fabric, and one for the diocesan bishop.[20] This corresponds with Hungarian regulations; it is clear from the sources that the bishop collected the tithe until the end of the eleventh century.[21]

Sources show similar confusion about the appellation or status of some churches. Even in eleventh-century English sources, the terms *ecclesia*, *capella*, and even *monasterium* were used interchangeably. Sources from East Central Europe show that the terminology does not define the role of a church clearly; its role should rather be sought in its right to hold funerals.[22]

In addition to general church law, Hungarian secular legislation contributes to understanding the local church system. The second law book of King Stephen states: *Decem ville ecclesiam edificent* ("ten villages shall build a church").[23] Even though this was used as a topos, it shows the ruler's goal of organized development at the level of local churches.[24] Furthermore, it ordered that the king should provide chalices and vestments, but the bishop was to provide liturgical books. An important point is that this law code already recognizes a general regulation of the tithe, the *decima*.

Subsequently, three more synods were held and churchyard cemeteries developed gradually. The synod of Szabolcs in 1092 made it compulsory to bury people in the sacred area of the churchyard. This appears in a milder form in the regulation from the synod of Tarcal, dated around 1100, stating only that burials should be around churches, and imposing a moderate penalty if not. The latest regulations, from the synod of Esztergom, held between 1104 and 1112/3, gave detailed orders on who could not be granted such a burial. All this marks a process, first ordering the act and giving a significant penalty for non-compliance, which marked the starting point for the introduction of a new custom, to the end, exceptional cases are noted.[25]

The question of the ecclesiastical hierarchy should also be examined. As noted above, the rough outline of the ecclesiastical system, the dioceses and the archbishoprics, was established rather early. For the local churches and the castle system, however, another, lower, category in the hierarchy is even more important: decanal churches. Mordovin investigated and compared the archaeological and historical sources and concludes that decanal churches did not appear before the end of the eleventh century. The development of this system connected to castles is only seen in charter evidence from the second half of the twelfth century onwards, thus churches before the turn of the eleventh century should rather be regarded as pastoral churches.[26]

Two further sources concern the regional development of a local church system. First, the less organized development of churchyard cemeteries is confirmed by a further source, the Legend of Saint Gerard, which says that "the bishop went together with his monks to visit his diocese, and to consecrate burial sites for those who want to build churches"[27] The second piece of legislation speaks about the demolition rate of local churches; in the law book of Ladislas I/7–8, the king ordered the renovation of churches that were demolished as either a consequence of pagan revolts or of age.[28] This shows that as early as the end of the eleventh century a significant number of churches can be presumed to have existed, definitely more than can be retrieved from written sources or archaeological remains. This makes it a challenge to reconstruct the contemporary state of the local church system.

Furthermore, from written sources and the legislation of general church law, it appears that a clear definition of the parish emerged only during the thirteenth century; before that it is better referred only as a local church system. This legislation, however, expressed the desire for parishes from the ninth century on and different areas may have developed at different rates. Hungarian secular law shows rapid development on the level of a local church system, with clear references to the pastoral functions of churches (regulation of the tithe, compulsory attendance, church ritual vessels and vestments) which can be connected to the top-down Christianization and church organization process tied to the state formation of the country, which – as the sources and historical events such as pagan revolts testify – took most of the century to stabilize.

The organization of counties and the castle system

Similarly to the Christianization and church organization process, the development of the castle and county system has long been studied, focusing mostly on the relations of the counties and the castles. The organization of the county system started during the reign of Stephen and was connected to the formation of the Christian state. According to Attila Zsoldos, a leading scholar of Árpádian-period political history, by the end of the eleventh century a good number of counties were already in existence: Bács, Baranya, Bars, Bihar, Bodrog, Borsod, Borsova, Csanád, Csongrád, Doboka, Esztergom, Fehér, Fejér, Győr, Hont, Nógrád, Nyitra, Somogy, Sopron, Szabolcs, Szolnok, Tolna, Újvár, Ung, Torda, Vas, Veszprém, and Zala.[29]

He also notes that the relationship between the organization of the counties and the emergence of castles is not always clear. He points out that some counties had more than one castle, sometimes with a *comes* for both. He regards this as characteristic for the earliest counties.[30]

Compared to counties, the origins of castles and the castle system are not as clear. Mordovin meticulously compared the dating of castles based on historical, archaeological, and typological evidence and concluded that neither archaeology nor history can provide an exact dating for them. Different types of evidence point towards a long development that probably started in the time of Stephen's father, Géza, and finished only in the second half of the eleventh century. Also, in Mordovin's opinion, it cannot yet be stated whether the organization of each county was preceded or followed by the construction of a castle.[31]

The problem with comparing the development of the parochial system and state formation (establishment of castles) starts with the ambiguous dating of castles, especially the missing archaeological evidence for central fortifications in some cases. In the present study, the comparison will be based on information collected by Mordovin on the 36 castles dated to the eleventh century,[32] supplemented by the fortifications of Csongrád, Nógrád, Sály, Szolnok, Trenčín, and Zvolen, where archaeological remains are either not known or not yet published, but their existence in the eleventh century can be presumed.

The impact of castles on the development of the local church system

The reorganization of power structures after the year 1000 shaped the landscape of the country in a different way than it had been organized before the state was founded. In this new system, the central elements of power were the county castles. As noted above, the foundation of the state, and with that the re-organization of power – the development of the system of county castles – took place in parallel with the process of Christianization. In the latter, the development of the local church system played an especially important role. As religion was also meant to express the new power of the state, the emergence of the local church system can be understood as a sort of auxiliary project. The county castles were power centers and the local churches were smaller centers of power that were to propagate the new religion and the power of the new state. Clearly, not only castles could and should be regarded as elements of power in this process. Monasteries and the royal curia system also played significant roles, and although it is not possible to discuss them in detail here, their role should not be ignored.

As described above, lacking written sources for this period, only the most important bishoprics and archbishoprics are known; the smallest, but in a way the most important, element of the church system – parishes – are not. These small elements, however, comprised the largest part of the local church system and thus influenced the largest segment of the population – the commoners – and so played a significant role in the process of Christianization and church organization. This paper focuses on this smallest element from a mostly archaeological point of view in order to draw an objective picture from the existing sources (archaeological finds and features – churches and field cemeteries), comparing their location, spread, and frequency to the castle system. This study encompasses all the recorded sites from the area of present-day Hungary, and all the published sites and known monuments from the area of the medieval Kingdom of Hungary.

With a large number of sites to analyze, all carefully investigated and put in a GIS system, new opportunities arise to explore their relation to the county castle system in more detail and in more ways than ever before, but with some variation in the limitations on the use of archaeological data and different states of research in various areas of medieval Hungary.

In this analysis, I had access to all the recorded archaeological sites from present-day Hungary;[33] here I used cemeteries and churches dated to the early Árpádian period, altogether over 250 sites. Besides published material, which only makes up the smaller part of the database, I used the online monument database of the churches in present-day Slovakia.[34] For Transylvania, I used the works of Erwin Gáll[35] and Géza Entz.[36] Another important monument database relevant for all the churches of the medieval Kingdom of Hungary is the monograph by János

Gyurkó.[37] The amounts of data on churches and cemeteries are not the same, resulting in two discrepancies. First, most of the data on cemeteries comes from the database of recorded archaeological sites in Hungary. This contains all the excavated (and published) material, but, as noted, this is only a small part of the number of recorded sites because most of them were recorded by field walking (site survey) and they were not researched further.[38] The number of recorded sites greatly exceeds the published material, even though it is hard to date the sites to the eleventh or the twelfth centuries solely by means of field walking (mainly relying on surface finds to offer dating opportunities). Here the only sites included date to the early Árpádian period, that is, more or less to the eleventh century. This also shows a significant difference in the state of research in different parts of the Carpathian Basin, as they lie almost completely within the area of present-day Hungary. This is a consequence of a discrepancy in the amounts of published and unpublished material. Such sites appear to be rather scarce in Transylvania and Slovakia as a result of gaps in the research; the territory of present-day Hungary is well covered. In consequence of the lack of data, the relationship among castles, churches, and cemeteries in Transylvania, it cannot be included here.

Churches complicate the picture. As is clear from the databases above, churches, especially standing churches, have attracted more research and thus more is known about their distribution in the Carpathian Basin. The dating of standing churches is also easier than archaeological remains in many cases, although some potential methodological problems present themselves. The dating of standing churches is mostly based on art historical evidence, which may not have preserved the earliest form of the church. The number of standing churches dated to the eleventh century is rather small; even taking into account the churches identified by field walking does not change the situation much. Dating a church to the High Middle Ages (eleventh through thirteenth century) is hard even with proper excavation, let alone only from field walking data. Therefore, most of the churches identified by this method can only be dated broadly within these three centuries. Thus, the number of churches must have been larger than is shown on this map because of the problematic dating and also because of the perishable material (wood) used for construction. All this, however, affects mostly the actual number of churches less than their spread.

Considering all this, the map (see Map 8.1) comparing the spread of churches, cemeteries, and castles is still rather telling on the impact of the castles. First, it is quite visible that the castles are more often located along the border areas of the kingdom, which is not surprising and can be explained by their defensive role. The relation of churches and castles is rather surprising, however. Lacking proper archaeological data, not all the castles appear to have had churches, which certainly was not the case. As Mordovin shows, most of the castles had at least one church, and many of them probably even had two.[39] Still, this is not the most surprising element of the map. With the exception of the castles that definitely pre-dated King Stephen's activity, such as Nitra and Visegrád, the early churches "avoided" the immediate surroundings of castles. This is rather surprising, as

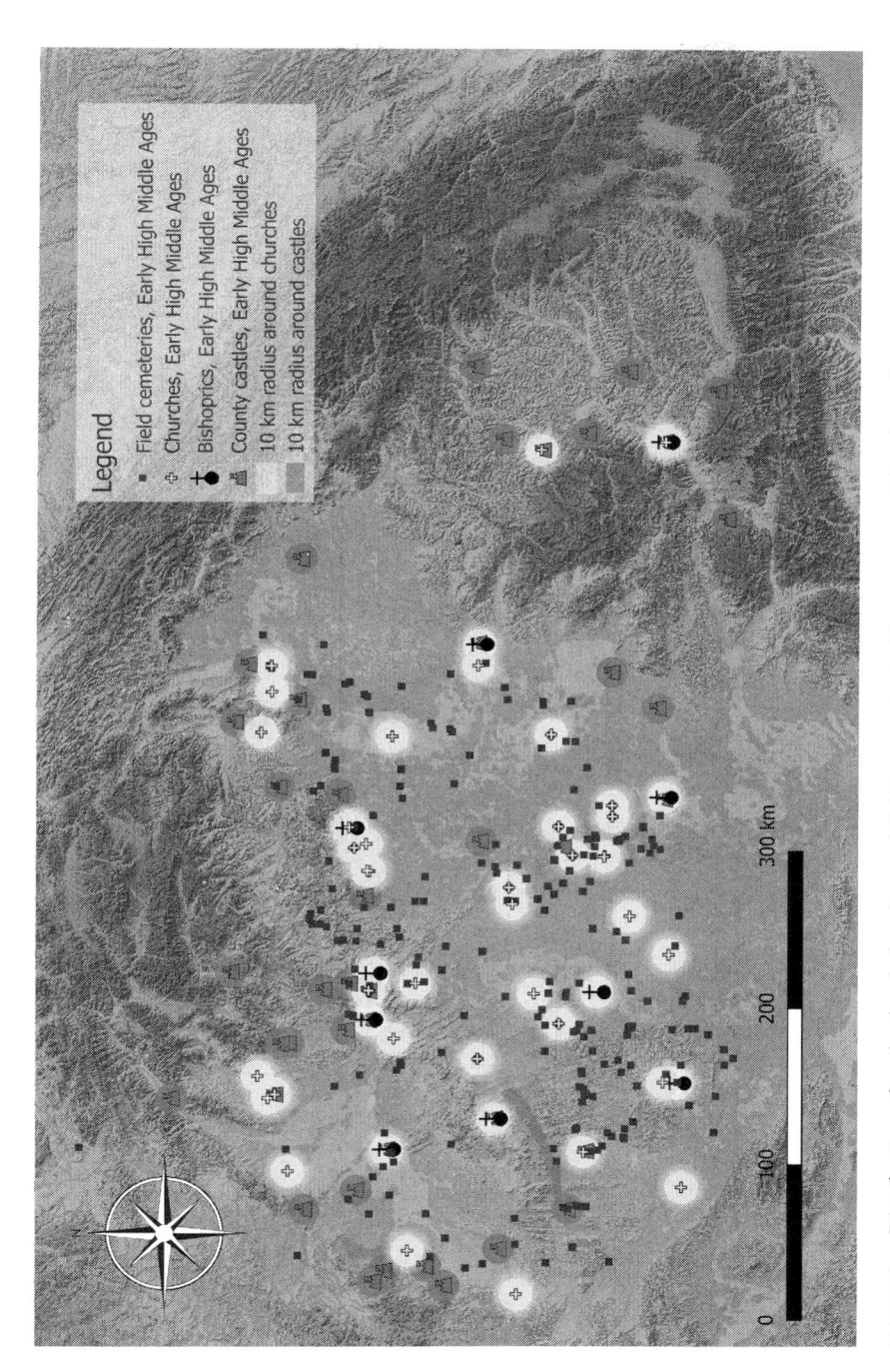

MAP 8.1   Distribution of castles, local churches, and field cemeteries in Hungary around the eleventh century

castles were the bastions of the new religion and probably the starting point for missions and Christianization movements in the countryside. One would have expected a dense appearance of churches around castles and a more scattered pattern with increasing distance, but the picture seems to be just the opposite. The lack of churches in the neighborhoods of castles, and the even density of the spread of churches (and the somewhat denser concentration in the central part of the Carpathian Basin where the absence of castles is the most visible) speaks of a different situation.[40]

The absence of churches and also the lower density of field cemeteries around castles show that the ecclesiastical institutions belonging to them probably had pastoral functions over the castle and its neighborhood. Secondly, the even spread of churches and their slightly higher density in the central part of the kingdom where castles are rare speaks of a well-designed plan for building up political power, and together with it, a state religion on the lowest social level. As was emphasized above, religion was employed to express the new power of the state, and its greatest power lay not in the foundation of bishoprics, but in converting the masses of commoners and creating a system of local churches. Thus, while castles may have been the power centers of secular state power and its representation, the emergence of the local church system – as is indicated in the law code of Stephen – should be regarded as a less visible but equally important complementary part of the development and consolidation of state power.

Notes

1 For an earlier example, see György Györffy, "Die Entstehung der ungarischen Burgorganisation," *Acta Archaeologica Academiae Scientiarum Hungaricae* 28 (1976): 323–358, here 324–326, and the most recent, pointing out the uncertainty of the dating: Maxim Mordovin, *A várszervezet kialakulása a középkori Magyarországon, Csehországban és Lengyelországban a 10–12. században* [The emergence of castle organization in medieval Hungary, Bohemia and Poland in the 10th–11th centuries] (Studia ad Archaeologiam Pazmaniensia, 5) (Budapest: Pázmány Péter Katolikus Egyetem Bölcsészettudományi Kar, Archaeolingua, 2016), 98–99.

2 For an exception, see Maxim Mordovin, "Templomok az ispánsági várakban" [Churches in the early royal centres], in *Népek és kultúrák a Kárpát-medencében. Tanumányok Mesteházy Károly tiszteletére* [Peoples and culture in the Carpathian Basin. Studies in honor of Károly Mesterházy], ed. László Kovács and László Révész (Budapest: Magyar Nemzeti Múzeum, 2016), 777–794.

3 Nora Berend, József Laszlovszky, and Béla Zsolt Szakács, "The Kingdom of Hungary," in *Christianization and the Rise of Christian Monarchy. Scandinavia, Central Europe and Rus' c. 900–1200*, ed. Nora Berend (Cambridge: Cambridge University Press, 2007), 319–368, here 327–330.

4 László Koszta, "State Power and Ecclesiastical System in Eleventh Century Hungary," in *"In My Spirit and Thought I Remained a European of Hungarian Origin." Medieval Historical Studies in Memory of Zoltán J. Kosztolnyik* (Szeged: JATE Press, 2010), 67–78 here 68–71.

5 Berend, Laszlovszky and Szakács, "The Kingdom of Hungary," 351.

6 László Koszta, "Fejezetek a korai magyar egyházszervezet történetéből" [Chapters from the history of the early church organization of Hungary], (DSc-diss., Hungarian Academy of Sciences, 2012).

7 See, for example, the recent synthesizing work of Attila Zsoldos, "Korai vármegyéink az újabb történeti kutatások fényében" [The early Hungarian counties in light of recent historical research], *A Castrum Bene Egyesület Hírlevele* 11, no. 1 (2010): 5–13.

8 József Dénes, "A honfoglalás és államszervezés korának várai" [Castles of the conquest and state organization period], *A Herman Ottó Múzeum Évkönyve* 30–31 (1993): 417–432.

9 István Bóna, *Az Árpádok korai várairól: 11–12. századi várak és határvárak* [On the early castles of the Árpáds: 11th–12th-century castles and borderline forts] (Debrecen: Ethnica Kiadás, 1995).

10 Gergely Buzás, "11. századi ispáni várainkról" [About the 11th-century Hungarian county castles], in *"Gondolják, látják az várnak nagy voltát …" Tanulmányok a 80 éves Nováki Gyula tiszteletére* ['Considering and seeing the greatness of castles.' Studies in honor of Gyula Nováki on his 80th birthday], ed. Gyöngyi Kovács and Zsuzsa Miklós (Budapest: Históriaantik, 2016), 43–53.

11 Katalin Szende, "Az ispánsági vártól a királyi városig. Miért, hogyan – vagy miért nem?" [From the *ispán's* castle to the royal town. Why, how – or why not?], in *Kő kövön. Dávid Ferenc 73. születésnapjára. Stein Auf Stein. Festschrift Für Ferenc Dávid*, I, ed. Klára Mentényi and Anna Simon (Budapest: Vince, 2013), 127–142.

12 Mordovin, *A várszervezet kialakulása*.

13 See, for example, the latest synthesis in English: Koszta, "State Power," 67–78 and the major work in Hungarian: Koszta, "Fejezetek a korai magyar egyházszervezet."

14 For a recent summary on the research on ecclesiastical topography in Hungary, see András K. Németh, "A középkori Magyarország egyházi topográfiai kutatása. Kutatástörténeti áttekintés" [Topographical research conerning the Church in medieval Hungary. A review of the research], in *A középkor és a kora újkor régészete Magyarországon / Archaeology of the Middle Ages and the Early Modern Period in Hungary*, I, ed. Elek Benkő and Gyöngyi Kovács (Budapest: Magyar Tudományos Akadémia Régészeti Intézete, 2010), 271–288.

15 Mordovin, "Templomok az ispánsági várakban," 783–786. See also idem, *A várszervezet kialakulása*, 105–108.

16 *Monumenta Germaniae Historica. Capitularia Regum Francorum*, II, eds. Alfred Boretius and Victor Krause (Hannover: Hahn, 1897) 221–222 (cap. XV): *De sepultura mortuorum. Restat propter instantem, quae tunc maxima occurrit, necessitatem, ubicunque facultas rerum et oportunitas temporum suppetat, sepulturam morientium apud ecclesiam, ubi sedes est episcopi, celebrari. Si autem hoc propter itineris longinquitatem aut difficultatem inpossibile videatur, expectet eum terra sepulturae suae, quo canonicorum aut monachorum sive sanctaemonialium congregatio sancta communiter degat, ut eorum orationibus iudici suo commendatus occurrat et remissionem delictorum, quam meritis non obtinet, illorum intercessionibus percipiat. Quodsi et hoc ineptum et difficile estimetur, ubi decimam persolvebat vivus, sepeliatur mortuus.*

17 *Burchardi Vormatiensis episcopi opera omnia [Decretorum Liber]* in *Patrologia Latina*, CXL, ed. Jacques-Paul Migne (Paris: Apud J.-P. Migne editorem, 1853), 676 (cap. XIII–XIV): *ecclesiam ubi paganus est, non liceat consecrare, neque Missas in ea celebrare … In ecclesia in qua cadavera mortuorum sepeliuntur, sanctificare altare non liceat. Si autem consecratum prius fuit, Missas licet celebrare in ea.*

18 Quoted from Elisabeth Zadora-Rio, "The Making of Churchyards and Parish Territories in the Early-Medieval Landscape of France and England in the 7th–12th Centuries: A Reconsideration," *Medieval Archaeology* 47 (2003): 1–19, here 13.

19 Szabolcs Anzelm Szuromi, *A temetésre vonatkozó egyházfegyelem a XII–XIII. században* [Canon law concerning burials during the 12th and 13th centuries] (Budapest: Szent István Társulat, 2002), 43–48.

20 John Eldevik, "Ecclesiastical Lordship and the Politics of Submitting Tithes in Medieval Germany. The Thuringian Dispute in Social Context," *Viator* 34 (2003): 40–56, here 45–46.

21 Mordovin, *A várszervezet kialakulása*, 117.

22 Mordovin, "Templomok az ispánsági várakban," 784.

23 *Decreta Regni Mediaevalis Hungariae. The Laws of the Medieval Kingdom of Hungary 1000–1301*, trans. and ed. János M. Bak, György Bónis, and James Ross Sweeney (2nd ed. Idyllwild, CA: Charles Schlacks, 1999), Decreta S. Stephani Regis, Liber Secundus, cap. 1.

24 Mordovin, *A várszervezet kialakulása*, 114–115.

25 Ibid., 107.

26 Mordovin, "Templomok az ispánsági várakban," 781.

27 ... *episcopus egredetur cum fratribus suis suam visitare dyocesim ut consecraret eorum cymiteria, qui erant ecclesias constructi* – *Legenda Sancti Gerhardi episcopii*, ed. Emericus Madzsar in *Scriptores rerum Hungaricarum*, II, ed. Emericus Szentpétery (Budapest: Academia litter. Hungarica, 1938), 461–506, here 495. See also József Laszlovszky, "Social Stratification and Material Culture in 10th–14th Century Hungary," in *Alltag und materielle Kultur im mittelalterlichen Ungarn*, ed. József Laszlovszky and András Kubinyi (Krems: Medium Aevum Quotidianum, 1991), 32–67, here 41.

28 Levente Závodszky, *A Szent István, Szent László és Kálmán korabeli törvények és zsinati határozatok forrásai* [The law codes and synods in the age of Saint Stephen, Saint Ladislas and Coloman] (Budapest: Szent István Társulat, 1904), 157.

29 Zsoldos, "Korai vármegyéink," 5–6.

30 Ibid., 8.

31 Mordovin, *A várszervezet kialakulása*, 191–192.

32 Ibid., 265–266.

33 http://archeodatabase.hnm.hu/ (last accessed: 11 June 2017)

34 https://dennikn.sk/160769/kostoly-slovenska-mapa-fotky/ (last accessed: 1 June 2017)

35 Erwin Gáll, "Krisztianizáció és régészet. Az Erdélyi-medencei 11–13. századi templomkörüli temetők kutatásának stádiuma" [Christianization and archaeology. The state of research of the 11th-13th century churchyard cemeteries in the Transylvanian Basin], in *Hadak útján XX. Népvándorláskor Fiatal Kutatóinak XX. Összejövetelének konferenciakötete* [On the path of armies, XX. XXth Assembly of Young Scholars on the Migration Period] (Budapest: Magyar Nemzeti Múzeum, 2012), 287–312, and Erwin Gáll, *Az Erdélyi-medence, a Partium és a Bánság 10–11. századi temetői* [10th and 11th-century burial sites, stray finds and treasures in the Transylvanian Basin, the Partium and the Banat] (Szeged; Budapest, 2013).

36 Géza Entz, *Erdély építészete a 11–13. században* [The architecture of Transylvania in the 11th to 13th centuries] (Kolozsvár: Erdélyi Múzeum-Egyesület, 1994).

37 János Gyurkó, *Árpád-kori templomok a Kárpát-medencében* [Árpádian-period churches in the Carpathian Basin] (Érd: Érdi Környezetvédő Egyesület, 2006). I would like to thank Gergely Buzás for providing me with this rare volume.

38 The surface survey method makes it rather hard, sometimes impossible, to differentiate between field cemeteries and churchyard cemeteries. If a church was constructed from a solid material (stone or brick), then it is easier to recognize in the field. Since the database

of recorded archaeological sites does not distinguish between field and churchyard cemeteries, neither will this present study.

39 Mordovin, *A várszervezet kialakulása*, 188.

40 Here it has to be noted that the somewhat denser appearance of churches between the Danube and Tisza rivers might also be the consequence of more intensive research activity in that area.

PART THREE

Trade Relations of East Central Europe in the Age of State Formation

9

THE LOGIC OF TRIBUTE VERSUS THE LOGIC OF COMMERCE

Why Did Dirhams Reach East Central Europe during the Tenth Century?

Dariusz Adamczyk

Ninth-century dirham networks generally encompassed the Russian interior and the Baltic Sea area. During the tenth century, however, a remarkable extension of commerce took place into the eastern parts of the Central European interior (Eastern, Central and Southern Poland, Hungary, and Bohemia). Arab sources, archaeological evidence, and numerous hoards with coins and fragmented silver emphasize the importance and intensity of social and economic contacts. Up to now almost 400,000 dirhams are known from several hundred hoards found in Russia, Ukraine, Belarus, Sweden, Poland, Denmark, the Baltic countries, Germany, and even the British Isles – most of them amassed during the tenth century.[1] The estimated amount of Arab silver may have fluctuated between about 125 and 250 million coins – most of them struck during the first half of the tenth century.[2] This context raises several questions: under what circumstances did such large quantities of dirhams reach the interior of East Central Europe? What historical processes led the Arab silver to be redistributed in these areas? And, why and by whom were these dirhams transferred and used: by merchants and craftsmen or by chieftains and their warriors? In other words, did the commercial or tributary logic stand behind the redistribution and circulation of silver? Or was there an intersection of these practices?

This paper comprises four main sections. The first sketch is the trade networks of Western Eurasia that developed from c. 900 onward. The following part deals with the rise of the Kievan Rus' from the perspective of their expansion along the Pripyat-Western Bug route in the early tenth century. The next section presents the extension of long-distance trade to Central and Southern Poland by the Piast networks in the mid-tenth century. Finally, the silver hoards along the Southern Bug, Dniester, and Tisza from the 920s/950s will be discussed in the context of Magyars' connections with the Kievan Rus' and the Volga Bulgars in the East and Bohemia in the West.

The cross-continental trade networks of Western Eurasia

Over the course of the ninth century, Arab silver was redistributed, generally speaking, by only a few networks. Networks of the Rus' and Khazars can be distinguished in the Russian interior; the Khazars acted as a key intermediary in the long-distance trade between the Arab world and the "barbarians". This situation changed significantly during the tenth century as several new networks developed (see Map 9.1). In this paper the silver redistribution networks are conceived of as an analytical category. There are three steps to reconstructing them: first, to locate the hoards and to find out the chronological and geographical structure of coins in them; second, to put the geography of the hoards into an archaeological context; third, to put the hoards into the context of written sources. The geography of hoards in the "barbarian" parts of Eastern Europe from the Early Middle Ages, their regional and chronological structure, and records of single finds, together with their archaeological contexts and an analysis of written sources allow one to define the network of redistribution:[3]

a) The networks had their own logic of transfer and structures of redistribution;
b) They were based on personal connections among merchants, ruling elites, clans, tribes, and mobile craftsmen and could equally have encompassed tribute, rent, and extortion as well as gifts or other, uncertain, forms of transfer more than on regular, anonymous relationships regulated by the economic mechanism of supply and demand. The only exceptions seem to have been cross-continental trade markets like the Bulgar or Atil, where Muslim merchants encountered "barbarian" people and exchanged silver for slaves and furs – here a commercial logic may have prevailed;
c) The redistribution networks could have expired with a generation or stretched over several generations with some possible changes in the logic of redistribution;
d) Within a network, precious metal could have had different functions: a means of payment for market transactions, rent, tribute or taxes, serving to remunerate a retinue and political clientele or to generally establish relationships within a society. Precious metal could also have been used to produce jewelry, bars, ingots, or coins or served as an object of prestige, cult, or magic.

Most dirhams flowed to Europe in the tenth century due to the strong political position of the Samanid dynasty in Central Asia and the Middle East. They controlled all the important silver mines in Western Eurasia – among others those of Panjhir in the Hindu Kush – and supported trade, above all the slave trade, with urban centers.[4] Besides slaves, Arab merchants imported attractive furs of beaver, black fox, sable, ermine, and others, which served as prestige goods. In the Middle East, slaves from Eastern Europe, mostly female, were used in households, frequently for prostitution. In contrast to the Middle East and Central Asia, in al-Andalus (Arabic Spain) several thousand slaves from Eastern Europe lived – especially under

Caliph Abd al-Rahman III (912–961) – in the palace-city of Madinat al-Zahra as domestic servants and members of the top echelons of the administration and guard.[5] Therefore, the demand for mainly slaves and furs in the Islamic world was the prime mover for commercial contacts with the "barbarians". But how were these relations established?

By the late eighth and early ninth century the Khazars, in reaction to the rising demand for furs and other forest products in the caliphate – above all Baghdad, which became the capital of the Abbasid Empire and evolved into a significant commercial and cultural center for the Islamic world – moved to the north and shifted the focus of their empire, the so-called Khaganate, from Northern Caucasia into the forest-steppe zone in present-day Ukraine and southern Russia.[6] In the basins of the Don, Donets, and Oskol rivers the Khazars and their allies created an elaborate system of forts and settlements which protected trade routes, served as stations for caravans, and formed strongholds for collecting tribute from the Slavic and Finno-Ugric tribes inhabiting the forest-steppe and forest zone. Generally, two settlement clusters can be distinguished: one in the core steppe lands of Khazaria along the lower Don; and another on the northern periphery of the khaganate along the Middle Don, Oskol, and Upper Donets.[7] The importance of the Khazar networks decreased significantly from the 880s/890s onward, however. Political shifts in the steppe zone such as the appearance of the Pechenegs, the expansion of the Rus' bands in the Dnepr and Desna Basins, and a new trade axis established between the Samanids and the Volga Bulgars changed the context of the commercial relationships in Western Eurasia. Archaeologically, the dissolution of the Saltov-Maiatskoe culture is reflected in the fate of some fortresses along the Don, Oskol, and Donets. Inhabited by Iranian-speaking Alans and Turkic-speaking Bulgars, who on "behalf" of the Khazars controlled the passing traffic, the stone forts of Dmitrievskoe and Maiatskoe seem to have been abandoned. In addition, several fortresses and settlements in the Donets Basin were destroyed.[8]

Despite the great loss caused by these shifts, some dirhams still flowed to the Slavic and Finno-Ugric interior through Khazaria along the Don, Donets, and Oskol rivers. At least the Vyatihs living along the upper Oka are said to have paid tribute to the Khazars by 964 in the form of a shilling per plowshare.[9] Additionally, strong evidence for caravan trade along the Don is revealed in camel bones found in two Slavic fortified settlements immediately to the north of the Maiatskoe fort, Titchikha and Bol'shoie Borshevo, both dating from the eighth to tenth century. Two small hoards have been unearthed in their vicinity: 106 coins (*terminus post quem* 927/928) in Maloe Borshevo and 22 dirhams (922/923) in Titchikha. In addition, a large hoard of 1092 dirhams has been recovered (Bezliudovka 935/936), approximately 125 kilometers east of the Titchikha and Bol'shoie Borshevo settlements in the upper Oskol Basin, where the important stone fortress of Dmitrievskoe stood in the ninth century. The finds of Maloe Borshevo and Bezliudovka are 88% to 90% imitation dirhams issued in Khazaria or Volga Bulgaria.[10]

The burial ground of Verkhne Saltovo along the upper Donets yielded finds of coins and silk. In approximately 1000 burials archaeologists found more than 150 dirhams and pieces of silk.[11] According to Roman K. Kovalev it is quite possible "that the burial complex along the upper Donets belonged to people who were situated on a major caravan route and were responsible for the collection of tolls in the form of silks and coins from the passing traffic."[12] As archaeologists have not yet analyzed all the graves and dirhams, it is not yet possible to say to what extent this statement applies to the tenth century.

Khazar, Jewish, and Arab merchant caravans brought dirhams to the Slavic or Finno-Ugric tribes and exchanged them for squirrel, beaver, marten, and fox furs. Beaver, marten, and fox skeletons have been recovered in several early medieval Slavic and Finno-Ugric settlements.[13] The inhabitants of the forest-steppe and forest-zone may have collected some of the dirhams to pay tribute. Thus, commercial logic intersected with the political-hierarchical logic. The chronology of dirham finds and information from the Russian Primary Chronicle show clearly that the Khazars still used the caravan route along the Don and Donets rivers in the tenth century to trade with Slavic and certainly Finno-Ugric tribes and collect tribute in the form of silver from them. Nonetheless, the wars between a strong alliance of Byzantium, the Pechenegs, Burtas, Ghuzz, and Black Bulgars and the Khazars during the reign of the Khagan Benjamin in the 880s/890s destabilized the Khazar trading networks in the steppe zone and made commerce more difficult.[14] As a consequence, new opportunities opened for the Volga Bulgars. Thomas S. Noonan comments on the situation around 900 as follows:

> Khwarazmian merchants were well aware of the disruption in the export of silver to European Russia via Khazaria and the pent-up demand that existed there. Khwarazm had very close military and economic ties with Khazaria and its merchants must have been aware for some time that the influx of dirhams into the Khaganate had been on the decline since ca. 880. Consequently, once Khwarazm was incorporated into the Samanid lands, its merchants convinced the Samanid rulers that they had to strike large quantities of dirhams to be exported to northern Russia. For their part, the Transoxiana and Khurasan worked out the infrastructure of this trade, i.e., the mechanics of moving large quantities of dirhams by caravan through an often hostile steppe to Volga Bulgaria where they were sold to Rus' and other traders … This, in brief, is how the great trade between the Samanids and Volga Bulgaria began around the year 900.[15]

There is strong evidence for this trade. First of all, there is Ibn Fadlan's account that shows clearly that large caravans traveled regularly from Khwarazm to Volga Bulgaria,[16] some of them consisting of 3000 pack animals and 5000 men. If one assumes that every merchant brought no less than 100 dirhams into Bulgaria, that would be half a million dirhams per year. Secondly, numismatic research in recent years has identified at least two basic stages in the development of Volga Bulgar money. The first occurred when the Bulgars imitated the dirhams struck by the

Samanids in Central Asia in the first half of the century. During the second stage, from the 950s onward, they issued their own coins.[17]

Additionally, their location near the confluence of the Volga and Kama rivers facilitated commercial ties with merchants coming from several other regions. The Bulgars created their own networks: 1) along the Kama and its tributaries, which linked them with the inhabitants of the entire Kama-Urals region; 2) along the upper Volga to connect with the networks of the Baltic Rus', which reached the upper Dnepr and northwestern Russia and from there the Baltic; and 3) the Oka, a tributary of the middle Volga, allowed connections to the networks of the Khazars in the Don, Donets, and Seim Basins as well as with the Kievan Rus' in the middle Dnepr.

The rise of the Kievan Rus' and the Pripyat-Western Bug route in the early tenth century

Trying to explain why dirhams flowed into Eastern Poland during the tenth century, one should first consider the political economy of the early Kievan Rus'. Johan Callmer, some years ago, clearly showed that Kiev underwent fundamental changes in the last decade of the ninth and the first half of the tenth century. Several dispersed agrarian settlements evolved into a significant political and economic center.[18] According to Callmer, the population was mixed, comprising various local and exogenous elements including elite Scandinavians. The explosive growth of this settlement and its dependence on goods from tributary tribes both as food for the population and as equivalents for long-distance trade are characteristics they had in common with the forts of the Saltov-Maiatskoe culture mentioned above.[19] Numismatic evidence as well as the Russian Primary Chronicle confirms the archaeological record. In the 900s at Kievan sites two dirham hoards have been recovered with the *terminus post quem* in 905/906 and 906/907.[20] The first one contained 2930 dirhams and six gold arm-rings, the other one 529 coins. The gold rings provide a good parallel to the collection of Peenemünde, West Pomerania, and are also well known from Gotland. According to Władysław Duczko:

> The rings were characteristic items of the elite culture of Viking-age Scandinavia, provided with a whole ideology that concerned both social hierarchy as well as religious manifestations. Gold arm-rings were objects of double value, an economic one because of the high price of this metal, and an even greater symbolic value. Norse rulers were called in skaldic poetry 'the dividers of rings,' the gold ring was a gift not only for a skald but for a retainer or other person worthy of it; the rings were connected with the gods and it was customary to sacrifice rings, either by depositing them in the soil, or by throwing them into rivers or lakes.[21]

In addition, for the years 882–885 the Russian Primary Chronicle records that Oleg, a Rus' chieftain from Northern Russia, conquered Kiev and imposed tribute

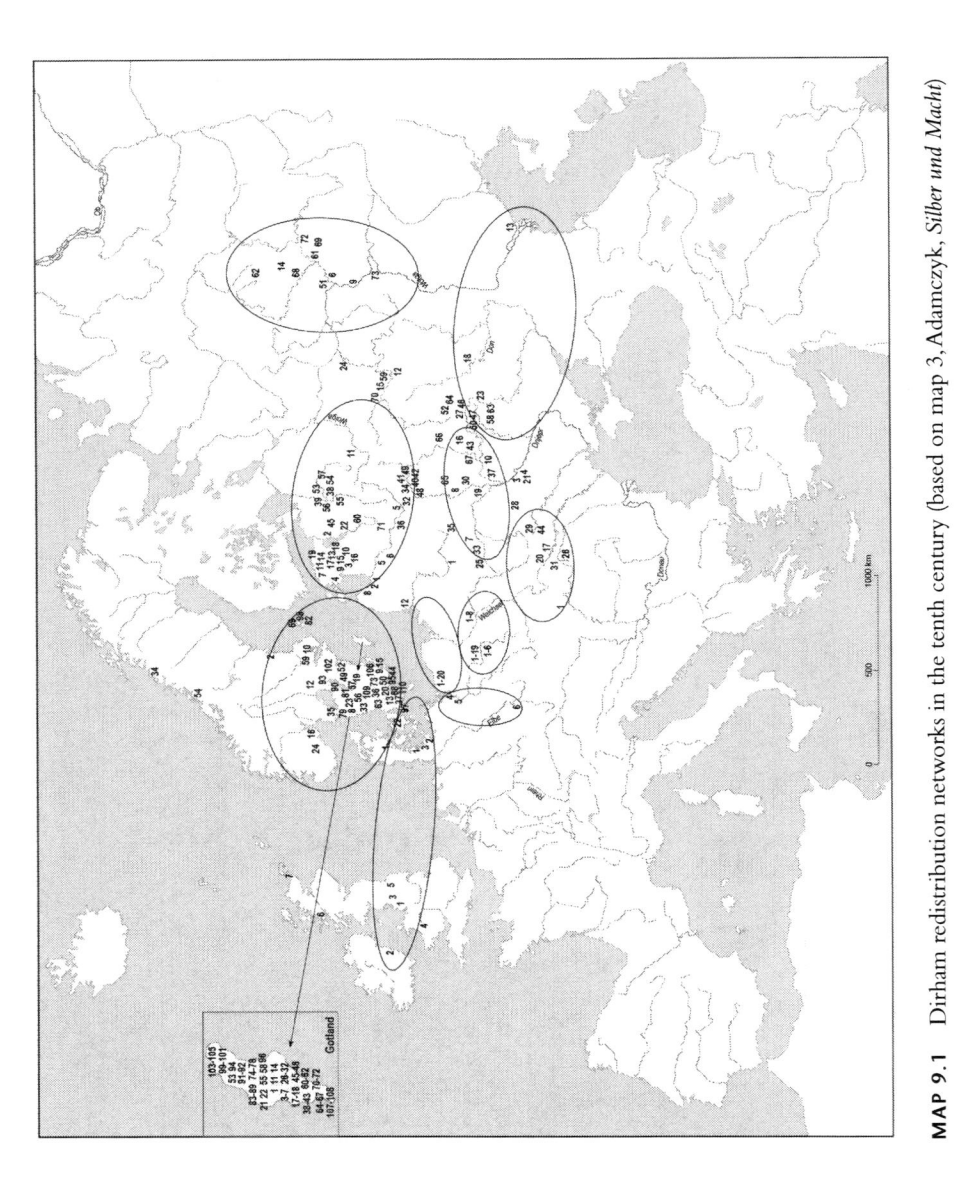

MAP 9.1 Dirham redistribution networks in the tenth century (based on map 3, Adamczyk, *Silber und Macht*)

on various East Slavic tribes inhabiting the left bank as well as the right bank in the Dnepr Basin. The Severians and Radimichs, who lived along the Desna, Seim, Psiol, Sula, and Vorskla or along the Sosh, are said to have paid tribute to the Khazars – among other types in the form of *shillings*, silver coins.[22] Interestingly, the two hoards from Kiev mentioned above differ significantly from each other. The larger find of 2930 dirhams contained only about 11% new Samanid coins and about 85% Abbasid dirhams, which were used most often by the inhabitants of the left bank of the Dnepr in the ninth century. No dirham hoards are known from Kiev from before 900. In contrast, the smaller hoard comprised approximately 70% new dirhams. This may indicate that the old Abbasid coins were being collected as tribute by the Rus', who had just appeared in the middle Dnepr Basin around 900.

According to the Russian Primary Chronicle for the year 883, the Rus' also imposed tribute on tribes occupying the right bank of the Dnepr. The Drevlyans, who lived along the Pripyat River, were forced to pay *po cerne kune*, a black marten skin.[23] Thus, the Chronicle clearly shows that around 900 the Rus' were penetrating the middle Dnepr Basin. Such *poliudia*, tribute collecting expeditions, probably also brought the chance to trade with subject clans for furs, which were not normally part of the tribute, and also for wax, honey, and slaves – as the Khazars already did during the ninth century. In this context, we have to look for an explanation as to why dirhams flowed into Eastern Poland during the tenth century.

More than 700 kilometers west of Kiev, along the middle Bug, a small cluster of early tenth century dirham hoards were secreted (see Map 9.2 marked with pentagons).

The largest, the hoard from Klukowicze with the *terminus post quem* of 901/902, contained about 1508 coins, among them 943 well-known dirhams and about 565 unknown coins. Approximately 100 kilometers west, in the vicinity of Liw, another find of 502 dirhams was discovered (also dating ca. 900/901), and 130 kilometers northwest of Klukowicze, at Góra Strękowa, a hoard of 33 dirhams and silver jewelry (dating to 900) has been recovered. Furthermore, an older hoard from Drohiczyn (dating ca. 893) and several smaller finds (less than ten coins and an unknown *terminus post quem*) have been noted in the region (at Grajewo-Prostki, dating to 906/907; at Pluty, dating to 910/911; and at Czaple Obrępalskie, dating to ca. 900).[24] Moreover, at the hill fort of Trzcianka, about 90 kilometers northeast of Góra Strękowa, a few single dirhams have been recovered from excavations.[25] It is striking that the hoards of Klukowicze and Liw especially show a similar structure because they included a very high percentage of non-fragmented Samanid dirhams struck shortly after 890 (80% to 90%; about 75% at Góra Strękowa). The hoard of Klukowicze also contained about 15% dirham imitations that were issued in Volga Bulgaria and perhaps Khazaria. In addition, two coins bore Scandinavian runes.[26] The chronology and structure of these early dirham hoards suggest that they can be traced back to a sole expedition of the Kievan Rus', who, after collecting tribute from the people living along the Pripyat, moved to the Western Bug Basin in search of new furs and slaves.

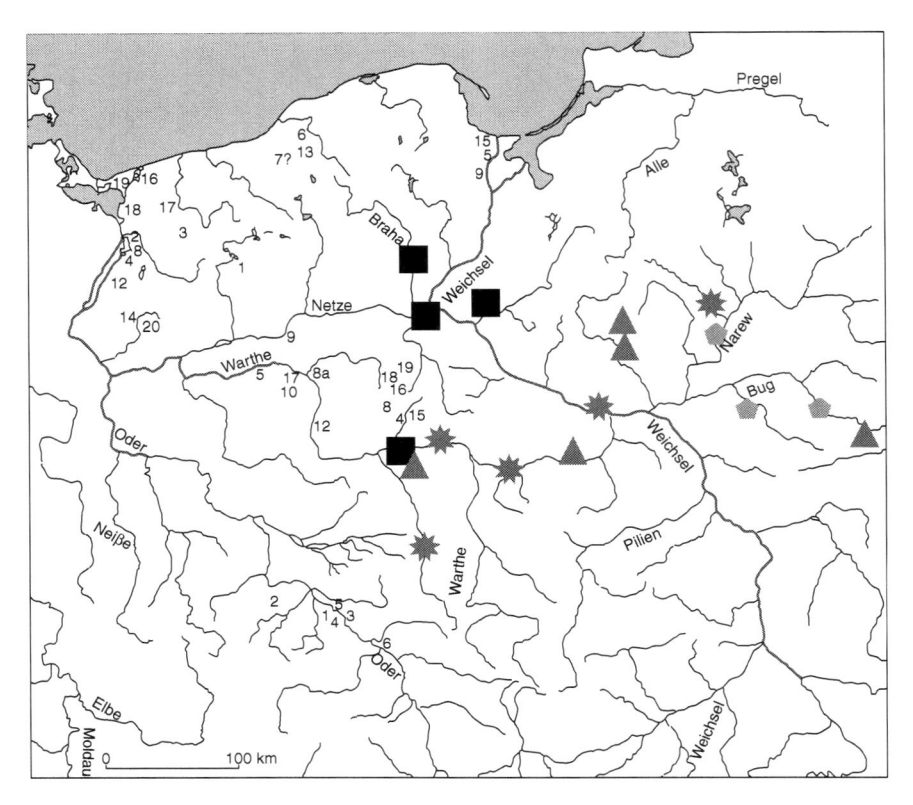

MAP 9.2 Hoards of at least 10 dirhams from Masovia and the neighboring regions (900s – pentagons; 930s/940s – stars; 950s – squares; 970s – triangles) (based on map 6, Adamczyk, *Silber und Macht*)

The extent to which these Rus' traders/warriors/robbers cooperated with local clans is unknown. Interestingly, all three hoards have been found in the vicinity of either settlements or hill-forts. Besides the settlement enclave established by around 900 along the Liwiec River, the left tributary of the Bug, some archaeologists connect the population with groups from east of the Western Bug,[27] where Slavic migrants to the Pripyat region settled, perhaps because they sought refuge from Rus' tribute-collecting expeditions. In the western part of Masovia at the same time, however, a range of strongholds emerged and disappeared after just a generation.[28] In the opinion of Marek Jankowiak, the rise of these well-fortified hill forts can be explained by raids of Scandinavian slave hunters in this area.[29] Nevertheless, the prospect of cooperation with local chieftains who were able to supply them with furs and slaves whenever they came seems to have attracted the Rus' to the Western Bug region.

The Russian Primary Chronicle illustrates how such raids may have looked. In the context of a Rus' attack on Iskorosten', the "capital" of the Drevlyan tribe that lived along the Pripyat, the Chronicle reports for 945:

Igor heeded their words [of his retinue] and he attacked Dereva in search of tribute. He sought to increase the previous tribute and collected it by violence from people with the assistance of his followers.[30]

One year later, after Igor had been killed by the Drevlyans, the Chronicle continues:

Thus she [Olga of Kiev] took the city [Iskorosten] and burned it, and captured the elders of the city. Some of the other captives she killed, while she gave others as slaves to her followers. The remnant she left to pay tribute. She imposed upon them a heavy tribute.[31]

It is striking to see that imposing and collecting tribute could have been accompanied by enormous exploitation and use of violence and may have evolved into mere robbery expeditions. At the same time, such raids brought with them the chance to trade with subject tribes and clans or with people living further west.

The Piast networks in central and southern Poland in the mid-tenth century

The next "waves" of the influx of silver into Masovia show a different geographical and structural pattern than in the early tenth century (see Map 9.2). From the 930s/940s onward dirhams reached the middle Vistula and the regions west of it, primarily Greater Poland. The analysis of several hoards from Greater Poland stresses that early dirhams flowed there, at least partly, from the East (and not via Pomerania).[32] In Greater Poland, archaeologists have excavated a range of strongholds dating to the 920s/930s that differ significantly from the older hillforts in this area. Six central strongholds are known, situated in a kind of square approximately 50 x 50 kilometers (Poznań, Gniezno, Ostrów Lednicki, Giecz, Grzybowo, Moraczewo).[33] The most hoards were discovered in their vicinity, several inside the square (Grzybowo-Rabieżyce, dating to c. 952/953 and Ostrów Lednicki, dating to ca. 985).[34] Moreover, scale balances are also known from the stronghold of Giecz, and at the burial ground of Sowinki (near Poznań) archaeologists discovered a scale with a balance set. Further, finds of scale balances come from Dziekanowice near Łubowo, where some graves that indicate Scandinavian or the Rus' presence have been excavated.[35] Several hoards from the core area of Piast power are really huge and contain mostly fragmented silver (Poznań, dating c. 961/976; Zalesie, dating c. 976; Dzierżnica II, dating c. 980/981; and Kąpiel, dating c. 983).[36] The find from Dzierżnica II includes at least nearly 21,000 fragmented dirhams and the silver weighs 15 kilograms – the equivalent of 50 female slaves. The hoard of Kąpiel consists of almost 2500 fragmented coins and jewelry of Scandinavian origin.[37] A similar pattern appears in some finds from Masovia. The hoard of Ciechanów III (nearly 100 kilometers north of Warsaw) is impressive, with the *terminus post quem* coin dating to around 975 (see Map 9.2). It contained 56 whole and 3824 fragmented dirhams, 92 German deniers, among which are seven so-called cross-deniers, and three fragmented Danish coins. Including jewelry of Rus' provenience (for example, earrings of the Borszczewka and Wołyń types), the hoard weighs about 1554 grams.[38] There is no doubt about the owner of this silver – whoever the person was, he or she must have belonged to the local elite.

But how did Arab silver reach Greater Poland? Was it only the Kievan Rus' and traders from Masovia cooperating with them or even Jewish and Khwarezm merchants? Not everything is known, but some information is provided by a Jewish merchant, Ibrahim ibn Yaqub from al-Andalus (Arabic Spain), around 965:

> [Mieszko] levies tribute in the form of *al-mathaqil al-marqatiyya* which he uses to pay his retinue; every month each of them [his followers] gets a certain sum of them. He has 3000 warriors, of every hundred of them as worth as a thousand others.[39]

The term *al-mathaqil* means a monetary unit equal to the *dinar*, a gold coin.[40] Thus, there is no doubt that Mieszko of the Piast dynasty paid his retinue in the form of *Hacksilber*, pieces of coins and jewelry which were weighed. As mentioned above, many of the hoards in Greater Poland (and the one from Ciechanów) contained fragmented dirhams, and balance scales have also been found there. Thus, Ibrahim ibn Yaqub al-Tartushi clearly shows that the Piast duke, Mieszko I, firstly, imposed tributes on undefined tribes, probably in neighboring regions, in the form of fragmented and weighed silver, and secondly, he paid his retinue in the form of these silver pieces. If some of these tributes Mieszko I or his ancestors collected in Masovia occur in hoards, it indicates clearly that the inhabitants of Eastern Poland were part of the Piast dirham circulation networks. German and Danish coins from the hoard of Ciechanów III, however, suggest that the redistribution mechanisms were more complicated and silver did not flow only from east to west.

Moreover, the Piast elite may have obtained dirhams and deniers by selling slaves and furs to Jewish, Rus', and Scandinavian traders. Archaeological excavations on the southwestern periphery of Greater Poland show that in the mid-tenth century several local hill forts were burnt down, probably by the neighboring Piast who had sold their inhabitants, presumably for silver.[41]

Furthermore, the chronology of several silver hoards from Lower Silesia indicates that some dirhams flowed there through the Piast redistribution networks.[42] The hoards of Kotowice II (c. 985) and Śląsk VII (c. 942/954–1019/1020) included, among German, Danish, and Bohemian deniers and jewelry, 570 and 1797 mostly fragmented dirhams, respectively.[43] Perhaps the Piasts tried to use silver as a bribe to get the local elites to cooperate – especially in the 980s when Mieszko I was about to usurp Silesia. Generally, precious metals may have been a universal medium of influence and a significant mechanism to regulate the social relationships between the "state" elites and various local clans or tribes.

Therefore, in the view of political economy, the early Piast state was nothing other than a hierarchical network of redistribution of silver and luxury goods acquired by violence or threat of force and long-distance trade. Tributary logic intersected with commercial logic. This seems to have been a constant in Viking Age Eastern and East Central Europe.

"One Generation" silver hoards in the Southern Bug, Dniester, and Tisza Basins: Magyar connections in the 920s to 950s?

As noted above, during the tenth century a significant extension of cross-continental long-distance trade occurred. One of the new dirham hoard clusters emerged in western Ukraine, in the upper Southern Bug, Dniester, and Tisza basins (see Map 9.3).

From this region at least six hoards are known. Two of them were located in the vicinity of Vinnitsa, about 270 kilometers west of Kiev: the hoards of Rajgorodok (941), 50 dirhams and jewelry, and Kopievka (955/956), 498 coins and also jewelry. About 350 kilometers west of Vinnitsa, in the upper Dniester Basin, several other hoards have been found: near Ivano-Frankovsk Nišnev (925/926) and Grabovec (919/944) of approximately 100 and 30 dirhams, and near Halytsch the huge hoard of Krylos containing 1110 dirhams and jewelry. The *terminus post quem*-coin in this case dated to 935/936. Furthermore, almost 200 kilometers west of Halytsch, in the upper Tisza Basin on the border between Ukraine and Hungary, another hoard was discovered. The find of Chust (Maramureş) comprised 371 dirhams, about 34% of them imitations issued in Volga Bulgaria and perhaps Khazaria, of which the youngest coin was struck in 934/935–941.[44] All the hoards between the 920s and the 950s cover the time span of one generation. Moreover, in Przemyśl, 200 kilometers northwest of the small dirham cluster along the upper Dniester, a hoard of 700 dirhams was recovered – unfortunately only dated generally to the tenth century.[45] How can we explain the appearance of these hoards from the 920s to the 950s?

Archaeological evidence indicates a Magyar presence in the first half of the tenth century at the sites of Krylos, Przemyśl, and Sudova Vyschnia (almost 50 kilometers east of Przemyśl), where burial grounds with human remains of warriors, women, and infants have been excavated.[46] It seems as if dirham hoards in the Southern Bug, Dniester, and Tisza basins belonged to Magyar migrants, who may have moved west from Kievan Rus' areas. According to the Russian Primary Chronicle under 898, the Magyars passed the settlement, and some items from Kiev's graves suggest Hungarian origins.[47] Interestingly, the archaeological record from Subboticy in the lower Dnepr Basin corresponds clearly with the tenth-century finds from the Carpathian Basin as well as with burial grounds from Bashkiria east of Volga Bulgaria. In addition, strong parallels to early Hungarian finds appear in the so-called Karaiakupovo culture located in the Samara region – just ca. 350 kilometers south of Volga Bulgaria in the Middle/Upper Volga Basin.[48] Also, Muslims from Volga Bulgar probably settled in the Carpathian Basin in the second half of the tenth century.[49] Consequently, the silver coins and jewelry of the Southern Bug, Dniester, and Tisza basins can be interpreted as a byproduct of Magyar "transit" networks spreading from the middle Volga through Kievan Rus' to Hungary.

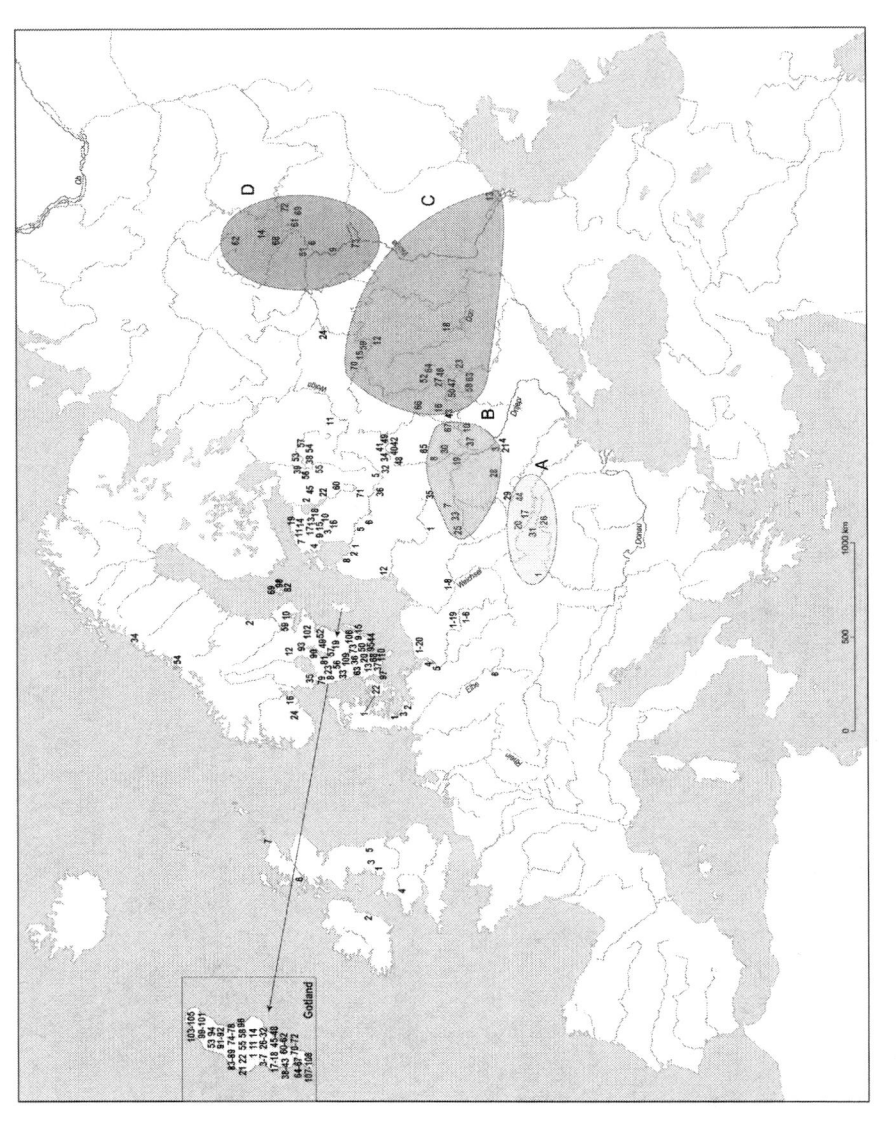

MAP 9.3 Dirham hoard clusters in the tenth century (A – Magyars; D – Volga Bulgaria; C – Khazars; B – Kievan Rus') (based on map 3, Adamczyk, *Silber und Macht*)

But what about the numismatic evidence from the Carpathian Basin? Just one hoard containing ten dirhams with the *terminus post quem* in 918/919 is known to me. It was discovered at the burial ground of Sárospatak-Baksahomok I, around 160 kilometers west of the Chust hoard.[50] Silver ornaments and cowry shells from the Indian Ocean have been found in Hungary. Byzantine, French, Italian, and German deniers have also been noted – they were probably brought by the Magyars from their raids into Western and Southern Europe.[51] Coins may have been melted down and used to make jewelry, which would explain why no or only few hoards have been found in Hungary for this period.

There is strong evidence for the circulation of Arab silver. Ibrahim ibn Yaqub's account from the 960s emphasizes that Muslim and Jewish merchants traveled from Hungary to Prague with *al-mathaqil al- marqatiyya* – probably silver pieces:[52]

> The Rus' and the Saqaliba [Slavs] go there [Prague] from Karaku [Cracow] with commodities, while from the country of the Turks [Magyars] and of the Muslims come to them Jews and Turks with commodities and *mathaqil al-marqatiyya* and carry away slaves, tin, and various kinds of wool.[53]

This report indicates two trade routes on the southern east-west axis: the first through Hungary and the second through Lesser Poland. As noted above, 200 kilometers northwest of the small dirham cluster along the upper Dniester a hoard of 700 dirhams has been found in Przemyśl and some Magyar presence inferred. About 200 kilometers west of Przemyśl and 80 kilometers east of Cracow, at the early medieval stronghold of Zawada Lanckorońska, a hoard of 49 glass beads and 30 silver beads or ear-rings has been recovered. These beads and earrings are of the Gnesdovo, Trnovec, and Břeclav-Pohansko types, among others, and reflect interactions or cultural influence among societies from the upper Dnepr (Gnesdovo) to Slovakia and Moravia.[54] The hoard of Zawada Lanckorońska may have dated to the first half of the tenth century.[55] Mieszko I is said to have given the infant emperor Otto III a camel as a gift in 986.[56] Because it is unlikely that camels were used by traders in the thick forests and swamps of the Pripyat route, one can assume the use of the more southern caravan road: Przemyśl–Zawada Lanckorońska–Cracow. Then, from Prague merchants went further west to Bavaria, France, and al-Andalus or northwest to the Elbe region. The hoard of at least 272 coins and jewelry unearthed in Meschwitz ca. 80 kilometers east of Meissen and dated to the 960s/970s may illustrate these connections.[57]

Conclusions

I have tried to respond to the question of why dirhams flowed to the East Central European interior during the tenth century. First, I examined the cross-continental long-distance trade networks of Western Eurasia around 900; second, the rise of Kievan Rus' and its expansion along the Pripyat River in the early tenth century; third, the emergence of Piast networks in the mid-tenth century; and finally, the context of silver hoards from the 920s to the 950s in the Southern Bug, Dniester, and Tisza basins.

First, around 900 the cross-continental long-distance trade in Western Eurasia underwent a fundamental change. Driven by demand, foremost for slaves and furs, the Samanids, who controlled the important silver mines in Central Asia and the Middle East, issued millions of dirhams which they exported to Bulgar and, to a lesser extent, Khazaria. Among other things, dirhams were transported from Bulgar or through the Khazar networks to Kiev, where at a mixed group of people had settled comprising various local and exogenous elements, including Scandinavian elite, who imposed tribute on the local East Slavic tribes. The right to collect tribute from the Drevlyans inhabiting the Pripyat Basin brought with it the chance to trade with them for furs or to catch slaves. We can probably assume that the early tenth-century dirham hoards in the Western Bug Basin were concomitant and reflect an extension of Rus' tributary expeditions along the Pripyat.

From the 930s to 940s onward, dirham hoards began to appear west of the middle Vistula River. It seems that new networks emerged and tried to drain the silver resources from the people who lived in Masovia – some coins and coin fragments may have been collected there as tribute. The prime mover and main beneficiary of extending commerce into Greater Poland and imposing tribute in Masovia were the Piasts, who used dirhams, among other things, to pay their retinue.

Finally, a small dirham hoard cluster was deposited in the upper basins of the Southern Bug, Dniester, and Tisza rivers. It seems that these coins and jewelry belonged to Magyar migrants who came from or through Kievan Rus' and settled there temporarily in the first half of the tenth century. Some evidence indicates a caravan silver road that ran from the east through Hungary or Lesser Poland to Prague and then to the west.

Notes

1 Roman K. Kovalev and Alexis C. Kaelin, "Circulation of Arab Silver in Medieval Afro-Eurasia," *History Compass* 5 (2007): 560–580.
2 Thomas S. Noonan, "Dirham Exports to the Baltic in the Viking Age: Some Preliminary Observations," in *Sigtuna Papers. Proceedings of the Sigtuna Symposium on Viking-Age Coinage 1–4 June 1989*, ed. Kenneth Jonsson and Brita Malmer (Stockholm: Kungl. Vitterhets historie och antikvitets Akademien, 1990), 251–257.
3 Dariusz Adamczyk, "Koniunkturalne cykle czy strukturalne załamania? Sieci redystrybucji srebra a fluktuacje w jego imporcie do Europy Środkowej i Wschodniej w IX–XI wieku" [Conjunctural cycles or structural collapse? Redistribution network of silver and fluctuations in its imports to Central and Eastern Europe in the 9th–11th centuries], in *Moneta czasów kryzysu – moneta czasów pomyślności* [Coins in times of crisis – coins in times of prosperity], ed. Borys Paszkiewicz (Nowa Sól: Muzeum Miejskie, 2015), 95–118.
4 Generally Peter Feldbauer, *Die islamische Welt 600–1250. Ein Frühfall von Unterentwicklung?* (Vienna: Promedia, 1995) and Maurice Lombard, *Blütezeit des Islam. Eine Wirtschafts- und Kulturgeschichte 8.–11. Jahrhundert* (Frankfurt am Main: Fischer Taschenbuch, 1992).

5 Dmitrij J. Mishin, "Saqlabi servants in Islamic Spain and North Africa in the Early Middle Ages," (PhD diss., Central European University, 1999), 109–110 (I thank Balázs Nagy for providing me with the work) and Marek Jankowiak, "Two Systems of Trade in the Western Slavic Lands in the 10th Century," in *Economies, Monetisation and Society in the West Slavic Lands AD 800–1200*, ed. Mateusz Bogucki and Marian Rębkowski (Szczecin: Wydawnictwo IAE PAN – Wydawnictwo WH US, 2013), 137–148, here 141.

6 Thomas S. Noonan, "Why Dirhams First Reached Russia: The Role of Arab-Khazar Relations in the Development of the Earliest Islamic Trade with Eastern Europe," *Archivum Eurasiae Medii Aevi* 4 (1984): 151–282.

7 Roman K. Kovalev, "Commerce and Caravan Routes Along the Northern Silk Road (Sixth-Ninth Centuries) – Part I: The Western Sector," *Archivum Eurasiae Medii Aevi* 14 (2005): 55–105, here 80–82 and 84–85; Svetlana A. Pletneva, *Sarkel i >shelkovyi put'<* [Sarkel and the Silk Road] (Voronezh: Izdat. Voronežskogo Gosudarstvennogo Univ., 1996), 129–130, and eadem, *Ot kochevii k gorodam. Saltovo-Maiatskaia kul'tura* [From nomadic camps to towns: the Saltovo–Maiatskoe culture] (Moskva: Nauka, 1967).

8 Simon Franklin and Jonathan Shepard, *The Emergence of Rus' 750–1200* (London and New York: Logman, 1996), 97–98.

9 *Polnoe sobranie russkich letopisej*, I/2 [Complete collection of Russian chronicles] (Leningrad: Nauka, 1926), 65.

10 Gert Rispling, "Islamiska mynt, särskilt volga-bulgariska" [Islamic coins with special regard to their presence in the Volga-Bulgar area], *Myntstudier* 4 (2005): 3–11, here 5.

11 Kovalev, "Commerce and Caravan," 90, and Pletneva, *Na slavjano-chazarskom*, 79 and 81.

12 Kovalev, "Commerce and Caravan," 90.

13 Ivan I. Ljapuškin, *Slavjane Vostočnoi Evropy nakanune drevnerusskogo gosudarstva (VIII-1ja pol. IX v.)* [The Slavs in Eastern Europe before the emergence of the Medieval Rus'] (Materialy i Issledovanija po Archeologii SSSR, 152) (Leningrad: Nauka, 1968), 140 and 153.

14 Thomas S. Noonan, "The First Major Silver Crisis in Russia and the Baltic, c. 875–c. 900," *Hikuin* 11 (1985): 41–50.

15 Thomas S. Noonan, "Volga Bulgharia's Tenth-Century Trade with Samanid Central Asia," *Archivum Eurasiae Medii Aevi* 11 (2000–2001): 140–218, here 157.

16 Ahmed Zeki Validi Togan, *Ibn Fadlans Reisebericht* (Leipzig: Brockhaus, 1939).

17 V. V. Kropotkin, "Bulgarian Tenth-Century Coins in Eastern Europe and around the Baltic. Topography and Distribution Route," in *Sigtuna Papers*, 197–200; idem, "Bulgarskie monety X veka na territorri Drevnej Rusi i Pribaltiki" [Bulgarian coins of the 10th century on the territory of ancient Rus and the Baltics], in *Volžskaja Bulgarija i Rus* [Volga Bulgaria and Rus] (Kazan: [N. p.], 1986), 38–62, and Gert Rispling, "Islamiska mynt," 3–11.

18 Johan Callmer, "The Archaeology of Kiev to the End of the Earliest Urban Phase," *Harvard Ukrainian Studies* 11 (1987): 323–364.

19 Ibid., 333 and Dariusz Adamczyk, *Silber und Macht. Fernhandel, Tribute und die piastische Herrschaftsbildung in nordosteuropäischer Perspektive (800–1100)* (Wiesbaden: Harrassowitz, 2014), Annex 1: Russland, no. 4.

20 Noonan, "Volga Bulgharia's Tenth-Century Trade," 148, Table B.

21 Władysław Duczko, *Viking Rus. Studies on the Presence of Scandinavians in Eastern Europe* (Northern World, 12) (Leiden and Boston: Brill, 2004), 228.

22 *Polnoe sobranie russkich letopisej*, I/2, 24.

23 Ibid.

24 Maria Czapkiewicz and Franciszek Kmietowicz, *Skarb monet arabskich z okolic Drohiczyna nad Bugiem* [Arabic coin hoard from Drohiczyn on the Bug] (Cracow: Państwowe wydawnictwo naukowe, 1960); Maria Czapkiewicz, Anatol Gupieniec, Anna Kmietowicz and Władysław Kubiak, *Skarb monet arabskich z Klukowicz* [Arabic coin hoard from Klukowicze] (Warsaw: Zakład Narodowy im. Ossolińskich, 1964); Anatol Gupieniec, Teresa Kiersnowski, and Ryszard Kiersnowski, *Wczesnośredniowieczne skarby srebrne z Polski Środkowej, Mazowsza i Podlasia* [Early medieval silver hoards from Central Poland, Masovia, and Podlachia] (Wrocław: Zakład Narodowy im. Ossolińskich, 1965), nos. 16 and 33; Sylwia Małachowska, "Srebrne ozdoby z wczesnośredniowiecznego skarbu z Góry Strękowej, gm. Zawady, woj. Łomżyńskie" [Silver ornaments from the early medieval hoard from Góra Strękowa], *Wiadomości Archeologiczne* 53 (1993–1994): 35–45, Andrzej Bartczak, "Islamic Dirhams from the Góra Strękowa Hoard," *Notae Numismaticae* 3/4 (1999): 263–290, and Dorota Malarczyk, "Klukowicze and Liw hoards," Paper read at the Conference Oriental Numismatic Workshop: Monetary Circulation in 10th-c. Northern Europe, Oxford 1–2 August 2011, ed. Marek Jankowiak and Luke Treadwell (forthcoming).
25 Aldona Andrzejewska and Urszula Stankiewicz, "Wczesnośredniowieczne grodzisko w Trzciance, gm. Janów, pow. Sokółka" [The early medieval hill fort from Trzcianka], *Podlaskie Zeszyty Archeologiczne* 5 (2009): 137–147, Jolanta M. Ścibior, "Zespół monet arabskich – dirhemów znalezionych w Trzciance, pow. Sokółka" [Arabic coins from Trzcianka, Sokółka District], *Podlaskie Zeszyty Archeologiczne* 4 (2008): 210–222.
26 Igor' G. Dobrovol'skii, Igor' V. Dubnov and Iurij K. Kuz'menko, *Graffiti na vostočnych monetach. Drevniaia Rus' i sopredel'nye strany* [Graffiti on Eastern coins. Medieval Rus' and the neighboring regions] (Leningrad, 1991), 108–109.
27 Wojciech Wróblewski, "U źródeł kasztelanii liwskiej. Wczesnośredniowieczne struktury osadnicze w dorzeczu Liwca" [The origins of the castellan system in Liw. Early medieval settlement in the Liw Basin], in *Najstarsze dzieje Podlasia w świetle źródeł archeologicznych* [The earliest history of Podlachia in the light of archaeological sources], ed. Bożena Bryńczak and Przemysław Urbańczyk (Siedlce: IH AP, 2001), 205–228.
28 Andrzej Buko, *Archeologia Polski wczesnośredniowiecznej. Odkrycia – hipozety – interpretacje* [The Archaeology of early medieval Poland. Discoveries – theses – interpretations] (Warsaw: Trio, 2005), 186–191, Marek Dulinicz, "Mazowsze w X wieku" [Masovia in the 10th century], in *Ziemie polskie w X wieku i ich znaczenie w kształtowaniu nowej mapy Europy* [Polish lands in the 10th century and their importance in the shaping of Europe], ed. Henryk Samsonowicz (Cracow: Universitas, 2000), 199–220, here 209–210.
29 Marek Jankowiak, "Wer brachte im 10. Jahrhundert die Dirhems in die polnischen Gebiete und warum," in *Fernhändler, Dynasten, Kleriker. Die piastische Herrschaft in kontinentalen Beziehungsgeflechten vom 10. bis zum frühen 13. Jahrhundert*, ed. Dariusz Adamczyk and Norbert Kersken (Wiesbaden: Harrassowitz, 2015), 41–54.
30 *Russian Primary Chronicle. Laurentian Text*, ed. Samuel H. Cross and Olgerd P. Sherbowitz-Wetzor (Cambridge, MA: Medieval Academy of Academia, 1953), 78.
31 Ibid., 81.
32 Dariusz Adamczyk, "Trzecia fala napływu srebra arabskiego a powstanie 'państwa' piastowskiego" [The third wave of Arabic silver inflow and the emergence of the Piast 'State'], *Wiadomości Numizmatyczne* 58, no. 1–2 (2014): 42–46.
33 Michał Kara, *Najstarsze państwo Piastów – rezultat przełomu czy kontynuacji? Studium archeologiczne* [The oldest Piast state – watershed or continuity? An archaeological study] (Poznań: Inst. Archeologii i Etnologii Polskiej Akad. nauk, 2009).

34 Adamczyk, *Silber und Macht*, Appendixex 1, Großpolen: no 19; Appendix II, Großpolen: no. 3.

35 See, for example, Anna Wrzesińska and Jacek Wrzesiński, "Odważniki z wczesnośredniowiecznego stanowiska w Dziekanowicach" [Weights from the early medieval site of Dziekanowice], in *Świat Słowian wczesnego średniowiecza* [The world of the early medieval Slavs], ed. Marek Dworaczek et al. (Szczecin and Wrocław: Instytut Archeologii i Etnologii, Polskiej Akademii nauk, 2006), 341–358.

36 Adamczyk, *Silber und Macht*, Appendixex 1, Großpolen: nos 12, 14, 16, and 18.

37 Anna Kmietowicz, "Wczesnośredniowieczny skarb srebrny Dzierżnica II: Uwagi o historii znaleziska i jego części orientalnej" [The early medieval hoard from Dzierżnica II. Some remarks about the history of the find and its oriental part], *Wiadomości Numizmatyczne* 38 (1994): 161–167, and Małgorzata Andrałojć, Mirosław Andrałojć and Mariusz Tuszyński, *Wczesnośredniowieczny skarb z Kąpieli gm. Czerniejewo, woj. wielkopolskie* [The early medieval hoard from Kąpiel, Czerniejewo District, Greater Poland] (Poznań: Poznańskiego Tow. Przyjaciół nauk, 2005).

38 Andrzej Bartczak, "The Early Medieval Silver Hoard of Ciechanów in the Light of Oriental Coins," *Wiadomości Numizmatyczne* 40, no. 1–2 (1996): 43–59, and Tomasz Nowakiewicz, "Ozdoby i srebro siekane z wczesnośredniowiecznego skarbu srebrnego z Ciechanowa" [Ornaments and hack-silver from the early medieval silver hoard from Ciechanów], *Studia Galindzkie* 1 (2003): 261–317.

39 *Relacja Ibrahima Ibn Ja'kuba z podróży do krajów słowiańskich w przekazie Al-Bekriego* [Ibrahim Ibn Yaqub's report of travels to the Slavic Lands in Al.-Bekri's interpretation], ed. Tadeusz Kowalski (Kraków: Skł. gł. w księg. Gebethnera i Wolffa, 1946), 50.

40 Andrzej Zaborski, "Bilans i przyszłość badań nad tekstem Ibrahima Ibn Jakuba" [Overwiew and future of research on Ibrahim Ibn Yaqub's text], in *Ibrahim Ibn Jakub i Tadeusz Kowalski w sześćdziesiątą rocznicę edycji* [Ibrahim Ibn Yaqub and Tadeusz Kowalski 60 years after the first edition], ed. Andrzej Zaborski (Cracow: Księgarnia Akademicka, 2008), 25–74, here 41 and 43–51; Władysław Kubiak, "Zagadnienie « odważników handlowych » u Ibrahima ibn Jakuba" [The question of the trade weights at Ibrahim Ibn Yaqub], *Slavia Antiqua* 5 (1954–1956): 368–376 and Marian Gumowski, "Moneta arabska w Polsce IX i X wieku" [Arabic coins in 9th- and 10th-century Poland], *Zapiski Historyczne* 24 (1958/1959): 7–61, here 24.

41 Michał Brzostowicz, "Wczesnośredniowieczne grodzisko w Spławiu, Gm. Kołaczkowo, woj. Poznańskie. Wstępne podsumowanie wyników badań ratowniczych z lat 1991–1992" [The early medieval hill fort at Spławie, Kołaczkowo District, Poznań voivodeship. Preliminary results of the archaeological excavations, 1991–1992], *Wielkopolskie Sprawozdania Archeologiczne* 2 (1993): 115–132, Michał Brzostowicz, "Bruszczewski zespół osadniczy w IX i X wieku" [The settlement complex of Bruszczewo from the 9th and 10th centuries], in *Centrum i zaplecze we wczesnośredniowiecznej Europie Środkowej* [Core and hinterland in early medieval Central Europe], ed. Sławomir Moździoch (Wrocław: Wydawn. Werk, 1999), 135–150; Michał Brzostowicz, *Bruszczewski zespół osadniczy we wczesnym średniowieczu* [The settlement complex of Bruszczewo in the Early Middle Ages] (Poznań: Wydawn. Poznańskiego Towarzystwa Przyjaciół Nauk, 2002), 232, *Katalog wystawy stałej "tu powstała polska" w muzeum archeologicznym w Poznaniu* [Catalogue of the permanent exhibition "Here Emerged Poland" in the Archaeological Museum in Poznań], ed. Michal Brzostowicz and Agnieszka Stempin (Poznań: Muzeum Archeologiczne, 2009), 60.

42 Dariusz Adamczyk, "Kruszec, moneta, tranzyt czy 'hybryda', czyli częścią jakiego systemu handlowego były ziemie Polski południowej w X wieku?" [Precious

metal, coin, transit or 'hybrid.' Which trade system were the southern Polish lands part of during the 10th century?], in *Argenti fossores et alii. Znaczenie gospodarcze wschodnich części Górnego Śląska i zachodnich krańców Małopolski w późnej fazie wczesnego średniowiecza (X–XII wiek)* [The economic importance of the eastern parts of Upper Silesia and the western parts of Lesser Poland in the later phase of the Early Middle Ages (10th–12th centuries)], ed. Piotr Boroń (Wrocław: Wydawnictwo Chronicon, 2013), 197–202.

43 *Frühmittelalterliche Münzfunde aus Polen. Inventar, IV. Schlesien*, ed. Mateusz Bogucki, Peter Ilisch, and Stanisław Suchodolski (Warsaw: Institut für Archäologie der Polnischen Akademie der Wisschenschaften, 2014), nos. 31 and 102.

44 Adamczyk, *Silber und Macht*, Annex 1, Russland: nos. 17, 20, 26, 29, 31, and 44.

45 *Frühmittelalterliche Münzfunde aus Polen. Inventar, IV: Kleinpolen*, no 79.

46 Buko, *Archeologia Polski*, 104, Andrzej Koperski, "Groby wojowników z koniem na cmentarzysku « staromadziarskim » w Przemyślu" [Warrior graves with horses from the 'Old Hungarian' cemetery at Przemyśl], in *Słowianie i ich sąsiedzi we wczesnym średniowieczu* [The Slavs and their neighbors in the Early Middle Ages], ed. Marek Dulinicz (Lublin and Warsaw: Wydawn. Uniwersytetu Marii Curie-Skłodowskiej, 2003), 365–374; Jan Tyszkiewicz, *Tatarzy na Litwie i w Polsce* (Warsaw: Państwowe Wydawn. Nauk, 1989), 36 and Michael Müller-Wille, "Zwei Grabfunde des 10 Jhs. in europäischer Perspektive: Rösta (Grab IV) im nördlichen Schweden und Gnezdowo (Grab Dn-4) im westlichen Russland," in *Zwischen Christianisierung und Europäisierung. Beiträge zur Geschichte Osteuropas in Mittelalter und Früher Neuzeit. Festschrift für Peter Nitsche zum 65. Geburtstag*, ed. Eckhard Hübner, Ekkehard Klug and Jan Kusber (Stuttgart: F. Steiner, 1998), 51–68.

47 Duczko, *Viking Rus*, 221.

48 Attila Türk, "Zu den osteuropäischen und byzantinischen Beziehungen der Funde des 10.–11. Jahrhunderts im Karpatenbecken," in *Die Archäologie der frühen Ungarn. Chronologie, Technologie und Methodik*, ed. Bendeguz Tobias (Mainz: Verlag des Römisch-Germanischen Zentralmuseum, 2012), 3–28, here 15–17, Charlotte Hedenstierna-Jonson, "Traces of Contacts: Magyar Material Culture in the Swedish Viking Age Context of Birka," in ibid., 29–48.

49 Hansgerd Göckenjan, *Hilfsvölker und Grenzwächter im mittelalterlichen Ungarn* (Wiesbaden: F. Steiner, 1972), 54–55.

50 Gert Rispling, "Osteuropäische Nachahmungen islamischer Münzen," in *Sylloge der Münzen des Kaukasus und Osteuropas im Orientalischen Münzkabinett Jena*, I, ed. Stefan Heidemann and Norbert Nebes (Wiesbaden: Harrassowitz, 2005), 172–220, here no. 155.

51 Gyöngyvér Bíró and Péter Langó, "«Deo odibilis gens Hungarorum» oder «auxilium Domini» – Die Ungarn und die christliche Welt im 10. Jahrhundert," in *Rauben – Plündern – Morden. Nachweis von Zerstörung und kriegerischer Gewalt im archäologischen Befund*, ed. Orsolya Heinrich-Tamáska (Hamburg: Kovac, 2013), 265–335, esp. table 1, 291–321; and László Kovács, *Münzen aus der ungarischen Landnahmezeit* (Budapest: Akadémiai, 1989), 120–134.

52 Kowalski, *Relacja Ibrahima Ibn Ja'kuba*, 49.

53 English translation after Jankowiak, *Two Systems of Trade*, 140.

54 Helena Zoll-Adamikowa, Maria Dekówna and Elżbieta Maria Nosek, *The Early Medieval Hoard from Zawada Lanckorońska* (Warsaw: Zakład im. Ossolińskich Zakład im. Ossolińskich, 1999).

55 *Frühmittelalterliche Münzfunde aus Polen. Inventar, IV: Kleinpolen,* no. 116.
56 Thietmar von Merseburg, *Chronicon* in *Monumenta Germaniae Historica. Scriptores Series Nova*, IX, ed. Robert Holtzmann (Munich: Monumenta Germaniae Historica, 1980), 140.
57 Adamczyk, *Silber und Macht*, Annex 1, Brandenburg und Sachsen: no. 6.

10

THE IMPORTANCE OF LONG-DISTANCE TRADE FOR THE SLAVIC PRINCES IN THE EARLY AND HIGH MIDDLE AGES

Matthias Hardt

Around the year 965, the Jewish-Arab merchant Ibrahim ibn Yaqub al-Tartushi traveled through Central Europe as an envoy of the caliph of Córdoba. His report has come down to us through the writings of Zakariya bin Muhammad al-Qazwini, who was born in northwestern Iran around 1200 and died in 1283. Ibrahim traveled from Mainz to Magdeburg, where he met the emperor, Otto the Great. From there, he visited the Slavic Abodrites in modern-day Mecklenburg and the Bohemians in Prague, although it is not clear in which order. He left the following remarks on a "King of the North:"

> In as far as Mesheqqo's country is concerned, it is the largest of their coun-
> tries and rich in grain, honey and fish. He collects his tribute in silver [*al-
> mathaqil al-marqtija*], and this forms the upkeep of his men; in each month,
> each man is given a certain amount thereof. He has 3000 men in armour, and
> these are warriors of whom a hundred are worth 10,000 others. He gives his
> men clothes, horses, weapons and everything they need … .[1]

The ruler whom Ibrahim describes here, who is providing his followers (termed *druzina* in Slavonic) with money and goods, is Mieszko I, the first definitely attested prince in Poland.[2] This description of Mieszko I's resources is an invitation to think about the beginnings and structures of princely rule in the Slavic countries of the Early and High Middle Ages. For instance, what role did silver play in these principalities? Where did the metal come from that clearly supported the power of the Slavic rulers? The earliest written sources which are definitely about Poland refer to events which are almost contemporary with the report of the Spanish envoy. According to Widukind of Corvey, the tenth-century Saxon chronicler, in the year 963 one of Otto the Great's margraves, a man called Gero, convinced the Redarians in the area of Lake Tollense in modern-day eastern Mecklenburg to attack their faraway neighbors under a king (*rex*), Misaca. Gero himself fought him further upstream along the Oder.[3] Finally, Misaca was forced to pay tribute to the east Frankish-Saxon king, Otto I, for the western part of his territory up to the Warthe River.[4]

In 997, Adalbert, the bishop of Prague, who came from the opposition family of the Slavnikids, left his bishopric to try his luck at missionary work among the heathens. On this occasion, Mieszko's son and heir, Bolesław, succeeded in mobilizing Adalbert against the Baltic Prussians, who bordered Boleslaw's territory to the northeast.[5] After initial successes, however, Adalbert was murdered there.[6] What happened then is related in both of the martyr's *vitae*[7] as well as in pictorial form on the bronze doors of Gniezno cathedral, which date to the first half of the twelfth century: Bolesław bought the missionary's body back from the Prussians by paying its weight in precious metal.[8] The relief on the bronze door shows this process very realistically; a person with a set of precise scales, such as those now used in pharmacies, is weighing coins and ingots provided by Bolesław and collecting them in a metal container nearby.[9] I will return to this procedure below. Bolesław took Saint Adalbert's body back to Gniezno, where it was buried.[10]

The grave of the Prague bishop, missionary to the Prussians and martyr for his faith, awakened the interest of the young Emperor Otto III. He had met Adalbert in the monastery San Alessio e Bonifacio in Rome and become friends with him. Besides political considerations, it was probably this personal relationship which led the young ruler of the Roman Empire to leave Rome in December 999 in order to visit the grave in Gniezno.[11] The party marched quickly, traveling via Ravenna, Verona, and the snow-covered Alps to Regensburg and from there through Jena-Kirchberg, Zeitz, and Meissen to Gniezno.[12] This was a state visit as much as a pilgrimage, since the court of the ruler of the "Polani," first mentioned historically at around this time, was also a destination.[13]

Gallus Anonymus describes the reception held in AD 1000 at the court of Bolesław Chrobry in honor of Otto III and the following banquet as an open demonstration of Bolesław's wealth. The aim was to be awarded a higher rank by the emperor in the course of the customary gift exchange: "We also think it worthy of note," writes Gallus Anonymus:

> that at this time Emperor Otto came to Saint Adalbert to pray ... and at the same time to see the fame of the glorious Bolesław for himself ... Bolesław received him as honourably and magnificently as it befitted a king to receive a Roman Emperor and so high a guest. ... And there was not only some cheap gaudiness in the furnishings, but everything was of the most valuable kinds that can be found among all the peoples. As at the time of Bolesław all knights and ladies at court wore cloaks instead of linen and woollen clothes. And at his court even very precious furs, even if they were new, were not worn without under-coats with gold brocade. Because in his time, everyone thought gold as common as silver, and silver was thought as cheap as straw. When the Roman Emperor saw his glory, his power and his wealth, he

exclaimed full of admiration: 'By the crown of my realm, what I see is greater than what I have heard tell.'[14]

This was allegedly followed by placing Otto's imperial diadem on Bolesław's head, raising him to the rank of king, and then by the banquet, which Gallus describes:

> At the end of the feast, the cup-bearers and foodrunners collected the gold and silver dishes – because there were none that were of wood – namely, the beakers and goblets, bowls, platters and drinking horns from all the tables used over the three days, and these were given to the Emperor as gifts of honor … In addition he also gave away a large number of other vessels, made of gold and silver and worked in different ways, as well as colorful cloaks, ornaments of unknown kinds, precious gems, and he showed so many and so great things of this kind that the Emperor believed all these gifts to be a miracle.[15]

Almost like a Migration Period king, Bolesław thus used his treasure to visualize his rule. Of course, much like his father, Mieszko, he also used it to equip his *družina*, his armed retinue, and his army and to keep them in good spirits. But where did the abundance described by Gallus come from? In contrast to the Migration Period kings,[16] Bolesław was no longer a neighbor of the Roman Empire, which collected taxes in the form of silver and gold and stored them in treasuries, which could then simply be plundered during large-scale raids. In what follows, I will try to show how one can explain the wealth of the Piast Dynasty and other Slavic rulers, mentioned so often in the written sources, and to explain thereby how they achieved their position in the early history of East Central Europe.

At a time relatively poor in written sources, certain kinds of material culture are particularly important for understanding questions of economic history. This is especially the case for research into methods of payment, or even money, which tells about far more than just the early economy.[17] The Slavic hoards from East Central Europe contain very large amounts of money,[18] for instance, this example from Cortnitz near Bautzen in Upper Lusatia[19] (see Fig. 10.1) or the hoard from Wrangels in Schleswig-Holstein.[20] These treasures are scattered far and wide in the eastern half of the continent, but the distribution is particularly dense across the Baltic area. The hoards were mostly hidden in pottery or metal vessels, but sometimes also in textile or leather containers. They consist of silver, complete and fragmentary jewelry, and coins from many different places of origin, both complete examples and items cut right down into very small pieces. This composition shows the economic context of these hoards. That precious metal jewelry and coins from the most diverse monetary systems were kept and hoarded together, as well as the frequent fragmentation, shows that this was a bullion currency.[21]

It has long been clear that starting from AD 800 and throughout the ninth and tenth centuries by far the greatest majority of the coins in hoards came from the Near East.[22] The religious inscriptions in Arabic as well as the place and time when

FIG. 10.1 Coin-hoard from his example from Cortnitz near Bautzen (after Friedland and Hollstein, "Der Schatz im Acker.")

the coins were minted clearly show[23] that this is so-called Kufic silver. Around 400,000 dirhams from Baghdad, Tashkent, Samarkand, and Bukhara have been found so far.[24] As just one example, the hoard from the coastal trading post of Ralswiek on Rügen was buried around 842/847 and not retrieved. It consists of 2211 dirhams weighing 2750 grams. Beside a few North African pieces, most come from Mesopotamia and the area of modern-day Iran.[25] However, one should not assume a direct route between the place where these coins were minted and the place of deposition; the silver would have passed through many hands and the hoard reached its final attested composition via unknown intermediate locations.[26]

The scales and weights necessary for the functioning of this kind of currency system are also known from many archaeological assemblages from the late ninth century onwards, sometimes in conjunction with hoards.[27] These are equal-armed pieces, many of which can be folded for transport.[28] They were associated with sets of very precise weights, again already in use in the Roman and Byzantine areas, but without reaching the standardization later evident in East Central Europe.[29]

Not only the silver itself came from the Arab world, but also these standardized weights, which were absolutely necessary for using the precision scales and were clearly valued and used in East Central Europe.[30] Their distribution is so similar that it is clear that these sets of weights were generally accepted. This led the Freiburg archaeologist Heiko Steuer to conclude that Eastern Europe in the ninth/tenth century was on its way into "the Islamic economic area"[31] or the "Islamic cultural circle,"[32] perhaps even to "Islamization."[33] Indeed, this focus on Near Eastern and

Central Asian coinage is remarkable, and so is the sudden re-orientation at the turn of the millennium, after which first Anglo-Saxon money and then coinage from what was to become the German areas was increasingly incorporated into Slavic hoards. This can be explained by the sudden deterioration of Arabic silver, which now contained increasing amounts of copper, a trend caused by the political repercussions of the decline of the Samanid Khaganate.[34] From the eleventh century onwards, the role of the dirham was increasingly taken over by coins from eastern Saxony, such as the Otto-Adelheid issues, coins of Otto III and his grandmother, the second wife of Otto the Great. Indeed, these early Ottonian-Salic denars are mainly known from hoards in the Slavic and Scandinavian areas.[35] In the tenth century, the Přemysl and Piast dynasties also began to mint their own coinage, initially from political motives.

The archaeological finds show clearly that silver in form of coins, ingots, and complete or fragmented jewelry drove the trade and exchange relationships of the Slavic world among the Baltic, the Black Sea, and the Adriatic in the Early and High Middle Ages. This was the case regardless of whether it was obtained from Near Eastern and Central Asian areas under Arab rule or, as later, from the Anglo-Saxon and Ottonian-Salic West. Great quantities of silver reached the Slavic principalities and were used there not least to show off the status[36] of a large number of people. The social elite tried ever harder to emulate its older neighbors in the East and West, in Byzantium, Baghdad, or the courts of the Western Roman Empire, such as Magdeburg, Quedlinburg, Merseburg, or Aachen. However, since the Slavic rulers could not exploit any silver sources of their own, they had to siphon off what they needed from their far-reaching trade contacts, as the origins of the coins show. And although the historical sources are rather silent on this matter, it is nevertheless clear that it was the trade in human beings in which people such as Bolesław must have been involved, not only through collecting tolls, but actively.[37]

The trade in people was virtually a bottomless source of profit in the early and High Middle Ages.[38] This is most famously shown by how the Slavs' own name for themselves changed in meaning to become the general term for unfree individuals, i.e., slaves,[39] throughout Europe, the Mediterranean area, and the Arab world (Saqaliba). But even at the very start of the relationships between the Slavic world and the West, the activities of the well-known Frankish slave trader Samo were recorded. He led a Slavic rebellion against the Avars in AD 630 and was proclaimed king after its success. Most likely, Samo was one of those who first organized the transfer of Slavic captives through the Frankish Empire and into the Mediterranean area.[40] About a hundred years later, around AD 740, Abbot Sturm was looking for a good spot to erect the monastery of Fulda along the eponymous river. There he met a group of Slavs and their "translator," probably on their way westwards.[41] Perhaps they were heading to Verdun, a city which became rich through the slave trade[42] in spite of many prohibitions by the synods.[43] After all, it was not Christians who were being sold nor the Arab recipients in the Emirate of Cordoba, and not even the often Jewish traders who organized these transfers.[44] There was thus no reason for the Frankish kings to act against this trade, especially since documents like the customs regulations of Raffelstetten[45] and Walenstatt[46] show that this brought large sums of silver to their own coffers.[47]

Charles Verlinden has traced the paths of the slave caravans and the fate of the men who were often turned into eunuchs, for whom there was such great interest in the Arab world.[48] Similarly, Heinrich Koller has pointed out that it was young girls who fetched the highest prices on the markets of the Moravians and for whom the highest tolls had to be paid.[49] The destination of slave traders and the enslaved people from the Slavic territories was not only Spanish Cordoba, but via Venice and also the whole of the Eastern Mediterranean, while the river system of East Central Europe distributed them to the Black Sea area, Mesopotamia, and Central Asia.[50] There may even have been a continental transit trade from Volga Bulgaria through East Central Europe and into Muslim Spain.[51] Reading high medieval historiography from this point of view, what happened to the oft-mentioned hundreds and thousands of captives taken by Slavic rulers in wars against their neighbors becomes clear. For example, in AD 867, the Moravian apostles Cyril and Methodius managed to free nine hundred slaves from the power of the Pannonian ruler Kocel.[52] As is shown on the bronze doors of Gniezno cathedral, the missionary and later martyr Adalbert bought prisoners at the Prague market.[53] In contrast, in the course of his wars against Henry II,[54] and perhaps even more on his raids against his eastern neighbors in Kievan Rus',[55] Bolesław Chrobry would have had many opportunities to capture people,[56] as shown by the occasional description of how they were split up amongst the members of his armies. At around 300 grams of silver, a slave cost about as much as a horse, while a sword or an ox could be obtained for 125 grams, and a cow cost 100 grams.[57]

Michael McCormick has suggested that the many small fortifications in the West Slavic area which date to between the ninth and the eleventh century were used to hold captives temporarily, but this seems hard to prove and also somewhat complicated.[58] Once people are restricted in their movement, watching over them can be successfully accomplished with simpler methods. Joachim Henning has connected the numerous iron shackles with such practices,[59] although there were also wooden items of this kind.[60] Of course, it cannot be excluded that defended sites and princely castles were repeatedly used as waypoints in the slave trade.

Following the sources summarized here, it is not unlikely that as early as the Carolingian Period, the trade in people determined the economic development not only of the emerging Slavic principalities but also of Europe as a whole. The early importance of Magdeburg and the east-west route crossing the Elbe at that point, which forms the eastward continuation of the Hellweg route from Cologne through Dortmund and Paderborn, is already shown in Charlemagne's Diedenhofen Capitulary. This document, which dates to AD 805, first mentions Magdeburg as a frontier post for monitoring the trade with Slavs and Avars, in particular to put a stop to the export of weapons. Beside Magdeburg, Bardowick, Schezla (probably located on the Elbe near Meetschow), Erfurt, Hallstatt on the Main near Bamberg, Forchheim, Premberg, Regensburg, and Lorch on the Enns are also mentioned.[61] Clearly, these were all destinations for important trade routes from the Frankish

Empire to the east, whether by river or on land. At the same time, the emporia or coastal trading sites which have become known over the last few decades opened inland areas to the Baltic trade. As examples, one could mention Hedeby, Gross-Strömkendorf on Wismar Bay, and perhaps also Rerik, Rostock-Dierkow, Menzlin on the Peene, Ralswiek on Rügen, Wolin, and Truso near Elbląg.[62]

The first markets and settlement agglomerations formed where long-distance routes intersected, where they crossed major rivers, and also near princely castles. Here, specialized craftsmen catered to the needs of the local elites and their military retinues, as well as to those of traveling and local merchants. The most important example was evidently Prague, the residence of the Přemysl dynasty, with a slave market then located in the Little Quarter and described in minute detail by Ibrahim ibn Yaqub in AD 965.[63] However, such multifunctional settlements were also established at Poznań,[64] Wrocław,[65] and Cracow.[66] It is likely that the smaller tribal centers and castle sites along the long-distance routes also profited from the slave caravans, for instance Lebus, Köpenick, Spandau, and Brandenburg on the Havel, which lay along the main west-east route from Magdeburg to Poznań.[67] So-called castle towns[68] developed, which in many cases became the chartered towns of later times.

I have shown in brief that the Slavic princes of the High Middle Ages, and to some extent also those of the Moravian principality, had large treasures at their command, mainly consisting of silver. These came from long-distance trade connecting Europe with Central Asia and North Africa, from which these princes either profited or in which they were directly involved. This was a large-scale trade in human beings who had either been captured during the numerous wars between the Slavic princes or were sourced from their "own" societies, that is to say, a demographic surplus. This way of acquiring people was practiced with the view to obtaining metal and thus maintaining one's power base. Whether this pattern is rooted in the far less developed agricultural economy of the Slavic early and High Middle Ages, which could only feed a relatively small population, must remain a topic for further research. One consequence of the power of Slavic princes maintained by trade in slaves was the recognition of Sclavinia as equal beside Germania, Gallia, and Roma.

Notes

1 Translated after: *Arabische Berichte von Gesandten an germanische Fürstenhöfe aus dem 9. und 10. Jahrhundert* (Quellen zur deutschen Volkskunde, 1), ed. Georg Jacob (Berlin and Leipzig: De Gruyter, 1927), 13f. On Ibrahim's account see also the translation of Dmitrij Mishin, "Ibrahim ibn-Ya'qub at-Turtushi's Account of the Slavs from the Middle of the Tenth Century," *Annual of Medieval Studies at CEU 1994–1995*, 184–199, here 187: "The country of Mashaqqah is the largest one among the countries [of the Slavs]. It abounds in food, meat, honey, and agricultural produce (or fish). The taxes are collected in market weights. Those are the salary of his men in every month, and each of them has a certain amount of them to get. He has three thousand warriors wearing coats of mail; a hundred of them is worth a thousand of other warriors in battle. He gives these men clothes, horses, arms, and everything they need." About al-mathaqil al-marqtija

see Christoph Kilger, "Mitqal, Gewichte und Dirhems – Aspekte monetärer Praxis in der frühmittelalterlichen Silberökumene des Ostseeraumes," in *Fernhändler, Dynasten, Kleriker. Die piastische Herrschaft in kontinentalen Beziehungsgeflechten vom 10. bis zum frühen 13. Jahrhundert* (Deutsches Historisches Institut Warschau; Quellen und Studien, 30), ed. Dariusz Adamczyk and Norbert Kersken (Wiesbaden: Harrassowitz, 2015), 17–40.

2 Przemysław Urbańczyk, *Mieszko Pierwszy Tajemniczy* [Mysterious Mieszko I] (Toruń: Wydawnictwo Naukowe Uniwersytetu Mikołaja Kopernika, 2012).

3 Widukind von Korvei, *Rerum gestarum Saxonicarum libri tres* in *Monumenta Germaniae Historica. Scriptores rerum Germanicarum in usum scholarum*, LX, ed. Paul Hirsch (Hannover: Hahn, 1935, 2nd ed. 1989), 141–142. See also Christian Lübke, *Regesten zur Geschichte der Slaven an Elbe und Oder*, II (Berlin: Duncker & Humblot, 1985), 168–171.

4 *Thietmari Merseburgensis episcopi Chronicon* in *Monumenta Germaniae Historica. Scriptores rerum Germanicarum, Nova Series,* IX, ed. R. Holtzmann (Berlin: Weidmannsche Buchhandlung, 1935), 75 and Lübke, *Regesten*, II, 226–228.

5 *Sancti Adalberti Pragensis episcopi et martyris vita prior* (Monumenta Poloniae Historica, Series nova IV, 1), ed. J. Karwasińska (Warsaw: Państwowe wydawnictwo naukowe, 1962), 40–41.

6 Ibid., 45–48.

7 Ibid., 40.

8 *Galli anonymi Cronicae et Gesta Ducum sive Principum Polonorum* (Monumenta Poloniae Historica, Nova Series, II), ed. Karol Maleczynski (Cracow: Acad. litt. Polonica, 1952), 17–18 and *Polens Anfänge. Gallus Anonymus: Chronik und Taten der Herzöge und Fürsten von Polen*, ed. Josef Bujnoch (Slavische Geschichtsschreiber, 10) (Graz, Vienna, and Cologne: Styria, 1978), 56–57.

9 Tadeusz Dobrzeniecki, *Die Bronzetür von Gniezno* (Warsaw: Państwowy Instytut Wydawniczy, 1954), 16 and Adam Bujak and Adam S. Labuda, *Porta regia. Drzwi Gnieźnieńskie* (Gniezno: Fundacja Świętego Wojciecha, 1998), Scena XVI, 162–167.

10 Tomasz Sawicki, "Gnesen (Gniezno)," in *Europas Mitte um 1000*, I–II, ed. Alfried Wieczorek and Hans-Martin Hinz (Stuttgart: Theiss, 2000), I, 471–474.

11 Gerd Althoff, *Otto III. Gestalten des Mittelalters und der Renaissance* (Darmstadt: Wissenschaftliche Buchgesellschaft, 1996), 96–99.

12 Matthias Hardt, "Verkehrs- und siedlungsgeschichtliche Bemerkungen zur Reise Ottos III. nach Gnesen," in *Trakt Cesarski. Iława – Gniezno – Magdeburg* (Bibliotheka Fontes Archaeologici Posnaniensis, 2), ed. Wojciech Dzieduszycki and Maciej Przybył (Poznań: Muzeum Archeologiczne w Poznaniu, 2002), 385–408.

13 Christian Lübke, "Frühzeit und Mittelalter (bis 1569)," in *Eine kleine Geschichte Polens*, ed. Rudolf Jaworski, Christian Lübke and Michael G. Müller (Frankfurt am Main: Suhrkamp, 2000), 13–141, here 37.

14 *Galli anonymi Cronicae*, 18. Translated according to Bujnoch, *Polens Anfänge*, 57. Considering the archaeological record, it seems that Gerd Althoff's criticism of the written sources of the Piast wealth only concerns the overemphasis on gold: idem, "Symbolische Kommunikation zwischen Piasten und Ottonen," in *Polen und Deutschland vor 1000 Jahren. Die Berliner Tagung über den "Akt von Gnesen"* (Europa im Mittelalter. Abhandlungen und Beiträge zur historischen Komparatistik, 5), ed. Michael Borgolte (Berlin: Akademie, 2002), 293–308, here 302–306.

15 *Galli anonymi Cronicae*, 20.

16 Matthias Hardt, *Gold und Herrschaft. Die Schätze europäischer Könige und Fürsten im ersten Jahrtausend* (Europa im Mittelalter, 6) (Berlin: Akademie, 2004).

17 For the following, see Matthias Hardt, "Fernhandel und Subsistenzwirtschaft. Überlegungen zur Wirtschaftsgeschichte der frühen Westslawen." in *Nomen et Fraternitas* (Ergänzungsbände zum Reallexikon der Germanischen Altertumskunde, 62), ed. Uwe

Ludwig and Thomas Schilp (Berlin and New York: De Gruyter, 2008), 741–763, Matthias Hardt, "Fernhandel, Markt und frühe Stadt im ostfränkischen Reich (9–10 Jahrhundert)," in *Das lange 10. Jahrhundert. Struktureller Wandel zwischen Zentralisierung und Fragmentierung, äußerem Druck und innerer Krise* (RGZM – Tagungen, 19), ed. Christine Kleinjung and Stefan Albrecht (Mainz: Verlag des Römisch-Germanischen Zentralmuseums, 2014), 283–293.

18 Sebastian Brather, "Frühmittelalterliche Dirham-Schatzfunde in Europa. Probleme ihrer wirtschaftsgeschichtlichen Interpretation aus archäologischer Perspektive," *Zeitschrift für Archäologie des Mittelalters* 23–24 (1995–1996): 73–153, here 115, S. Brather, *Archäologie der westlichen Slawen. Siedlung, Wirtschaft und Gesellschaft im früh- und hochmittelalterlichen Ostmitteleuropa* (Ergänzungsbände zum Reallexikon der Germanischen Altertumskunde, 30) (Berlin and New York: De Gruyter, 2001), 223–237.

19 Sarah Nelly Friedland and Wilhelm Hollstein, "Der Schatz im Acker – Ein Hacksilberfund des 11. Jahrhunderts aus Cortnitz, Stadt Weißenberg (Lkr. Bautzen)," *Arbeits- und Forschungsberichte zur sächsischen Bodendenkmalpflege* 50 (2008): 211–229.

20 R. Wiechmann, *Edelmetalldepots der Wikingerzeit in Schleswig-Holstein. Vom "Ringbrecher" zur Münzwirtschaft* (Offa-Bücher, 77) (Neumünster: Wachholtz, 1996), no. 26.

21 Heiko Steuer, "Feinwaagen und Gewichte als Quellen zur Handelsgeschichte des Ostseeraumes," in *Archäologische und naturwissenschaftliche Untersuchungen an ländlichen und frühstädtischen Siedlungen im deutschen Küstengebiet vom 5. Jahrhundert v. Chr. bis zum 11. Jahrhundert n. Chr. 2. Handelsplätze des frühen und hohen Mittelalters*, ed. Georg Kossack and Albert Bantelmann (Weinheim: Acta Humaniora, 1984), 273–292, here 274–277; Heiko Steuer, "Gewichtsgeldwirtschaften im frühgeschichtlichen Europa," in *Untersuchungen zu Handel und Verkehr der vor- und frühgeschichtlichen Zeit in Mittel- und Nordeuropa 4. Der Handel der Karolinger- und Wikingerzeit* (Abhandlungen der Akademie der Wissenschaften in Göttingen, Philologisch-Historische Klasse, Dritte Folge, 156) (Göttingen: Vandenhoeck & Ruprecht, 1987), 405–527, here 508–516; idem, "Waagen und Gewichte vom Burgwall in Berlin-Spandau. Aspekte der Währungsgeschichte." *Neue Forschungsergebnisse vom Burgwall in Berlin-Spandau* (Berliner Beiträge zur Vor- und Frühgeschichte, NF, 9 = Archäologisch-historische Forschungen in Spandau, 5), ed. Adrian von Müller and Klara von Müller-Muči (Berlin: Staatliche Museen zu Berlin and Preußischer Kulturbesitz, 1999), 80–103, here 80; Heiko Steuer, Wilhelm B. Stern, and Gert Goldenberg, "Der Wechsel von der Münzgeld- zur Gewichtsgeldwirtschaft in Haithabu um 900 und die Herkunft des Münzsilbers im 9. und 10. Jahrhundert," in *Haithabu und die frühe Stadtentwicklung im nördlichen Europa* (Schriften des archäologischen Landesmuseums, 8), ed. Klaus Brandt (Neumünster: Wachholtz, 2002), 133–166, here 133–141; Heiko Steuer, "Münzprägung, Silberströme und Bergbau um das Jahr 1000 in Europa – wirtschaftlicher Aufbruch und technische Innovation," in *Aufbruch ins zweite Jahrtausend. Innovation und Kontinuität in der Mitte des Mittelalters*, eds. Achim Hubel and Bernd Schneidmüller (Ostfildern: Thorbecke, 2004), 117–149, here 122; Heiko Steuer, "Waagen und Gewichte," in *Reallexikon der Germanischen Altertumskunde*, XXXIII, ed. Heinrich Beck, Dieter Geuenich and Heiko Steuer (Berlin and New York: De Gruyter, 2007), 539–586, here 584–586; Brather, *Archäologie der westlichen Slawen*, 223–237, and Marek Jankowiak, "Two Systems of Trade in the Western Slavic Lands in the 10th Century," in *Economies, Monetisation and Society in the West Slavic Lands 800–1200 AD* (Wolińskie Spotkania Mediewistyczne, 2), ed. Mateusz Bogucki and Marian Rębkowski (Szczecin: Wydawnictwo IAE PAN: Wydawnictwo WH US, 2013), 137–148.

22 Csanád Bálint, "Einige Fragen des Dirhem-Verkehrs in Europa," *Acta Archaeologica Academiae Scientiarum Hungaricae* 33 (1981): 105–131; Steuer, "Gewichtsgeldwirtschaften,"

480; Brather, "Frühmittelalterliche Dirham-Schatzfunde," 90–103; Sebastian Brather, "Frühmittelalterliche Dirham-Schatz- und Einzelfunde im südlichen Ostseeraum. Die Anfänge der Gewichtsgeldwirtschaft bei den Westslawen," in *Archäologie als Sozialgeschichte. Studien zu Siedlung, Wirtschaft und Gesellschaft im frühgeschichtlichen Mitteleuropa*, ed. idem, Christel Bücker, and Michael Hoeper (Rahden: M. Leidorf, 1999), 179–198, here 181; Dariusz Adamczyk, "Fernhandelsemporien, Herrschaftszentren, Regional- und Lokalmärkte: Die ökonomischen Funktionen von Silber oder: Wie lässt sich der Grad der Monetarisierung in den frühmittelalterlichen Gesellschaften des Ostseeraums 'messen'?" in *Economies, Monetisation and Society*, 115–136, here 120–126; idem, *Silber und Macht. Fernhandel, Tribute und die piastische Herrschaftsbildung in nordosteuropäischer Perspektive (800–1100)* (Deutsches Historisches Institut Warschau, Quellen und Studien, 28) (Wiesbaden: Harrassowitz, 2014), Marek Jankowiak, "Wer brachte im 10. Jahrhundert die Dirhems in die polnischen Gebiete und warum?" in *Fernhändler, Dynasten, Kleriker*, 41–54 and Kilger, "Mitqal."

23 Brather, *Archäologie der westlichen Slawen*, 223.

24 Heiko Steuer, "Geldgeschäfte und Hoheitsrechte im Vergleich zwischen Ostseeländern und islamischer Welt," *Zeitschrift für Archäologie* 12 (1978): 255–260, here 257; Brather, *Archäologie der westlichen Slawen,* 230–232; Roman K. Kovalev, "The Mint of al-Shash. The Vehicle for the Origins and Continuation of Trade Relations between Viking-Age Northern Europe and Sāmānid Central Asia," *Archivum Eurasiae Medii Aevi* 12 (2002–2003): 47–79; and Jankowiak, "Wer brachte im 10. Jahrhundert," 41.

25 Joachim Herrmann, "Ralswiek auf Rügen – ein Handelsplatz des 9. Jahrhunderts und die Fernhandelsbeziehungen im Odergebiet," *Zeitschrift für Archäologie* 12 (1978): 163–180, here 168–171 and 175 Fig. 13.

26 Brather, "Frühmittelalterliche Dirham-Schatzfunde," 108.

27 Joachim Herrmann, *Ralswiek auf Rügen. Die slawisch-wikingischen Siedlungen und deren Hinterland 3. Die Funde aus der Hauptsiedlung* (Beiträge zur Ur- und Frühgeschichte Mecklenburg-Vorpommerns, 37) (Schwerin: Archäologisches Landesmuseum für Mecklenburg-Vorpommern, 2005), 228–232; Steuer, "Waagen und Gewichte vom Burgwall," 85–98; idem, "Feinwaagen," 277–286; and idem, "Gewichtsgeldwirtschaften," 459–466.

28 Steuer, "Feinwaagen," 277–280; idem, "Gewichtsgeldwirtschaften," 462–466; idem, "Waagen," 556–569; Brather, *Archäologie der westlichen Slawen*, 230; and Andrzej Krzyszowski, "Frühmittelalterliches Grab eines Kaufmannes aus Sowinki bei Poznan in Großpolen," *Germania* 75 (1997): 639–671, here 646–650.

29 Joachim Werner, *Waage und Geld in der Merowingerzeit* (Sitzungsberichte der Bayerischen Akademie der Wissenschaften, Philologisch-historische Klasse 1, 8) (Munich: Verlag der Bayerischen Akademie der Wissenschaften, 1954), and Steuer, "Gewichtsgeldwirtschaften," 431–459.

30 Steuer, "Feinwaagen," 280–283; idem, "Gewichtsgeldwirtschaften," 466–479 and 500–503; idem, "Waagen und Gewichte vom Burgwall," 80 and 91–94; idem, "Waagen," 569–584; Brather, *Archäologie der westlichen Slawen*, 231; Krzyszowski, "Frühmittelalterliches Grab," 641–646 and 667–671; and Kilger, "Mitqal."

31 Steuer, "Geldgeschäfte," 258; idem, Stern, and Goldenberg, "Der Wechsel," 140; Steuer, "Gewichtsgeldwirtschaften," 479; Heiko Steuer, "Münzprägung, Silberströme und Bergbau um das Jahr 1000 in Europa – wirtschaftlicher Aufbruch und technische Innovation," in *Aufbruch ins zweite Jahrtausend. Innovation und Kontinuität in der Mitte des Mittelalters*, ed. Achim Hubel and Bernd Schneidmüller (Ostfildern: Thorbecke, 2004), 117–149 and 123.

32 Steuer, "Münzprägung, Silberströme und Bergbau," 124.

33 Ibid., 132.
34 Steuer, "Feinwaagen," 291; Brather, "Frühmittelalterliche Dirham-Schatzfunde," 103–106; Steuer, Stern, and Goldenberg, "Der Wechsel," 152; Brather, *Archäologie der westlichen Slawen*, 232–234; and Kovalev, "The Mint of al-Shash," 70.
35 Steuer, "Gewichtsgeldwirtschaften," 481–483; idem, "Münzprägung, Silberströme und Bergbau," 132 and 136; idem, "Frühmittelalterliche Dirham-Schatzfunde," 106 and 119–121; idem, *Archäologie der westlichen Slawen*, 234; Peter Ilisch, "Die Pfennigströme aus dem römisch-deutschen Reich im Spiegel der Funde aus Pommern, Masowien und Großpolen (ca. 980–1050)," in *Fernhändler, Dynasten, Kleriker*, 55–65.
36 In contrast to the passages cited above, Brather also thinks it possible that silver was hoarded as a prestige good, idem, "Frühmittelalterliche Dirham-Schatz- und Einzelfunde im südlichen Ostseeraum," 184 and 191; Steuer, Stern and Goldenberg, "Der Wechsel," 141, also point to the representative function of silver.
37 Michael McCormick, "Verkehrswege, Handel und Sklaven zwischen Europa und dem Nahen Osten um 900: Von der Geschichtsschreibung zur Archäologie?" in *Europa im 10. Jahrhundert. Archäologie einer Aufbruchszeit*, ed. Joachim Henning (Mainz: Philipp von Zabern, 2002), 171–180, here 173; Brather, "Frühmittelalterliche Dirham-Schatzfunde," 79; Matthias Hardt, "'Silber, so wohlfeil wie Stroh.' Der Reichtum der Piasten," *Mitropa. Jahresheft des Geisteswissenschaftlichen Zentrums Geschichte und Kultur Ostmitteleuropas (GWZO) 2014*, 13–19.
38 Michael McCormick, *Origins of the European Economy. Communications and Commerce A. D. 300–900* (Cambridge: Cambridge University Press, 2001), 741–777; Mary A. Valante, "Castrating Monks: Vikings, Slave Trade, and the Value of Eunuchs," in *Castration and Culture in the Middle Ages*, ed. Larissa Tracy (Cambridge: Boydell & Brewer, 2013), 174–187; Christian Delacampagne, *Geschichte der Sklaverei* (Düsseldorf and Zürich: Artemis & Winkler, 2004), 102–127; and Fritz Rörig, *Magdeburgs Entstehung und die ältere Handelsgeschichte* (Deutsche Akademie der Wissenschaften zu Berlin Vorträge und Schriften, 49) (Berlin: Akademie, 1952), 17–23.
39 Maurice Lombard, *Blütezeit des Islam. Eine Wirtschafts- und Kulturgeschichte. 8.–11. Jahrhundert* (Frankfurt am Main: Fischer Taschenbuch, 1992), 198–200; Michael Zeuske, *Handbuch Geschichte der Sklaverei. Eine Globalgeschichte von den Anfängen bis zur Gegenwart* (Berlin and Boston: De Gruyter, 2013), 526–531.
40 *Chronicarum quae dicuntur Fredegarii scholastici libri IV cum continuationibus* in *Fredegarii et aliorum Chronica. Vitae sanctorum* in *Monumenta Germaniae Historica, Series Rerum Merovingicarum*, V, ed. Bruno Krusch (Hannover: Hahn, 1888), 1–193, here 154. See also Hansjürgen Brachmann, "Als aber die Austrasier das castrum Wogastisburc belagerten … [Fredegar IV, 68]," *Onomastica Slavogermanica* 19 (1983): 17–33, here 17–19; Rörig, *Magdeburg*, 22; against an interpretation of Samo as a slave trader, see Peter Johanek, "Der 'Außenhandel' des Frankenreiches der Merowingerzeit nach Norden und Osten im Spiegel der Schriftquellen," in *Untersuchungen zu Handel und Verkehr der vor- und frühgeschichtlichen Zeit in Mittel- und Nordeuropa 3. Der Handel des frühen Mittelalters* (Abhandlungen der Akademie der Wissenschaften in Göttingen, Philologisch-Historische Klasse 3, 150), ed. Klaus Düwel et al. (Göttingen: Vandenhoeck & Ruprecht, 1985), 214–254, here 245. McCormick, *Origins*, 739 seems less sceptical.
41 *Die Vita Sturmi des Eigil von Fulda. Literarkritisch-historische Untersuchung und Edition* (Veröffentlichungen der Historischen Kommission für Hessen und Waldeck, 29), ed. Pius Engelbert (Marburg: Elwert, 1968), 139. *Tunc quadam die cum pergeret, pervenit ad viam, quae a Turingorum regione mercandi causa ad Mogontiam pergentes ducit, ubi platea illa super flumen Fulda vadit; ibi magnam Sclavorum multitudinem repperit, eiusdem fluminis alveo gratia*

lavandis corporibus se immersisse. – Ibid., 82 assumes with further literature that it was not about a slave caravan, but about a Slavic population resident at the Fulda River. This assumption should not be exluded either. E.g., Rolf Sprandel, "Gerichtsorganisation und Sozialstruktur Mainfrankens im früheren Mittelalter," *Jahrbuch für fränkische Landesforschung* 38 (1978): 7–38, here 10. In this case, Johanek, "Der 'Außenhandel'," 246 does not exclude the interpretation of a slave caravan. Helmut Roth, "Handel und Gewerbe vom 6. bis 8. Jh. östlich des Rheins," *Vierteljahrschrift für Sozial- und Wirtschaftsgeschichte* 58 (1971): 323–358, here 324; and Rörig, "Magdeburg," 21, assumed an evidence for slave trade.

42 Liutprandi, *Antapodosis* in *Monumenta Germaniae Historica. Scriptores rerum Germanicarum in usum scholarum*, XLI, ed. Joseph Becker (Hannover and Leipzig: Hahn, 1915), 155. For a more recent edition: Liudprandi Cremonensis, *Opera omnia. Antapodosis, Homelia paschalis, Historia Ottonis, Relatio de legatione Constantinopolitana* (Corpus Christianorum. Continuatio Mediaevalis, 156), ed. Paolo Chiesa (Turnhout: Brepols, 1998); *Antapodosis*, 148, lib. VI; Walther Stein, *Handels- und Verkehrsgeschichte der deutschen Kaiserzeit* (2nd ed. Darmstadt: Wissenschaftliche Buchgesellschaft, 1977), 106–110; Hartmut Hoffmann, "Kirche und Sklaverei im frühen Mittelalter," *Deutsches Archiv für Erforschung des Mittelalters* 42 (1986): 1–24, here 18; and Lombard, *Blütezeit des Islam*, 200. At the time of Henry II, coins with Arabic inscriptions were produced, which clearly met the needs of slave trade, see Heiko Steuer, "Münzprägung, Silberströme und Bergbau," 127–130 and 144.

43 Hoffmann, "Kirche," 14, Harald Siems, *Handel und Wucher im Spiegel frühmittelalterlicher Rechtsquellen* (Schriften der Monumenta Germaniae Historica, 35) (Hannover: Hahn, 1992), 487–489.

44 *Ibn Fadlān and the Land of Darkness. Arab Travellers in the Far North*, ed. P. Lunde and C. Stones (London: Penguin, 2012), 111; Methodie Kusseff, "St. Nahum," *The Slavonic and East European Review* 29 (1950): 139–152, here 143; Lombard, *Blütezeit des Islam*, 199–201 and 212. Cf. Michael Toch, '*Dunkle Jahrhunderte'. Gab es ein jüdisches Frühmittelalter? 3. Arye Maimon-Vortrag an der Universität Trier, 15. November 2000* (Kleine Schriften des Arye-Maimon-Instituts, 4) (Trier: Kliomedia, 2001), 23; idem, "Mehr Licht: Eine Entgegnung zu Friedrich Lotter," *Aschkenas – Zeitschrift für Geschichte und Kultur der Juden* 11 (2001): 465–487, here 478–483; Undine Ott, "Europas Sklavinnen und Sklaven im Mittelalter. Eine Spurensuche im Osten des Kontinents," in *Europas Sklaven* (WerkstattGeschichte, 66–67), ed. Doris Bulach and Juliane Schiel (Essen: Ruhr Klartext, 2015), 31–53, here 38–42.

45 *Inquisitio de theloneis Raffelstettensis* in *Monumenta Germaniae Historica. Capitularia II. Capitularia regum Francorum*, II/1, ed. Alfredus Boretius and Victor Krause (Hannover:Hahn, 1897), 249–252 (no. 253), Konrad Schiffmann, "Die Zollurkunde von Raffelstetten," *Mitteilungen des Instituts für Österreichische Geschichtsforschungen* 37 (1917): 479–488, here 479–487; Michael Mitterauer, "Wirtschaft und Verfassung in der Zollordnung von Raffelstetten," *Mitteilungen des Oberösterreichischen Landesarchivs* 8 (1964): 344–373; and Peter Johanek, "Die Raffelstetter Zollordnung und das Urkundenwesen der Karolingerzeit," in *Festschrift für Berent Schwineköper zu seinem siebzigsten Geburtstag*, ed. H. Maurer and H. Patze (Sigmaringen: Thorbecke, 1982), 87–103.

46 *Churrätisches Reichsurbar* in *Bündner Urkundenbuch I, 390–1199*, ed. Elisabeth Meyer-Marthaler and Franz Perret (Chur: Bischofberger, 1955), 382–383, here 382.

47 Peter Johanek, "Der fränkische Handel der Karolingerzeit im Spiegel der Schriftquellen," in *Untersuchungen zu Handel und Verkehr der vor- und frühgeschichtlichen Zeit in Mittel- und Nordeuropa 4. Der Handel der Karolinger- und Wikingerzeit* (Abhandlungen der

Akademie der Wissenschaften in Göttingen, Philologisch-Historische Klasse, Dritte Folge, 156), ed. Klaus Düwel (Göttingen: Vandenhoeck & Ruprecht, 1987), 7–68, here 39.

48 Charles Verlinden, *Wo, wann und warum gab es einen Großhandel mit Sklaven während des Mittelalters?* (Kölner Vorträge zur Sozial- und Wirtschaftsgeschichte, 11) (Cologne: Forschungsinstitut für Sozial- und Wirtschaftsgeschichte an der Universität zu Köln, 1970), 4–16, Stein, "Handels- und Verkehrsgeschichte," 108 and Lombard, *Blütezeit des Islam,* 197.

49 Heinrich Koller, "Die Raffelstetter Zollordnung und die mährischen Zentren," in *Burg, Burgstadt, Stadt. Zur Genese mittelalterlicher nichtagrarischer Zentren in Ostmitteleuropa* (Forschungen zur Geschichte und Kultur des östlichen Mitteleuropa), ed. Hans-Jürgen Brachmann (Berlin: Akademie, 1995), 283–295, here 291.

50 Lombard, *Blütezeit des Islam,* 198–200. Cf. Ott, "Europas Sklavinnen," 33–38.

51 Joachim Henning, "Gefangenenfesseln im slawischen Siedlungsraum und der europäische Sklavenhandel im 6. bis 12. Jahrhundert. Archäologisches zum Bedeutungswandel von 'sklabos – sakaliba – sclavus'," *Germania* 70 (1992): 403–426, here 417.

52 *Zwischen Rom und Byzanz. Slavische Geschichtsschreiber,* I, ed. Josef Bujnoch (Graz, Vienna, and Cologne: Styria, 1958), 71 and McCormick, "Verkehrswege," 176f.

53 Dobrzeniecki, *Die Bronzetür,* pl. 8, and Bujak and Labuda, *Porta regia,* Scena VIII, 94–101.

54 Stefan Weinfurter, "Neue Kriege. Heinrich II. und die Politik im Osten," in *Europas Mitte um 1000,* II, 819–824.

55 *Thietmari Merseburgensis episcopi Chronicon,* 528–532, *Galli anonymi Cronicae,* 21–25; translated according to Bujnoch, *Polens Anfänge,* 59–63. See also Christian Lübke, *Das östliche Europa. Die Deutschen und das europäische Mittelalter* (Berlin: Siedler, 2004), 224.

56 *Thietmari Merseburgensis episcopi Chronicon,* 262–264, 370, 472 and 478.

57 Brather, *Archäologie der westlichen Slawen,* 236.

58 McCormick, "Verkehrswege," 176.

59 Henning, "Gefangenenfesseln," 405–425.

60 McCormick, "Verkehrswege," 175.

61 Matthias Hardt, "Das Diedenhofener Kapitular und die Ostgrenze des Karolingerreiches," in *Magdeburg 1200. Mittelalterliche Metropole, preußische Festung, Landeshauptstadt. Die Geschichte der Stadt von 805 bis 2005,* ed. Matthias Puhle (Stuttgart and Magdeburg: Theiss, 2005), 42–43; Matthias Hardt, "Erfurt im Frühmittelalter. Überlegungen zu Topographie, Handel und Verkehr eines karolingerzeitlichen Zentrums anlässlich der 1200sten Wiederkehr seiner Erwähnung im Diedenhofener Kapitular Karls des Großen im Jahr 805," *Mitteilungen des Vereins für Geschichte und Altertumskunde von Erfurt* 66 [NF 13] (2005): 9–39.

62 Brather, *Archäologie der westlichen Slawen,* 246, pl. 66.

63 *Arabische Berichte,* 12, Mishin, "Ibrahim," 186; Dusan Třeštík, "Eine große Stadt der Slawen namens Prag. Staaten und Sklaven in Mitteleuropa im 10. Jahrhundert," in *Boleslav II. Der tschechische Staat um das Jahr 1000,* ed. Petr Sommer (Prague: Filosofia, 2001), 93–138.

64 Michal Kara, "Posen (Poznan)," in *Europas Mitte,* I, 475–478.

65 Pawel Rzeźnik, "Breslau (Wrocław)," in *Europas Mitte,* I, 483–486.

66 Zbigniew Pianowski, "Krakau (Kraków)," in *Europas Mitte,* I, 479–482.

67 Joachim Herrmann, "Magdeburg-Lebus. Zur Geschichte einer Straße und ihrer Orte," *Veröffentlichungen des Museums für Ur- und Frühgeschichte Potsdam* 2 (1963): 89–106.

68 *Burg, Burgstadt, Stadt.*

11

THE HEYDAY AND FATE OF AN EARLY TRADE CENTER

Graphite Pottery in Early Óbuda

Bence Péterfi*

The Italian writer known as Master Roger, in his account of the Mongol invasion of 1241–1242, described the town of Óbuda[1] as a *locus communior* ("an easily accessible place"). According to scholarly opinion, the town was considered the administrative center and capital of the Kingdom of Hungary.[2] The collegiate church[3] of Óbuda and the royal palace (later the residence of queens)[4] are important monuments of the Árpádian period which are known not only from written sources but also from archaeological and art historical analysis. Óbuda was certainly a settlement of great importance in the Kingdom of Hungary, but its unprecedented blossoming came to an end in the second half of the twelfth and first third of the thirteenth century. This interruption in the town's development cannot be attributed solely to the plundering of the Mongol troops in 1241–1242; its development was also very much halted by the foundation of the new settlement of Buda on the hill opposite Pest on royal initiative.

Nevertheless, before the mid-thirteenth century Óbuda stood out in a political sense from many of the settlements in the Kingdom of Hungary. Apart from Esztergom – the seat of the kings of Hungary and of the first archbishopric – Óbuda as well as a few other trade centers by the Danube, may well have provided the basis for the remark of Odo of Deuil, a Benedictine monk and participant of the Second Crusade (1147–1149), that "the Danube carries the wealth of many lands to the noble town of *Estrigun*."[5] Contemporary merchants liked spending time not only in Esztergom, but anywhere they smelled good business. The map of the Sicilian Arab geographer al-Idrīsī from the middle of the twelfth century based on accounts from Eastern travelers, depicts the settlements of the Kingdom of Hungary that were important in commerce as well as their distance from each other. Apart from Esztergom, which he called the "governmental place" of the country, actually meaning capital, the map lists – among others – a certain *B.dwār.h* or *B.zwār.h*.[6] These terms, in the opinion of Hungarian scholars, can be identified with Budavár

(Buda Castle) or Budavára (Buda's Castle), which at some point settled to Buda.[7] Budavár can be identified with present-day Óbuda, not with the town on Castle Hill, which only came into existence a century later.

The aim of this study is primarily to draw attention to the economic importance of Óbuda in the period before the Mongol invasion, usually considered in the historiography as the "golden age" of the town, and to some extent demonstrate that even in the early period of the Kingdom of Hungary important long-distance trade routes connected the country with other powers. Due to the lack of narrative sources – with the exception of the few mentioned above – there is hardly any information available on these questions. One can only presume the importance of the town based on vague references to its administrative role and its function as a seat.[8] If one is interested in the economic and commercial role of Óbuda, one has to consider the methods and results of a discipline other than history: medieval archaeology – only this field can give at least some hints to address the problem. It is almost a century-long tradition to use objects in medieval and Early Modern economic history that are considered indicators of trade, which, apart from a few prestige objects kept in private or public collections, were unearthed during excavations.[9] However, it is important to draw attention to the fact that archaeology does not provide results in historical logic, thus attuning the two fields without hurting their methodological barriers is possible only to some extent, even if the questions the two disciplines ask are the same.[10]

The obvious indicators of trade: scales and coins

The presence of so-called balance scales is indicative of trade and the exchange of goods. Based on the investigations of Heiko Steuer, some examples of a type of balance scale characteristic for the surroundings of Budapest can be identified in present-day Óbuda. Two of them were found within the borders of early Óbuda, in the area of the Roman remains (131–139 Szentendrei Road, the civic town of Roman Aquincum) and further from early Felhévíz (a settlement close to Óbuda to the south). It should be noted here that a few finds from Esztergom and one from Mende-Leányvár (some 20 kilometers from Budapest) also belong to this group. This type of scales occurred in the Carpathian Basin in the eleventh century and its use can be considered widespread for the twelfth through thirteenth centuries. The common feature of finds of this type is a cube-shaped element at the end of the 8 to 30 centimeter-long scale-beam. This semi-circular closing ornament is a general form, thus it cannot be considered specific to this type. We have a more schematic picture of the scale-pans as they are much more vulnerable to damage than the arms. There is a (debated) theory that the most complete piece from Óbuda (see Fig. 11.1) was marked with an authentication stamp. If so, then it was probably used as a currency exchange scale.[11] In general, however, these scales are associated with merchandizing (spices, etc.) rather than measuring precious metals.[12] The spread of this type of scale in the Carpathian Basin shows a rather peculiar pattern. Most of these objects were unearthed at the clearly important Esztergom and Óbuda, but in similarly significant Bratislava – at least according to Steuer and to my knowledge – no scale has been found so far.[13]

There is another important but much more hypothetical find that was allegedly unearthed in Óbuda: a late twelfth-century coin-hoard (475 full and 20 fragmented Byzantine bronze coins).[14] However, as it disappeared during World War Two it has virtually been forgotten and hardly any information is available about it. According to András Kerényi, the rescuer of the hoard and identifier of the scientific value, it consisted of almost 500 coins from the period between 1143 and 1195 – issued by Manuel I Komnenos, Andronikos II Komnenos, and Isaac II Angelos – the period when strong Hungarian-Byzantine diplomatic ties are attested.[15] Since Isaac II had only six coins in the ensemble the hoard can be dated to the first period of his reign (perhaps from the 1180s). As the coins are not made of precious metals but of bronze, I think Kerényi's assessment is fully acceptable: "with these [bronze] coins the face value was always higher than their actual material or metal value. Such non-precious metal coins can only be found in foreign countries if there were strong political and commercial ties between two states."[16] This is entirely true for the period covered by the issue years of the coins. The serious doubts around the provenance, however, put us on guard.[17] It is nonetheless true that the existence of this find at Óbuda would reinforce what written sources imply – the blossoming of the town in the second half of the twelfth century – and would certainly be telling of the town as a center of long-distance trade.

Graphite-tempered ceramics as indicator of trade activity

Regarding the economic connections of Óbuda there is, however, one more source, not as rare as balance scales and certainly not as difficult of reconstruction as a once existing coin hoard: a group of graphite-tempered ceramics unearthed in large quantities, primarily in the surroundings of the medieval market square of Óbuda. The leading field archaeologist at the excavation, Vilmosné Bertalan (1923–2008), may have implied this when, in a study of hers, she represented the find spots of medieval fine ware vessels, pot fragments of the so-called "later" graphite group, and scales on two maps. These were found in the greatest density at the sites of the houses that had encircled the medieval market square and at those in their immediate neighborhood.[18]

Graphite is a gray form of carbon that occurs naurally as a mineral. But what do we mean by graphite ceramics? This is not merely about refining the surface of a pot; potters mixed graphite with the clay and other components in order to enhance it in some way. It is not self-evident what the real function of this additive was, but it seems that pots made of this mixture increased the capacity to hold water, decreased in expansion and resisted damage from high heat. The positive impacts of the additive, however, decreased over time, as the graphite content gradually diminished due to the frequent use of these ceramics in fireplaces.[19] Some believe that the role of this additive lies in the better malleability of the clay-graphite mixture, because material analysis of large storage vessels of Silesian origin found in Polish areas has shown the

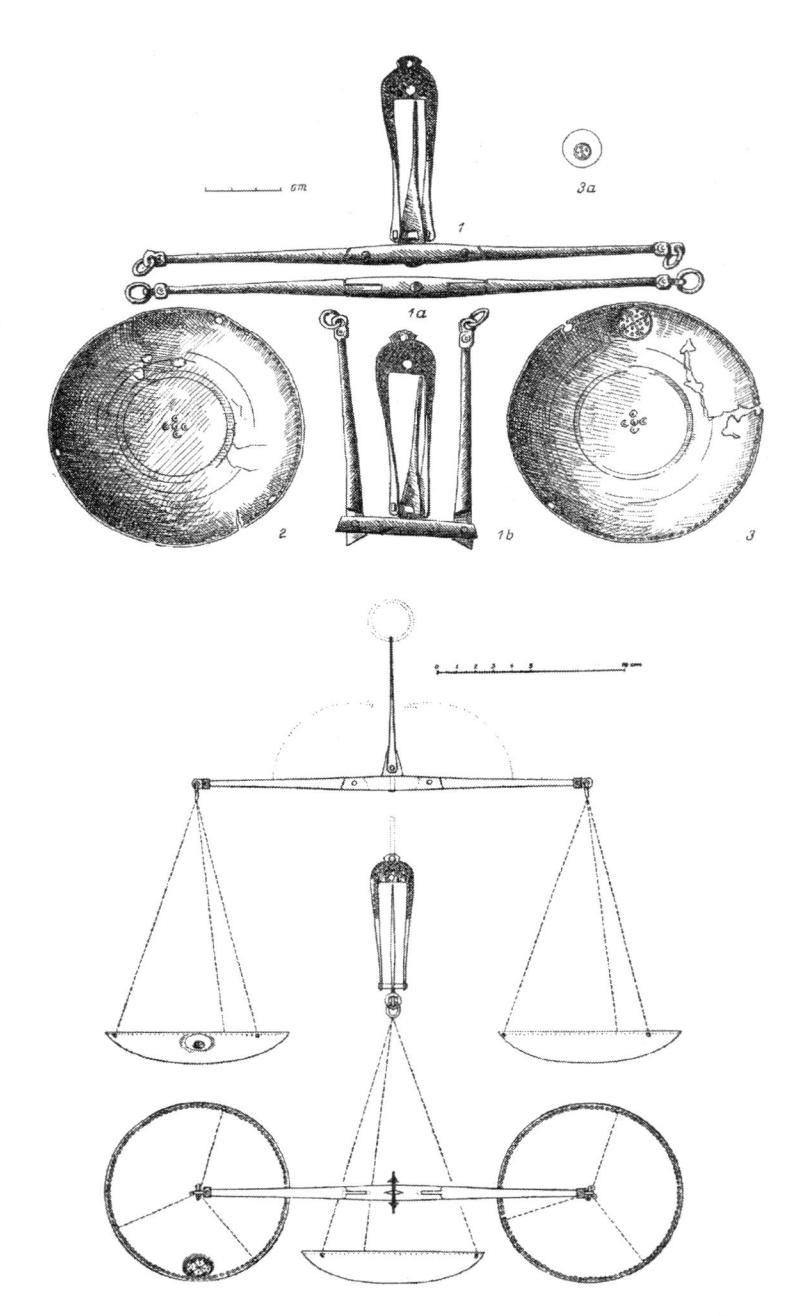

FIG. 11.1 Currency exchange scale from Kórház Street plot 20, Óbuda (First image by Nándor Fettich; reconstruction by István Méri).

presence of larger graphite particles in higher frequency than in smaller pots.[20] The fact, however, that large vessels were also made without adding graphite starting in the Neoolithic era goes against the assumption of better malleability.

Graphite is not available everywhere; although there are some quarries in the Carpathian Basin, their output is limited and most of them were probably discovered only in modern times. While there is a chance that quarrying took place at these sites prior to the modern era, it is not certain whether it was expressly for graphite or for some other material.[21] If one disregards the negligible domestic graphite deposits, it is evident that these materials were transported from elsewhere. Where could this indispensable material have come from? The most evident sources are Austrian, Bavarian, and Moravian–Bohemian quarries. Important mines can be found in some areas of the Bohemian Massif (southern Bohemian and southern Moravia), in the Waldviertel in Lower Austria, in the Dunkelsteinerwald south of the Danube, and in the Mühlviertel in Upper Austria – and also in the Bavarian Forest. Graphite can also be quarried in Styria, Carinthia, and Tyrol. The exact place of quarrying can be identified with scientific methods but few analyzes have been carried out on medieval pieces so far, unlike in the case of Iron Age Celtic graphite ceramics, for which significant differences in the material quarried in Bavaria (Passau, Kropfmühl) and southern Bavaria have been found.[22] Concerning ceramic finds from some Celtic sites in Hungary, research has shown that the graphite used originated from southern Moravia while the other "ingredients" were obtained locally.[23] The same can be presumed based on an extraordinary find from the early Iron Age (early La Tène) in Germany: a graphitic clay block, which was preserved in a burnt-out form measuring 5.4 kilograms – this supports the idea of some kind of transportation or trade of raw materials already back then.[24]

Because the clay was not purified and contained a lot of rough gravel some believe that in this "early period" potters used graphitic clay/soil that accumulated naturally rather than quarried graphite on its own. Jiří Waldhauser, based on his observations on the graphite ceramics of the Celtic period, distinguished three ranges of use for this pottery. The first is the location of graphite quarrying and a roughly 50-kilometer radius. Here, 20 to 57% of the ceramics unearthed were graphite-tempered ceramics (at some sites there were exceptionally high proportions of this type of ceramic, even 70 to 80%). This area was surrounded by another zone, spanning 50 to 100 kilometers from the quarry where proportion of graphite-tempered wares was 3 to 12%. According to Waldhauser, in this area graphite-tempered pots were still produced and the raw material was acquired by trade. However, one cannot disregard the possibility that graphite reached this area as a finished good (i.e., in pottery) and that it was only the "wrapping" of something else that was transported in it. In the third zone (100 to 170 kilometers from the quarry), the presence of graphite-tempered ceramics is even more scattered (0.6 to 3%)[25] and local production is dubious. It is likely that graphite ware arrived there by trade.[26] Independent of the period, the Carpathian Basin could only belong to this third zone.[27] Not only are written sources lacking for the Celtic period, but even in case of the medieval period, which is allegedly relatively rich in documentary historical evidence. The frequently referred to customs' register from Stein from the first half of the thirteenth century is unique.[28] The items listed under the names *havendach* and *prevhaven* in the register seem to attest that graphite or graphitic clay was once present in trade.[29] The Kingdom of Hungary, however, lacks such extraordinary sources and thus the export–import of these wares is entirely invisible in the historical record.

In the Kingdom of Hungary during the Middle Ages two major groups of graphite ceramics can be identified, "earlier" and "later," which can be divided – perhaps allowing some overlapping – by the middle of the thirteenth century.[30] The "later" group is particularly well known, which can be attributed to the abundance of these wares. This is why the secondary literature has paid more attention to this group from early on. It has been generally accepted that because of the connectivity of the Danube, graphite ware must have originated in Lower and/or Upper Austria and thus can only be considered an import. This conclusion came about for three reasons: first, because of the highly influential works of Imre Holl,[31] second, because of classic archaeological methods working with analogues, and third, because of the lack of materials' analysis. This position is totally understandable if one looks at the existing analogues, as they are surprisingly many and close. However, the objection that the overall picture is not that simple is also worth consideration. In addititon to the import of ceramics in some areas of the Carpathian Basin local pottery with southern German-Austrian roots may have existed as well.[32] This would also be logical because of the abundance of the finds and the fact that grey-burnt ceramics with entirely the same forms, but without graphite, are also known in major quantities in the Kingdom of Hungary.

The "earlier" graphite group is in sharp contrast with that discussed above as these pieces are known in smaller numbers from most sites;[33] in the majority of cases it is represented only by a few fragments, thus local production seems unlikely.[34] Yet it is also true that based on scientific investigations some ceramics were proven to have been produced locally (e.g., at Bácsa, present-day part of Győr).[35] The appearance of these pots can be connected either to trade or perhaps to some other reason, such as personal objects[36] or war booty.[37]

Based on ninth- through tenth-century analogues, the petrographic analysis of wares from Nitra,[38] carried out some ten years ago, and a new study from northwestern Transdanubia (Bácsa, Győr, Mosonmagyaróvár, Sopron[39]), the "Moravian direction" certainly seems to be underestimated in Hungarian scholarship, which can be attributed to the general archaeological interpretation of the later graphite ceramics.[40] Moreover, both northwestern Slovakian and western Transdanubian (western Hungary) fragments lead to the assumption that the spread and "popularization" of these ceramics, as well as the existence of trade and other relations, go back to the ninth and tenth centuries. It is telling that such fragments are known from the eastern confines of the Carolingian Empire, from the surroundings of Bratislava, the valley of the Váh River,[41] Mosonszentmiklós,[42] and from the emblematic site of Zalavár-Vársziget (called *Mosaburg* in Carolingian times).[43] In the case of the latter two, the ninth-century dating seems more probable.

The importance of the medieval market square of Óbuda

To what extent are the graphite ceramics unearthed at Óbuda unique? The answer is "only" in that they were found at a unique site. Similar published fragments are known in major quantities only from the territories of Bratislava and Nitra[44] in the Carpathian Basin. Along with these two sites the medieval market square of Óbuda (see Figs 11.2 and 11.3), more specifically the triangular space enclosed by the classicist synagogue (plot 163 Lajos Street), the cubical building on plot 160–162 Lajos Street), and the only standing medieval building (plot 158 Lajos Street) with the modern row of houses added to it on the south (plot 154–156 Lajos Street) is one of the most important sites of early graphite ceramics in the Carpathian Basin.

Luckily the medieval market square has remained to our time more or less in the same shape as it once was. This is only a continuation in shape, as with the exception of the house on plot 158 Lajos Street, the buildings, their function, and their memory have faded away with the medieval town and its population. The leading archaeologist of plots 163–167 Lajos Street, Vilmosné Bertalan, was aware of the importance of the architectural remains and finds unearthed there. This is why she started to prepare a final report on the work carried out there some time at the beginning of the 1990s.[45] Her death in 2008, however, put an end to the processing of the information from these excavations, although there is every reason to believe that she had been planning to complete this work for a long time because she also systematically analyzed and published her previous excavations. Her death – despite the indeed exemplarily accurate documentation – makes it difficult to study and synthesize the highly scattered urban excavations with fairly complex stratigraphy, as she fully understood. This is why a short article by István Vörös, which analyzed the bone finds from plots 165–167 Lajos Street, includes the most detailed description of the objects discovered at plot 165 Lajos Street up to now.[46] It would be in vain to search for this information in the published works of Vilmosné Bertalan. Only certain aspects of the excavations were covered in her lifetime, thus, for instance, unlike the "later"[47] graphite ceramics, the "earlier" ones recovered there sank more or less into oblivion.

Many fragments, of course – from an urban, much disturbed area – have been found accompanied by later finds, which in this case makes the exact dating of the finds impossible. Regrettably – due to the missing excavation report – hardly any information is available on the excavation at plot 160 Lajos Street, which defined the market square on the north, however, almost facing it, on the odd-numbered side of Lajos Street, plot plots 163 luckily provides the opposite example. During the excavations in 1963 and subsequently in 1970, stratigraphy and features free of late medieval or post-medieval disturbance were observed over a relatively large surface. In 1970, post holes belonging to a feature measuring 3.8 × 4 meters were discovered. The layer(s) containing "earlier" graphite ceramics may have come into existence during a leveling on the top of Roman layers. A number of post holes cut into the Roman layers and one feature with an outline that was difficult to

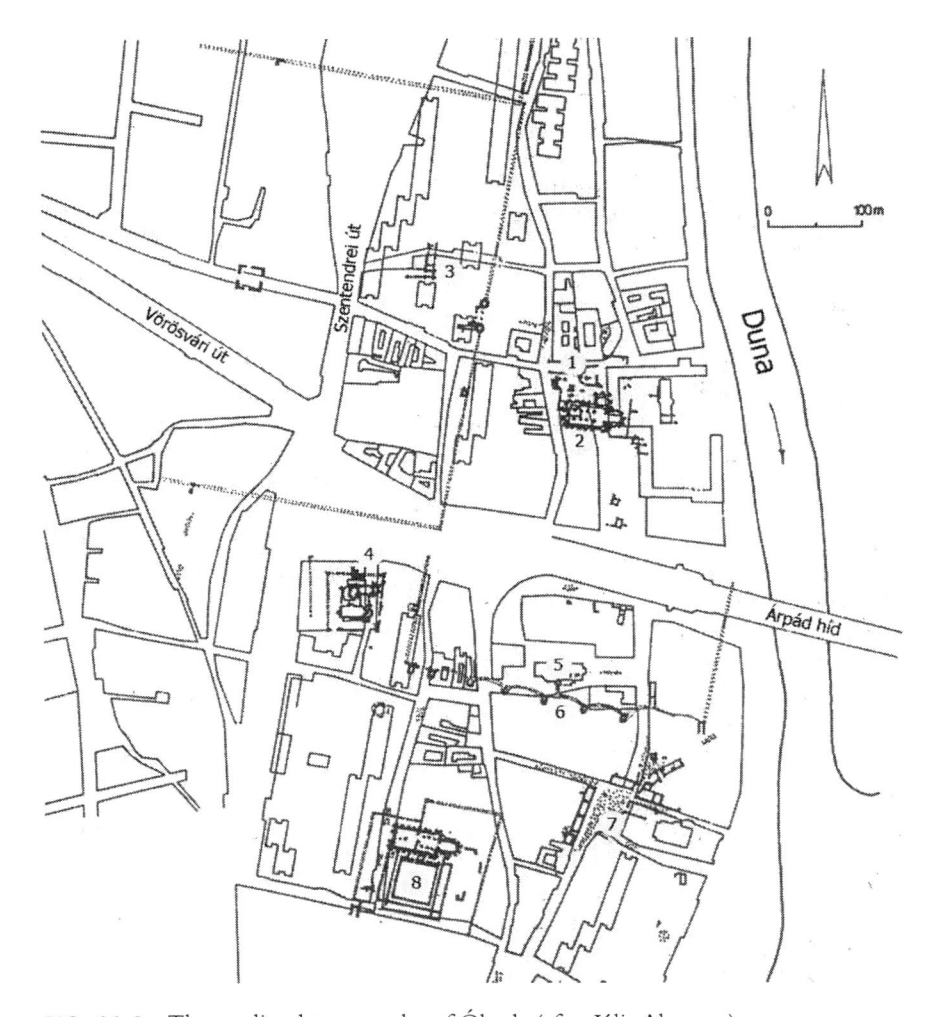

FIG. 11.2   The medieval topography of Óbuda (after Júlia Altmann)

1. St. Peter's Church, 2. Virgin Mary's Chruch, 3. Franciscan friary, 4. Royal, later queenly castle, 5. St. Mary's Chapel, 6. Walls of the Roman *castrum*, 7. The medieval market square with the surrounding row of houses, 8. Church of the Poor Clares.

define, was also filled in with the same debris, which was rich in graphite ceramics.[48] However, the richest deposit of Árpádian-age graphite ceramics and also the ones in the best context were preserved at plot 165 Lajos Street at the northeastern corner of the medieval market square. Here it was possible to excavate layers that were probably untouched even by the disturbances of the second half of the thirteenth century.

The most obvious basis for comparison would be the immediate neighborhood of the square, but these materials are as yet unprocessed. Our image of

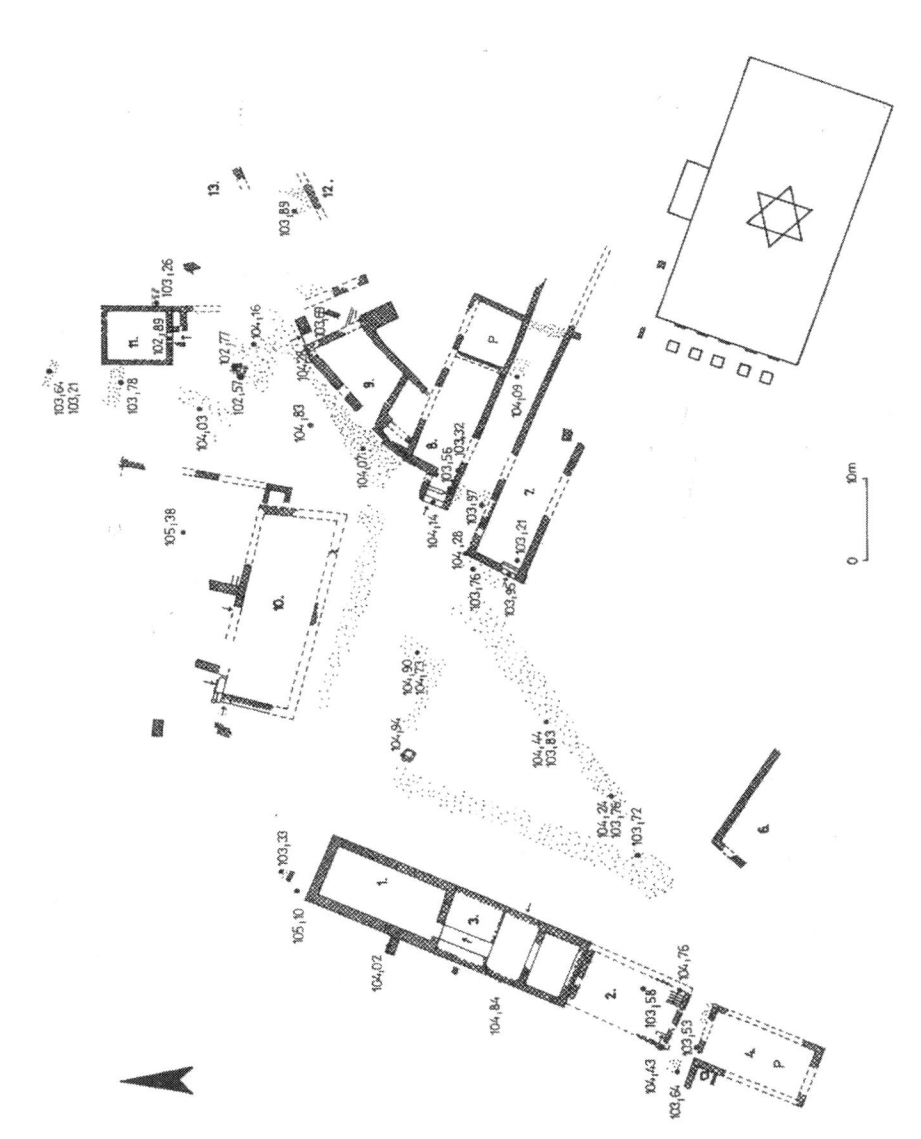

FIG. 11.3 Medieval market square of Óbuda (after Vilmosné Bertalan)

early Árpádian-age Óbuda can only be complemented by two excavations in the neighboring area: one carried out south of the Buda bridgehead of the Árpád Bridge on the site of a present-day hotel building, led – following the footsteps of János Szilágyi and Vilmosné Bertalan – by Júlia Altmann between 1985 and 1987,[49] and second, the site of a portion of a sunken house with associated graphite ceramics from the eleventh through twelfth centuries south of the synagogue, excavated by Vilmosné Bertalan.[50]

Fifty shades of graphite pottery

The secondary literature has probably dealt the most with graphite storage vessels. With the exception of a piece from Sankt Pölten considered to be from the fifteenth century, no complete vessel, to my knowledge, has been unearthed at any other site including Óbuda. However, more complete pieces of storage vessels with a slightly different "quadratic" profile, widespread in Moravian-Bohemian areas, are known. From Óbuda, pieces that exceed 20–30 centimeters in height or that have at least a relatively long part of their rims preserved (see Fig. 11.4/1–2) are rare. In most cases, 10–15-centimeter-long rim fragments or small fragments of sides were found. Thus, there are major uncertainties in the reconstruction of these vessels; the variety of fragments with different ornaments, rims, sides, and bases has so far been impossible to reconstruct.[51]

Gabriele Scharrer-Liška identified two major group types based on the rims of the ceramics. The rims of the first type are relatively thick compared to the sides and usually have a rectangular cross-section ("Bohemian–Moravian"). No piece of this type from Óbuda (or from the area of present-day Hungary) has ever been unearthed to my knowledge. This type is known, however, from a number of sites in present-day southwestern Slovakia, mostly in Nitra.[52] The second group consists of pieces with "club-shaped" (*keulenförmig*) rims, which are known from Óbuda. The 2/b sub-type (rounded, everted rim with oval cross-section and seemingly very thin sides compared to the robust size), known from Austria from the thirteenth century onwards, is rare in Óbuda. There are no fragments of this type in the early layers of Óbuda at all. Most of the storage vessels found in the layers at plots 163–165 Lajos Street belong to Gabriele Scharrer-Liška's 2/a sub-type, characterized by articulated, "club-shaped," and thickened rims. The excavation circumstances did not allow any more classification within this sub-type or building some kind of chronology. The basic forms are the same as the 2/a sub-type, but the rims and decorations on the shoulders of the vessels vary somewhat. They are all reduction fired with graphite, although I do not know of storage vessels of the same form but without graphite at either Óbuda or other sites. Though they differ greatly in diameter (33–63 centimeters), the character of the profile remains the same.

According to the secondary literature, the *ummäntelte Graphittonkeramik*, or mixed-fired ceramics, started to spread from the eleventh century onwards.[53] During the firing process first an oxygen-poor space was produced in a firing kiln, in consequence of which the material faded to grey, then after some time, air was

FIG. 11.4 Ceramic finds from the excavations at 165 Lajos Street, Óbuda. For the inventory number of the ceramics on Fig 11.4 and 11.5, see Bence Péterfi, "Egy hajdani 'locus communior' és ami belőle megmaradt. Grafitos kerámia az Árpád-kori Óbudán" [A former 'locus communior' and what remained of it. Graphite ceramics at Árpádian-age Óbuda] in *Pénz, posztó, piac: Gazdaságtörténeti tanulmányok a magyar középkorról* [Money, cloth, market. Studies in the economic history of medieval Hungary], ed. Boglárka Weisz (Budapest: MTA BTK Történettudományi Intézet, 2016), 457–493

gradually let into the firing chamber, which then burnt the surface of the ceramics red. Most of the finds from Óbuda, and especially the finds from the two plots mentioned above, where most of the storage vessels came from, were produced with this special technique. The brownish-grey, sometimes roseish, surface caused by the oxidation of the wares went only a tenth of a millimeter deep. Medium-grey fragments are rare. It should be noted that the oxidation of the wares did not always produce a homogeneous color, in many cases after the burning the color of the ceramic became patchy (probably because the surface of the ware did not redden after the firing).

In many cases the storage vessels were perforated, normally around the neck (sometimes even before the firing). The remains of wires can frequently be identified in these holes. There is no visible pattern in the placement of the holes; in a number of cases they can be found on the sides of the vessel. Based on this, there is reason to assume that the vessels with thin sides and comparatively heavy rims were strengthened by wiring, but there is a chance that the wiring was done in order to ease the moving of the ware. The perforation of the sides of the ware raises questions about the products transported in them; for instance, liquids can be ruled out. Also in the case of some cooking pots, the holes on the sides or at the neck testify to similar trussing.

We have surprisingly close analogues in the Lower and Upper Austrian territories, not only in the case of storage vessels, but also for cooking pots.[54] In the case of the former type there was a long-lasting form, which[55] – mostly based on parallels – is usually dated to the eleventh through twelfth centuries.[56] However, in the case of the cooking pots from the territory of Óbuda north of plots 163–165 Lajos Street – the surroundings of the bastions of the late Roman fortification (the find spot in itself raises questions) – we have some "earlier" pieces that, based on an analysis of their forms, seem confusingly early (tenth through eleventh century).[57] In most cases, however, based on analogues they can be dated to the twelfth rather than to the eleventh through twelfth century. Gabriele Scharrer-Liška devised a scheme, which, though lacking accurate references, helps with the classification of the Óbuda finds.[58] The works of Sabine Felgenhauer-Schmidt also support a similar chronology. Based on these works – which at this point form a working hypothesis that cannot be confirmed – the fragments can be classified into two groups, an eleventh-century group (more arcuate and with everted rims, see Fig. 11.5/6) and a twelfth-century group (arcuate or angularly splaying cut rims, see Fig. 11.5/3 and 11.5/5).[59]

After storage vessels, the highest number of finds are bowl fragments, followed by spindle whorls. Apart from these we have single fragments of some more unique types of vessels. Compared to the storage vessels and pots the cooking-pans and bowls are (much) later. Scattered cooking-pan fragments (from Bavaria) were identified, but none of them included graphite. The spread of these objects can be attested only from the beginning of the thirteenth century. Bowls treated with graphite were probably used already in the eleventh century, but the earliest object with certain dating comes only from the second half (?) of the twelfth century. Gabriele

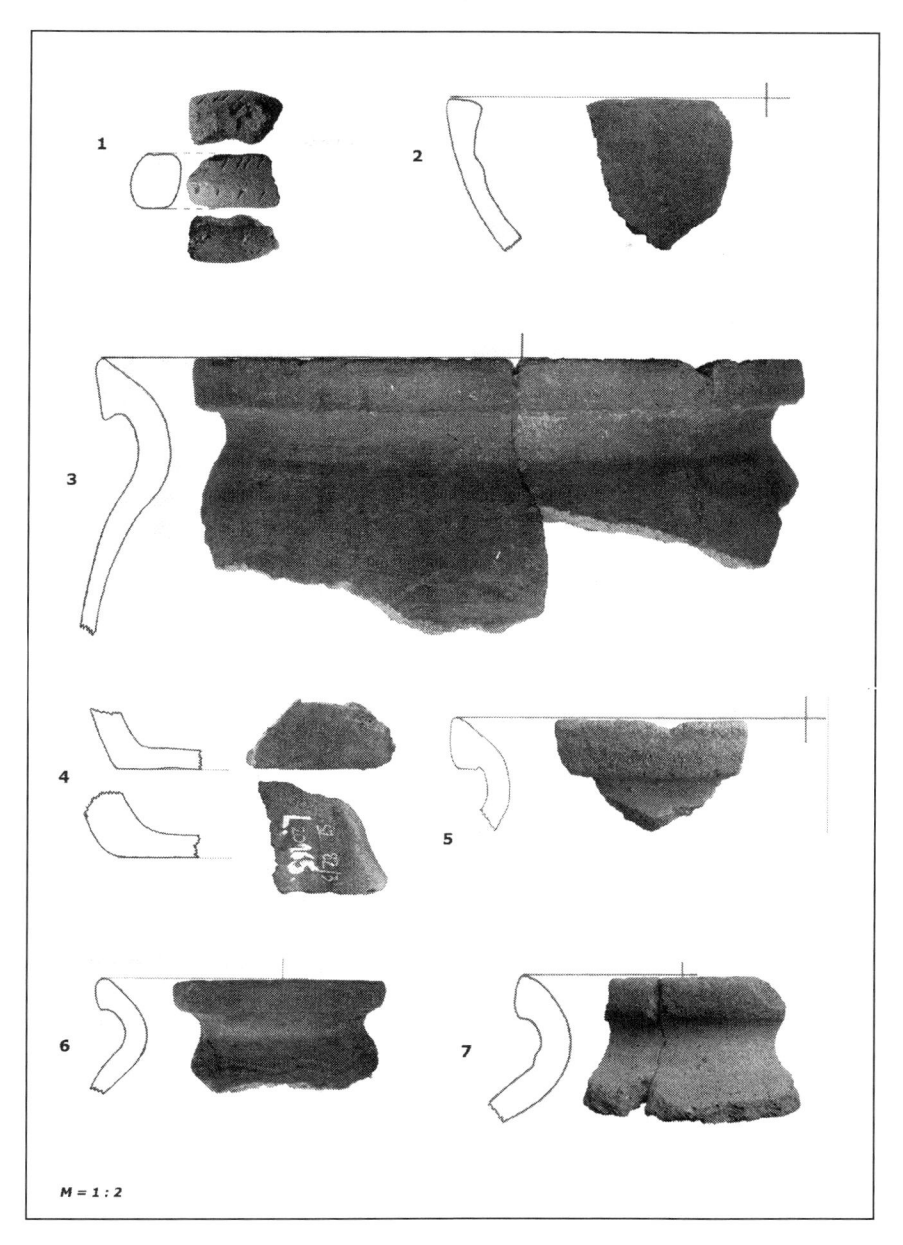

FIG. 11.5   Ceramic finds from the excavations at 165 Lajos Street, Óbuda

Scharrer-Liška classified the bowls into three groups based on their forms.[60] In the material studied here the first group is most often represented, but there are pieces belonging to the second group as well (see Fig. 11.5/2). There is also a piece that does not fit any of the groups set up by Scharrer-Liška.[61] This single cooking-pan fragment looks negligible, the only characteristic feature of it is that the one part of the side thickens heavily, which is likely to be the part that connected the side of the pan to the handle (see Fig. 11.5/4).

We also have one single fragment (see Fig. 11.5/7) of Scharrer-Liška's type 1 two-handled jar (*Doppelhenkelkanne*; everted rim, two handles starting from below the rim, rounded body, spout on the shoulder of the vessel). The difference between this piece and the graphite cooking pots is only that in the case of the aforementioned jar (independent of the type) the diameter of the base is "relatively small" compared to how the sides belly out. Much more important is the close analogue provided by a twelfth-century complete vessel from Möllersdorf. The vessel form in itself is a long-standing one; some scholars think it may go back to the seventh or eighth century. The emergence of type 1 jars can be dated to the eleventh century and they were popular up to the turn of the twelfth century, when stirrup jars (*Bügelkanne*) surpassed them in popularity.[62]

Lastly, a few words should be dedicated to spindle whorls. Their mention only at the end of this text is due to the fact that in most cases they were drilled out of the thick sides of other wares, mostly storage vessels. I only know of one piece that was originally made as a spindle whorl, and not as a secondary product. This conic piece was ornamented with notches (see Fig. 11.5/1). Because of recycling and the eminently functional form, the accurate dating of these objects is almost impossible.

Conclusions

As in many cases, there are no "usable" coin finds from either plot 163 Lajos Street or plot 165. From the surroundings of the medieval market square altogether four Árpádian-age coins were found, of which three are entirely useless in establishing a more precise dating, while the fourth does not help in dating the eleventh- through twelfth-century ceramics.[63] Thus, the most important supporting tool is the stratigraphy. The finds in the fill date to the eleventh and twelfth centuries. The most important question is how long the "earlier" group was in use, either up to the Mongol invasion (and the end of the golden age of Óbuda) or only to the turn of the twelfth century, by when the "absolute prevalence" of the graphite ceramics ceased to exist in Austria. One thing is for sure, the forerunners of the "later" graphite type appeared even before the Mongol invasion, as attested by, for instance, some finds from Budaújlak.[64]

It would be nice to confirm or refute the picture based on archaeological evidence with other sources or at least to provide some further considerations. The study of the material composition is self-evident. Vilmosné Bertalan, the archaeologist, already had this in mind as on some ceramics regular cut traces are visible and other signs also point to archaeometric analyzes carried out in Vienna. Ceramics, as well as some slag pieces, were sampled. The results of these analyzes, however, are not known.

It is baffling, however, that from the area of the town of Pest, which can be compared to early Óbuda in importance, no eleventh- or twelfth-century datable graphite ceramics have been unearthed, unlike at some other settlements in the surroundings of Óbuda and Pest such as Kána,[65] Soroksár,[66] and the territory of the later Víziváros.[67] How shall we evaluate the features sunken in the ground, filled-up with major quantities of graphite ceramics? Could they be the traces of a "pre-urban" settlement, perhaps those of the earliest Óbuda? Or were they – taking into an account the refuse found at plot 165 Lajos Street and the large kiln of unknown function excavated by Júlia Altmann in the second half of 1980 in the neighborhood[68] – only "workshops" and "farm-buildings" (i.e., not dwelling houses) close to the Danube landing. Even if at this point – with the excavations of Vilmosné Bertalan and Júlia Altmann as yet unprocessed – one cannot answer these questions with certainty, nonetheless, it cannot be doubted that the presence of the "earlier" graphite group testifies to the early long-distance trade connections of Óbuda, the artery of which was the Danube, and the heart the town's medieval market square.

Notes

* The research was supported by the "Lendület" Research Group on Hungarian Economic History at the Institute of History, Research Centre for the Humanities, Hungarian Academy of Sciencies, Budapest, Hungary (LP2015-4/2015). The present study is based on the author's MA thesis defended in 2013 at the Institute of Archaeology at Eötvös Loránd University, Budapest: Bence Péterfi, "Árpád-kori grafitos kerámia a Kárpát-medencében. Az óbudai Lajos utca 163–165. sz. telkek korai kerámiaanyaga" [Árpádian-period pottery with graphite from the Carpathian Basin. The early ceramics finds of plots 163–165 Lajos Street in Óbuda] (MA thesis, ELTE, 2013). I am thankful to István Feld (Eötvös Loránd University, Budapest) for his supervision during the work as well as to the members of the Budapest History Museum, especially to Eszter Kovács. This article was translated by András Vadas.

1 Óbuda, part of present-day Budapest, will be referred to in this form; however, until the Mongol invasion it was referred to as Buda and the differentiation only became systematic from the fourteenth century onwards.

2 Bernát L. Kumorovitz, "Buda (és Pest) 'fővárossá' alakulásának kezdetei" [The formation of Buda (and Pest) as 'capital' of Hungary], *Tanulmányok Budapest Múltjából* 18 (1971): 7–57, here 43. On the administrative role of Óbuda before the Mongol invasion, see Enikő Spekner, *Hogyan lett Buda a középkori Magyarország fővárosa? A budai királyi székhely története a 12. század végétől a 14. század közepéig* [How did Buda become the capital of medieval Hungary? The history of the Buda seat from the end of the 12th to the mid-14th century] (Monumenta Historica Budapestinensia, 17) (Budapest: BTM, 2015), 17–41.

3 Most recently, Júlia Altmann, Vilmosné Bertalan and Zoltán Kárpáti, "A budai (óbudai) társaskáptalan Péter temploma" [The St. Peter's Church of the Buda (Óbuda) Collegiate Chapter], *Budapest Régiségei* 37 (2003): 39–62.

4 Krisztina Havasi, "A király új palotája. Megjegyzések a kora 13. századi óbudai rezidencia művészettörténeti helyéhez," [The new palace of the king. Notes on the art historical position of the early 13th-century residence of Óbuda], in *In medio regni Hungariae. Régészeti, művészettörténeti és történeti kutatások "az országközépén"* [Archaeological, art historical, and historical research in the middle of the kingdom], ed. Elek Benkő and Krisztina Orosz (Budapest: MTA Bölcsészettudományi Kutatóközpont, 2015), 405–469 (with further literature on the topic).

5 [...]*multarum regionum divitias nobili civitati Estrigun navigio convehit* [...] – *Ex rerum Francogallicarum scriptoribus. Ex historiis auctorum Flandrensium Francogallica lingua scriptis* in

Monumenta Germaniae Historica. Scriptores, XXVI, ed. G[eorg] Waitz (Hannover: Hahn, 1882), 62.

6 István Elter, "Magyarország Idrīsī földrajzi művében (1154)" [Hungary in the geographic work of Idrīsī (1154)], *Acta Universitatis Szegediensis de Attila József nominatae. Acta Historica* 82 (1985): 53–63, here 57–58 and 60 (citing *Opus geographicum, sive "Liber ad eorum delectationem qui terras peragrare student,"* consilio et auctoritate E. Cerulli et al. una cum aliis ediderunt A. Bombaci et. al. [Naples–Rome: E. J. Brill, 1978], fasc. 8, 876, row 15 to 879, row 4, Clima VI, Sectio secunda as well as 882, row 1 to 889, row 11, Clima VI, Sectio tertia).

7 On this most recently, see Spekner, *Hogyan lett Buda*, 21–22 and 30–31.

8 Because of space restrictions I will not be able to discuss the objects found in Lajos Street plots 163 and 165 in this text; I aim to publish my findings on that matter in a separate paper.

9 Cf. István Feld, "Import Objects as Sources of the Economic History of Medieval Hungary," in *The Economy of Medieval Hungary* (East Central and Eastern Europe in the Middle Ages, 450–1450), ed. József Laszlovszky et al. (Leiden and Boston: Brill, 2018, forthcoming).

10 Cf. for instance: Barbara Scholkmann, "Die Tyrannei der Schriftquellen? Überlegungen zum Verhältnis materieller und schriftlicher Überlieferung in der Mittelalterarchäologie," in *Zwischen Erklären und Verstehen? Beiträge zu den erkenntnistheoretischen Grundlagen archäologischer Interpretation*, ed. Marlies Heinz, Manfred K. H. Eggert and Ulrich Veit (Muenster, New York, Berlin and Munich: Waxmann, 2003), 239–257.

11 István Méri, "Árpád-kori pénzváltó mérleg" [Árpádian-age currency exchange scales], *Folia Archaeologica* 6 (1954): 110–112, and Nándor Fettich, "Ötvösmester hagyatéka Esztergomban a tatárjárás korából" [Inheritance of a smith at Esztergom from the age of the Mongol invasion], *Komárom-Esztergom Megyei Múzeumok Közleményei* 1 (1968): 157–196, esp. 160 note 5.

12 Vilmosné Bertalan, "XIII. századi csuklós bronzmérlegek Óbudán" [13th-century balance scales from Óbuda], *Budapest Régiségei* 32 (1998): 171–180, esp. 171–172.

13 Heiko Steuer, "'Objektwanderung' als Quelle der Kommunikation. Die Möglichkeiten der Archäologie," in *Kommunikation und Alltag in Spätmittelalter und früher Neuzeit. Internationaler Kongress, Krems an der Donau, 9. bis 12. Oktober 1990*, ed. Helmut Hundsbichler (Vienna: Verlag der Österreichischen Akademie der Wissenschaften, 1992), 401–440, esp. 418. Abb. 6. For this type of scale in general see Heiko Steuer, *Waagen und Gewichte aus den mittelalterlichen Schleswig. Funde des 11. bis 13. Jahrhundert aus Europa als Quellen zur Handels- und Währungsgeschichte* (Zeitschrift für Archäologie des Mittelalters. Beiheft, 10) (Cologne and Bonn: [N. p.], 1997), 172–230. Both of these works were used and slightly modified by Vilmosné Bertalan (see note 12).

14 Cf. Péter Rostás, "Schmidt Miksa hagyatéka" [The inheritance of Miksa Schmidt], in *Egy közép-európai vállalkozó Budapesten. Schmidt Miksa bútorgyáros magyarországi tevékenysége és hagyatéka* [A Central European businessman in Budapest. The Hungarian activities and inheritance of the furniture-contractor Miksa Schmidt], ed. Éva Horányi and Éva Kiss (Budapest: BTM, 2001), 11–83, esp. 39 and 77 notes 221–222.

15 See, e.g., Ferenc Makk, *The Árpáds and the Comneni: Political Relations Between Hungary and Byzantium in the 12th century* (Budapest: Akadémiai Kiadó, 1989).

16 András Kerényi, "Egy XII. századi óbudai bizánci pénzlelet" [A 12th-century Byzantine coin-hoard], *Budapest Régiségei* 15 (1950): 541–547, esp. 541–542 and 546 (translation mine, BP). On the historical-archaeological evaluation of Byzantine trade, see Károly Mesterházy, "Régészeti adatok Magyarország 10–11. századi kereskedelméhez"

[Archaeological data on the 10th–11th-century trade of Hungary], *Századok* 127 (1993): 450–468, esp. 453–456 and 464–465 Figs. 11.1; András Kubinyi, "A magyar várostörténet első fejezete" [The first chapter of urban development in Hungary], in *Társadalomtörténeti tanulmányok* [Studies in social history] (Studia Miskolcinensia, 2), ed. Csaba Fazekas (Miskolc: Miskolci Egyetem, 1996), 36–46, esp. 38–39; András Kubinyi, *Városfejlődés és vásárhálózat a középkori Alföldön és az Alföld szélén* [Urban development and market network in the Great Hungarian Plain and its margins in the Middle Ages] (Dél-Alföldi Évszázadok, 14) (Szeged: Csongrád Megyei Levéltár, 2000), 171–173.

17 Cf. István Gedai "Fremde Münzen im Karpatenbecken aus den 11.–13. Jahrhunderten," *Acta Archaeologica Academiae Scientiarum Hungaricae* 21 (1969): 105–148, esp. 110.

18 Bertalan, "XIII. századi csuklós bronzmérlegek," 174–175 maps 1–2.

19 György Duma and Csaba Ravasz, "Graphithaltige Gefäße aus Österreichs Mittelalter," *Archaeologia Austriaca* 59–60 (1976): 225–242; György Duma, "Cserépedények grafittartalmának gyakorlati jelentősége" [The practical importance of the graphite content of pottery], *Múzeumi Műtárgyvédelem* 7 (1980): 13–26, and idem, "Középkori grafitos kerámiák Magyarországon" [Medieval graphite pottery in Hungary], *Építőanyag* 39 (1987): 177–182.

20 Paweł Rzeźnik and Henryk Stoksik, "Silesian *Graphittonkeramik* of the 12th–13th Centuries in the Light of Specialist Analyses of Vessels from Racibórz," *Archeologické Rozhledy* 56 (2004): 321–342, esp. 325–335. The same content, but with less background material, is published in Paweł Rzeźnik and Henryk Stoksik, "Weakening and Structural Temper. A New Approach to the Interpretation of Results of Physico-Chemical Tests on Medieval Pottery Pastes," *Archaeologia Polona* 46 (2008): 251–270, esp. 255, 257 and 264–267.

21 Cf. Duma, "Középkori grafitos kerámiák," 177 and Zoltán Zentai, "Tények és remények. Nyersanyagkutatás és a bányászkodás története a Kőszegi-hegységben" [Facts and hopes. The history of research into raw materials and mining in the Kőszegi Mountains], *Vasi Szemle* 52 (2000): 310–324, esp. 317, 320 and 322. On prehistoric graphite quarries in the territory of today's Northern Hungary (without mentioning the supporting data), see Magdolna B. Hellebrandt, "A nyersanyagok hatása a vaskor és a császárkor településeire a Sajó és a Bódva vidékén" [The role of raw materials in the settlements of the Iron Age and the Roman Imperial period in the region of the Sajó and Bódva rivers], *A Herman Ottó Múzeum Évkönyve* 43 (2004): 103–126, esp. 115 and 119–121.

22 For an overview (with the earlier scholarship), see C[laus] von Carnap-Bornheim, "Graphit und Graphittonkeramik," in *Reallexikon der Germanischen Altertumskunde*, XII, ed. Heinrich Beck, Heiko Steuer and Dieter Timpe (2nd ed. Berlin and New York: De Gruyter, 1998), 596–597, and Gabriele Scharrer-Liška, *Die hochmittelalterliche Grafitkeramik in Mitteleuropa und ihr Beitrag zur Wirtschaftsgeschichte. Forschungsstand – Hypothesen – offene Fragen* (Mainz: Verlag des Römisch-Germanischen Zentralmuseums, 2007), 15–16.

23 Izabella Havancsák et al., "Kelta grafitos kerámia: elmélet és gyakorlat. Dunaszentgyörgyi kerámiák ásványtani, petrográfiai és geokémiai vizsgálatának tükrében" [Celtic graphite pottery: theory and practice. The Dunaszentgyörgy ceramics in light of mineralogical, petrographic, and geochemical analyzes], *Archeometriai Műhely* 6, no. 1 (2009): 39–51, esp. 49–50; Izabella Havancsák et al., "A petrográfiai vizsgálatok jelentősége a kelta kerámiák grafitos soványítóanyagának provenicia meghatározásában" [The significance of petrographic investigations in the determination of provenance of graphitic temper in Celtic ceramics], *Archeometriai Műhely* 6, no. 4 (2009): 1–14, esp. 11–12, and Attila Kreiter et al., "Kelta kerámiák makroszkópos és petrográfiai vizsgálata / Macroscopic and petrographic analysis of Celtic ceramics," in *Település- és temetőfeltárás Dunaszentgyörgy határában*

/ *Settlement and Cemetery Excavations at the Borders of Dunaszentgyörgy*, ed. Judit Kvassay (Budapest: KÖSZ, 2009), 159–199, esp. 164–170.

24 Irene Kappel, "Zum Handel mit Graphiterde in der Frühlatènezeit," *Germania* 14 (1963): 13–18, esp. 17–18.

25 I do not think it makes sense to identify a low limit because even one single piece that can be dated with some certainty can be indicative.

26 Jiří Waldhauser, "Keltische Distributionssysteme von Graphittonkeramik und die Ausbeutung der Graphitlagerstätten während der fortgeschrittenen Latènezeit," *Archäologisches Korrespondenzblatt* 22 (1992), 377–392, here 379–383. Cf. also: Carnap-Bornheim, "Graphit und Graphittonkeramik," 596–597.

27 Miklós Takács has estimated the proportion of graphite pottery in the finds of the villages of Western Transdanubia: idem, "Österreichische Importgefäße in der Árpádenzeit," in *Der pannonische Raum um die Jahrtausendwende (vom 9. bis 12. Jahrhundert)*, ed. Margarete Wagner and Rudolf Kropf (Eisenstadt: Amt der Burgenländischen Landesregierung, 2010), 131–143, esp. 136. For further concrete numbers, see Szabina Merva, "'Rejtélyes bélyegű cserépedények.' Adatok a kisalföldi kora középkori grafitos kerámia régészeti és archaeometriai kutatásához" [Pottery with mysterious stamps. Data on the archaeometry and archaeology of early graphite pottery from the Little Hungarian Plain], in *Népek és kultúrák a Kárpát-medencében. Tanulmányok Mesterházy Károly tiszteletére* [Peoples and cultures in the Carpathian Basin. Studies in honor of Károly Mesterházy], ed. Ádám Bollók et al. ([N. p.]: MNM–Déri Múzeum–MTA BTK Régészeti Intézet–Szegedi Tudományegyetem, 2016), 521–541 (with an appendix by György Szakmány and Zsolt Bendő, "Kora középkori kisalföldi grafitos kerámiák petrográfiai és SEM-EDX vizsgálati eredményei" [Results of the petrographic and SEM-EDX analysis of the early medieval graphite pottery of the Little Hungarian Plain], in ibid., 542–562) as well as Péter Tomka and Szabina Merva, "Bácsa-Szent Vid domb. Eine Siedlung des 9.–10. Jahrhunderts an der Wieselburger Donau," *Antaeus. Communicationes ex Instituto Archaeologico Academiae Scientiarum Hungaricae* 34 (2016): 253–286.

28 Herbert Knittler, "Zum ältesten Steiner Zolltarif. Eine handelsgeschichtliche Untersuchung," *Mitteilungen des Kremser Stadtarchivs* 17–18 (1977–1978): 27–75.

29 The certainty of this statement is dubious: Scharrer-Liška, *Die hochmittelalterliche Grafitkeramik*, 14 and Tilman Mittelstraß, "Graphitkeramik des Mittelalters und der frühen Neuzeit in Altbayern. Ein Beitrag zum Beginn und zur Frühzeit der Obernzeller Produktion," *Bayerische Vorgeschichtsblätter* 72 (2007): 235–318, esp. 260. On the graphite quarried around Passau (earliest from 1453) see: W. Rudolph, "Geschichtliches über den bayerischen Graphit," *Verhandlungen des historischen Vereins für Niederbayern* 72 (1939): 43–90, esp. 46–47.

30 The forerunners of the "later" graphite group appeared even before the Mongol invasion, attested by, for instance, the finds at Budaújlak (today in the northwest part of Budapest, a bit south of Óbuda), see Zoltán Kárpáti, "Árpád-kori majorság Budaújlak területén" [An Árpádian age manor in the territory of Budaújlak], *Budapest Régiségei* 35 (2001): 587–615, esp. 589, 601 Fig. 8 (BTM KO (Budapesti Történeti Múzeum Középkori Osztály [Budapest History Museum, Medieval Department]) No 99.70.10.), 604 Figs. 11 (BTM KO No 99.70.6.) and 19 (BTM KO Nos 99.71.4, 99.71.5, 99.71.8, 99.71.43, 99.71.17, 99.71.6).

31 Imre Holl, "Külföldi kerámia Magyarországon (XIII–XVI. század)" [Foreign ceramics in Hungary (13th–16th-centuries], *Budapest Régiségei* 16 (1955): 147–197, esp. 163–176; idem, "Középkori cserépedények a budai várpalotából," *Budapest Régiségei* 20 (1963): 335–394, esp. 340–343, and idem, "Angaben zur mittelalterlichen Schwarzhafnerkeramik mit

Werkstattmarken," *Mitteilungen des Archäologischen Instituts der Akademie der Wissenschaften* 5 (1974–1975): 129–150, esp. 135–150.

32 Cf. Feld, "Imported Objects." During field walking at deserted sites in Lower Austria raw graphite blocks (Rohgrafit) have been found. This study does not include how far graphite quarries – perhaps known from the Middle Ages – were from these settlements; Kurt Bors, "Einzelwüstungen in Niederösterreich. Ein Bericht zu 81 verstreut liegenden Fundstellen," *Unsere Heimat* [NF] 74 (2003): 180–207, esp. 192 no. 30 and 194 no. 31.

33 For an overview of only the "earlier" graphite group in the whole of the Carpathian Basin, see: Takács, "Österreichische Importgefäße." For present-day Slovakia, see: Gabriel Fusek and Ján Spišiak, "Vrcholnostredoveká grafitová keramika z Nitry-Šindolky. Archeológia a minearológia" [Late medieval graphite ceramics from Nitry-Šindolka. Archeology and mineralogy], *Slovenská archeológia* 53 (2005): 265–336. With some further find spots for earlier graphite ceramics, see Péterfi, "Árpád-kori grafitos kerámia," 57–63 and Merva, "Rejtélyes bélyegű cserépedények," 524–530.

34 Based on the Slovakian graphite ceramics Fusek and Spišiak came to the same conclusion: Fusek and Spišiak, "Vrcholnostredoveká grafitová keramika," 334.

35 Merva, "Rejtélyes bélyegű cserépedények," 530 and 535.

36 Ibid., 535.

37 "aufgrund von Kriegsoperationen in unser Gebiet gelangt sein" – Fusek and Spišiak, "Vrcholnostredoveká grafitová keramika," 334.

38 "eine Rohstoffherkunft im Moravikum angenommen; die moldanubischen Graphitlagerstätten sind auszuschließen" – ibid., 333.

39 Merva, "Rejtélyes bélyegű cserépedények." The petrographic examinations were carried out by György Szakmány and Zsolt Bendő (ELTE TTK Institute of Geography and Earth Sciences, Department of Petrology and Geochemistry). For further petrographic investigation on the ceramics of some sites of the Western Transdanubian region, see Szabina Merva, "Adatok a IX. és X–XI. századi fazekasság működéséhez. Néhány északnyugat–magyarországi lelőhely kerámiájának archaeometriai elemzéséből levonható tanulság" [Data on the function of 9th- and 10th–11th-century pottery. Some lessons based on the archaeometric analysis of the ceramics finds of sites from northwestern Hungary], in *Beatus hono qui invenit sapientiam. Ünnepi kötet Tomka Péter 75. születésnapjára* [Jubilee volume in honor of Péter Tomka's 75th birthday], ed. Teréz Csécs and Miklós Takács (Győr: Lekri Group Kft., 2016), 463–476, with a petrographic analysis by György Szakmány ("Északnyugat-magyarországi IX–XI. századi kerámiák petrográfiai vizsgálati eredményei" [Results of the petrographic analysis of 9th–11th-century ceramics from northwestern Hungary], ibid., 477–494).

40 Perhaps the Austrian scholars were also driven by the same premises when they searched for the origin of the Austrian graphite pottery in Austria. Scharrer-Liška, *Die hochmittelalterliche Grafitkeramik in Mitteleuropa*, 94–95.

41 For a list of ninth- to tenth-century find spots in the territory of Slovakia, see Fusek and Spišiak, "Vrcholnostredoveká grafitová keramika," 306–307 and Fig. 14.

42 Balázs Martinschich, "A VIII–IX. századi települések kronológiája a Kisalföldön. Telepkerámia" [Chronology of the eighth- through ninth-century settlements of the Little Hungarian Plain. Ceramics from settlement] (MA thesis, ELTE, 2011), 76–79 and 87–88. I am thankful to the author for sharing his work with me.

43 Cf. Katalin Gergely, "Die Überreste des karolingerzeitlichen Herrenhofes un der Befestigung in Mosaburg/Zalavár," *Antaeus: Communicationes ex Instituto Archaeologico Academiae Scientiarum Hungaricae* 34 (2016): 287–372, esp. 296.

44 Fusek and Spišiak, "Vrcholnostredoveká grafitová keramika," 307–308 and Fig. 15.

45 BTM RA (Régészeti Adattár [Archaeological Data Collection]) no. 1678–92.

46 István Vörös, "Előzetes jelentés Budapest III. ker. Lajos u. 165–167. sz. alatti 11–13. sz.-i állatcsontleletekről" [Preliminary report on the 11th–13th-century animal bones from plots 165–167 Lajos Street, Budapest, District III], *Budapest Régiségei* 25 (1984): 439–440, esp. 439.

47 Vilmosné Bertalan, "Bélyeges ausztriai edények Óbudáról" [Austrian vessels with stamps from Óbuda], *Budapest Régiségei* 32 (1998): 181–209.

48 For the archaeological documentation, see: 1962: BTM RA no. 423–77 and 1970: BTM RA no. 446–77.

49 Júlia Altmann, "Piactér a középkori Óbudán" [The market square of medieval Óbuda], in *Változatok a történelemre. Tanulmányok Székely György tiszteletére* [Variations on history. Studies in honor of György Székely], ed. Gyöngyi Erdei and Balázs Nagy ([Budapest]: BTM, 2004), 59–63.

50 BTM RA no. 1635–91. Cf. [Vilmosné Bertalan], "A Középkori Osztály munkatársainak ásatásai és leletmentései 1981–1991 között" [Excavations and rescue excavations of the Medieval Department between 1981 and 1991], *Budapest Régiségei* 29 (1992): 237–251, esp. 248.

51 I do not have information concerning any complete ninth- to thirteenth-century Hungarian or Austrian piece. There is only one mostly complete piece from Sankt Pölten, see Scharrer-Liška, *Die hochmittelalterliche Grafitkeramik*, 39 Abb. 7. I think the reasoning behind the exclusively fifteenth-century dating of the piece is not convincing. On "Moravian" storage vessels cf., for instance, Rzeźnik and Stoksik, "Weakening and Structural Temper," 265 Fig. 13.

52 Fusek and Spišiak, *Vrcholnostredoveká grafitová keramika*, 288–293, 304, 333, and 335.

53 E.g., Hannelore Elfriede, Karin Kühtreiber, and Gabriele Scharrer, "Die Keramikformen des Hoch- und Spätmittelalters im Gebiet der heutigen Stadt Wien sowie der Bundesländer Niederösterreichs und Burgenland," in *Beiträge vom 34. Internationalen Hafnerei-Symposium auf Schloß Maretsch in Bozen / Südtirol, 2001* (Nearchos, 12 = Veröffentlichungen des Arbeitskreises für Keramikforschung, 3), ed. Werner Endres and Konrad Spindler (Innsbruck: Univ.-Buchhandlung Golf-Verl., 2003), 43–66, esp. 45.

54 Apart from Scharrer-Liška's work (Scharrer-Liška, *Die hochmittelalterliche Grafitkeramik*), see: Sabine Felgenhauer-Schmiedt, "Die hochmittelalterliche Burg Möllersdorf," *Beiträge zur Mittelalterarchäologie in Österreich* 2 (1986): 1–45, esp. 16, 33–34 Taf. 6–7, 43 Taf. 16, and Alice Kaltenberger, "Das Fundmaterial des Burgstalles Ober-Blasenstein in St. Thomas am Blasenstein, Bez. Perg, Oberösterreich," *Jahrbuch des O[ber]ö[sterreichischen] Musealvereines Gesellschaft für Landeskunde* 142 (1997): 53–127, esp. 57, 80–93 Taf. 1–7.

55 "ist anhand ethnographischer Parallelen als gesichert anzusehen, dass diese Art von Vorratskeramik sehr langlebig war" – Takács, "Österreichische Importgefäße," 135.

56 According to Szabina Merva, "A 10–11. századi kerámia keltezésének problematikája egy kisalföldi esettanulmány tükrében" [The problem of dating 10th–11th-century ceramics in light of a case study from the Little Hungarian Plain], in *Hadak útján 20. Népvándorláskor Fiatal Kutatóinak XX. Összejövetelének konferenciakötete* [On the path of armies. Proceedings of the 20th conference of young scholars working on the age of migrations], ed. Zsolt Petkes (Budapest: Magyar Nemzeti Múzeum Nemzeti Örökségvédelmi Központ, 2012), 271–286, esp. 277 – based on stratigraphic considerations – a limit starting in the tenth century is quite possible. The dating of the graphite pottery to the ninth to tenth centuries should not be refused. Szabina Merva, "A korai Árpád-kori sáncvárak keltezési lehetőségeiről" [On the possibilities

of dating early Árpádian-age hillforts], *Castrum: A Castrum Bene Egyesület Hírlevele* 9, no. 1–2 (2012): 5–31, esp. 12 and Figure 1. Cf. Scharrer-Liška, *Die hochmittelalterliche Grafitkeramik*, 40.

57 As there is little information on the find context I am not discussing the fragment: BTM KO no. 93.85.1.1., 93.85.2.1. Scharrer-Liška published a typology of the graphite cooking pots based on which one of the fragments (BTM KO no. 93.85.1.1) with its straight rim could be dated to the first half of the eleventh century. Cf. Scharrer-Liška, *Die hochmittelalterliche Grafitkeramik*, 37 Abb. 6.

58 Scharrer-Liška, *Die hochmittelalterliche Grafitkeramik*, 45.

59 Cf. *Keramische Bodenfunde aus Wien. Mittelalter – Neuzeit* ([N. p.]: [N. p.], [1982]), 46. Fig. 5, 52 and Fig. 6.

60 Scharrer-Liška, *Die hochmittelalterliche Grafitkeramik*, 52–55.

61 The fragmentary inner wall is ground down and ribbed on the outside: BTM KO No 97.31.87.1.

62 Scharrer-Liška, *Die hochmittelalterliche Grafitkeramik*, 57–60. The spout of this piece is not preserved. However, these otherwise extremely rare jar fragments are not unknown in Óbuda, see, for example: BTM KO no. 96.8.16.1. (7 Zichy Street). For the excavation, see BTM RA no. 653–78. For the fragments of the graphitic stirrup jar, see: BTM KO nos. 88.48.1.1. and 88.49.1.1 (Árpád Fejedelem Road and 179 Lajos Street).

63 1) BTM KO no. 92.148.7.1. (an obulus of Coloman I [1095–1116]); 2) BTM KO no. 92.149.21.1. (a denar of Eberhard II, archbishop of Salzburg [1200–1246], Friesach mint); 3) BTM KO no. 92.183.1.1. (a copper coin imitating Arabic coin of Stephen IV [1162–1163]); 4) BTM KO no. 93.77.21.1. (Stephen IV [1162–1163]) – ceramics dated to the thirteenth have been unearthed from this layer.

64 Kárpáti, "Árpád-kori majorság Budaújlak területén."

65 György Terei and Mária Vargha, "Madár alakú bronzcsat az Árpád-kor Kána faluból" [Bird shaped brooch from the Árpádian-age village of Kána], *Budapest Régiségei* 46 (2013): 151–166, esp. 157.

66 BTM KO no. 88.54.1. Cf. Irásné Melis, "Kerekegyháza középkori falu," 74.

67 Communication from Judit Benda (BTM).

68 Cf. Altmann, "Piactér a középkori Óbudán."

PART FOUR

Trade Relations of East Central Europe in the Late Medieval Period

12

MINING, COINAGE, AND METAL EXPORT IN THE THIRTEENTH CENTURY

The Czech Lands and Italy in Comparative Perspective

Roman Zaoral

A whole range of internal and external factors conditioned the economic growth of thirteenth-century East Central Europe.[1] Mining, coinage, and the metal trade had a multiplying effect on the economy of East Central Europe during the later Middle Ages. New settlers were interested increasingly in Bohemia and Hungary not only seeking free arable land, but also due to the opening of new silver and gold mines. Foreign prospectors, mining entrepreneurs, and financiers took technical innovations in various fields of life with them, including the Law of Emphyteusis (adopted from Roman law), which made it possible to convert agricultural products into money through paying rent. The general dissemination of fixed money rent made it possible to transform payment-in-kind into a monetary system. Economic changes in the thirteenth century laid the foundation for further development in the following century.

Failure to control supply during the initial upswing in golden and silver mining led to local money markets in East Central Europe being flooded with coin. Overpricing of domestic products caused most of the silver and gold to pass into the hands of merchants who exported it, receiving manufactured goods from Western and Southern Europe in exchange.[2] A manuscript compiled in the last third of the thirteenth century provides a detailed picture of the nature of this trade, listing the most important goods transported to Bruges. The references to Hungary, Bohemia, and Poland contain special information about the wares traded in this period:

> *Dou royaume de Hongrie vient cire, or et argent en plate. Dou royaume de Behaingne vient cire, or et argent et estain. Dou royaume de Polane vient or et argent en plate, cire, vairs et gris et coivre.*[3]

The same structure of commodities probably also applied to export to Venice.

Metals from East Central Europe were as important for the Venetian trade as thread from the West. The growth of Venice and its trade dominance was based on a balance between the volume of overseas trade and metal production, in which German miners and merchants played a part besides the Italians. Regensburg, a city with a high level of goldsmiths' trade, stayed at the forefront of the precious metals' market until the 1370s, when Nuremberg took over its position. A great deal of silver and gold, however, was transferred to Southern and Western Europe in more complicated ways than through direct trade connections. State and church payments moved precious metals, but more complicated ways were used in trade, too. Due to merchants from south German towns, some exported precious metal was converted into coins in the Holy Roman Empire or used to manufacture jewelry and only some of it reached Italy and Flanders as compensation for exported goods.[4]

Developments in the twelfth century

In the twelfth century, Italy established close relations with East Central European mining districts, which was affected by trade and political barriers. Intensive exchanges of trade goods began after a peace treaty was concluded between the Holy Roman Emperor Frederick I Barbarossa (1155–1190) and Venice, after which a new type of silver coin – the Venetian *grossi* – started to be struck. The first German silver suppliers appeared in Venice in the period between the third (1189–1192) and the fifth crusade (1213–1221). The richest foreigner there was a Regensburg merchant, Bernardus Teutonicus, who brought silver from Eastern Alpine mines (Friesach, Villach), Upper Hungary (present-day Slovakia), and Transylvania (present-day Romania).[5] He headed a private society which held a monopoly on the silver supply in Venice. From 1221 to 1225, the number of merchants coming from South German and Austrian towns increased considerably. German suppliers were vested with special rights which enabled them to build their own establishment (*Fondaco dei Tedeschi*) near the Rialto with about twenty brokers who dealt in the import of silver and copper ores.[6]

A regular flow of silver assisted Venice in surviving competition with Genoa and Pisa and at the same time it became a dynamic factor in the development of commodity-monetary relations for countries with sufficient supplies of raw materials.[7] At the same time, silver passing from Bohemia permitted mint masters to stabilize the main circulatory media in the West – the English sterling and Brabant denier.[8]

Prospectors in East Central Europe supplied both German and Italian towns not only with precious metals, but also with non-ferrous metals necessary for the production of weapons, various instruments, and ship's equipment.[9] Hungary concluded the first contract with merchants in Venice as early as 1217.[10] At that time, the volume of trade exchange was about 9,500 to 10,000 marks of silver.[11] A certain amount of Hungarian gold was also sent southwards in the thirteenth century, but the quantities available before 1320 were still insignificant in comparison with

West African gold. The Venetians were interested in the chambers connected with mining and the processing of precious metals, where they replaced the Jews who had dominated the economic administration of Hungary until then.[12] The first documentary proof of merchants from Venice traveling to the Holy Roman Empire to trade supported by the authority of the doge of Venice is from 1232.[13] As early as the first half of the thirteenth century, trade contacts had spread widely, as is evident from the customs regulations issued for Wiener Neustadt in 1244 by Frederick II, duke of Austria (1230–1246). The road to Venice via the Pyhrn Pass seems to have been in operation at that time.[14] Nevertheless, crucial developments in long-distance trade came only in the second half of the thirteenth century. The accurate specification of duties in the *Fondaco dei Tedeschi*, building a road across the Brenner Pass, and the opening of new trade routes via Nuremberg and West European passes directed at the Rhineland, Flanders, and England all laid the ground for the booming late medieval long-distance trade.

Further developments in the thirteenth century

The relatively rapid establishment of trade connections between Venice and Bohemia was not only a result of the expansion of silver production in the Bohemian-Moravian highlands from the late 1230s, but also of the expanding power of Ottokar II Přemysl, king of Bohemia (1253–1278), to the Alpine lands and the Venetian region in the 1260s and 1270s. He used the power struggle between the patriarchate of Aquileia and the local nobility to his own benefit; in 1270 he acquired Friuli and in the spring of 1272 his commissioner in Carinthia, Ulrich of Drnholec, captured Cividale. This added the patriarchate of Aquileia, centered in Udine, to the king's sphere of power and the local canonry elected Ottokar its captain general.[15] Ottokar and his allies had control of most of the towns situated on the way to Venice (Aquileia, Cividale, Pordenone, Treviso, Feltre, and Verona). Essentially the entire road from Prague or Brno via Vienna or Linz to Venice passed through the demesne of the king of Bohemia at that time.

The north Italian currency reform and its consequences

Ottokar, as a ruler related to the Hohenstaufen dynasty, seems to have been inspired by the economic reforms of Emperor Frederick II (1220–1250). The aim of his three reforms in 1253, 1260–1261, and 1268–1270 was to make trade contacts with Venice easier.[16] The solution lay in creating a system of measures to strengthen the quality of coins and make the exchange of coins minted earlier more practical. That is why the king ordered that measures and weights be renewed and marked.[17] Coins of lower weight but high quality (970–980/1000) and denominations of half value (*oboli*) were included in the currency systems of the Czech and Austrian lands and have been discovered in coin hoards. Coins of the same type were no longer struck in two different weights and new issues of pfennig-type deniers were put into circulation in Bohemia and Moravia; in addition, the weight of bracteates of the small flan became compatible with the weight of pfennigs. All this serves as proof of more advanced currency conditions than had previously existed.[18] At the same time, a new heavy pound of 280 grams seems to have been introduced in Moravia, seen in the modified bronze weight, originally much lighter, found at the Upper Square in Olomouc and dated to the second half of the thirteenth century.[19] Although Ottokar's daring and basically unrealistic plan to unify different currency units, weights, and measures remained unfinished,[20] it became a basis for introducing a Prague groschen in 1300 as one of the most stable currencies in late medieval Europe.

The timing of these changes in connection with the legal and administrative reforms in Venice is notable. The doges of Venice and the Major Council (*Maggior Consiglio*) took a number of measures to bring the booming long-distance trade under control. During the 1260s and 1270s, in Venice as well as in Bohemia, three and later four officers were entrusted with financial powers over trade transactions in precious metals,[21] silver circulation began to be taxed and regulated, and a law was passed concerning coinage. In Venice, moreover, a public debt and a permanent deposit were established, both indicative of an ever-more-complex financial sphere.[22]

During the second half of the thirteenth century, the number of mints leased to burghers increased considerably in both northern Italy and the Czech lands. The decentralization and "privatization" of coinage by means of leasing mints contrasted with centralization in the distribution of coin metal and assays of its quality. This is evident from the centralization of mining rights in Jihlava, where royal officials from all of Bohemia and Moravia were concentrated in 1272, responsible for the management of the proceeds from silver mining (the so-called *urburéři*).[23]

Assay offices in Venice and Prague serving for the quality control of coin metal are documented in the early 1260s.[24] Nevertheless, their effectiveness seems to have been insufficient. This is evident from the fact that precious metal control became more restrictive in 1278. The council of Venice ordered appraisers to weigh all silver offered for sale at their bank or in the mint. The mint master was obliged to buy it back for mintage and had the right to remove anyone who overpaid the silver price from the exchange office. Purchased silver could only be in the form of mined silver, coins, and alloys made in Venice. At the same time, silver alloys started to be marked with coining dies. Silver in coin form was allowed to be melted down only at the mint or state refinery in the Rialto.[25]

In order to find a reason for the rapid expansion of the money supply it is necessary to search for the uncontrolled mass production of coins that basically had an inflationary character. This is how the kings of Bohemia and Hungary were able to multiply their incomes and thus create conditions for enforcing a royal domain in mining and coinage, but taxation also played an important role. The sale of real estate was taxed at the amount of one sixteenth of a mark in weight, as is evident from the deed issued by the Vyšehrad chapter on 12 September 1279.[26] Nevertheless, regular re-coinage or coin renewal (*renovatio monetae*), pursued twice a year on St. Peter's day (29 June) and Candlemas (2 February),[27] were the most effective forms of taxing the population at that time.

The first mentions of silver taxation and regulation in Venice come from 1268 and 1270. They presumably referred to the regular supply of "German" silver (which seems to have come mainly from Jihlava), which had become dominant in Venice from the late 1260s.[28] German merchants arriving at the *Fondaco dei Tedeschi* were required to register their wares with the officials (*vicedomini*) supervising activity at the *Fondaco* within two days of their arrival. Should they fail to register a single mark of silver or coin they were to be subject to draconian penalties. By 1270, they had to pay a 2.5% tax on all their goods, including *argentin et platas argenti*.[29] These rules had not changed much even in the first half of the fourteenth century, as is evident from the merchant manual of Francesco Balducci Pegolotti, a Florentine factor for the Bardi banking house, according to which every merchant had to declare his supply in three days after his arrival and complete the sale in a week. In 15 to 20 days he was to be paid in Venetian *grossi*.[30] A similar ordinance was in force at Prague. In 1304, King Wenceslaus II (1278/83–1305) confirmed the decision of the Old and Lesser Towns that every foreign merchant was obliged to unload his goods and put them on the market for five days of his stay in Prague.[31]

In the thirteenth century, coins brought a temporary increase in the price of silver owing to mintage. This seems to have been the reason why cheaper unminted metal became widespread as a means of payment at the market.[32] To merchants it represented an advantageous counter-value for imported goods. It could often be carried without high customs duties; transporting it was less expensive than coins and also provided a guarantee of greater independence from weather conditions. Jiří Majer calculated that about 90% of the silver mined in the thirteenth-century Czech lands was sold in unminted form[33] and a similar situation has been demonstrated for Hungary as well.[34] The use of unminted metal was established primarily by larger payments and taxes.[35] The Venice mint allowed silver ingots to be purchased in 1273 and thus assisted in their spread. This practice was still common at the beginning of the fourteenth century. South German and Italian merchants took precious metals in various forms with them: silver ore, silver and gold jewelry, valid and devalued coins as well as silver ingots.[36] Such a variety of metal objects can be found, for example, in the hoard of Fuchsenhof, Upper Austria, concealed in the years 1276/78, which can be interpreted as one of many silver supplies for the *Fondaco dei Tedeschi*.[37]

The profit on unminted metal seems to have been greater than has been judged until now.[38] One of the principles in the capitulary of the "German" nation in 1278 is evidence of this; the price for silver alloys stipulated by the doge and his council is to be accepted, but the price for minted silver is not mentioned at all.[39] In his manual from the early fourteenth century, Zibaldone da Canal, a merchant of Venice, gives instructions for converting unminted metal and suggests that Venetian money-dealers purchase unminted silver from Germany and Hungary.[40] Silver supplies directly influenced the productive efficiency of the Venice mint, particularly after 1273, when the sale of silver ingots was authorized. Data published by Alan Stahl explicitly support this connection; the first marked upsurge of mintage came in the 1260s and 1270s with the peak of production in 1278.[41]

Payments in unminted metal are also documented in the Czech lands. The last will of Bruno of Schauenburg, bishop of Olomouc (1245–1281), dating to 1267, refers to unminted denier flans as a specific medium of payment. Bruno's efforts to avoid loss in the incomes of clerics caused by the mintage of light coins lay behind these measures. It is evident from the rule that wages for two hundred priests in the amount of 12 deniers each were to be paid not in a common devalued coin but in unminted metal.[42]

Silver production in Bohemia increased considerably from the 1270s to the 1350s. The exact output is, however, unknown. Ian Blanchard, referring to Jan Kořán, estimates that it increased to some 5 tons a year in ca. 1270, before finally rising to a peak of 6.5 tonnes of silver a year from 1298 to 1306.[43] Jiří Majer also mentions an output of 5 tons in the 1260s and 1270s. After the discovery of silver ore in Kutná Hora, however, the annual yield increased, according to him, to 10 tons at the end of the thirteenth century and to 20 tons in the first half of the next century.[44] Gold production in Hungary increased in the 1330s after the gold price had increased by 30 to 40% and Kremnica, one of the major mining towns in Hungary, had been founded in 1328.[45] From the 1330s to the 1370s, the annual gold production in Kremnica reached up to 400 kilograms in some years, while the total production of all the gold-panning sites and gold mines in Bohemia is estimated to have been 100–200 kilograms a year.[46]

The restrictive policy of Venice followed towards German merchants in the 1280s and 1290s created an opportunity for the Florentine entrepreneurs who controlled international financial operations. Moreover, Venice ceased to be the sole terminal destination in Italy for Bohemian silver which may have been re-exported from there to Florence.[47]

As early as 1262 Ottokar's court was in contact with the papal banker Dulcis de Burgo, a merchant of Florence, who settled the king's debt to the Papal Curia that had originated from Ottokar's divorce from his first wife Margaret of Austria and secured the legalization of his three natural children. The money transfer was handled through the treasury of St. Mark's Basilica in Venice.[48] In the 1280s, the papal collector Gerardus de Mutina raised tithes in cooperation with the Florence banking house of Jacopo Alfani[49] and in 1300 Andrew III, king of Hungary, deposited 4,500 florins from the sale of gold in the bank of Mozzi.[50] The insecurity caused by the 1299 Black versus White coups in Florence, as well as the anticipated profit from the mining and minting of precious metals, was probably the reason why some Florentine merchants started to take an interest in East Central Europe.[51]

The role of the private Florentine trading and financial company in Bohemia formed by Rinieri, Apardo, and Cyno called Lombardian is the best known. These partners acted as a bank and rented the office of mint master and a mine from the king, including royal income from smelted precious metals (the so-called *urbura*) with the aim of carrying out a complete monetary reform.[52] These Florentine financiers were able to improve their knowledge and experience thanks to the good quality of Bohemian and Moravian coins that had resulted from previous reforms.[53] They acquired the exclusive status in the framework of the Prague trade with abroad because they were exempt from the ordinance that goods of foreign provenience could only be sold with a written authentication of their origin. Thus, they could deal in luxury goods without restraints. Up to 1305, they carried on business in real estate and for a short time were charged with important powers related to economic administration. Nevertheless, the anticipation of fabulous gains from conducting business in the lands of the "silver" king clearly did not prove true, because Apardo traveled to Bohemia in 1311 to recover his claims. Many owed him money. In 1316, King John of Luxemburg (1310–1346) acknowledged the debt of his predecessors on the Bohemian throne in the amount of 28,000 silver marks. Such a high sum in fact could not be collected.[54]

The introduction of the Prague groschen in 1300 was accompanied by King Wenceslaus II issuing the Mining Code (*Ius Regale Montanorum*), which was drawn up by Gozzius of Orvieto, an Italian professor of law, based on the older German Mining Code of Jihlava. This code introduced Roman law into Bohemia by specifying the administrative and technical terms and conditions necessary for the operation of mines, such as the king's portion in mining and coinage, rules of labor safety, legislation on wages, and on work hours.[55]

Bohemian silver (*bracciali cioe buenmini* or *braccali coniata*) in the form of quality Prague groschen was not melted at the Venice mint but re-exported from Venice to other Italian towns as well as to Famagusta (Cyprus) and Lajazzo (Lesser Armenia).[56] Zibaldone da Canal traced silver from Germany (*l'argento che vien d'Alemagna*) in 1320 and Francesco Pegolotti states that the Prague groschen from the Kutná Hora mint, referred to as *buenmini dalla magna* ("Bohemian from Germany"), came to Venice via Vienna.[57] The Prague groschen (*grossi boemi*) became thus one of the most frequent silver denominations in fourteenth-century Italy, as is evident, for example, from the Pilgrimage Book of Siena.[58]

High earnings of the Prague patricians from colonization, mining, and the silver trade enabled the upper class settled in Bohemia and Moravia to purchase foreign luxury goods in larger quantities. The demand was considerable. They could purchase from foreign merchants "cheap" (in terms of silver) cottons and linens woven in Syria and Egypt, silk,[59] painted or enameled glass manufactured in Italy and Syria as well as a whole range of spices from India and Arabia that passed through the Levant. Silver of Bohemian origin flowed in the form of Venetian *grossi* to the Eastern Mediterranean and from 1261 to 1278 even towards the capital of the Mongol il-khanate in Persia, Tabriz, where a mint was opened in 1271 to process these burgeoning supplies.[60] In the opposite direction, luxury medieval textiles not only of Mediterranean, but also of Chinese and Persian origin were imported to Prague Castle, where fragments of some them are still preserved.[61]

Imported glass, primarily cups and dishes (bottles and beakers occur rarely), originated in Syria (Aleppo), northern Italy (Murano), Byzantium (Constantinople, Corinth), and in southwestern Germany. It was possible to buy these articles in Prague and Brno, so they seem to have become available even to persons outside the royal and bishop's courts.[62] Glass beakers decorated with colored enamels, made in Murano between 1280 and 1350, have been discovered in the holdings of Bohemian and Moravian patricians in Prague, Brno, Olomouc, and Jihlava.[63] The Prague finds do not only come from Prague Castle; they mostly come from places connected with the activities of foreign merchants, which means that they cannot be interpreted only as gifts and souvenirs from crusades but also as part of long-distance trade.[64]

Although hollow glassware came to transalpine countries mostly from 1270 to 1350, both in terms of the number of finds and of types and variants, some researchers are of the opinion that most products in fact originated concurrently in the last third of the thirteenth century when this high quality glass was spread over a major part of Europe.[65] This glass was connected with a high dining culture focused on wine consumption, which also gave the exchange of silver for glass an important cultural context. Archaeological finds from the fourteenth century show that imported glass gradually disappeared and was replaced by local glass production.[66] The "cheap" import of luxury goods to East Central Europe had, however, a negative impact as well. It was one of the reasons why industrial specialization did not develop to a sufficient degree nor a local trader stratum with strong capital, which would have kept foreign trade on a larger scale. The import of foreign goods was therefore reimbursed by the export of precious metals throughout this period by those who participated as customers.

The effects of collecting money for the Papal Curia

Papal financial administration gave another important impulse towards general monetization. Venice occupied a key position in the management of papal money collection in East Central Europe. Money collected in the southeastern areas of the Holy Roman Empire (Austria, Bohemia, Moravia, and Silesia), Poland, and Hungary was usually sent to Rome via Venice, while Bruges played a decisive role for the Baltic region of the Hanseatic towns, Scandinavia, and northern parts of Poland. During the Avignon papacy (1309–1377), however, the payment flow via Venice weakened as more money was transferred via Bruges.[67]

The clergy in Bohemia had paid a regular tithe to Rome since 1229.[68] Master Simon, scribe of Pope Gregory IX (1227–1241), the first known papal money collector for Bohemia, Moravia, Poland, and Pomerania, is named in a papal letter dating to 29 May 1230.[69] Collecting money was made possible thanks to the more favorable conditions which had recently been established in Bohemia. In 1222, Ottokar I Přemysl, king of Bohemia (1198–1230), concluded a concordat with the church and, roughly at the same time, began to coin bracteates as a new form of higher quality denier.[70]

In the early 1260s, the Czech lands seem to have played an important role in the management of papal collections.[71] On 26 September 1261, Pope Urban IV (1261–1264) appointed his nuncius, Petrus de Pontecurvo (Peter of Pontecorvo), *clericus capellae*, archdeacon of Hradisko Monastery, to deposit money collected from Poland, Hungary, Bohemia, and Moravia at the court of Bruno of Schauenburg, bishop of Olomouc (1245–1281), and to secure its transfer to the treasury in St. Mark's Basilica in Venice.[72] At the same time, the pope issued an order with the aim of providing security for the transfer of this money from Olomouc to Venice.[73] There is no doubt that the concentration of papal collections in Olomouc stimulated long-distance trade. Nevertheless, in 1263, the place where the money collected from Poland by Petrus de Pontecurvo and Master Stephan, archdeacon of Opole, was to be deposited was moved to the Abbey of Our Lady of the Scots in Vienna, where it was taken over by brothers of the Teutonic Order and transferred to Venice.[74] Vienna then became the most important place for papal collectors and traders in East Central Europe for many decades.

The thirteenth century, briefly

In the absence of traveler's checks in thirteenth-century East Central Europe, papal collectors or special messengers were forced to transport ready cash and precious metals. The East Central European region was, in general, regarded as insufficiently secure. The danger of robbery was high for both churchmen and merchants. For this reason, amounts sent from East Central Europe were usually smaller than 1,000 florins.[75] Such sums were often transferred in unminted metal. The accounts of Master Gerardus, tax collector in Hungary and Poland from 1281 to 1286, distinguished two types of silver: smelted silver (*argenti fusi*) and black silver (*argenti nigri*). The prescribed gold-black silver rate was 1:15.[76]

Favorable conditions for trade and money transactions created in the thirteenth century were fully developed in the following period, mainly thanks to the expansion of the South German towns. When the council of Vienne imposed a veto on trade with Muslims in 1312, Bohemia and Hungary became the most important producers of precious metal in late medieval Europe. The silver and gold supplies to the Venice mint culminated in the years of 1330 to 1380.

The acceptance of the basic principles of the north Italian currency reform which consisted of improving the fineness and weight of coins, creating a flexible currency system, and integrating gold denominations in a new system of the traditional European silver standard, was important for consolidating economic development in East Central Europe. Extremely large supplies of silver and quality coin in the form of Prague *groschen* attracted the attention of prospectors, merchants, and financial entrepreneurs from distant countries. The influx of luxury goods, however, had a drawback; it took on such dimensions in the fourteenth and fifteenth centuries that it suppressed the expansion of home craft production.[77]

Precious metals became an instrument for a more effective connection of East Central Europe with the advanced hub of the European economy. Not only mining and coinage but also collecting money for the Papal Curia assisted the penetration of Italian financiers and merchants into East Central Europe. Their expansion in the 1290s made Prague "a city with extraordinary consumption conditions within the scope of a local market," in which a relatively numerous Italian colony was settled.[78] Trade helped to connect different cultural regions of Europe and to reduce differences among them, which I take as one of the most important processes of late medieval history.

Notes

1 This paper was supported by the Czech Ministry of Education, Youth and Sports – Institutional Support for Long-term Development of Research Organizations – Charles University, Faculty of Humanities, 2015.

2 Bálint Hóman, "La Circolazione delle monete d'oro in Ungheria dal X al XIV secolo e la crisi europea dell' oro nel secolo XIV.," *Rivisita Italiana di Numismatica*, second series 5 (1922): 109–156, here 134 and 140.

3 *Hansische Urkundenbuch*, III, ed. K. Höhlbaum (Halle: Verlag der Buchhandlung des Waisenhauses, 1882–1886), 419 note 1. As is evident from this report as well as from the finds, ingots were more widespread in Hungary and Poland than in Bohemia.

4 Josef Janáček, "Stříbro a ekonomika českých zemí ve 13. století" [Silver and economy of the 13th-century Czech Lands], *Československý časopis historický* 20 (1972): 875–906, here 903–904.

5 Wolfgang von Stromer, "Bernardus Teutonicus und die Geschäftsbeziehungen zwischen den deutschen Ostalpen und Venedig vor Gründung des Fondaco dei Tedeschi," in *Beiträge zur Handels- und Verkehrsgeschichte* (Grazer Forschungen zur Wirtschafts- und Sozialgeschichte, 3), ed. Paul W. Roth (Graz: Selbstverlag der Lehrkanzel für Wirtschafts- und Sozialgeschichte am Institut für Geschichte der Universität, 1978), 1–15; Wolfgang von Stromer, "Venedig und die Weltwirtschaft um 1200. Ein neues Bild," in *Venedig und die Weltwirtschaft um 1200* (Studi / Centro Tedesco di Studi Veneziani, 7), ed. idem (Stuttgart: Thorbecke, 1999), 1–9. See also Gerhard Rösch, *Venedig und das Reich. Handels- und verkehrspolitische Beziehungen in der deutschen Kaiserzeit* (Bibliothek des Deutschen Historischen Instituts in Rom, 53) (Tübingen: Niemeyer, 1982).

6 Sources on the history of the *Fondaco dei Tedeschi* have been published by Georg Martin Thomas, *Capitular des Deutschen Hauses in Venedig* (Berlin: A. Asher & Co., 1874, repr. Vaduz: Topos, 1978). See also Henry Simonsfeld, *Der Fondaco dei Tedeschi in Venedig und die deutsch-venetianischen Handelsbeziehungen*, I–II (Stuttgart: Cotta, 1887); Karl-Ernst Lupprian, "Zur Entstehung des Fondaco dei Tedeschi in Venedig," in *Grundwissenschaften und Geschichte. Festschrift für P. Acht* (Münchener Historische Studien. Abt. Geschichtliche Hilfswissenschaften, 15), ed. Waldemar Schlögl and Peter Herde (Kallmünz: Lassleben, 1976), 128–134; Karl-Ernst Lupprian, *Il Fondaco dei Tedeschi e la sua funzione di controllo del comercio tedesco a Venezia* (Venice: Centro Tedesco di Studi Veneziani, 1978) and Rösch, *Venedig und das Reich*, 85–96.

7 Trade relations between Venice and Central Europe are the subjects of many studies by Wolfgang von Stromer. See particularly idem, "Binationale deutsch-italienische Handelsgesellschaften im Mittelalter," in *Kommunikation und Mobilität im Mittelalter. Begegnungen zwischen dem Süden und der Mitte Europas (11.–14. Jahrhundert)*, ed. Siegfried de Rachewiltz and Josef Riedmann (Sigmaringen: Thorbecke, 1995), 135–158. This topic was also a subject of discussion at the conference in Prato (Wolfgang von Stromer, Frederic C. Lane, and Peter Spufford), taken down in the proceedings *La moneta nell'economia europea: secoli XIII–XVIII: atti della "settima Settimana di studio" (11–17 aprile 1975)*, ed. Vera Barbagli Bagnoli (Firenze: Le Monnier, 1981), 145, 157–158, and 879. From the Czech side, see Josef Janáček, "L'argent tchèque et la Méditerranée (XIVe et XVe siècles)," in *Mélanges en l'honneur de Fernand Braudel*, I (Toulouse: Privat, 1972), 245–261; Roman Zaoral, "Silver and Glass in Medieval Trade and Cultural Exchange between Venice and the Bohemian Kingdom," *The Czech Historical Review / Český časopis historický* 109 (2011): 235–261. See also idem, "Wirtschaftsbeziehungen zwischen Bayern

und Böhmen. Die Handelskontakte Prags mit Eger, Regensburg, Nürnberg und Venedig im 13. Jahrhundert," in *Bayern und Böhmen. Kontakt, Konflikt, Kultur*, ed. Robert Luft, Ludwig Eiber (Munich: Oldenbourg, 2007), 13–34, and Roman Zaoral, "České země a Benátky: k obchodním stykům ve 13. století" [The Czech Lands and Venice: trade contacts in the 13th century], in *Odorik z Pordenone: z Benátek do Pekingu a zpět / Odoric of Pordenone: from Venice to Peking and Back*, ed. Petr Sommer and Vladimír Liščák (Prague: Centrum medievistických studií: Filosofia, 2008), 75–94.

  8 Ian Blanchard, *Mining, Metallurgy and Minting in the Middle Ages, III. Continuing Afro-European Supremacy, 1250–1450* (Stuttgart: F. Steiner, 2005), 938–956.

  9 Tin, copper, and lead occur most often among non-ferrous metals exported from Central Europe. See in detail Blanchard, *Mining*, 1451–1572.

10 *Monumenta spectantia historiam Slavorum meridionalium*, I, ed. Šime Ljubić (Zagreb: Academia Scientiarum et Artium Slavorum Meridionalium, 1868), 29–31 (no. 38; 1217). On the beginnings of trade contacts between Hungary and Venice see Zsuzsanna Teke, *Velencei-magyar kereskedelmi kapcsolatok a XIII–XV. században* [Trade contacts between Venice and Hungary in the 13th to 15th centuries] (Budapest: Akadémiai, 1979), Martin Štefánik, "Počiatky obchodných stykov Uhorska s Benátskou republikou za dynastie Arpádovcov" [The Beginnings of the trade contacts of Hungary with the Republic of Venice under the Árpádian dynasty], *Historický časopis* 50 (2002): 553–568.

11 Ibid., 564.

12 Boglárka Weisz, "Zsidók a budai jogkönyvben" [Jews in the Law Code of Buda], in *Magyaroknak eleiről. Ünnepi tanulmányok a hatvan esztendős Makk Ferenc tiszteletére* [On the forerunners of the Hungarians. Studies in honor of the 60th birthday of Ferenc Makk], ed. Ferenc Piti (Szeged: Szegedi Középkorász Műhely, 2000), 681–694; Zoltán Batizi, "Mining in Medieval Hungary," in *The Economy of Medieval Hungary* (East Central and Eastern Europe in the Middle Ages, 450–1450, 49), ed. József Laszlovszky et al. (Leiden and Boston: Brill, 2018), 166–181. Katalin Szende, "Traders, 'Court Jews', Town Jews: The Changing Roles of Hungary's Jewish Population in the Light of Royal Policy between the Eleventh and Fourteenth Centuries," in *Intricate Interfaith Networks in the Middle Ages: Quotidian Jewish-Christian Contacts*, ed. Ephraim Shoham-Steiner (Turnhout: Brepols Publishers, 2016), 119–151.

13 Simonsfeld, *Fondaco*, II, 31.

14 Rösch, *Venedig und das Reich*, 87.

15 Roberto Cessi, *Venezia nel Duecento: tra Oriente e Occidente* (Venice: Deputazione editrice, 1985), 257 and Václav Novotný, *České dějiny*, I/4 [History of Bohemia] (Prague: Laichter, 1937), 252.

16 Zaoral, "Silver and glass," 245–246.

17 *Codex diplomaticus et epistolaris regni Bohemiae*, V/2, ed. Jindřich Šebánek and Saša Dušková (Prague: Sumptibus Academiae scientiarum bohemoslovacae, 1981), 478–479 (no. 794). See also *Fontes rerum Bohemicarum*, II, ed. Josef Emler and Václav Vladivoj Tomek (Prague: Nakladatelství Musea Království českého, 1874), 300.

18 Roman Zaoral, "Die böhmischen und mährischen Münzen des Schatzfundes von Fuchsenhof," in *Der Schatzfund von Fuchsenhof* (Studien zur Kulturgeschichte von Oberösterreich, 15), ed. Bernhard Prokisch and Thomas Kühtreiber (Linz: Oberösterreichisches Landesmuseum, 2004), 95–132.

19 Jiří Doležel, "Středověká miskovitá (lotová) závaží v českých a moravských nálezech" [Medieval bowl-shaped weights from the finds in Bohemia and Moravia], *Přehled výzkumů* 49 (2008): 183–215, here 198–201.

20 His bracteates from the mints of Sankt Veit and Völkermarkt, following Bohemian patterns, are indicative of it, see Tomáš Krejčík, "Mincovnictví Přemysla Otakara II. v alpských zemích" [The Coinage of Přemysl II Ottokar in the Alpine lands], *Folia historica bohemica* 1 (1979): 209–224 and Vratislav Vaníček, *Velké dějiny zemí Koruny české*, III, 1250–1310 [History of Czech crown lands] (Prague: Paseka, 2002), 328–329.

21 Miloš Dvořák, "Císař Karel IV. a pražský zahraniční obchod I" [Emperor Charles IV and Prague's foreign trade], *Pražský sborník historický* 34 (2006): 7–91, here 22.

22 Alan M. Stahl, *Zecca. The Mint of Venice in the Middle Ages* (Baltimore, London, and New York: Johns Hopkins University Press in association with the American Numismatic Society, 2000), passim. See also Lucia Travaini, "Mint organization in Italy between the twelfth and fourteenth centuries: a survey," in *Later Medieval Mints: Organisation, Administration, Techniques. 8th Oxford Symposium on Coinage and Monetary History* (BAR International Series, 389), ed. Nicholas John Mayhew and Peter Spufford (Oxford: B.A.R., 1977), 39–60.

23 *Codex diplomaticus et epistolaris regni Bohemiae*, V/2, 320 (no. 681).

24 Ibid., V/2, 478–479 (no. 794).

25 Stahl, *Zecca*, 138–139 and 169.

26 *Regesta diplomatica nec non epistolaria Bohemiae et Moraviae*, I–VII, ed. Karel Jaromír Erben, Josef Emler, and Bedrich Mendl (Prague: Wiesner, 1855–1963), II, 515–516 (no. 1189).

27 Ibid., II, 1014–1015 (no. 2334).

28 Janáček, "L'argent tchèque," 245–261.

29 *Problemi monetari veneziani*, ed. Roberto Cessi (Padua: A. Milan, 1937), 11–12 (nos. 14–15).

30 Francesco Balducci Pegolotti, *La pratica della mercatura*, ed. A. Evans (Cambridge, MA: Mediaeval Academy of America, 1936). The most recent discussion of Pegolotti is in Lucia Travaini, *Monete, mercanti e matematica: le monete medievali nei trattati di aritmetica e nei libri mercatura* (Rome: Jouvence, 2003), 118–130.

31 Prague, Archiv hlavního města Prahy [Prague City Archives], Manuscript collection, no. 986, fol. 64. Quoted according to Miloš Dvořák, "Zahraniční a vnitřní obchod" [Foreign and internal trade], *Lucemburská Praha, 1310–1437* [Prague in the age of the Luxemburgs], ed. Jaroslava Mendelová, Pavla Státníková and Jan N. Assmann (Prague: Scriptorium, 2006), 124.

32 The supply of unminted metal in Venice is analyzed in more detail by Louise Buenger Robbert, "Il sistema monetario," in *Storia di Venezia*, II, ed. Rodolfo Pallucchini (Rome: Istituto della Enciclopedia italiana, 1995), 409–436. See also Blanchard, *Mining*, 936–970 and Stahl, *Zecca*, passim.

33 Jiří Majer, "Development of Quality Control in Mining, Metallurgy, and Coinage in the Czech Lands (up to the 19th Century)," in *History of Managing for Quality*, ed. Joseph M. Juran (Milwaukee, WI: ASQC Quality Press, 1995), Ch. 8, 264–266; Jiří Majer, *Rudné hornictví v Čechách, na Moravě a ve Slezsku* [Ore mining in the Czech lands, Moravia and Silesia] (Prague: Libri, 2004), 60.

34 See, for example, Márton Gyöngyössy, "Magyar pénztörténet: 1000–1526" [Hungarian coinage], in *Magyar középkori gazdaság- és pénztörténet. Jegyzet- és forrásgyűjtemény* [Sources on the medieval economy and coinage in Hungary], ed. idem (Budapest: Bölcsész Konzorcium, 2006), 227–286, and idem and Heinz Winter, *Münzen und Medaillen des ungarischen Mittelalters: 1000–1526* (Vienna: Kunsthistorisches Museum and Milano: Skira, 2007).

35 The unpunished use of unminted metal for large payments is, for example, documented in the report of the so-called Saar memorials from 1250, according to which a magnate weighed out 10 marks of gold and 104 marks of silver to his son-in-law. See *Fontes rerum Bohemicarum*, II, 528.

36 Klaus Fischer, *Regensburger Hochfinanz. Die Krise einer europäischen Metropole* (Regensburg: Univ.-Verl. Regensburg, 2003), 185. Fine silver and gold ingots were also changed into Venetian grossi and ducats later, as is evident from the account book of the Runtinger family of Regensburg from 1383–1407. Franz Bastian, *Das Runtingerbuch 1383–1407 und verwandtes Material zum Regensburger-südostdeutschen Handel und Münzwesen*, I–III (Regensburg: G. Bosse, 1935–1944).

37 *Der Schatzfund von Fuchsenhof*, 130–132.

38 Attention to this fact has been drawn in Frederic C. Lane and Reinhold C. Mueller, *Money and Banking in Medieval and Renaissance Venice I.: Coins and Money of Account* (Baltimore and London: Johns Hopkins University Press, 1985), 134–142. See also Frederic C. Lane, "Exportations vénitiennes d'or et d'argent de 1200 à 1450," in *Études d'histoire monétaire XIIe–XIXe siècles*, ed. John Day (Lille: Presses universitaires de Lille, 1984), 29–48.

39 *Capitular*, ch. 73.

40 Zibaldone da Canal, *Manoscritto mercantile del sec. XIV*, ed. Alfredo Stussi (Venice: Comitato per la pubblicazione delle fonti relative alla storia di Venezia, 1967).

41 Alan M. Stahl, "Venetian Coinage: Variations in Production," in *Rythmes de la production monétaire, de l'antiquité à nos jours. Actes du colloque international organisé à Paris du 10 au 12 janvier 1986* (Publications d'histoire de l'art et d'archéologie de l'Université catholique de Louvain, 50 = Numismatica Lovaniensia, 7), ed. Georges Depeyrot, Tony Hackens, and Ghislaine Moucharte (Louvain-la-Neuve: Séminaire de numismatique Marcel Hoc, Collège Erasme, 1987), 467–481, here 476–479.

42 *Codex diplomaticus et epistolaris Moraviae*, III, ed. Antonín Boczek (Olomouc: Skarnitzl, 1841), 402–408 (no. 402).

43 Blanchard, *Mining*, 930 prefers the figures of Jan Kořán, *Přehledné dějiny československého hornictví*, I [The history of Czechoslovak mining] (Prague: Nakladatelství Československé akademie věd, 1955), 89–90 and 195, based on actual mine revenues, to the hearsay and chronicle evidence presented by Peter Spufford, *Money and Its Use in Medieval Europe* (Cambridge and New York: Cambridge University Press, 1988), 125 or the estimations of Janáček, "L'argent tchèque," 259 note 12, which yield an exaggerated annual output figure of 20–25 tons.

44 Jiří Majer, "Konjunkturen und Krisen im böhmischen Silberbergbau des Spätmittelalters und der frühen Neuzeit. Zu ihren Ursachen und Folgen," in *Konjunkturen im europäischen Bergbau in vorindustrieller Zeit. Festschrift für Ekkehard Westermann zum 60. Geburtstag* (Vierteljahrschrift für Sozial- und Wirtschaftsgeschichte. Beihefte, 155), ed. Christoph Bartels and Markus A. Denzel (Stuttgart: Franz Steiner, 2000), 73–83, here 73 and 76–78.

45 Martin Štefánik, "Podoby ekonomickej spolupráce pri počiatkoch stredovekej Kremnice" [The forms of economic cooperation in the early years of the medieval town of Kremnica], in *Stredoveké mesto ako miesto stretnutí a komunikácie* [The medieval town as a place of meeting and communication], ed. Ján Lukačka and Martin Štefánik (Bratislava: Historický ústav SAV, 2010), 169–176, here 169.

46 Majer, *Rudné hornictví*, 52.

47 Unminted "German" silver appears in the early (ca. 1290) list for Florence, compiled some forty years later, under the guise of "della bolla di Venegia," bars of silver sealed at the Venice mint. See Philip Grierson, "The Coin List of Pegolotti," in *Studi in onore di Armando Sapori*, I (Milan: Instituto editoriale cisalpino, 1957), 485–492.

48 *Regesta diplomatica nec non epistolaria Bohemiae et Moraviae*, II, 146 (no. 374). See also Jaroslav Čechura, "Peněžní a finanční aktivity ve středověkých Čechách" [Money and financial activities in medieval Bohemia], in *Dějiny bankovnictví v českých zemích* [History

of banking in the Czech lands] (Prague: Bankovní Institut, 1999), 2–16 and 28–29. This report seems to relate to questionable data mentioned by F. L. Hübsch, *Versuch einer Geschichte des böhmischen Handels* (Prague: G. Haase, 1849), 112–113. Simonsfeld, *Der Fondaco*, II, 80 takes a critical stand to this report.

49 *Monumenta Vaticana historiam regni Hungariae illustrantia, I / 1. Rationes collectorum pontificiorum in Hungaria 1281–1375* (Budapest: Szent István Társulat, 1884, repr. Budapest: METEM, 2000), 1–12 (no. 1: 1281–1286).

50 Ibid., I / 1, 434 (no. 95: 25 October 1300).

51 Antonella Astorri, *La Mercanzia a Firenze nella prima metà del Trecento. Il potere dei grandi mercanti* (Florence: L. S. Olschki, 1998), 116 and 128.

52 In the light of recent research attesting Rinieri's presence to Bohemia since 1299, Josef Šusta's still- accepted commentary on a mediating role for Peter of Aspelt in real-izing Wenceslaus II's currency reform seems to be mere fiction. See Libor Jan, *Václav II. a struktury panovnické moci* [Wenceslaus II and the structures of sovereign power] (Brno: Matice moravská, 2006), 144–146. The activities of the Florentines in Bohemia have been described in detail by Winfried Reichert, "Oberitalienische Kaufleute und Montanunternehmer in Ostmitteleuropa während des 14. Jahrhunderts," in *Hochfinanz. Wirtschaftsräume. Innovationen. Festschrift für Wolfgang von Stromer*, I, ed. Uwe Bestmann, Franz Irsigler, and Jürgen Schneider (Trier: Auenthal, 1987), 269–356; W. Reichert, "Mercanti e monetieri italiani nel regno di Boemia nella prima metà del XIV secolo," in *Sistema di rapporti ed élites economiche in Europa (secoli XII–XVII)*, ed. Mario Del Treppo (Napoli: Liguori, 1994), 337–348.

53 Ivo Pánek, "Das Münzvermächtnis des 13. Jahrhunderts in Böhmen," *Numismatický sborník* 12 (1973): 65–74.

54 Jan, *Václav II.*, 147–148.

55 *Codex juris Bohemici*, I, ed. Hermenegild Jireček (Prague: Kober, 1867), 265–435. The mining code has been recently analyzed by Guido Ch. Pfeifer, *Ius Regale Montanorum. Ein Beitrag zur spätmittelalterlichen Rezeptionsgeschichte des römischen Rechtes im Mitteleuropa* (Ebelsbach: Aktiv Druck & Verlag, 2002).

56 Pegolotti, *La pratica della mercatura*, 60 and 81. See also Blanchard, *Mining*, 951–952.

57 Spufford, *Money*, 137–138.

58 Gabriela Piccinni and Lucia Travaini, *Il Libro del pellegrino (Siena 1382–1446). Affari, domini, monete nell'Ospedale di Santa Maria della Scala* (Naples: Liguori, 2003). See also Roman Zaoral and Jan Hrdina, "Peněžní hotovosti římských poutníků ve světle poutnické knihy ze Sieny, 1382–1446" [Cash of pilgrims to Rome in the light of the Pilgrim's Book of Siena, 1382–1446], *Numismatický sborník* 23 (2008): 191–204.

59 A list of home and foreign textiles in archaeological finds has been published by Helena Březinová, *Textilní výroba v českých zemích ve 13.–15. století* [Textile manufacture in the Czech Lands in the 13th to 15th centuries] (Prague and Brno: Ústav pro pravěk a ranou dobu dějinnou, Filozofická fakulta, Univerzita Karlova, 2007).

60 Blanchard, *Mining*, 946–947.

61 Milena Bravermanová, "Archeologický textilní fond na Pražském hradě" [Archaeological textile resources at the Prague Castle], in *Sborník semináře historie odívání* [Seminar in the history of clothing] (Zlín: Martina Hřibová, 2011), 109–138; see also Milena Bravermanová, "Historický textil na Pražském hradě" [Historical textiles at the Prague Castle], *Zprávy památkové péče* 65 (2005): 113–125.

62 A piece of written evidence for the Venetian glass trade in Prague at the end of the thir-teenth century has been traced by František Graus, "Die Handelsbeziehungen Böhmens zu Deutschland und Österreich im 14. und zu Beginn des 15. Jahrhunderts," *Historica*

2 (1960): 77–110, here 94, note 119. It concerns an entry in the deed of the Břevnov monastery from 1296: *It. cristalinam monstranciam Venetiis emptam pro 7 mar.* See *Regesta diplomatica nec non epistolaria Bohemiae et Moraviae*, II, 1202–1204, (no. 2752). The finds of Venetian and Islamic glass in Bohemia and Moravia are the subject of a number of works. See, for example, *Středověké sklo v zemích Koruny české* [Medieval glass in the lands of the Bohemian Crown], ed. Eva Černá (Most: Ústav archeologické památkové péče severozápadních Čech, 1994), and eadem and Jaroslav Podliska, "Sklo – indikátor kulturních a obchodních kontaktů středověkých Čech" [Glass – the indicator of cultural and trade contacts of medieval Bohemia], in *Odorik z Pordenone: z Benátek do Pekingu a zpět. Setkávání na cestách Starého světa ve 13.-14. století. = Odoric of Pordenone: From Venice to Peking and Back. Meetings on the Roads of the Old World in the 13th–14th Centuries. Sborník příspěvků z mezinárodní konference Plzeň, 13.-14. listopadu 2006. = Proceedings of the International Conference Pilsen, 13th to 14th November 2006* (Colloquia mediaevalia Pragensia, 10), ed. Petr Sommer and Vladimír Liščák (Prague: Filosofia, 2008), 237–256, Hedvika Sedláčková, "Ninth- to Mid-16th Century Glass Finds in Moravia," *Journal of Glass Studies* 48 (2006): 191–224, and Zdeněk Smetánka, *Archeologické etudy* [Archaeological studies] (Prague: Lidové noviny, 2003), 56 deals with the sale of imported glass in thirteenth-century Prague.

63 See the map of Italian glass finds in medieval Moravia published by Hedvika Sedláčková, "Italské sklo ve středověku na Moravě" [Italian glass in medieval Moravia], in *Gotika severní Itálie. České země a Furlansko ve středověku* [Gothic style of northern Italy. The Czech Lands and Friuli in the Middle Ages] (Mikulov: Regionální museum, 2009), 42–51, here 46.

64 Černá and Podliska, *Sklo*, 240–245.

65 Marta Janovíčková and Hedvika Sedláčková, "Obchod se sklem ve střední Evropě ve 13. a 14. století na příkladu konvic typu »Mečová« a stolních láhví typu »Norimberk«" [Glass trade in Central Europe in the 13th and 14th centuries by an example of pots of the "Mečová" type and table bottles of the "Nuremberg" type], in *Odorik z Pordenone*, 257–278, here 263.

66 See Hedvika Sedláčková, "Ninth- to Mid-16th-Century Glass Finds in Moravia," *Journal of Glass Studies* 48 (2006): 191–224, here esp. 216–217 supporting the increase of domestic glass production in Bohemia during the fourteenth century with concrete examples showing how Bohemian glassmakers adopted Venetian and German techniques. Similar glass forms were also produced later by Moravian and Silesian glassworks.

67 Yves Renouard, *Les relations des papes d'Avignon et des compagnies commerciales et bancaires de 1316 à 1378* (Paris: E. de Boccard, 1941), 147. See also Arnold Esch, "Bankiers der Kirche im großen Schisma," *Quellen und Forschungen aus italienischen Archiven und Bibliotheken* 46 (1966): 277–398.

68 The fundamental work on the Papal Curia and the church administration of the Czech lands in the pre-Hussite period has been published by Kamil Krofta, "Kurie a církevní správa zemí českých v době předhusitské" [Curia and church administration of the Czech Lands in the pre-Hussite period], *Český časopis historický* 10 (1904): 15–36, 125–132, 249–275; 12 (1906): 7–34, 178–191 and 14 (1908): 18–34; see recently Zdeňka Hledíková, *Počátky avignonského papežství a české země* [The beginnings of the Avignon Papacy and the Czech Lands] (Prague: Karolinum, 2013).

69 *Regesta diplomatica nec non epistolaria Bohemiae et Moraviae*, I, 356 (no. 759).

70 The conditions under which the first Bohemian bracteates began to be coined within the Meissen–Bohemian currency union have been analyzed by Roman Zaoral, "Die Anfänge der Brakteatenwährung in Böhmen," in *XII. Internationaler Numismatischer*

Kongress – Berlin 1997. Akten – Proceedings – Actes, II, ed. Bernd Kluge and Bernhard Weisser (Berlin: Staatliche Museen zu Berlin, 2000), 993–999.

71 In detail see Roman Zaoral, "The Management of Papal Collections and Long-Distance Trade in the Thirteenth-Century Czech lands," *Mélanges de l'École française de Rome – Moyen Âge* 127, no. 2 (2015). Online: http://mefrm.revues.org/2732 (last accessed: 27 October 2015).

72 *Regesta diplomatica nec non epistolaria Bohemiae et Moraviae*, II, 125–126 (no. 328).

73 Ibid., II, 141 (no. 368).

74 *Monumenta Poloniae Vaticana*, I/1 (1207–1344), ed. Jan Ptaśnik (Cracow: Sumptibus Academiae Polonae Litterarum et Scientiarium, 1913), 7–9 (no. 14).

75 Kurt Weissen, *Florentiner Bankiers und Deutschland (1275–1475). Kontinuität und Diskontinuität wirtschaftlicher Strukturen.* Habilitationsschrift (Basel: Universität Basel, 2001), 60. Available online: http://kweissen.ch/docs/weissen%20-%202000%20-%20Habil%20-%20ganz.pdf (last accessed: 26 June 2015).

76 *Monumenta Poloniae Vaticana* I/1, 17–24 (no. 26).

77 Jiří Janáček, "Der böhmische Aussenhandel in der Hälfte des 15. Jahrhunderts," *Historica* 4 (1962): 39–58.

78 Peter Spufford, *Power and Profit: The Merchant in Medieval Europe* (London: Thames & Hudson, 2002), 134.

13

LATE MEDIEVAL GDAŃSK AS A BRIDGE BETWEEN REGIONS

Western European, Hanseatic, and East Central European Contacts

Beata Możejko

In the late medieval period, Gdańsk played a key role as an intermediary in contacts between East Central Europe (the Kingdom of Poland[1]), the towns of the Hanseatic League, and, finally, Western Europe. This role was enacted during the rule of the Polish king Kazimierz Jagiellończyk (Casimir IV Jagiellon[2]), whose reign (1447–1492) featured thirteen years (1454–1466) of war with the Teutonic Order. Its end was marked by the Second Treaty of Toruń (Thorn),[3] concluded in 1466, which gave Kazimierz Jagiellończyk control of Royal Prussia, and with it authority over Gdańsk. The privileges that Gdańsk was granted by this monarch clearly stated that the city had the right to independence in maritime policy, and thus effectively in foreign policy.[4]

This placed Gdańsk in a new position. Up until this juncture, from the moment that the city became involved in Hanseatic politics in the latter half of the fourteenth century, attending assemblies of Hanseatic towns, Gdańsk[5] had always been able to rely on the diplomatic support of the Teutonic Order's Grand Master.[6] However, this situation, which had been advantageous in the fourteenth century, had become a hindrance by the second decade of the fifteenth century – for example when Grand Master Paul von Russdorf prevented Gdańsk and other Prussian towns (Elbląg and Toruń) from becoming too actively involved on the side of Lübeck in its war against Denmark and King Eric of Pomerania.[7]

The town council of Gdańsk shaped its diplomatic relations thanks to the commercial contacts of Gdańsk's merchants. In the late fourteenth and the first half of the fifteenth century, they not only reached Hanseatic ports such as Lübeck and Hamburg, but also Hanseatic *kontors* that lay much further from Gdańsk: in Bergen[8] (on the Norwegian North Sea coast), in Bruges (in this case stopping at one of the ports on the Zwin),[9] and in London. They were well acquainted with the western coast of France and even Spain and Portugal. Historical sources show that by 1435 ships from Gdańsk had reached Iceland.[10] In the fifteenth century (particularly after the Second Treaty of Toruń) the transport of goods – both imports and exports – was important. The commodities exported to Western Europe were partly products connected to forestry (timber, wax, and animal hides) and partly agricultural goods, mostly grain. By the 1470s, amber was also being exported (up until the mid-fifteenth century the Teutonic Knights held a monopoly on the amber trade with Western Europe, especially Bruges). Imports included woolen and silk textiles, salt, spices, and exotic fruits for the Polish market, such as figs.[11]

Thanks to these trade contacts, news from Western Europe reached Gdańsk either by word-of-mouth or in writing. Gdańsk's envoys held diplomatic meetings in the first half of the fifteenth century with merchants from Flanders, the Dutch nobility (including the lords of Veere and the duke of Burgundy, Philip the Good), and the regency council of Henry VI, king of England. Here it is worth mentioning the diplomatic missions of Heinrich Vorrath, mayor of Gdańsk, who acted on behalf of the town council of Gdańsk, Grand Master Paul von Russdorf, and the Hanseatic towns.[12] As Marian Biskup observed, despite having authorization from the Grand Master, Heinrich Vorrath endeavored to pursue Gdańsk's line of diplomatic relations. This Gdańsk diplomat frequently visited Lübeck, which he viewed as a model for Gdańsk, striving for the town's independence in foreign policy.[13]

In Gdańsk the East was also borne in mind, as demonstrated by the town's increasing influence in the Lithuanian city of Kaunas (where, however, conflicts arose with local merchants, who were supported by the then-grand duke of Lithuania, Kazimierz).[14] Nonetheless, in the latter half of the fifteenth century, Gdańsk's attention was focusing on the West.

Meanwhile, Poland's royal diplomatic service, with its chancellors and secretaries, was concentrating on other aims and different courses for foreign policy than those pursued by Gdańsk. Their principal interests were the kingdoms of Bohemia and Hungary. A major influence in this was the bishop of Cracow, Zbigniew Oleśnicki,[15] a long-time political "player," who had been a grey eminence during the reign of Władysław III. Bishop Oleśnicki devised plans concerning Hungary and crusades against the Ottomans. However, even after his death in 1455, the main target of Polish diplomacy was not Western Europe but East Central Europe. Under the reign of Kazimierz Jagiellończyk, having won the war against the Teutonic Order, the thrones of Bohemia and Hungary remained important targets.[16] Kazimierz's marriage to Elizabeth of Habsburg, sister of Ladislas (the Posthumous) of Habsburg, who was ruler of Hungary in 1454, was also not without significance.[17]

Naturally, Poland also placed importance on relations with the pope in Rome as well as with the king of Germany and Holy Roman emperor, Frederick III.[18] Gdańsk's Western European relations became a significant challenge for the royal chancery – more of which will be discussed later. In 1479, King Kazimierz Jagiellończyk famously said that the son of Bohemia (Władysław Jagiellończyk) was not so dear to him as to dictate his politics at the expense of Royal Prussia. He pledged his commitment to his new territories, stating that: "we hold you and the Prussian nations in higher esteem than the Czech crown."[19] However, the monarch's practices left no illusions as to his priorities. The diplomatic machine and the country's finances were focused on securing the Czech and Hungarian thrones for the descendants of Kazimierz Jagiellończyk. These efforts, which were ultimately successful, were undertaken with financial support from Gdańsk.[20]

The sources examined here permit me to risk suggesting that Gdańsk attempted to involve King Kazimierz Jagiellończyk in relations with the Hanseatic realm, Western Europe, England, France, and the Duchy of Burgundy.[21] Sometimes, however, these endeavors ended in blunders made by the Polish chancery. Such a situation came about in 1466. On 31 March 1466, at the request of Gdańsk, the royal chancery issued a letter in Piotrków, addressed to the king of France – an intercession in support of the efforts and activities of Gdańsk's merchants and city authorities. This episode was linked to the attacks carried out by the French against Hanseatic ships near Dunkerque in the spring of 1466. Unfortunately, the status of this letter was badly compromised by a grave error made by the royal chancery, who referred to the French king as Charles instead of Louis.[22] The town council of Gdańsk noticed the chancery's mistake, and so added to this correspondence a letter written by Kazimierz Jagiellończyk himself, on 23 April 1466.[23] In this, he apologized to Louis XI for the Polish chancery clerk's mistake and expressed his hope that it would not cause offence. This *faux pas* was particularly regrettable as the father of Louis XI, Charles VII (with whom Louis had maintained hostile relations), had been dead since 1461. As I have demonstrated elsewhere,[24] the letter from Kazimierz Jagiellończyk to the king of France was written in haste, when the clerks were effectively packed and ready to travel (in Poland the king still remained an itinerant *rex ambulans*), and the chancellor – Wojciech of Żychlin – did not verify the letter. French diplomacy had already made contact with Poland during the reign of Louis XI. On 28 January 1463, Louis XI had sent Kazimierz Jagiellończyk a letter of recommendation for the diplomat Antonio de Gracianopoli.[25] Thus, the error cannot be explained by ignorance of the facts; nevertheless, this change on the throne had failed to register in the mind of the scribe who made the hapless mistake. There is yet another example of royal correspondence written on behalf of Gdańsk, where a similar mistake was made with a monarch's name. A letter in support of the citizens of Gdańsk, written by Kazimierz Jagiellończyk in April 1482, mentions Christian, king of Denmark, when in fact it was his son John who was then in power.[26] As in the previous instance, we do not know exactly who was to blame for this error. At the time in question, the head of the royal chancery was a vacant post. In the end, Gdańsk decided not to send the letter addressed to the wrong king. They had learned from bitter experience not to follow the same course of action as they had with the letter to Louis. The king of France had not agreed to their requests and Gdańsk believed that the Polish chancery's diplomatic blunder was to blame for this failure.

Gdańsk did not give up trying to involve King Kazimierz Jagiellończyk in relations with France, as illustrated by the town council's petitions to the monarch in September 1487, asking him to intercede with King Charles VIII on behalf of Gdańsk's shipmasters and merchants. This time the Polish chancery did its job well.[27] Gaining diplomatic support was important for Gdańsk, not least because of its commercial contacts with France, from which the city imported Atlantic salt.[28] As for

Poland, it was only after the death of King Kazimierz Jagiellończyk that Polish diplomacy recognized the need to establish somewhat closer ties with France because of marital plans. These concerned the sons of Kazimierz Jagiellończyk: Władisłas Jagiellończyk (Ladislas Jagiellon or Władysław II) and Jan Olbracht (John I Albert), who were to marry the French princesses Anne and Germaine de Foix – cousins of Anne, wife of Louis XII. It was also planned that Elżbieta Jagiellonka (Elizabeth Jagiellon) should marry a French prince. Eventually, in May 1501, King Jan Olbracht permitted Jan of Pilcza and Jan Bochotnicki to travel on a mission to France. Ultimately, the only planned marriage that actually took place was that of Władisłas and Anne de Foix.[29]

The Kingdom of Poland also maintained contacts with Italian cities. The presence of Italians in Poland was not limited to Cracow,[30] but also extended to the royal chancery. In the mid-1470s, the Italian Filippo Buonaccorsi – royal adviser and tutor to the king's sons – had a marked impact on royal diplomacy. He played an important role in 1474, when a delegation sent by Charles the Bold, duke of Burgundy, visited Toruń.

The Kingdom of Poland was embroiled in this affair by Gdańsk – or more precisely by the actions of one of the city's privateers – Paul Beneke. In the spring of 1473 he carried out a brazen attack near Dunkerque, capturing a galley operated by the Medici family sailing under the Burgundian flag. The ship was carrying a valuable cargo owned by Italian and English merchants, Pope Sixtus IV, and the banker and broker Tommaso Portinari.[31] The aforementioned delegation was led by the knight Anselm Adornes, who was well known in Bruges (having, among other things, founded the Jerusalem Church). The duke of Burgundy entrusted Adornes with the task of obtaining compensation for the losses inflicted by the Gdańsk privateer. Traveling via Hamburg, Lübeck, and then on to Rostock, Stralsund, Greifswald, and Wołogoszcz (Wolgast), the delegation finally reached Gdańsk. After their negotiations with Gdańsk, the envoys went on to attend an assembly in Malbork (Marienburg). They visited Ścibor Bażyński, governor of Royal Prussia in Sztum (Stuhm), and in June 1474 they appeared in Toruń at an assembly of the Royal Prussian estates attended by King Kazimierz Jagiellończyk. However, some form of intrigue prevented them from being admitted into the Polish monarch's presence. Adornes met only with Filippo Buonaccorsi, who promised assistance in the Tommaso Portinari affair. He never kept his promise.[32]

It must be admitted that royal diplomacy proved useful in relations with England, with whom Gdańsk, Lübeck, and Hamburg were at war in the early 1470s (ending with the Treaty of Utrecht).[33] The Polish monarch managed to persuade Hanseatic Cracow (which no longer sent envoys to Hanseatic assemblies, leaving the mandate to Gdańsk) to boycott English broadcloth. He also supported Gdańsk by giving assurances to King Edward IV that he was favorably disposed towards English merchants, and requesting that the English monarch adopt the same attitude towards Gdańsk's merchants.[34]

King Kazimierz Jagiellończyk did not intervene in any way in Gdańsk's decisions regarding shipbuilding. His interest in maritime affairs was limited to issuing letters of marque authorizing Gdańsk to attack its enemies – the enemies of the Hanseatic League. A sensitive issue for which Gdańsk sought approval – namely, permission to build ships at its shipyards for non-Hanseatic clients (such as the Italians and the Dutch) – was not appreciated by either Lübeck or the Grand Master. It was not until the second half of the fifteenth century that Gdańsk decided independently to build ships for cities outside the Hansa,[35] breaking up (somewhat short-sightedly) the solidarity of the Hanseatic union. The consequences of this decision did not take effect until the sixteenth century.

Focusing on Western and Hanseatic relations, Gdańsk remained almost entirely indifferent to the Turkish threat, which was significant from the perspective of Polish state interests. This became clear in the latter half of the 1480s. In the summer of 1484, the army of the Ottoman Sultan Bayezid II captured the Black Sea ports of Kiliya (on 14 July) and Cetatea Albă (on 22 August). His forces also entered Moldavia, forcing Stephen III of Moldavia to turn for help to the king of Poland, Kazimierz Jagiellończyk, and the king of Hungary, Matthias Corvinus. For King Kazimierz Jagiellończyk, the issue of financial assistance became a subject for debate at assemblies of the estates (burghers and nobility) of Royal Prussia. In Toruń, where these assemblies took place, the king's envoys appeared with dramatic appeals for help. However, Gdańsk remained unmoved, making any potential financial help dependent on the city receiving confirmation of its existing privileges, and on castles in Royal Prussia being handed over to the local nobility and burghers and not to Poles.[36]

In discussing Gdańsk as a link between Central Europe and the Hanseatic world or Western Europe, we have to acknowledge the influence of the wealthy patrician families who held power in the city from the fifteenth to the late seventeenth century. One example is the Ferber family, who came to Gdańsk in the fourteenth century. Their descendant, Eberhard Ferber, represented Gdańsk at the First Congress of Vienna in 1515, which witnessed a meeting between King Zygmunt (Sigismund) I of Poland, King Wladislas II of Hungary, and Emperor Maximilian, making vital decisions for this part of Europe (the Jagiello-Habsburg alliance – a double marriage – was agreed: Louis II Jagiello, prince of Bohemia and Hungary, was to marry Archduchess Mary, granddaughter of the emperor, whilst Anna Jagiellon, queen of Hungary and Bohemia, was to marry Archduke Ferdinand of Austria or his brother Charles V). It was at this congress that nobility was conferred on Eberhard Ferber by Zygmunt I and subsequently by Emperor Maximilian.[37]

Conclusions

Late medieval Gdańsk took advantage of the royal privileges it had been granted and pursued its own policies relatively freely, based on commercial and diplomatic relations with the Hanseatic League and Western Europe. Gdańsk's actions also had an impact on Polish diplomacy, to some degree forcing Poland to take an interest in the West. Even a cursory glance at letter collections or account books from France,

Flanders, or England, or at Hanseatic documents, reveals that King Kazimierz Jagiellończyk appears in them because of Gdańsk.[38]

Notes

1 The directions and operational methods of Polish diplomacy during the reign of King Kazimierz Jagiellończyk are outlined by Marian Biskup and Karol Górski, "Czasy Kazimierza Jagiellończyka (1447–1492)" [The age of Casimir IV Jagiellon (1447–1492)], in *Historia dyplomacji polskiej, t. I połowa X w.–1572* [The history of Polish diplomacy, vol. 1, first half of the 10th century to 1572] (Warsaw: Państwowe Wydawnictwo Naukowe, 1982), 431–529.

2 For a biography of this king, see Maria Bogucka, *Kazimierz Jagiellończyk i jego czasy* [Casimir IV Jagiellon and his times] (Warsaw: Państwowy Instytut Wydawniczy, 1981). See also Marian Biskup and Karol Górski, *Kazimierz Jagiellończyk. Zbiór studiów o Polsce drugiej połowy XV wieku* [Casimir IV Jagiellon. Collected studies on Poland in the latter half of the 15th century] (Warsaw: Państwowe Wydawnictwo Naukowe, 1987). For a list of more recent literature on the subject of this monarch (and others) see Urszula Borkowska OSU, *Dynastia Jagiellonów w Polsce* [The Jagiellonian dynasty in Poland] (Warsaw: Wydawnictwo Naukowe PWN, 2011) and *Europa Jagiellonica 1386–1572. Sztuka, kultura i polityka w Europie Środkowej za panowania Jagiellonów* [Europe Jagiellonica 1386–1572. Arts, culture and politics in Central Europe during the reign of the Jagiellonian dynasty], ed. Przemysław Mrozowski, Paweł Tyszka, and Piotr Węcowski (Warsaw: Zamek Królewski w Warszawie-Muzeum Studia i Materiały V, 2015).

3 The Thirteen Years' War is covered in the monograph by Marian Biskup, *Trzynastoletnia wojna z Zakonem krzyżackim 1454–1466* [The Thirteen Years' War with the Teutonic Order 1454–1466] (Warsaw: Wydawnictwo Ministerstwo Obrony Narodowej, 1967), which remains relevant to this day. For details of Gdańsk's participation in this war, see Marian Biskup, *Stosunek Gdańska do Kazimierza Jagiellończyka w okresie wojny trzynastoletniej 1454–1466* [Gdańsk's stance towards Casimir IV Jagiellon during the Thirteen Years' War, 1454–1466] (Toruń: Towarzystwo Naukowe w Toruniu, 1952), and Henryk Samsonowicz, "Gdańsk w okresie wojny trzynastoletniej" [Gdańsk during the Thirteen Years' War], in *Historia Gdańska*, I–V [The history of Gdańsk], ed. Edmund Cieślak (Gdańsk: Wydawnictwo Morskie, 1978–1997), II, 7–76.

4 Three royal privileges were granted during the course of the war: in 1454, 1455, and 1457; they are published in Paul Simson, *Geschichte der Stadt Danzig*, IV (Danzig: A. W. Kafemann, 1913), nos. 137, 138, 141 and 142. For a discussion of the provisions of these privileges, see Biskup, *Stosunek Gdańska*, 76–80 and 119–120; Beata Możejko, *Czynsz gdański w polityce Kazimierza Jagiellończyka i jego synów (1468–1516)* [The Gdańsk rent in the policy of Casimir IV Jagiellon and his sons (1468–1516)] (Gdańsk: Wydawnictwo Uniwersytetu Gdańskiego, 2004), 17–20; eadem, "The Gdańsk Rent as a Subject of Communications between King Kazimierz Jagiellończyk, the Polish Nobility and Gdańsk," in *Komunikace ve středověkých městech* [Communication in medieval cities], ed. Martin Čapský et al. (Prague and Opava: European Social Fund and Silezská univerzita v Opavě, 2014), 81–94, here 81–82.

5 For details of Gdańsk's participation in Hanseatic assemblies, see Marian Biskup, "Rola Gdańska w Związku Miast Hanzeatyckich" [Gdańsk's role in the Hanseatic League], in *Historia Gdańska*, I, 428–436 and idem, "Gdańsk a Hanza w połowie XV stulecia" [Gdańsk and the Hansa in the mid-fifteenth century], in ibid., I, 541–553.

6 On the subject of the Teutonic Order's diplomatic service see Klaus Neitmann, *Die Staatsvertäge des Deutschen Ordens in Preußen 1230–1449. Studien zur Diplomatie eines spätmittelalterlichen deutschen Territorialstaates* (Cologne and Vienna: Böhlau, 1986). For an outline of power-society relations in the Teutonic state see Roman Czaja, *Miasta pruskie a zakon krzyżacki. Studia nad stosunkami między miastem a władzą terytorialną w późnym średniowieczu* [Prussian towns and the Teutonic Order: Relations between towns and territorial authorities in the late medieval period] (Toruń: Wydawnictwo Uniwersytetu Mikołaja Kopernika, 1999) with details of the economic relations between the burghers of Gdańsk and local Teutonic officials detailed on 173–176. See also chapters in this monograph addressing the relationship between the central government and towns in Prussia. This issue is also dealt with by Renata Skowrońska, *Posłowie wielkich miast pruskich w latach 1411–1454* [Envoys of the great Prussian cities in 1411–1454] (Malbork: Muzeum Zamkowe w Malborku, 2007).

7 The war in question was that waged during 1426–1435 by Wendish towns against Eric of Pomerania, king of Denmark, Sweden, and Norway, details of which can be found in Biskup, *Gdańsk a Hanza w połowie XV stulecia*, 544–547. See also Carl August Lückerath, *Paul von Rusdorf Hochmeister des Deutschhen Ordens 1421–1441* (Bad Godesberg: Verlag Wisssenschaftliches Archiv Bad Godesberg, 1969), 90–96.

8 For more on the dealings of members of the Hansa (including Gdańsk) with the Bergen *Kontor*, see Mike Burkhardt, *Der hansische Bergenhandel im Spätmittelalter. Handel-Kaufleute-Netzwerke* (Quellen und Darstellungen zur hansischen Geschichte, 60) (Cologne, Weimar and Vienna: Böhlau, 2009).

9 For information on Bruges' dealings with the Hansa, see James M. Murray, *Bruges. Cradle of Capitalism 1280–1390* (Cambridge: Cambridge University Press, 2009), 219–229.

10 Theodor Hirsch, *Danzig Handels – und Gewerbsgeschichte unter der Herrschft des Deutschen Ordens,* (Leipzig: Hirzel, 1858), 154; Ernst Daenell, *Die Blütezeit der deutsche Hanse,* I (Berlin: Reimer, 1905), 335; Biskup, *Handel*, 398–416; and Marian Biskup, "Przeobrażenia w handlu i rzemiośle" [Changes in trade and crafts], in *Historia Gdańska*, I, 507–536.

11 On Gdańsk's foreign trade in the latter half of the fifteenth century, see Henryk Samsonowicz, "Handel zagraniczny Gdańska w drugiej połowie XV wieku (rejonizacja handlu na podstawie ksiąg cła palowego)" [Gdańsk's foreign trade in the latter half of the 15th century (Regionalization of trade based on mooring toll registers)], *Przegląd Historyczny* 47 (1956): 283–352.

12 Eduard Reibstein, *Heinrich Vorrath, Bügermeister von Danzig, als hansiscger Diplomat* (Zeitschrift des Westpreussischen Geschichtsvereins, 42) (Danzig: [N. p.], 1900).

13 Biskup, *Stosunek*, 24–25.

14 Ibid.

15 Literature on the subject of Oleśnicki is collated by Maria Koczerska, *Zbigniew Oleśnicki i kościół krakowski w czasach jego pontyfikatu (1423–1455)* [Zbigniew Oleśnicki and the Cracow Church during his pontificate (1423–1455)] (Warsaw, Wydawnictwo DiG: 2004). For more on the role of Oleśnicki after the death of King Władysław Jagiełło, see Bożena Czwojdrak, "Królowa Zofia Holszańska a biskup krakowski Zbigniew Oleśnicki – konflikt, współpraca czy rywalizacja" [Queen Sophia of Halshany and Zbigniew Oleśnicki, bishop of Cracow – conflict, cooperation or rivalry], in *Zbigniew Oleśnicki. Książę Kościoła i mąż stanu* [Zbigniew Oleśnicki. Prince of the church and statesman], ed. Feliks Kiryk and Zdzisław Noga (Cracóv: Wydawnictwo Secesja, 2006), 143–155, and Bożena Czwojdrak, *Zofia Holszańska. Studium o dworze i roli królowej w późnośredniowiecznej Polsce* [Sophia of Halshany. A study of the court and the queen's role in late medieval Poland] (Warsaw, Wydawnictwo DiG, 2012), 42–74.

16 A good account of this issue is given in the literature by Krzysztof Baczkowski, *Walka Jagiellonów z Maciejem Korwinem o koronę czeską w latach 1471–1479* [The struggle between the Jagiellonians and Matthias Corvinus for the Czech crown] (Cracow: Nakładem Uniwersytetu Jagiellońskiego, 1980) and idem, *Walka o Węgry w latach 1490–1492. Z dziejów rywalizacji habsbursko-jagiellońskiej w basenie środkowego Dunaju* [The struggle for Hungary from 1490 to 1492. From the annals of the Jagiellonian–Habsburg rivalry in the Middle Danube Basin] (Cracow: Nakładem Uniwersytetu Jagiellońskiego, 1995).

17 Biskup and Górski, "Czasy Kazimierza Jagiellończyka," 441–442.

18 Ibid., 439–441, 444–446, and 448–450.

19 *Acten der Ständetage Preussens Königlischen Antheils*, I, ed. Franz Thunert (Danzig: A. W. Kafemann, 1896), 483; Biskup and Górski, "Czasy Kazimierza Jagiellończyka," 483.

20 Możejko, *Czynsz*, 106–108.

21 Biskup and Górski, "Czasy Kazimierza Jagiellończyka," 467. In searching for sources, I focused primarily on those held among the archival materials of the Archiwum Państwowe Gdańsk ([APG] State Archives in Gdańsk), in particular a set of letters and documents catalogued as 300 D, 1–80, but also copy books of correspondence with Gdański: 300/27, no. 6.

22 *Hansisches Urkundenbuch*, I–XI, ed. Konstantin Höhlbaum et al. (Leipzig, Munich, and Halle: Duncker und Humbolt and Verl. der Buchh. des Waisenhauses, 1876–1916), IX, no. 257. APG 300/27, no. 6, 572–573. Cf. APG 300 D/2, no. 84. For further details, see Beata Możejko, "W sprawie jednej pomyłki polskiej kancelarii z II połowy XV w., czyli przyczynek do funkcjonowania służby dyplomatycznej Kazimierza Jagiellończyka" [The story of an error in the Polish chancery in the second half of the 15th century: an insight into the functioning of Casimir IV Jagiellon's diplomatic service], in *Studia z dziejów średniowiecza, nr 14* [Studies in medieval history], ed. Błażej Śliwiński (Malbork: Wydawnictwem Zamku w Malborku, 2008), 215–225.

23 APG 300/27, no. 6, 579.

24 Możejko, "W sprawie jednej pomyłki."

25 *Matricularum Regni Poloniae summaria, excussis codicibus, qui in Chartophylacio Maximo Varsoviensi asservantur, I. Casimiri IV regis tempora complectens (1447–1492)* ed. Theodorus Wierzbowski (Varsoviae: C. Kowalewski, 1905), no. 625, cf. Biskup and Górski, "Czasy Kazimierza Jagiellończyka," 458–459.

26 APG 300 D/3, no. 254a and *Acten der Ständetage Preussens*, I, 112–113.

27 APG 300D/3. no 367, *Hansisches Urkundenbuch*, XI, no. 155 (a register with extensive extracts from letters) and *Acten der Ständetage Preussens*, I, 463.

28 Samsonowicz, *Handel zagraniczny.*

29 Aleksander Hirschberg, *Koalicja Francji z Jagiellonami z r. 1500* [Coalition of France and the Jagiellonians from 1500] (Lviv: Przewodnik Naukowy i Literacki, 1882); Marian Biskup, "Czasy Jana Olbrachta i Aleksandra Jagiellończyka (1492–1506)" [Times of Johan Albrecht and Alexander Jagiellon (1492–1506)], in *Historia Dyplomacji*, I, 531–547.

30 On the subject of Italians in medieval Cracow, see Jan Ptaśnik, *Kultura włoska wieków średnich w Polsce* [Medieval Italian Culture in Poland] (Warsaw: Instytut Wydawniczy "Biblioteka Polska," 1922).

31 The story of the raid on this galley and the consequences is related in detail by Beata Możejko, *Peter von Danzig, Dzieje wielkiej karaweli 1462–1475* [Peter von Danzig. The Story of a Great Caravel 1462–1475] (Gdańsk: Wydawnictwo Uniwersytetu Gdańskiego, 2011), 166–226 and Beata Możejko, "Maritime Gdańsk in the second half of the fourteenth and the fifteemth century: The phenomenon of privateer Paul Beneke and the

great caravel Peter von Danzig," in *New Studies in Medieval and Renaissance Poland and Prussia. The impact of Gdansk*, ed. Beata Możejko (London and New York: Routledge, 2017), 102–114.

32 Key sources on this subject are held in the Stadsarchief Brugge (Bruges Town Archive), Archief van de Familie Adornses (Archive of the Adornses family), Ls 29–32. For more details of this mission, see Beata Możejko, "Die Gesandtschaft des Anselm Adornes im Jahr 1474 nach Polen. Zur Geschichte der Kontakte zwischen dem Herzogtum Burgund und dem König Kasimir IV. Jagellonicus," *Handelingen van het Genootschap voor Geschiedenis te Brugge* 149 (2012): 45–69.

33 Biskup and Górski, "Czasy Kazimierza Jagiellończyka," 495.

34 APG 300/27.6, k. 212^v–213; k. 286v (kop. 1), k. 286^v–287 (kop. 2), APG 300 D16. 106 (register: *Hansisches Urkundenbuch*, IX, no. 173).

35 For more on this subject, see Beata Możejko, "Z dziejów floty gdańskiej w XV wieku" [Episodes from the history of the Gdańsk fleet in the fifteenth century], in *Studia z dziejów średniowiecza. Komturzy. Rajcy, Żupani* [Studies in medieval history. Commanders, councilors, and zupans], ed. Błażej Śliwiński (Malbork: Muzeum Zamkowe w Malborku, 2005), 165–200, here 174.

36 For further details, see Beata Możejko, "Odległe pogranicze. Stanowisko stanów Prus Królewskich, a zwłaszcza Gdańska, wobec problemu zagrożenia tureckiego w latach 1485–1488" [Distant frontier. The attitude of Royal Prussia, and in particular Gdańsk, towards the problem of the Turkish threat from 1485 to 1488], *Średniowiecze Polskie i Powszechne* 3 [7] (2011): 151–170.

37 For further details of this congress, see Krzysztof Baczkowski, *Zjazd wiedeński 1515. Geneza, przebieg i znaczenie* [The congress of Vienna, 1515. Its origins, course, and significance] (Warsaw: Państwowe Wydawnictwo Naukowe, 1975). On the subject of Eberhard Ferber's ennoblement, see Ewa Bojaruniec, "Nobilitacje patrycjuszy gdańskich w okresie panowania Kazimierza Jagiellończyka i jego synów" [The Ennoblement of Gdańsk patricians during the reign of Casimir IV Jagiellon and his sons] (PhD diss., Uniwersytet Gdański, 2010).

38 As can be seen, for example, in Noël Geirnaert, *Het archief van de familie Adornes en de Jeruzalemstichting te Brugge / II, Regesten van de oorkonden en brieven tot en met 1500* (Brugge: Stadsarchief, 1989), 83 (no. 224).

14

A SILESIAN TOWN AND THE HUNGARIAN MONARCHY

Economic Contacts between Wrocław and Hungary, ca. 1250–1500

Grzegorz Myśliwski

It is generally accepted in the scholarly literature that the economy of East Central Europe developed significantly between the thirteenth and fifteenth centuries.[1] As part of this process the economies of the "Third Europe" (Hungary, Bohemia, and Poland), as Jenő Szűcs referred to it, continued to tighten their ties with Western Europe.[2] Long-distance trade played a leading role in this process. From the turn of the thirteenth century, the integration of the continent progressed in the field of financial and credit interrelations, prompted particularly by holding great trade fairs.[3] Although this period was not always profitable for all the states in the region (e.g., the Kingdom of Hungary was devastated by the Mongols in 1241–1242 and the anti-Hussite campaigns and internal wars heavily impacted the Kingdom of Bohemia from 1419 to 1436), comparing the state of these countries and the quality of their economies in the middle of the thirteenth century and towards the end of the fifteenth century shows plainly that they went through a long period of development.

Studying multiple intraregional connections in the "Third Europe" is as interesting as researching the links with "Old Europe." In this article, I examine these economic relations with particular emphasis on the commercial relations between Wrocław, one of the leading East Central European towns, and the Kingdom of Hungary, including both its commercial centers and individual merchants. Although scholars have repeatedly grappled with the economic ties of the town with its southern neighbor,[4] they have usually left it out of their central argument.

Both Wrocław and the Kingdom of Hungary were deeply affected by the Mongol invasion of 1241–1242.[5] In the subsequent decades, however, both the Hungarian state and the Silesian town recovered and managed to set off on a path of long-term development. Wrocław was rebuilt; before April 9, 1242, it was re-located and became an autonomous town governed by Magdeburg Law.[6] The town flourished, particularly in the last thirty years of the thirteenth century during the reign of Henryk IV Probus; in 1274, for instance, it was granted a staple right. In 1327 Henry VI, the last duke of Wrocław, paid homage to King John of Bohemia. Subsequently, in 1335, Wrocław came under direct Bohemian (Luxemburg) rule;[7] Wrocław thrived and quickly attained the status of the city second to Prague in the kingdom. In the fifteenth century the town's population approached, or perhaps even exceeded, 20,000 people.[8] For many years, the Wrocław authorities acted as *starosta* (the highest royal representative in the land) in the duchy of Wrocław, formally still in existence, which inspired Richard Hoffmann to consider the town a city-state.[9] The significance of the developments in the fifteenth century, however, is not so unequivocal; there was a sinister side to the economic history of the town: the incursions of Hussite armies and a corresponding agrarian crisis in Wrocław's immediate vicinity; an increase in crime; and more frequent natural disasters than in the preceding century. Nevertheless, long-distance trade embracing Flanders, Venice, Novgorod the Great, and the Kingdom of Hungary flourished until the 1460s.[10] The agrarian crisis came to an end around 1480.[11]

The Kingdom of Hungary also recovered from the Mongol destruction; in the later Middle Ages the country rose to a peak of splendor. This process began with the great reformer Charles I of Anjou.[12] The Hungarian state covered over 300,000 square kilometers and included two highly developed regions in an economic sense: Upper Hungary (present-day Slovakia) and Transylvania (now in Romania), as well as large swathes of land in the Balkan Peninsula: Croatia (from 1091) and parts of Serbia, including Belgrade.[13] In 1358, King Louis I (the Great) snatched Dalmatia from Venice, putting it under the Hungarian control for over 50 years.[14] Furthermore, from 1370 to 1382 Louis ruled the Kingdom of Poland, depriving it of Ruthenia (Galician Rus'),[15] which was annexed to the Kingdom of Hungary.[16]

In the Kingdom of Hungary, the period of Angevin rule (until 1386) and the subsequent rule of Sigismund of Luxemburg accelerated urbanization, a development that was significant earlier in Upper Hungary and Transylvania as well.[17] Consequently, towards the end of the Middle Ages the urban elite comprised about 30 *civitates*, that is, free royal towns and royal mining towns.[18] The Kingdom of Hungary reached an advanced level of development under the government of King Matthias Corvinus (d. 1490) that lasted until the beginning of the sixteenth century.[19] In contrast to the Polish territories, for instance, grain cultivation did not play a major role in the Kingdom of Hungary.[20] Other economic domains of the primary economic sector were more important: highly developed wine production for export[21] and especially breeding heavy-bodied cattle which were driven as far as Nuremberg and Venice as well as many other Austrian, South German, and Swiss towns in the Late Middle Ages.[22]

Another great asset of the Hungarian economy was mining (gold, silver, copper, iron ore, and salt). Thanks to the new legislation introduced by Charles I, mining the deposits in Upper Hungary and Transylvania started as early as the 1320s, and considerable amounts (1 to 1.5 tons per year) were extracted in a number of locations: Kremnica, Smolník, Baia Mare, Baia de Arieş, and others.[23] Hungarian copper mining, also in Upper Hungary and Transylvania,[24] exploited the largest ore deposits in Europe. The high quality of Hungarian copper was a result of the high content of silver in the ore.[25] In addition, iron ore was extracted and processed for export.[26] It is a controversial issue whether the extensive Hungarian silver deposits were mostly used in the domestic economy or for export.[27]

Thanks to these dominant assets, the Warsaw school of economic history (M. Małowist, H. Samsonowicz, A. Mączak) considered the Kingdom of Hungary and the region of Silesia as components of the same economic zone, the so-called Sudeto-Carpathian zone. From the perspective of European commercial exchange, the fundamental assets of this region were mining products. According to H. Samsonowicz and A. Mączak, each such zone comprised "regions with similar basic geographies which because of that have economies that depend on a similar external factor."[28] Besides Hungary and Silesia (rich in gold and silver), the Sudeto-Carpathian zone embraced other countries and regions with great deposits of minerals: the Kingdom of Bohemia (except Lusatia) with considerable silver deposits, southern Poland (Lesser Poland) with rich salt and lead deposits, and Ruthenia with salt mines (Drohobych, Zhydachiv).[29]

The Kingdom of Hungary is an example of a land where the borders of various economic zones overlapped. Transylvania was not only a mining center but also part of the Black Sea economic zone (called sometimes the Black Sea–Caspian zone). The dominant activity there was cattle breeding.[30] Furthermore, the Black Sea functioned as a route to Byzantium and the Middle East,[31] and this had serious implications for the trading routines of Hungarian towns.[32] Parts of the Balkan Peninsula belonging to Hungary also linked the country to the Balkan economic zone.[33]

Trade routes

Many different routes linked Silesia and Wrocław to the Kingdom of Hungary. A direct route led through Racibórz[34] to the Jablunkov Pass, crossing the border between Silesia and the Kingdom of Hungary.[35] One could also arrive there through Brzeg, Grodków, Nysa, Głubczyce, Opava, and Nový Jičín.[36] From Nový Jičín roads diverged in multiple directions.[37] Focusing exclusively on the routes leading to the Kingdom of Hungary, the following can be identified:[38] 1) to Trenčín to the valley of the Váh River to Bratislava, with further travel opportunities to Vienna and Buda; 2) to Košice (after 1364 through Žilina, Ružomberok, Liptovský Mikuláš, and Prešov),[39] and from Szikszó or Eger through Debrecen and Oradea to Cluj in Transylvania;[40] 3) beginning from Nový Jičín, then to Ružomberok, then Banská Bystrica[41] to the Danube; 4) the route Brno–Hranice–Trnava–Esztergom was known from the 1240s at the latest (and then also Buda after its foundation in ca. 1244 and intense growth in importance).[42] From Buda there were multiple roads going to Transylvania and from there to Moldavia and the Black Sea.[43] The route through Oradea lead to Cluj and on to the main trading centers at the edges of the Kingdom of Hungary: Sibiu and Brașov. Another route to the latter passed through Szeged, Timișoara, and Sibiu. A route through Cracow was indirect, but a significant connection worth mentioning. The great trans-European Cologne–Ruthenia route (the so-called *Hoher Weg*, known also as *Hohe Strasse, Königstrasse*), crossed Wrocław.[44] For the present paper, discussing the connection between Wrocław and Cracow is essential, since the latter had close economic and political ties with the Kingdom of Hungary. The road from Wrocław to Cracow went through, among other places, Brzeg, Opole, Toszek, Bytom, Będzin, and Olkusz (a center of lead mining).[45] Sometimes a circuitous detour was preferred that led to Olkusz through Psie Pole, Namysłów, Kluczbork, Krzepice, and Częstochowa.[46] A parallel connection to the *Hohe Strasse* went through Nysa, Głubczyce, Racibórz, Żory, Oświęcim, and Skawina.[47] Thus, for the merchants of Wrocław the Kingdom of Hungary was accessible through Cracow, often chosen as a destination anyway. The route from Cracow passed through Czchów, Nowy Sącz, and Prešov to Košice.[48] Towards the end of the fourteenth century, the town of Bardejov, located on the way from Nowy Sącz to Prešov, significantly developed by King Louis the Great, grew in importance.[49] From Košice, passing through Szikszó and Eger, the road led to Buda.[50]

Commercial contacts

Trade relations between Hungary and Wrocław were first established in the period when the town was governed by Polish dukes. Until 1335 trade links were chiefly one-way and unilateral, that is, Hungarian commodities were imported to Wrocław. The Wrocław customs tariff from before 1266 mentioned *vino Ungarico vel de Austria*.[51] It is difficult to decide, but this may have meant that Wrocław merchants traveled to Austria to buy Hungarian wine.[52] Importing Hungarian wine would prove that the Wrocław merchants established commercial contacts with Hungary in the same period as the merchants of Cracow did.[53] In time, the assortment of goods in trade increased. It is fortunate that the great customs tariff of 1327, an invaluable source for analyzing the long-distance trade of Wrocław shortly before its incorporation into the Kingdom of Bohemia, has been preserved.[54] According to its records, Hungarian cattle (*ungarische ochsin*)[55] were driven to Wrocław. The scholarly literature has assumed that the copper registered in the tariff also originated in Hungary.[56] This may be true, but it should still be noted that small copper deposits were also extracted in Silesia at the time.[57] Presumably, the Hungarian copper arrived in Wrocław via Cracow. After 1306, the latter was granted a staple right for copper and the merchants of Cracow then exported it further, as far as Bruges.[58] It is almost certain that goods from Hungary were brought to Wrocław by foreign suppliers.[59] Hungarian commodities were carried into the town by people called *gast*, which in this context can be translated as "guest" or "foreign [merchant]",[60] although one cannot totally exclude the participation of merchants from Wrocław. The sources attest their presence in Bruges and northern Italy even earlier.[61]

After Wrocław became part of the Kingdom of Bohemia contacts with Hungary developed further and strengthened. It is claimed that in 1335 the rulers of Bohemia and Hungary embarked on a joint project to advance Central European trade.[62]

Perhaps at the summit in Visegrád (19–23 November) or not long afterwards they agreed to grant Brno a staple right, which aimed at undermining the role of Vienna in the transit trade.[63] This ambitious project did not bear fruit. Despite Charles IV's efforts, commanding Austrian, Hungarian, and Polish merchants to travel through Brno,[64] Vienna preserved its firm position in the transit trade in Central Europe. Another important initiative that proved important was the Bohemian-Hungarian agreement (6 January 1336)[65] on commercial exchange and Bohemian-Hungarian routes.

In general, the kings of Hungary looked with favor on the Wrocław merchants. In 1364, Louis the Great ordered a road to be built to connect Silesia with Košice, the third most important town in the Kingdom of Hungary and the center of the copper trade, through the Jablunkov Pass and Žilina.[66] In 1365, the king granted the Wrocław merchants the right to trade freely in his kingdom.[67] Building on similar acts issued for the Nuremberg and Prague merchants, King Louis levied the so-called thirtieth (*tricesima*) customs tax on the Wrocław merchants, that is, a payment collected at the kingdom's border and calculated as 1/30 of the overall value of the imported goods.[68] Louis's successors followed in his footsteps. Between 1419 and 1437 Silesia and Wrocław were ruled by Sigismund of Luxemburg, who was resented by the Hussites. In March 1421, he renewed Louis's privilege.[69] Later (in March 1440), after his death, his daughter, Queen Elisabeth, reasserted the Wrocław right to collect customs for grain imported during a famine.[70] In 1441 Władisłas III Jagiello, king of Poland as well as Hungary (Władisłas I), allowed the Wrocław merchants to trade all commodities freely in the Hungarian part of his vast yet ephemeral lordship.[71]

Contacts among Silesia, Wrocław, and the Kingdom of Hungary tightened during the conflict with the Kingdom of Bohemia when Matthias Corvinus conquered the entire region. Formally this happened in July 1479 (the peace treaty of Olomouc), but in fact Silesia and Wrocław had been subjugated in May 1469.[72] Matthias's strong-arm government impacted the region and its capital Wrocław considerably. Many royal economic initiatives were harmful: a failed and detrimental monetary reform, fiscal oppression, and curbing the town's autonomy by obstructing the election of the town council.[73] The negative feelings about Matthias's policy towards Wrocław can best be seen in the fact that after the king's death in 1490 his *starosta*, Heinz Dompnig of Wrocław, was sentenced to death.[74] Nevertheless, the king's trade policy was beneficial for Wrocław. In 1474, he commanded that security on the trade routes to Hungary be assured.[75] In 1481, he banned his customs officers from increasing tolls on Wrocław merchants.[76] Supposedly, this decision was ineffective because the town council dispatched envoys requesting the king to renew the 1365 privilege. In 1484, Matthias acceded to their plea and confirmed Louis the Great's charter.[77] In 1481, the king established a fourth annual fair in Wrocław that was scheduled for a full week beginning with the Feast of the Exaltation of the Cross (September 14).[78] It is possible that by requesting an additional period for another fair the petitioners intended to forge stronger ties with towns at the Silesian-Polish border and to weaken those border towns' commercial bonds with Cracow.[79] Besides these allowances, the king defended Wrocław merchants in their quarrels with Cracow and with the Kingdom of Poland.[80]

On the whole, in the period after 1335, circumstances were usually favorable for commercial contacts between Wrocław and the Hungarian towns. The most intense relations developed with the capital Buda and with few Upper Hungarian towns north of the Danube: Bratislava, Košice, Levoča, Bardejov, Smolník, Spišská Sobota, Kremnica, Esztergom, Trnava, Ľubietová, Trenčín, and Sankt Georgen.[81] Once someone from Croatia even reached Wrocław.[82] In terms of contacts with Sopron, it is not clear whether the Wrocław merchants traveled to this city with a Silesian product or whether it was brought to the town by merchants from other towns or countries. In the Hungarian part of the the Black Sea economic zone, in the Saxon areas of Transylvania, there were two towns of special importance for Wrocław: Sibiu and Braşov.[83] Sebeş was less significant.

The import of wine from Hungary (*ungarisch weyn*) continued throughout the entire fifteenth century.[84] Presumably, Wrocław also gained access to a particular Mediterranean wine (*malvasia*) through Hungary. This sweet and highly desirable wine was produced in Italy, Sicily, Crete, Sardinia, and in the vicinity of Tyre.[85] There is evidence that it appeared in Wrocław during the rule of Sigismund of Luxemburg at the latest.[86] Nuremberg merchants might have brought the wine from Venice,[87] although, as noted above, Hungary had close ties to the Black Sea and to the Mediterranean economic zones.[88] This Hungarian "link" can be substantiated with the help of another source: the 1469 Wrocław town council's list of gifts to numerous towns, rulers, and individuals.[89] Most of the gifts on the list were wines, including malmsey (*malvasia*). This would not be extraordinary unless if it were compared with a similar list from a year before. In 1468, a long list of transalpine wines did not mention malmsey;[90] 1469, however, was the year when Silesia became subject to Matthias Corvinus.

Besides wine, another product was livestock. The question already raised above is: did cattle continue to be driven to Wrocław from Hungary in the fifteenth century? In 1441 a charter of privilege issued by Władisłas III, king of Poland and Hungary, granted the cattle trade to Wrocław merchants.[91] The import of cattle into Wrocław reached its peak during the fifteenth century.[92] According to previous studies, it mainly came from Ruthenia, Moldavia, and Mazovia.[93] It is quite revealing to note that in the fifteenth century there are no records of Hungarian cattle in Wrocław. The 1441 privilege pertained not only to Hungary, but also to the lands of the Kingdom of Poland, and thus, to the lands of Ruthenia as well. Due to the international importance of the cattle exported from the Kingdom of Hungary in the fifteenth century (until 1425 and from 1470 onwards), however, it is reasonable not to rule out entirely a continuation of driving Hungarian cattle to this region and Wrocław.

Regarding copper from Hungary there is no doubt that the Wrocław merchants imported it after 1335. One of the resolutions of the diet of the Hanseatic League in Stralsund (1376) serves as clear evidence: Wrocław is named there as one of the towns whose merchants were trading in copper and transporting it to Hanseatic cities.[94] The Wrocław import of copper continued in the fifteenth century. This can best be seen in an invaluable source, the extant excerpts from the accounting records of the Wrocław company of Hans Hesse, Karl Kunze and Jorge Zebrecht (1438), who traveled to the Kingdom of Hungary to buy copper, among other things.[95] They bought 143½ hundredweight (cwt) and 14 pounds (approx. 7,200 kg) of copper for 777 Hungarian florins in total.[96] They did not sell their entire load in Wrocław, but they took some of it to the market in Nysa (19 cwt = approx. 1,000 kg). It is unknown where Zerbrecht transported the largest part of the load (73 cwt and 14 pounds = approx. 3,700 kg).[97] It is certain, however, that 50½ cwt of copper (over 2,500 kg) reached Wrocław.[98] It remains unclear in which Hungarian town this valuable mineral was acquired. It is likely that it was bought somewhere in Upper Hungary rather than in Transylvania as Wrocław had quite sporadic contacts with the mining towns there, and even these connections were established later. Instead, it is evident that copper on the Wrocław market was traded from Levoča (but was not mined there) and from Smolník (an important mining center at the time).[99] However, the origin of the copper brought to Wrocław was not always registered.[100] Therefore, it is quite possible that it was imported from other mining centers in Upper Hungary (perhaps via Cracow).[101] It cannot be excluded that copper traveled to Wrocław at least until the end of the period under study.[102]

Hungarian minerals were significant in the trade relations between Hungary and Wrocław. Compared to copper, Hungarian gold was certainly less important to Wrocław merchants because there were quite considerable gold deposits in Silesia,[103] which were extracted throughout the thirteenth and in the early fourteenth centuries and exported to Bruges.[104] Some data exist on the trade in Hungarian gold, however. For instance, in 1364, a certain Wrocław trader brought gold coins from Kremnica, a Hungarian mining town and the center of a minting chamber.[105] It is unsure whether these coins, made on his commission, were minted from Silesian gold or – what is more plausible – from gold acquired on the spot. According to extant sources, the amount of gold collected or traded outside Silesia was very small. Importing it became unnecessary after Silesian gold mining was restored in the fifteenth century (Zlaté Hory, Złoty Stok).[106]

The situation with silver was similar. A recently published document from 1458 can serve as a good example. The document reports that Magdalena Morsztyn, a certain townswoman from Cracow, bought silver from two burghers of Bardejov and then sent it to Wrocław.[107] There it turned out, however, that the silver was of poor quality (*nicht fertig* – unprocessed), and the Wrocław authorities put a seal on it and sent it back, putting Morsztyn's envoys in jail. The inadequate quality of the silver and the lack of data on the amount make it difficult to decide whether the import of silver from Hungary to Wrocław was occasional or regular.

The Wrocław merchants were interested in importing spices via the Kingdom of Hungary (chiefly pepper and saffron). Before 1428, Niklas Ferber bought (probably in Buda) 2860 pounds of pepper of the Buda weight, i.e., ca. 1607–1681 kg.[108] Even more was acquired by the merchants Hans Hesse, Karl Kunze, and Jorge Zebrecht in 1438.[109] According to their accounting records, they spent 1808 florins, presumably in Buda, on 362 stones of pepper (4,344 kg).[110] It is remarkable that the acquisitions of pepper in the Kingdom of Hungary significantly exceeded the considerable quantities brought in the 1420s by merchants from Regensburg, Passau, and – presumably – Venice.[111] The Wrocław merchants traded for saffron, too. For instance, the same Hesse, as well as Alexius Banke, Wenzlaw Scherer, and Niklas Koppen sold, among other things, Hungarian saffron (*ungerisch und mark zaffran*) to Prussia.[112] Presumably, it was East Central European saffron, perhaps from present-day Slovakia.[113]

Concerning raw products, the Wrocław merchants were interested in furs available for sale in Hungary. One chronologically late account is extant that reports on an extraordinary delivery: in 1475, the Wrocław merchant Baltazar Hornig received, by the intermediary Jan Kiełbaska of Cracow, over 120,000 items of "black furs" from the Košice merchant Jorgen Melka.[114] This could have been Hungarian "black martens," which Lviv merchants imported through Moldova in the fifteenth century.[115]

Goods from the primary sector of the economy were clearly dominant in the commodities imported to Wrocław from the Kingdom of Hungary. The only exception which confirms this general tendency was the acquisition of a gilded silver goblet, or vase (*eyn silber gegultene komp*), in Buda for 200 florins.[116] Other examples seem to provide evidence for methods of final settlement rather than for imports.[117] Wrocław imports differed from the variety of Hungarian exports in the fifteenth century, which was dominated by livestock (cattle and horses).[118] The structure of exports from Wrocław to the Kingdom of Hungary was entirely different. It is uncertain whether the merchants of Wrocław provided Buda with the renowned beer from Świdnica.[119] Even if this was so, exports from Wrocław included mostly fully processed products, mainly cloth. In the period examined, the Wrocław merchants traded local cloth as well as that of foreign origin. The origin of "Polish cloth" (*pannus polonicalis, polensch tuch*) is particularly controversial. Some historians have suggested that it was produced in Silesia while others have considered other Polish regions.[120] Although these terms could refer to textiles from other centers in Silesia (e.g., Strzegom and Świdnica), the development of textile production in Wrocław makes it possible to assume that some amount of Wrocław cloth was exported.[121] "Polish" cloth was delivered to Sopron as early as 1352[122] but its export intensified only in the fifteenth century. According to D. Poppe, *Polensch tuch* was known in Buda (from the early 1400s) and in towns of Slovakia (Bratislava and Bardejov in the second half of the fifteenth century),[123] although Silesian cloth began arriving in Bratislava somewhat earlier. In 1438, the Wrocław merchants mentioned above (Hesse, Zebrecht, and Kunze) bought a quantity of 102 bales of cloth made in Strzegom (*CII stregener tuch*),[124] part of which was transported to Buda.

Wrocław merchants exporting foreign textiles to Hungary are attested from the first half of the fifteenth century. The earliest product that was brought to Hungary was high-quality cloth from Tienen (in Brabant). A shipment of 16 to 17 bales was delivered to Buda in the first quarter of the fifteenth century to be sold to the representatives of the archbishop of Esztergom and a local merchant.[125] Sporadically, the merchants of Wrocław brought German cloth (made in Cologne and Aachen) and Moravian cloth (produced in Brno) to the customs' house at Bratislava.[126] From the late 1430s, data show that cloth of poorer quality from Görlitz (86 bales) was brought to Buda and Bratislava.[127] In Hesse's, Kunze's, and Zebrecht's accounting records there are 452 bales of an unspecified type of cloth that was exchanged for pepper.[128] It is unsure whether the absence of information about the origin of this textile in otherwise meticulous records can indirectly serve as evidence for its local, Wrocław-based, production. This is likely because apparently the merchants did not distinguish between Silesian and Görlitz cloth in their records, counting them as the same.

Textiles also reached the Hungarian towns in the Black Sea economic zone. According to H. Ammann, as early as 1400 "Polish cloth" (*Polonicali panno*), considered the product of Silesia, reached Sibiu.[129] Further accounts about this textile in Sibiu, this time clearly of Wrocław origin (*pallen Presler, pecia Bresler*), are very late (the beginning of the sixteenth century).[130] Nevertheless, in the first quarter of the fifteenth century Braşov merchants delivered "Polish cloth" to Transylvania, Moldova, and Wallachia. This material is mentioned in the customs tariffs in Rodna, a border town, issued in 1412 by the voivode of Transylvania for the inhabitants of Bistriţa and Braşov[131] as well as in the trade concessions Mircea the Old granted the merchants of Braşov in 1413.[132]

Thus, it was not the Wrocław merchants who arrived there, although the content of the tariffs, literally interpreted, does not deny this. In my opinion, it was rather Braşov traders who came to Buda to buy Silesian cloth rather than Silesian Wrocław merchants traveling as far as Transylvania. Analogically, the Sebeş suppliers would buy the cloth of Tienen from Wrocław merchants in Buda.[133]

Besides cloth, Wrocław tradesmen brought other goods to Hungary. In the third quarter of the fifteenth century, they delivered stoat fur. According to the records of Hesse, Kunze, and Zerbrecht, they brought almost 2,000 sacks of this high-quality commodity in 1438.[134] It might have originated from the northern areas of the Rus'. If so, it suggests circular methods of supply and points to Wrocław as one of the centers of the fur trade in Central Europe.[135] It is unclear whether stoat fur had been exported to Hungary earlier.[136]

For the record, one should mention a complaint filed by the Wrocław belt makers about the export of locally produced belts to Hungary, among other places.[137] In my opinion, it is difficult to consider this as an example of commercial exchange. Export of goods to Hungary carried out by the Wrocław merchants fit into Hungary's general balance of foreign exchange; foreign textiles constituted 79% of its imports.[138]

TABLE 14.1 Debtors of Wrocław merchants in the Kingdom of Hungary

Town of origin	Debt in currencies and units of account	Debt calculated in Hungarian Florins[139]	Proportion (in %) of debts owed by the townsmen of the Kingdom of Hungary	Chronology of loans' records
Buda	a. 1 mark + 6 groschen b. 874 ½ Hungarian florins[140]	876 ½	44.91%	1491–1494
Svätý Jur (Sankt Georgen)	400 marks[141]	684	35.05%	1438
Košice	391 Hungarian florins[142]	391	20.04%	1465
Total	a. 401 marks b. 874 ½ Hungarian florins	1951 ½	100%	1438–1494

Credits and rents

Economic contacts between Wrocław and the towns of the Kingdom of Hungary were also manifested in the field of money lending. Its scope was limited, though. The Wrocław merchants made loans mainly to the inhabitants of Buda and Svätý Jur and also to people in Levoča and Spišská Sobota, but the sums are unknown. Also, an enigmatic record reporting a 400-Hungarian-florin payment made by a burgher of Košice to the Wrocław council seems to be linked to a previous credit operation (see Table 14.1).[143]

Altogether, the amount of money lent to the residents of the Kingdom of Hungary, counted in gold, reached almost 2,000 florins, although the amount must have been much higher because other records did not list detailed loan sums.[144] The language of these other records suggests that there must have been considerable money involved. For instance, two burghers of Levoča and their partner, a judge from Ľubietová (*uff der Luebeth*), ceded their entire property to repay their debt.[145] An account registering a payment by a burgher of Spišska Sobota mentions that the sum was high.[146] Moreover, another merchant of Wrocław received permission as a creditor to enforce his claims in Hungary and elsewhere.[147] Lamentably, the data are too sporadic to attempt any assessment of the values of loans. Credit operations were mostly registered in the second half of the fifteenth century, particularly in the 1490s, but the dates of these registrations are only the *termini ante quem* of the loans. Furthermore, according to the sources I used, the Wrocław merchants borrowed virtually no money in the Kingdom of Hungary. I am aware of only two loans, taken out in Košice and Buda (see Table 14.2).

TABLE 14.2 Debts of the burghers of Wrocław in the Kingdom of Hungary

Towns of origin of the creditors	Debt in currencies and units of account	Debt calculated in Hungarian florins[148]	Chronology of loan records
Buda	60 marks[149]	120	1418
Košice	89 Hungarian florins[150]	89	1394

It is evident that the credit balance was favorable to the residents of Wrocław, as it was with their contacts with particular centers: Buda (876½ Hung. florins vs 120 Hung. florins), Košice (391 Hung. florins vs 89 Hung. florins), and Sväty Jur (684 Hung. florins vs 0). The dynamics of moneylending are particularly interesting if one keeps in mind that the dates in the tables often signify the time of repayment requests, the time of establishing the repayment arrangement, the sizes of installments (after prior disagreements), and the time of credit return transactions. Wrocław merchants were the first to start borrowing money from the subjects of the Hungarian kings and not the other way around. One possible explanation could be the Wrocław merchants' higher mobility towards the east and southeast compared to their Hungarian counterparts. It is tempting to link the more frequent loans taken out by Hungarians to Matthias Corvinus's rule in Silesia. The records appear a few years after his death, which means that in some cases these credits had been arranged earlier.[151] In addition, the absence of earlier registrations could derive from transactions made in Hungary or in secret, that is, without entering them into the official town books. In fact, Matthias Corvinus's monetary reforms and the bans (on using old coins) related to them did not favor unregulated money-lending activities.

In contrast to the towns of Bohemia and Moravia, Hungarians did not buy annuities in Wrocław and vice versa. The only exception that attests this practice is the case of Johann Stadler from Buda[152] who for his life (*ad vite sue tempora*) bought 125 marks of rent in Wrocław.

Craftsmen's contacts

In the history of contacts between Wrocław and the towns of the Kingdom of Hungary, craftsmen's mobility requires some attention. I found an archival source on migration from Hungary to Wrocław. In the 1470s, a certain goldsmith (*Goltsloer*) from Košice owned a workshop in Wrocław.[153] A possible context for this migration could have been Corvinus's rule in Silesia. After the king's death, craftsmen of Wrocław origin were invited to Transylvania. Just to mention but one case, in 1495 the Sibiu authorities invited Hieronimus Rinke (*Jeronimus Rÿnke*),[154] a cannon-founder, to come for a year. Judging from the political context, the date of his trip as well as its destination justify linking this migration with the Ottoman threat.

Wrocław as the center of transactions and financial settlements

For the merchants from the Kingdom of Hungary Wrocław was not really an important center for contacting tradesmen from outside Wrocław; there are only a few instances of such contacts. Particularly striking is the lack of contact between the Hungarian merchants and burghers of Silesian towns apart from Wrocław.[155] There are single examples of contact between Hungarian merchants and their trade partners from Prussia, Southern Germany, Bohemia, and Lusatia via Wrocław. For instance, Grand Master Michael Küchmeister of the Teutonic Order repaid his debt of 4000 Hungarian florins in Wrocław to the above-mentioned Johann Stadler from Buda.[156] Merchants of Pécs asserted in Wrocław that they owed burghers of Buda for copper that had not been delivered.[157] Moreover, a burgher of Košice pledged to pay off his debt to a creditor from Regensburg in Wrocław.[158] In Wrocław, a local money-lender(?), Hans Giger, pledged to deliver furs and fur products from a Košice merchant to a Toruń tradesman.[159] The Wrocław town councilors investigated a transaction between a Prague merchant and his copper supplier from Levoča.[160] Another example of Wrocław's role in supervising financial transactions is the delivery of a testated sum left by a burgher named Arnold de Pak (otherwise unknown) to a certain Albert of Vasvár (Eisenburg) from 1367.[161] A 1479 transaction is a separate instance: Gregor Krekwitz from Croatia (*aws Croacien*) arrived in Wrocław to sell three villages near Głogów on his father's behalf to his cousins, also Krekwitzs, for 200 Bohemian marks.[162] Whether the Krekwitzs were originally from Wrocław is unclear; it is likely, however, since their place of origin (and of residence) was not noted otherwise in the registry.

Participants in the Hungarian–Wrocław contacts

Fewer than 40 inhabitants of Wrocław were engaged in economic contacts between Wrocław and the towns of the Kingdom of Hungary. It is striking that only a few of them held offices in the town's administration. They were, among others: Hans Hesse, Niklas Banke (of the famous lineage of Johann Banke, his father),[163] Dawid Jentsch (also the *iuratus* of the furriers' guild),[164] three Hornigs – two Pauls and Baltazar[165] – and Sebald Sauermann.[166] In addition, there were also Paul Wiener,[167] Wenzlav Reichel, and Konrad Glesel; the latter two both became Wrocław councilors shortly after having concluded their transactions with the Hungarian burghers.[168] It is not clear if Jorge Saffran was born into a lineage of councilors, as simultaneously two people with the same name had careers in the town.[169] An analogous assumption does not stand for Margaretha Hildebrand because there was a gap of over 100 years between her trading activity and a short episode of her namesakes' careers in the town council (and the name was quite popular anyway).[170] The majority of economic contacts with Hungary remained outside the town's political elite. Some of the agents were wealthy merchants, like Hieronimus Rindfleisch or Hesse's partners Karl Kunze, Jorge Zebrecht, and Niklas

Rymer, a commission agent (*lieger*) in Buda. Three partners, Hans Mumeler, Peter Geil, and Martin Neckil, were also among this group; they established a company operating in Hungary, especially Kremnica.[171] They maintained chiefly economic contacts with Buda[172] which remained important for them even after the death of Matthias Corvinus.[173] There were also contacts with Kremnica[174] and Košice[175] as well as with unidentified places (*in Unghern, in Ungarie regione*).[176] There were also a few merchants carrying out business with Spišská Sobota, Smolník, Svätý Jur, and Sebeş in Transylvania.[177] The Wrocław burghers mentioned above were also active in Bratislava and Levoča.[178] Wrocław merchants had 27 Hungarian trade partners,[179] besides the contacts between the Wrocław councilors and the authorities in Hungarian towns (see below), and Hungarian incomers of unknown professions (who were registered exclusively for their offenses) as well as five visitors from Pécs who pledged before the Wrocław court to reimburse the claims of residents of Buda. Defining their status is difficult. Due to the lack of relevant literature, I can only say something about a few of them; probably the majority were professional tradesmen. In addition, there was a thirtieth customs collector (Peter Edlasberger, *burger und dreysiger zcu-o Offen*),[180] two judges, one from Levoča (Hieronimus Selin) and another from Ľubietová (Peter Lange),[181] a trade factor (Jakub Hocheimer),[182] a treasurer of the archbishop of Esztergom, and a butcher, Johann (Svätý Jur), who took a considerable loan and provided generous guarantees to secure its repayment.[183]

Trade did not occur solely among individual merchants but also between the town councils of Wrocław and several towns in the Kingdom of Hungary. Councilors of Hungarian towns – such as Buda – authorized plenipotentiaries to collect debts,[184] on occasion notified the Wrocław authorities about particular transactions – e.g., Buda and Levoča – [185] and intervened – Trnava, for instance – on behalf of a merchant who had suffered damages in Wrocław.[186]

Conclusions

Summarizing the nearly 250-year history of economic relations between Wrocław and the Kingdom of Hungary, it has to be emphasized that the exchange of goods was the most important. Lending money and buying/selling rents were sporadic, but when they occurred considerable money was involved.

Towards the end of the Middle Ages, the legal status of Wrocław merchants trading with Hungary was reinforced. The organizational frameworks of the Wrocław trade were expanded with the establishment of a new annual fair. All these changes were inspired by Matthias Corvinus's subjugation of Silesia and his understanding of the economy. Corvinus's rule in Wrocław can be perceived as an example of a confrontation between proto-absolutist state policy and a long tradition of town autonomy, which was anything but unique in late medieval Europe.[187] A better understanding of the economic contacts between Wrocław and the Kingdom of Hungary in the Late Middle Ages is an important contribution not only to the economic history of the "Third Europe" but also to the economic and political-constitutional history of the entire continent.

Notes

1 Henryk Samsonowicz, *Miejsce Polski w Europie* [Poland's place in Europe] (Warsaw: Bellona, 1995), 67, 71–72, 76, 86, 90, 92 and 95; Jörg Hoensch, *Geschichte Böhmens. Von der slavischen Landnahme bis zur Gegenwart* (Munich: C. H. Beck, 1997), 93–96, 98–100, 134 and 151, and Pál Engel, *The Realm of St. Stephen. A History of Medieval Hungary*, trans. Tamás Pálosfalvi (London and New York: I. B. Tauris, 2001), 101, 112–113, 154–156 and 244–275.

2 Jenő Szűcs, *Les trois Europes* (Paris: L'Harmattan, 1985).

3 Henryk Samsonowicz, "Jarmarki w Polsce na tle sytuacji gospodarczej w Europie w XV–XVI wieku" [The annual fairs in Poland against a background of the economic situation in Europe in the 14th and 15th centuries], in *Europa – Słowiańszczyzna – Polska. Studia ku uczczeniu Profesora Kazimierza Tymienieckiego* [Europe – Slavic areas – Poland. Studies offered in honor of Professor Kazimierz Tymieniecki] (Poznań: Uniwersytet im A. Mickiewicza, 1970), 523–532; Markus Denzel, "Der Beitrag von Messen und Märkten zum Integrationsprozess des internationalen bargeldlosen Zahlungsverkehrsystems in Europa (13–18 Jahrhundert)," in *Fiere e mercati nella integrazione delle economie europee. Secc. XIII–XVIII.*, ed. Simonetta Cavacciocchi (Florence: Le Monnier, 2001), 819–836, here 822.

4 Samuel Benjamin Klose, *Von Breslau. Dokumentierte Geschichte und Beschreibung in Briefen,* I–III (Breslau: Korn, 1781–1783), I, 353–354; Heinrich Wendt, *Schlesien und der Orient. Ein geschichtlicher Rückblick* (Breslau: Hirt, 1916), 7, 51–53, 55, 57–63, 80 and 81; Gerhard Pfeiffer, *Das Breslauer Patriziat im Mittelalter,* (Breslau: Trewendt & Granier, 1929), 229, 237, 239, 279 and 298; Wolfgang Kehn, *Der Handel im Oderraum im 13. und 14. Jahrhundert* (Cologne and Graz: Böhlau, 1968), 17–18, 50, 80 and 87–88; and Herbert Patzelt, "Schlesien und Ungarn. Geschichtliche Wechselbeziehungen," *Jahrbuch der Schlesischen Friedrich–Wilhems–Universität zu Breslau* 34 (1993): 73–91.

5 Karol Maleczyński, "Dzieje Wrocławia od czasów najdawniejszych do roku 1618" [A history of Wrocław from the earliest times to 1618], in Wacław Długoborski, Józef Gierowski and Karol Maleczyński, *Dzieje Wrocławia do roku 1807* [A history of Wrocław to 1807] (Warsaw: Państwowe Wydawnictwo Naukowe, 1958), 11–336, here 71–72, and Engel, *The Realm*, 102–103.

6 Maleczyński, "Dzieje," 74; Th. Goerlitz, *Verfassung, Verwaltung und Recht der Stadt Breslau, Part. 1 (Mittelalter)* (Würzburg: Holzner, 1962), 15; Marta Młynarska–Kaletynowa, *Wrocław w XII–XIII wieku. Przemiany społeczne i osadnicze* [Wrocław in the 12th to 13th centuries. The social and settlement transformations] (Wrocław: Zakład Narodowy im. Ossolińskich, 1986), 125, 130 and 158.

7 Karol Maleczyński and Wacław Hołubowicz, *Historia Śląska*, I/1 [The history of Silesia] (Wrocław: Zakład Narodowy im. Ossolińskich, 1960), 544–550; Mateusz Goliński, "Wrocław od połowy XIII do początków XVI wieku" [Wrocław between the mid-13th and the beginning of the 16th century], in Cezary Buśko et al., *Historia Wrocławia. Od pradziejów do końca czasów habsburskich* [A history of Wrocław. From its prehistory until the end of the Habsburg period] (Wrocław: Wydawnictwo Dolnośląskie, 2001), 133–135.

8 Roman Heck, "Struktura społeczna średniowiecznego Wrocławia na przełomie XIV/XV w." [The structure of Wrocław society at the turn of the 14th and in the 15th century], *Sobótka* 7 (1952): 57–94, here 86; Goliński, "Wrocław," 207.

9 Richard C. Hoffmann, "Towards a City-State in East-Central Europe: Control of Local Government in the Late Medieval Duchy of Wrocław," *Societas. A Review of Social History* 5, no. 3 (1975): 173–199.

10 Grzegorz Myśliwski, *Wrocław w przestrzeni gospodarczej Europy (XIII–XV wiek). Centrum czy peryferie?* [Wrocław in the economic space of Europe between the 13th and 15th

century. Core or periphery?] (Wrocław: Wydawnictwo Uniwersytetu Wrocławskiego, 2009), 502.

11 Richard C. Hoffmann, *Land, Liberties, and Lordship in a Late Medieval Countryside: Agrarian Structures and Change in the Duchy of Wrocław* (Philadelphia: University of Pennsylvania Press, 1989), 319–320 and 326.

12 Engel, *The Realm*, 124–156; Stanisław A. Sroka, "Methods of Constructing Angevin Rule in Hungary in the Light of Most Recent Research," *Quaestiones Medii Aevi Novae* 1 (1996): 77–90.

13 For more details about the Balkan domains of the Hungarian monarchy, see Engel, *The Realm*, 33, 35, 110, 134, 162, 164–165, 232–234 and 237.

14 Frederic C. Lane, *Venice. A Maritime Republic* (London & Baltimore: The Johns Hopkins University Press, 1973), 183–184.

15 For more details about the rich variety of names for this territory, see Olha Kozubska-Andrusiv, *"'… propter disparitatem linguae et religionis pares ipsis non esse …'* Minority Communities in Medieval and Early Modern Lviv," in *Segregation – Integration – Assimilation. Religious and Ethnic Groups in the Medieval Towns of Central and Eastern Europe*, ed. Derek Keene, Balázs Nagy, and Katalin Szende (Farnham: Ashgate, 2009), 51–66, here 51.

16 Krzysztof Baczkowski, *Dzieje Polski późnośredniowiecznej (1370–1506)* [A history of late medieval Poland] (Cracow: Fogra Oficyna Wydawnicza, 1999), 35–55 and 72.

17 Engel, *The Realm*, 113–114 and 244–245; Richard Marsina, "O kształtowaniu się pozycji społeczno–gospodarczej miast średniowiecznych na Słowacji" [On the development of the socio-economic significance of towns in Slovakia], *Kwartalnik Historii Kultury Materialnej* 23 (1975): 567–588, here 567; Danuta Molenda, "Powstawanie miast górniczych w Europie Środkowej w XIII–XVIII w." [The emergence of mining towns in Central Europe between the 13th and the 18th centuries], in *Czas, przestrzeń, praca w dawnych miastach. Studia ofiarowane Henrykowi Samsonowiczowi w sześćdziesiątą rocznicę urodzin* [Time, space, work in pre–industrial towns. Studies offered to Henryk Samsonowicz on the occasion of his 60th birthday], ed. Andrzej Wyrobisz et al. (Warsaw: Wydawnictwo PWN, 1991), 157–175, here 166–168 and István Petrovics, "The Cities and Towns of Medieval Hungary as Economic and Cultural Centres and Places of Coexistence. The Case of Pécs," *Colloquia* 18 (2011): 5–26, here 7–8.

18 András Kubinyi, "Die Märkte Ungarns im Spätmittelalter," in *Messen, Jahrmärkte und Stadtentwicklung in Europa* (Beiträge zur Landes- und Kulturgeschichte, 5), ed. Franz Irsigler and Michel Pauly (Trier: Porta Alba, 2007), 253–262, here 254.

19 Engel, *The Realm*, 323.

20 László Makkai, "Economic Landscapes: Historical Hungary from the Fourteenth to the Seventeenth Century," in *East-Cental Europe in Transition. From the Fourteenth to the Seventeenth Century*, ed. Antoni Mączak et al. (Cambridge: Cambridge University Press, 1985), 24–35, here 26 and 30–31.

21 Ibid., 27 and 32–33. In the Late Middle Ages wine for export was produced in the region of Srijem, in the vicinity of Bratislava, in Sopron, and to the north of the Lake Balaton, as well as in the Tokaj region (Engel, *The Realm*, 275). Hungarian wine was exported to Germany, Bohemia, and Poland, ibid., 249.

22 Márta Belényesy, "Viehzucht und Hirtenwesen in Ungarn im 14. und 15. Jahrhundert," in *Viehzucht und Hirtenleben in Ostmitteleuropa. Ethnographische Studien*, ed. László Földes (Budapest: Akadémiai, 1961), 13–82, here 20–23 and 76; István M. Kiss, "Agricultural and Livestock Production: Wine and Oxen. The Case of Hungary," in *East-Central Europe in Transition*, 84–96, here 88; Friedrich Lütge, *Strukturwandlungen im ostdeutschen und osteuropäischen Fernhandel des 14. bis 16. Jahrhunderts* (Munich: Verlag

der Bayerischen Akademie der Wissenschaften. Philosophisch-Historische Klasse. Sitzungberichte, 1964), 36 and 41; Ian Blanchard, "The Continental European Cattle Trades, 1400–1600," *Economic History Review* NS 39 (1986): 427–460, here 429–430, 433–434 and 436.

23 Engel, *The Realm*, 155–156 and 247–248; Molenda, "Powstawanie," 166–168. The main mining centers in this region were Banská Bystrica, Ľubietová, and Gelnica near Košice (Engel, *The Realm*, 248).

24 On Slovak mining, see Marian Małowist, *Wschód a Zachód Europy w XIII–XVI wieku. Konfrontacja struktur społeczno–gospodarczych* [East and West Europe in the 13th to 16th century. A comparison of their socio-economic structures] (Warsaw: Państwowe Wydawnictwo Naukowe, 1973), 143–144, Molenda, "Powstawanie," 166–168 and Engel, *The Realm*, 248.

25 Ibid.

26 Ibid.

27 Wolfgang von Stromer, "Nürnberger Unternehmer im Karpatenraum. Ein oberdeutsches Buntmetall–Oligopol 1396–1412," *Kwartalnik Historii Kultury Materialnej* 16 (1968): 641–662, here 649; Josef Janáček, "L'argent tchèque et la Méditerranée (XIVᵉ et XVᵉ siècles)," in *Histoire économique du monde méditerranéen 1450–1650. Mélanges en l'honneur de Fernand Braudel*, I (Touluse: Privat, 1973), 245–261, here 247; Małowist, *Wschód*, 143–144; Engel, *The Realm*, 62 and 248. Some silver was brought to Venice, where it was used for minting groschen (von Stromer, "Nürnberger Unternehmer," 649).

28 Antoni Mączak and Henryk Samsonowicz, "La zone baltique: l'un des éléments du marché européen," *Acta Poloniae Historica* 11 (1965): 71–99, here 71.

29 Małowist, *Wschód*, 25. On Ruthenian salt mines, see Jan Ptaśnik, *Kultura włoska wieków średnich w Polsce* [Medieval Italian culture in Poland] (Warsaw: Państwowe Wydawnictwo Naukowe, 1959), 95–96.

30 Małowist, *Wschód*, 30; Samsonowicz, "L'économie de l'Europe du Centre-Est du haut moyen âge au XVIᵉ siècle," in *Histoire de l'Europe du Centre-Est* (Paris: Presses Universitaires de France, 2004), 621–641, here 629.

31 Lane, *Venice*, 79; Małowist, *Wschód*, 27–29; Janet L. Abu-Lughod, *Before European Hegemony. The World System A.D. 1250–1350* (New York and Oxford: Oxford University Press, 1989), 153–184.

32 Zs[igmond] P[ál] Pach, "Levantine Trade Routes und Eastern Europe in the Middle Ages," in *XVᵉ Congrès des Sciences Historiques*, II (Bucuresti: Editura Academiei Republicii Socialiste Romania, 1980), 222–230, here 227–229; idem, "La route du poivre vers la Hongrie médiévale. Contribution à l'histoire du commerce méditerranéen au XVᵉ siècle," in *Mélanges en l'honneur de Fernand Braudel*, I, 449–458; idem, "Le commerce du Levant et la Hongrie au Moyen Âge," *Annales É.S.C.* 31 (1976): 1176–1194; Myśliwski, *Wrocław*, 348 and 350–351; Katalin Szende, "Towns Along the Way. Changing Patterns of Long-distance Trade and the Urban Network in Medieval Hungary," in *Towns and Communication*, vol. 2: *Communication between Towns. Proceedings of the Meetings of the International Commission for the History of Towns*, ed. Hubert Houben and Kristjan Toomaspoeg (Lecce: Mario Congedo Editore, 2011), 161–226, here 211–216; Mária Pakucs-Willcocks, "Economic Relations Between the Ottoman Empire in the Sixteenth Century: Oriental Trade and Merchants," in *Osmanische Orient und Ost. Perzeptionen und Interraktionen in den Grenzzonen zwischen dem 16. und 18. Jahrhundert*, ed. Robert Born and Andreas Puth (Stuttgart: Franz Steiner, 2014), 207–227, here 211.

33 Małowist, *Wschód*, 27; Samsonowicz, "L'économie," 629.

34 For general comments, see Janina Nowakowa, *Rozmieszczenie komór celnych i dróg handlowych na Śląsku do końca XIV wieku* [The situation of customs points and trade routes

within Silesia until the end of the 14th century] (Wrocław: Wrocławskie Towarzystwo Naukowe, 1951), 99.

35 Wendt, *Schlesien*, 53; Heinrich von Loesch, "Die Verfassung im Mittelalter," in *Geschichte Schlesiens*, I, ed. Hermann Aubin (Stuttgart: Priebatsch, 1961), 242–321, here 246–247.

36 Wendt, *Schlesien*, 54.

37 For the characteristics of the transit significance of the pass, see ibid., 53–54, and Patzelt, "Schlesien," 74.

38 Wendt, *Schlesien*, 54.

39 Jan Dąbrowski, "Kraków a Węgry w wiekach średnich" [Cracow and Hungary in the Middle Ages], *Rocznik Krakowski* 13 (1911): 187–250, here 208.

40 Wendt, *Schlesien*, 54; Engel, *The Realm*, 375; Petrovics, "The Cities," 11; and Szende, "Towns," 185, 212, and 215–216.

41 Wendt, *Schlesien*, 54.

42 Based on the privilege of January 6, 1336, in which the customs-collecting locations and tariffs were determined (and thus the route itself) for merchants traveling between *Alba Ecclesia* (Hranice) and Buda. See *Codex diplomaticus et epistolaris Moraviae*, VII, ed. Peter von Chlumecký (Olomouc: Skarnitz, 1858), 76–77 (no. 102). The document has been discussed by Georg Juritsch, *Handel und Handelsrecht in Böhmen bis zur husitischen Revolution. Ein Beitrag zur Kulturgeschichte der österreichischen Länder* (Leipzig and Vienna: Deuticke, 1907), 64; Theodor Mayer, *Der auswärtige Handel des Herzogtums Österreich im Mittelalter* (Innsbruck: Wagner, 1909), 30; Balázs Nagy, "Transcontinental Trade from East-Central Europe to Western Europe (Fourteenth and Fifteenth Centuries)," in … *The Man of Many Devices, Who Wandered Full Many Ways. Festschrift in Honor of János M. Bak*, ed. idem and Marcell Sebők (Budapest: Central European University Press, 1999), 347–356; György Rácz, "The Congress of Visegrád," in *Visegrád 1335*, ed. idem (Bratislava: International Visegrad Fund, 2009), 17–29, here 27–28. For an introduction to this route, see Miloš Dvořák, "Císař Karel IV. a pražský zahraniční obchod" [Emperor Charles IV and the foreign trade of Prague], *Pražský sborník historický* 34 (2006): 7–91, here 82. On the significance of Esztergom and its gradual decline as a nodal and commercial point in favor of Buda see: Szende. "Towns," 193–194.

43 Engel, *The Realm*, 375; Petrovics, "The Cities," 11; and Szende, "Towns," 212 and 215–216.

44 Wolfgang Herborn, "Die mittelalterliche Messen im deutschsprachigen Raum," in *Brücke zwischen den Völkern – Zur Geschichte der Frankfurter Messe,* I (Frankfurt im Messennetz Europas – Erträge der Forschung), ed. Hans Pohl (Frankfurt am Main: Historisches Museum, 1991), 51–66, here 59. See also Konrad Wutke, "Die Versorgung Schlesiens mit Salz während des Mittelallters," *Zeitschrift des Vereins für Geschichte und Alterthum Schlesiens* 27 (1893): 238–290, here 284; Roman Heck, "Wrocław w latach 1241–1526" [Wrocław in 1241–1526], in *Wrocław, jego dzieje i kultura* [Wrocław, its history and culture], ed. Zygmunt Świechowski (Warsaw: Arkady, 1978), 56–76, here 62; Werner Mägdefrau and Erika Langer, "Die Entfaltung der Stadt von der Mitte des 11. bis zum Ende des 15. Jahrhunderts," in *Geschichte der Stadt Erfurt*, ed. Willibald Gutsche (Weimar: H. Böhlaus Nachfolger, 1986), 53–102, here 60; Herbert Eiden, "The Fairs of Leipzig and Eastern European Economies (15th–18th centuries)," in *Fiere*, 723–739; here 724. For a detailed description of the *Hohe Strasse*, see Friedrich Bruns and Hugo Weczerka, *Hansische Handelsstrassen. Textband* (Weimar: Böhlau, 1967), 467–470, 539–548, 550–552, 568–570 and 681–690; Nowakowa, *Rozmieszczenie*, 78–87, and Myśliwski, *Wrocław*, 75–80.

45 Wutke, "Die Versorgung," 284; Stanisław Kutrzeba, *Handel Krakowa w wiekach średnich na tle stosunków handlowych Polski* [The trade of Cracow in the Middle Ages against a

background of the commercial relations of Poland) (Cracow: Akademia Umiejętności, 1902), 12. Cf. Nowakowa, *Rozmieszczenie*, 59–66.

46 According to Konrad Wutke, they used to transport salt from around Cracow to Wrocław (Wutke, "Die Versorgung," 284).

47 Nowakowa, "Rozmieszczenie," 96–99. About the transit significance of Nysa, see Józef Leszczyński, "Zarys dziejów miasta do roku 1740" [Outline of history of Nysa to 1740), in *Miasto Nysa. Szkice monograficzne* [Nysa. The monographic articles], ed. Janusz Kroszel (Wrocław: Państwowe Wydawnictwo Naukowe, 1970), 17–61, here 28.

48 Kutrzeba, *Handel, 9.*

49 About the origins of the town, see Adrienne Körmendy, *Melioratio terrae. Vergleichende Untersuchungen über die Siedlungsbewegung im östlichen Mitteleuropa im 13.–14. Jahrhundert* (Poznań: Wydawnictwo Poznańskiego Towarzystwa Przyjaciół Nauk, 1995), 69. About the development of the town and the turning points in the course of its history, see Dąbrowski, "Kraków," 215 and Engel, *The Realm*, 257.

50 Engel, *The Realm*, 375.

51 *Quellen zur Schlesischen Handelsgeschichte bis 1526*, I, ed. Marie Scholz–Babisch and Heinrich Wendt (Breslau: Trewendt & Granier, 1940), 163 (no. 236). For a more recent edition, see *Schlesisches Urkundenbuch*, III, ed. Winfried Irgang (Cologne: Böhlau, 1984), 348 (no. 555). See also Hermann Markgraf, "Zur Geschichte des Breslauer Kaufhauses," *Zeitschrift des Vereins für Geschichte und Alterthum Schlesiens* 22 (1888): 249–280, here 269; Mateusz Goliński, *Podstawy gospodarcze mieszczaństwa wrocławskiego w XIII wieku* [The economic basis of Wrocław burghers in the 13th century) (Wrocław: Wydawnictwo Uniwersytetu Wrocławskiego, 1991), 46–47.

52 Myśliwski, *Wrocław*, 397–398.

53 Kehn, *Der Handel*, 80. About the Wrocław–Hungarian contacts through Cracow, see Dąbrowski, "Kraków," 109. See also Belényesy, "Viehzucht," 20.

54 *Breslauer Urkundenbuch,* I, ed. Georg Korn (Breslau: Korn, 1870), 111–114 (no. 122). This source has also been discussed by Maleczyński, "Dzieje," 120–121; idem and Hołubowicz, *Historia*, 470–471; Goerlitz, *Verfassung*, 57; Kehn, *Der Handel*, 68 and 79–80; Goliński, *Podstawy*, 26; and Gregorz Myśliwski, "Strefa sudecko–karpacka i Lwów. Miejsce Śląska, Małopolski i Rusi Czerwonej w gospodarce Europy Zachodniej (połowa XIII w. – początek XVI w." [The Sudeto-Carpathian economic zone and Lviv. The significance of Silesia, Lesser Poland and Red Ruthenia in the European economy (between the mid-13th and early-16th century], in *Ziemie polskie wobec Zachodu. Studia nad rozwojem średniowiecznej Europy* [The Polish lands vs the West. Studies on the development of medieval Europe], ed. Sławomir Gawlas (Warsaw: DiG, 2006), 247–319, here 285–286.

55 *Breslauer Urkundenbuch*, I, 113 (no. 122). See also Lütge, "Strukturwandlungen," 28 and Kehn, *Der Handel*, 50 and 87.

56 Kutrzeba, *Handel*, 83, and Kehn, *Der Handel*, 80.

57 Karol Maleczyński, "Aus der Geschichte des schlesischen Bergbaus in der Epoche des Feudalismus," in *Beiträge zur Geschichte Schlesiens*, ed. Ewa Maleczyńska (Berlin: Rütten & Loening, 1958), 236–283, here 244–245.

58 Kutrzeba, *Handel*, 24 and 28–29.

59 Ibid., 83.

60 Matthias Lexer, *Mittelhochdeutsches Handwörterbuch*, I–III (Leipzig: Hirzel, 1872–1878), III, 742.

61 About earlier contacts with Flanders, see Wendt, *Schlesien*, 12; Hektor Ammann, "Zur Geschichte der wirtschaftlichen Beziehungen zwischen Oberdeutschland und dem deutschen Nordosten im Mittelalter," *Schlesische Geschichtsblätter* no. 3 (1927): 49–57, here 52; Maleczyński, "Dzieje," 117 and 119; Kehn, *Der Handel*, 81, and Goliński, "Wrocław,"

150. About earlier contacts with northern Italy, see Ammann, "Zur Geschichte," 53; Franz Bastian, *Oberdeutsche Kaufleute in den älteren Tiroler Raitbüchern (1288–1370)*. *Rechnungen und Rechnungsauszüge samt Einleitungen und Kaufmannsregister* (Munich: Verlag der Kommission, 1931), 76–78, and Myśliwski, *Wrocław*, 449–454.

62 František Graus, *Český obchod se suknem ve 14. a počátkem 15. stoleti. K otázce významu středověkého obchodu* [The Bohemian trade in cloth in the 14th and the beginning of the 15th century. On the significance of medieval trade] (Prague: Melantrich, 1950), 30–31; von Stromer, "Nürnberg Unternehmer," 642; Wolfgang von Stromer, *Oberdeutsche Hochfinanz 1350–1450*, I (Wiesbaden: Steiner, 1970), 90–91; Nagy, "Transcontinental trade," 348–350; Engel, *The Realm*, 137.

63 It is unclear whether any charter concerning economic matters was ever issued. According to the extant documents which are the legacy of the Visegrád summit, political matters remained central. See Maleczyński and Hołubowicz, *Historia*, 560–561; Stanisław Szczur, "Zjazd wyszehradzki z 1335 roku" [The Visegrád summit in 1335], *Studia Historyczne* 35 (1992): 3–18, here 15–16; Rácz, "The Congress," 22–27. Granting Brno the staple right is known from a letter (February 22, 1336) from John of Luxemburg to the town council of Frankfurt am Main, see *Urkundenbuch der Reichstadt Frankfurt*, II, ed. Johann F. Boehmer (Frankfurt am Main: Baer & Co., 1905), 418 (no. 548). The king of Bohemia notified the council that three monarchs confirmed the Brno staple right and promised to secure free and safe passage on all routes leading to that town, see František Graus, "Die Handelsbeziehungen Böhmen zu Deutschland und Österreich im 14. und zu Beginn des 15. Jahrhunderts," *Historica* 2 (1960): 77–100, here 87; Nagy, "Transcontinental trade," 349. The Bohemian–Hungarian agreement of January 6, 1336, concerning free trade between them is considered to be an outcome of the pact of three monarchs (see note 42).

64 *Codex diplomaticus et epistolaris Moraviae*, VII, 552 (no. 761).

65 See note 42.

66 Dąbrowski, "Kraków," 195 and 209. For the position of Košice in the hierarchy of towns in Angevin-period Hungary, see Engel, *The Realm*, 257. About the town's role in the copper trade, see Dąbrowski, "Kraków," 223. See also Kazimierz Myśliński, "Rola miast małopolskich w handlu międzynarodowym późnego średniowiecza" [The role of the Lesser Poland towns in the late medieval international trade], in *Czas*, 417–429, here 420. About Sigismund of Luxemburg's ideas about launching fustian production in Košice, see Martin Štefánik, *Obchodná vojna krala Žigmunda proti Benátkam. Stredovekový boj o trhy medzi uhorsko-nemeckým králom a Republikou svätého Marka* [The trade war of King Sigimund against Venice. A medieval struggle for markets between the Hungarian-German king and the Republic of St. Mark] (Bratislava: Slovenská Akademie Vied, Historický Ústav, 2004), 74–76.

67 *Breslauer Urkundenbuch*, I, 209–210 (no. 243). For a summary of Louis's charter, see Klose, *Von Breslau*, II/1, 354; see also Wendt, *Schlesien*, 56; Graus, *Český obchod*, 58; von Stromer, "Nürnberger Unternehmer," 643; idem, *Oberdeutsche Hochfinanz*, I, 106.

68 von Stromer, "Nürnberger Unternehmer," 643. About the privileges of the burghers of Nuremberg and Prague in the Kingdom of Hungary, see Graus, "Die Handelsbeziehungen," 90; Wolfgang von Stromer, "Der Kaiserliche Kaufmann – Wirtschaftspolitik unter Karl IV.," in *Kaiser Karl IV. Staatsman und Mäzen*, ed. Ferdinand Seibt (Munich: Prestel, 1978), 63–73, here 65–66, and Engel, *The Realm*, 260. About the customs' system in Hungary and about the *tricesima* (thirtieth), see Dąbrowski, "Kraków," 212; Marsina, "O kształtowaniu się," 577; Engel, *The Realm*, 156 and 226; Balázs Nagy, "The Problem of Financial Balance in the Foreign Trade of Late Medieval Hungary. A Century–Long Historiographical Debate," *Transylvanian Review*, 18, no. 3 (2009): 13–20, here 13.

69 See APWr. (Wrocław, Archiwum Państwowe we Wrocławiu [State Archive of Wrocław] DmWr. (Dokumenty miasta Wrocławia [Archive of the town of Wrocław]), no. 1495. Regarding all the documents from this collection, I have followed a recently established new numerical order after Roman Stelmach, *Katalog średniowiecznych dokumentów przechowywanych w Archiwum Państwowym we Wrocławiu* [Catalog of medieval documents stored in the State Archive in Wrocław] (Wrocław and Racibórz: Archiwum Państwowe, 2014). For the charter's summary, see Klose, *Von Breslau*, II/1, 353. See also Schieche, "Politische Geschichte," 247 (erroneously dated to 1420).

70 APWr. DmWr., no. 2429.

71 Roman Stelmach, ed. "Listy i dokumenty Jagiellonów w WAP we Wrocławiu (1413– 1503)" [The Jagiellonian letters and charters in the State Archive at Wrocław], *Teki Archiwalne* 18, no. 4 (1981): 12–84, here 19 (no. 5); August Mosbach, *Przyczynki do Dziejów Polskich z Archiwum Miasta Wrocławia* [Articles on the history of Poland based on the documents from the Wrocław Town Archive] (Poznań: Poznańskie Towarzystwo Przyjaciół Nauk, 1860), 18; Schieche, "Politische Geschichte," 261; Roman Heck and Ewa Maleczyńska, *Historia Śląska*, I/2 [A history of Silesia] (Wrocław: Zakład Narodowy im. Ossolińskich, 1961), 138; Kazimierz Myśliński, "Lublin a handel Wrocławia z Rusią w XIV i XV w." [Lublin and the Wrocław trade with Ruthenia in 14th and 15th centuries], *Rocznik Lubelski* 3 (1960): 5–36, here 12.

72 Heck and Maleczyńska, *Historia*, 290; Patzelt, "Schlesien," 78; Hoensch, *Geschichte Böhmens*, 162 and 164; András Kubinyi, *Matthias Rex* (Budapest: Balassi, 2008), 87–88, 95, 97 and 100; Krzysztof Baczkowski, *Między czeskim utrakwizmem a rzymską ortodoksją, czyli walka Jagiellonów z Maciejem Korwinem o koronę czeską w latach 1471–1479* [Between the Czech utraquism and the Roman ortodoxy or the fight of Jagiellonians against Matthias Corvinus for the crown of the Kingdom of Bohemia] (Oświęcim: Wydawnictwo Napoleon, 2014), 178–188.

73 Hermann Markgraf, "Einleitung," in *Breslauer Stadtbuch enthaltend die Rathslinie von 1287 ab und Urkunden zur Verfassungsgeschichte der Stadt* in *Codex Diplomaticus Silesiae*, XI, ed. Hermann Markgraf and Otto Frenzel (Breslau: Josef Max & Comp., 1882), XLIV–XLV; Ferdinand Friedensburg, *Schlesiens Münzgeschichte im Mittelalter, Part 2 (Münzgeschichte und Münzbeschreibung)* in *Codex Diplomaticus Silesiae*, XIII (Breslau: Max, 1888), 85 and 89; Maleczyński, "Dzieje," 291; Heck, "Wrocław," 73 Goliński, "Wrocław," 197; Kubinyi, *Matthias Rex*, 101–102.

74 Hermann Markgraf, "Heinz Dompnig, der Breslauer Hauptmann," *Zeitschrift des Vereins für Geschichte und Alterthum Schlesiens* 20 (1886): 157–196, here 192.

75 Wutke, "Die Versorgung," 266.

76 Klose, *Von Breslau*, III/2, 309; Wendt, *Schlesien*, 59.

77 Klose, *Von Breslau*, III/2, 319–320; Schieche, "Politische Geschichte," 286.

78 Klose, *Von Breslau*, III/2, 308; Myśliwski, *Wrocław*, 134.

79 Grzegorz Myśliwski, "Did Silesia Constitute an Economic Region between the 13th and the 15th century? Survey of Region-Integrating and Region-Disintegrating factors," in *The Long Formation of a Region Silesia (c. 1000–1526))*, ed. Przemysław Wiszewski (Wrocław: Publishing House Wydawnictwo ebooki, 2013), 93–128, here 112–115.

80 See *Przyczynki*, 114–115 (1485); see Max Rauprich, "Der Streit um die Breslauer Niederlage (1490–1515)," *Zeitschrift des Vereins für Geschichte und Alterthum Schlesiens* 27 (1893): 54–116, here 55.

81 I am using the German name due to identification problems (*in opido sancti Georgii*), see APKrak. (Cracow, Archiwum Państwowe w Krakowie [State Archive of Cracow]), DmKr. (Dokumenty miasta Krakowa [Archive of the town of Cracow]), no. 245 (1438/

1452). The most likely is to link it with the town of Svätý Jur (Hungarian: *Szentgyörgy*), located near Bratislava.

82 See the section on Wrocław as the center of transactions and financial settlements.

83 About their origins and importance in the period under study, see the syntheses: Engel, *The Realm*, 114; and Szende, "Towns," 214–216.

84 See Myśliwski, *Wrocław*, 374. Cf. *Der Rechte Weg. Ein Breslauer Rechtsbuch des 15. Jahrhunderts*, ed. Friedrich Ebel (Cologne: Böhlau, 2000), 505 (no. 51).

85 Rolf Sprandel, *Von Malvasia bis Kötschenbroda. Die Weinsorten auf den spätmittelalterlichen Märkten Deutschlands* (Stuttgart: Steiner, 1998), 21 and 25–26.

86 APWr., DmWr., no. 2260 (1439). Albrecht Habsburg's charter confirms the customs tariffs for wine in the period of Sigismund of Luxemburg.

87 See Marie Scholz–Babisch, "Oberdeutscher Handel mit dem deutschen und polnischen Osten nach Geschäftsbriefen von 1444," *Zeitschrift des Vereins für Geschichte und Alterthum Schlesiens*, 64 (1930): 56–74, here 66.

88 Venetian merchants appeared in the Kingdom of Hungary no later than 1255 as a consequence of the trade agreement of 1217 made by the doge of Venice and Andrew II, king of Hungary (Szende, "Towns," 175 and 190). Hungarian merchants arrived in Venice in the 1320s (Henry Simonsfeld, *Der Fondaco dei Tedeschi in Venedig und die deutsch–venetianischen Handelsbeziehungen*, II [Stuttgart: Cotta, 1887]). In this context it is important to point out that in the Late Middle Ages malvasia was imported to Lviv. See Łucja Charewiczowa, *Handel średniowiecznego Lwowa* [The trade of medieval Lwów] (Lwów: Zakład Narodowy im. Ossolińskich, 1925), 17. There is no evidence, however, that the Wrocław merchants bought the wine there. Bringing malvasia to Lviv asserts its delivery to the edge of the Black Sea economic zone. Hence, this makes it more probable that malvasia was imported to Wrocław from the Kingdom of Hungary, which was located much closer to the malvasia's production centers than Lviv.

89 Peter Eschenloer, *Historia Vratislaviensis et que post mortem regis Ladislai sub electo Georgio de Podiebrat Bohemorum rege illi acciderant prospera et adversa* (Scriptores Rerum Silesiacarum. 7), ed. Hermann Markgraf (Breslau: Max, 1872), 208–210, and Peter Eschenloer, *Geschichte der Stadt Breslau,* II, ed. Gunhild Roth (Münster: Waxmann, 2003), 763–764.

90 Eschenloer, *Historia*, 174–175.

91 ... *civibus et omnibus incolis civitatis dicte Wrathislaviensis ... cum ... bobus ... ire, equitare et fluitare ... plenam damus ... libertatem* (Stelmach, ed. "Listy i dokumenty Jagiellonów," 19 [no. 5]). See Stanisław Kutrzeba and Jan Ptaśnik, "Dzieje handlu i kupiectwa krakowskiego w wiekach średnich" [A history of trade and merchants of Cracow in the Middle Ages], *Rocznik Krakowski* 14 (1910): 1–183, here 17.

92 Goerlitz, *Verfassung*, 66. See also remarks in Lütge, *Strukturwandlungen*, 6–8, 29 and 31, and Samsonowicz, "L'économie," 38, on the increase of cattle imported from the Sudeto-Carpathian zone (1475–1500).

93 Kutrzeba, *Handel*, 82; Charewiczowa, *Handel*, 15; Blanchard, "The Continental," 431; and Myśliwski, *Wrocław*, 274 and 347.

94 A. L. Choroškevič, *Torgovlâ Velikogo Novgoroda s Pribaltikoj i zapadnoj Evropoj v XIV–XV vekah* [The trade of Novgorod the Great with Livonia and Western Europe in 14th and 15th centuries] (Moscow: Izdatelstvo Akademii Nauk SSSR, 1963), 314–315.

95 Otto Stobbe, ed., "Mittheilungen aus Breslauer Signaturbücher," *Zeitschrift des Vereins für Geschichte und Alterthum Schlesiens* 8, no. 2 (1867): 151–166 and 438–453, here 446–449 (no. 205). Stobbe's edition contains misreadings, hence in such cases I am referring to

the manuscript (APWr., AmWr. [Akta miasta Wrocławia] Lib. exc. sign. [Libri excessuum et signaturarum], XXXIII, 126–28). No mistakes were made by Samuel B. Klose while discussing the extensive record very briefly, see Klose, *Von Breslau*, II/2, 354–356.

96 Stobbe, "Mittheilungen [1867]," 447. In the Middle Ages the Wrocław hundredweight equaled 50 kilograms (Myśliwski, *Wrocław*, 542). Later its weight rose to approx. 52.8–53 kilograms. See Danuta Molenda, *Polski ołów na rynkach Europy Środkowej w XIII–XVIII wieku* [Lead from Poland in the Central European markets between the 13th and 18th centuries] (Warsaw: Wydawnictwo Instytutu Archeologii i Etnologii PAN, 2001), 26.

97 *Item primo Jorge Zebrecht hot vorkoufft 73 centener 14 lb. zu 5 ½ guldin, facit 402 guldin 8 g.g.* (Stobbe, "Mittheilungen [1867]," 448).

98 *Item so quam her ken Breslou 50 ½ centener coppers das ist vorkoufft zu 6 guldin, facit 303 guldin* (APWr., Lib. exc. sign., XXXIII, 127 and Stobbe, "Mittheilungen [1867]," 448).

99 APWr, Lib. exc. sign., XX, 108 (1415). A certain Jorge *thwrszy* [Thurzo?] of Levoča (*aus der Lewcz*) also owed a cwt of copper (ibid., XXXIII, 127) to the company of Hesse, Kunze and Zebrecht. About the copper from Smolník, see ibid., XX, 121 (1416).

100 Ibid., XXXIX, 68 (1452). See also Myśliwski, *Wrocław*, 421.

101 See the remarks by S. Kutrzeba and J. Ptaśnik about copper available in Cracow and about its source of origin (iidem, "Dzieje handlu," 5).

102 This can be supported by a case from 1493 when Hungarian merchants of Pécs (*aller von Petsch*) were ordered to the Wrocław town council and did not bring the promised copper to Wrocław. For some unexplained circumstance the copper had been left in Trenčin (APWr., Lib. exc. sign., LXI, 121). See note 157.

103 Maleczyński, "Aus der Geschichte," 239–240.

104 Marian Małowist, "Le développement des rapports économiques entre la Flandre, la Pologne et les pays limitrophes du XIIIᵉ au XIVᵉ siècle," *Revue belge de Philologie et d'Histoire* 10 (1931): 1013–1065, here 1020–1021.

105 Myśliwski, *Wrocław*, 522.

106 Colmar Grünhagen, "Schlesien am Ausgange des Mittelalters," *Zeitschrift des Vereins für Geschichte und Alterthum Schlesiens* 18 (1884): 26–67, here 37–38; Karl Peter, "Die Goldbergwerke bei Zuckmantel und Freiwaldau," *Zeitschrift des Vereins für Geschichte und Alterthum Schlesiens* 19 (1885): 35–62, here 42.

107 Stanisław A. Sroka and Wojciech Krawczuk, eds., "Dokumenty i listy miasta Krakowa z drugiej połowy XV wieku z archiwum w Bardiowie" [The Cracow charters and letters from the second half of the 15th century from the Archive at Bardejov], *Rocznik Krakowski* 71 (2005): 55–65, here 57–58.

108 … *czweytawsnt mynus fierczig pfunt und newn czenten pfeffers ofenisch gewichtes* (APWr., Lib. exc. sign., XXVII, 88). The record concerns the ways of managing the property which Niklas Ferber and his children left in Buda. It is noteworthy that Hans Hesse, who himself had been trading pepper, was involved there. I do not have data about the Buda hundredweight. This is why I am supplying the calculation based on the Bratislava hundredweight for pepper (58.8 kg) and on the hundredweights of Brașov and Sibiu (56.2–56.7 kilograms): Pach, "Levantine," 226 and 229.

109 Mentioned by Pach (ibid., 225).

110 Stobbe, "Mittheilungen [1867]," 448 (no. 205).

111 Myśliwski, *Wrocław*, 422 and 468.

112 Stobbe, "Mittheilungen [1867]," 156 (no. 161 [1433]). About this record, see Krzysztof Kopiński, *Gospodarcze i społeczne kontakty Torunia z Wrocławiem w późnym średniowieczu* [The economic and social relations between Toruń and Wrocław in the Late Middle Ages] (Toruń: Towarzystwo Naukowe, 2005), 117. *Mark, marche* stood for the synonym

of saffron (Lexer, *Mittelhochdeutsches Handwörterbuch*, I, 2048–2050). Cf. the usage of the term in the correspondence of a Nuremberg merchant residing in Wrocław: Wolfgang von Stromer, "Die Zeringer: Steirisch–Nürnberger innovatorische Montanunternehmer und Fernhändler im 15. Jahrhundert," in *Festschrift Othmar Pickl zum 60. Geburtstag*, ed. Herwig Ebner (Graz and Vienna: Leykam, 1987), 603–662, here 620.

113   Hektor Ammann, *Die Diesbach–Watt Gesellschaft. Ein Beitrag zur Handelsgeschichte des 15. Jahrhunderts* (Sankt Gallen: Fehr, 1928), 85.

114   *...dreytawsent und newn czeuling* [?] *swarcz ungerisch wergk* (APWr., Lib. exc. sign., LIII, 63). I think that this dubious word, which could be also read as *czenling*, can be taken as a distorted version of the word *zingel* (= belt, Lexer, *Mittelhochdeutsches Handwörterbuch*, III, 1124). It is probable that this refers to some unit of measurement. In the Polish lands the measure of 40 units was employed, see Leon Koczy, *Handel Poznania do poł. XVI w.* [The trade of Poznań until the mid-16th century] (Poznań: Poznańskie Towarzystwo Przyjaciół Nauk, 1930), 344, which originated in northern Rus. Cf. P. K. Kovalev, "K voprosu o proishoždenii soročka: po materiałam berestânyh gramot" [The issue of the origins of the measure <sorotschoc>. On the basis of the birch bark manuscripts], in *Berestânye gramoty: 50 let otkrytiâ i izučeniâ: materialy meždunarodnoj konferencii Velikij Novgorod, 24–27 sentâbrâ 2001 g.* [The birch bark manuscripts: the 50th anniversary of their first excavation and the beginnings of the relevant studies: papers from the international conference at Novgorod the Great], ed. Valentin L. Janin (Moscow: Indrik, 2003), 57–72. Also in Wrocław the same Russian measure was used exclusively under the German term *czymmer* (Myśliwski, *Wrocław*, 533). I suspect that the same unit was referred to in the quoted source, only again with in a garbled form.

115   See Charewiczowa, *Handel*, 67; Myśliwski, *Strefa*, 275. About marten furs, see Agnieszka Samsonowicz, *Łowiectwo w Polsce Piastów i Jagiellonów* [Hunting in Poland in the period of the Piast and Jagiello dynasties] (Wrocław: Zakład Narodowy im. Ossolińskich, 1991), 94–96.

116   *Komp* → *kumpf*, see Lexer, *Mittelhochdeutsches Handwörterbuch*, I, 1671 and 1770. Hans Hartenberg of Wrocław bought it in Buda (*Inn Unger in der Stat zu Offen*) from certain Lorenz Spore (APWr., DmWr., no 6062 [1495]). Even if he was from Wrocław (see note 179), this transaction – due to its location and, perhaps, the country of origin of this valuable object – can still be viewed as part of the history of Wrocław–Hungarian trade contacts.

117   In the records of Hesse, Kunze, and Zebrecht there is a note that Hans Gleibitz of Bratislava owed the Wrocław merchants 12 bales of undefined cloth (*tenetur 12 tuch pro 51 guldin*, APWr., Lib. exc. sign., XXXIII, 128). That this commodity belonged to the Wrocław merchants can be determined from the title of this section of the records: *Nota was die leute schuldig seynt*. One can assume that Gleibitz was still (*noch*) supposed to pay 50 florins, which he decided to pay off with the cloth of undefined origin. In a similar manner one can perhaps explain a piece from the last will of Hieronimus Rindfleisch. He noted there that a certain inhabitant of Košice (*Kaschawer*) owed him two bales of white cloth and 34 bales of red cloth for 214 florins and 6 shillings altogether (APWr., Lib. exc. sign., LIX, 165, [1491]).

118   Belényesy, *Viehzucht*, 76; Nagy, "The Problem," 15; about the demand for Hungarian horses, see von Stromer, *Oberdeutsche Hochfinanz*, I, 92–93.

119   See Hermann Aubin, "Die Wirtschaft im Mittelalter," in *Geschichte Schlesiens*, I, 322–387, here 373.

120   See, for instance, Hans Schenk, *Nürnberg und Prag* (Wiesbaden: Harrasowitz, 1969), 48; Danuta Poppe, "'*Pannus polonicalis.*' Z dziejów sukiennictwa polskiego w średniowieczu"

[*Pannus polonicalis*. From the history of the medieval cloth industry in Poland], *Kwartalnik Historii Kultury Materialnej* 36 (1988): 617–636, here 623, 627, and 629. Hektor Ammann took into consideration that under this name cloth could be produced in Greater Poland (idem, "Wirtschaftsbeziehungen zwischen Oberdeutschland und Polen im Mittelalter," *Vierteljahrschrift für Sozial- und Wirtschaftsgeschichte* 48 [1961]: 433–443). However, F. Graus considered it a Polish product that had been manufactured in other Polish regions (idem, *Český obchod*, 46–47).

121 About textile centers in Silesia, see Poppe, "'*Pannus polonicalis*'," 625. On the development of a textile industry in Wrocław at the beginning of the fourteenth century, see Wendt, *Schlesien*, 15; Maleczyński, "Dzieje," 94; Kehn, *Der Handel*, 61; Goliński, *Podstawy*, 49–50, and idem, *Wrocław*, 150. In the Late Middle Ages the textile industry became the most popular craft in Wrocław. See Mateusz Goliński, *Socjotopografia późnośredniowiecznego Wrocławia (podatnicy – przestrzeń – rzemiosło)* [The sociotopography of late medieval Wrocław (tax payers – area – industries)] (Wrocław: Wydawnictwo Uniwersytetu Wrocławskiego, 1997), 510.

122 Poppe, "'*Pannus polonicalis*'," 618.

123 Ibid., 618 and 631.

124 Stobbe, "Mittheilungen [1867]," 447 (no. 205). See György Székely, "Deutsche Tuchnamen im mittelalterlichen Ungarn," *Annales Universitatis Scientiarum Budapestinensis de Rolando Eötvös nominatae. Sectio Historica* 6 (1975): 43–76, here 71. About the term used and about textile production in Strzegom, see Poppe, "'*Pannus polonicalis*'," 625–626, and Irena Turnau, *Historia europejskiego włókiennictwa odzieżowego od XIII do XVIII w.* [The history of the European textile industry between the 13th and 18th century] (Wrocław: Zakład Narodowy im. Ossolińskich, 1987), 94.

125 APWr., Lib. exc. sign., XIX, 9 (1412) and Otto Stobbe, ed., "Mittheilungen aus Breslauer Signaturbüchern," *Zeitschrift des Vereins für Geschichte und Alterthum Schlesiens* 7, no. 1 (1866): 176–191 and 344–362, here 189–190 (no. 15 [1420]).

126 Székely, "Deutsche Tuchnamen," 45, 49 and 69, on the basis of the thirtieth customs register of 1457–1458. On this source, see Balázs Nagy, "Old Interpretations and New Approaches: the 1457–1458 Thirthieth Customs Register of Bratislava," in *Money and Finance in Central Europe during the Later Middle Ages,* ed. Roman Zaoral (Basingstoke and New York: Palgrave Macmillan, 2016), 192–201, here 193–196.

127 Stobbe, "Mittheilungen [1867]," 447 (no. 205). According to Horst Jecht, cloth of Görlitz was available in the Kingdom of Hungary as early as the middle of the fourteenth century. Besides the Polish lands, the Kingdom of Hungary was one of the main markets for this particular commodity, idem, "Zur Handelsgeschichte der Stadt Görlitz im Mittelalter," in *Oberlausitzer Forschungen. Beiträge zur Landesgeschichte*, ed. Martin Reuther (Leipzig: Koehler & Amelang, 1961), 121–127, here 124 and 126. See also Myśliwski, *Wrocław*, 372.

128 APWr., Lib. exc. sign., XXXIII, 126. Stobbe mistakenly gave the number 4052 of cloth units (Stobbe, "Mittheilungen [1867]," 447 [no. 205]). One should read: *IIII-c LII* as was written correctly and earlier by Klose (*Von Breslau*, II/2, 355).

129 Ammann, "Wirtschaftsbeziehungen," 440.

130 *Rechnungen aus dem Archiv der Stadt Hermannstadt und der sächsischen Nation,* I, ed. Verein für siebenbürgische Landeskunde (Hermannstadt: Ausschluss des Vereins für siebenbürgische Landeskunde, 1880), 317 (1505) and 523 (1509). See also Karl Borchardt, "Handel i polityka w póznosredniowiecznym Wrocławiu" [Trade and politics in medieval Wrocław], *Śląski Kwartalnik Historyczny Sobótka* 56 (2006): 249–257, here 255.

131 Graus, *Český obchod*, 59; Ammann, "Wirtschaftsbeziehungen," 440; Marian Małowist, "The Trade of Eastern Europe in the Later Middle Ages," in *The Cambridge Economic*

History of Europe, II, ed. Michael M. Postan and Edward Miller (Cambridge: Cambridge University Press, 1987), 525–612, here 567; Poppe, "'*Pannus polonicalis*'," 618. See *Urkundenbuch zur Geschichte der Deutschen in Siebenbürgen*, I–VII, ed. Franz Zimmermann, Carl Werner, and Gustav Gündisch (Cologne: Michaelis, 1892–1991), III, 528 (no. 1679) and 546 (no. 1692).

132 Ibid., IV, 425 (no. 2106). The sources also included customs tariffs from the transit settlement Dambowica.

133 APWr., Lib. exc. sign., XIX, 29 (1412).

134 APWr., Lib. exc. sign., XXXIII, 126. Otto Stobbe mistakenly read this number as 2960 (Stobbe, "Mittheilungen [1867]," 447 [no. 205]), and Rudolf Stein followed his reading (idem, *Der Rat und die Ratsgeschlechter des alten Breslau* [Würzburg: Holzner 1962], 181). However, the source states: *I-m IX-c LX harmbalge*. The number was properly identified by Klose (*Von Breslau*, II/2, 353–355).

135 Wendt, *Schlesien*, 5 and 7. About Novgorod's fur trade, see Choroškevič, *Torgovlâ*, 45–121.

136 In 1429 Hesse's factor, Johann Lilgenstein denied that he had transported ermine furs from Vienna to Buda to present them to his wife (APWr., Lib. exc. sign., XXVII, 60). This note confirms the export of ermine furs to Vienna rather than Buda.

137 Myśliwski, *Wrocław*, 251.

138 Engel, *The Realm*, 246, and Nagy, "The Problem," 14.

139 For the exchange rate of the mark to the Hungarian florin, see Myśliwski, *Wrocław*, 522–527.

140 APWr., Lib. exc. sign., LVIII, 106 (1491–298 Hungarian florins, 54 Bohemian groschen), LIX, 165 (1491/1492–139 ½ Hungarian florins), LX, 130 (1492–200 Hungarian florins), LXII, 148 (1494–228 Hungarian florins), 159 (1494–9 Hungarian florins).

141 APKr., DmKr., no 245. The loan was granted in 1438; this is known from a transumpt made in 1452.

142 APWr., Lib. exc. sign., XLV, 184 (1465).

143 This refers to the records of 1465 that assert that three Wrocław merchants (Holikro, Krapse, and Dachs) dropped their claims against the town council of Wrocław. The council was entrusted with 391 florins deposited there in the name of Jürgen Melber of Košice. The money was then picked up by two other Wrocław merchants, Brendel and Wolzindorff (APWr., Lib. exc. sign., VL, 184). From the later records it was revealed that Brendel had shares in the company of Dachs and Berger (ibid., LI, 41 [1473]). I would think Jürgen Melber of Košice deposited his debt for the company in a safe place (the town hall) and the creditors withdrew their claims against the council because the money was taken by their co-partner. Supposedly this course of events resulted from some internal financial settlements in the company or from arrangements carried out in private.

144 For instance: ibid., XL, 19 (1453).

145 Ibid., XXII, 18 (1418).

146 ... *eyne Mechtliche summe* ... – ibid., XXXIX, 76 (1452).

147 Ibid., XLIII, 199 (1453).

148 For the exchange rate of the mark to the Hungarian florin, see Myśliwski, *Wrocław*, 522–527.

149 Ibid., XXII, 93 (1418).

150 The record of a payment from 1395: *Acta iudiciaria civitatis Cassoviensis (1393–1405)*, ed. Ondrej R. Halaga (Munich: Oldenbourg, 1994), 92 (no. 1151).

151 See especially APWr., Lib. exc. sign., LIX, 165 (1491), LX, 130 (1492).

152 APWr., Antiquarius, II, 310 (1418). About Johann Stadler's descent from Buda, see Lib. exc. sign., XXII, 25 (1418) and 149 (1419). He was the treasurer of Barbara of Cilli, queen-consort to Sigismund of Luxemburg. *Regesta Historico–diplomatica Ordinis S. Mariae Theutonicorum*, II, ed. Erich Joachim and Walther Hubatsch (Göttingen: Vandenhoeck & Ruprecht, 1948), 225 (no. 1498) (1419). About Stadler and his links with the Teutonic Order see Kopiński, *Gospodarcze*, 165.

153 APWr., Lib. exc. sign., LIV, 18 (1476).

154 *Rechnungen aus dem Archiv der Stadt Hermannstadt*, I, 198.

155 This does not mean that there were no Hungarian-Silesian contacts at all (excluding Wrocław merchants). See APWr., Lib. exc. sign., XIX, 86 (1413), XXXII, 175 (1439) and XLVI, 157 (1467).

156 It took place in the presence of Rosenfeld and Witche Morser of Gdańsk (ibid., XXII, 148 [1419]). For more details, see: Krzysztof Kopiński, "Mieszczanin Dawid Rosenfeld w dyplomatycznej i gospodarczej służbie zakonu krzyżackiego w Prusach w pierwszej połowie XV w." [A townsman, David Rosenfeld, in the service of the Teutonic Order in Prussia in the first half of the 15th century], *Zapiski Historyczne* 56, no. 2–3 (2001): 41–51, here 49.

157 APWr., Lib. exc. sign., LXI, 121 (1493). See note 102.

158 Ibid., XIV, 90 (1404).

159 Ibid., XVI, 7 (1406).

160 Ibid., XX, 108 (1415).

161 APWr. AmWr., Laurentius Nudus, f. 227; for more details about this transaction, see Myśliwski, *Wrocław*, 390.

162 APWr. Lib. exc. sign., LVI, 94.

163 R. Stein was mistaken when he linked Niklas with the lineage of Michael Banke (Stein, *Der Rat*, 147). See Pfeiffer, *Das Breslauer Patriziat*, 322 and *Breslauer Stadtbuch*, 24, where, contrary to Stein's assertion, only one councilor – Niklas Banke – was mentioned.

164 Myśliwski, *Wrocław*, 149.

165 Stein, *Der Rat*, 155–56 (nos. 1, 4 and 5; about Paul Hornig, see Myśliwski, *Wrocław*, 474).

166 About Sebald Sauermann, see Markgraf, "Zur Geschichte," 265; Pfeiffer, *Das Breslauer Patriziat*, 224; Hans Jürgen von Witzendorff–Rehdiger, "Herkunft und Verbleib Breslauer Ratsfamilien im Mittelalter. Eine genealogische Studie," *Jahrbuch der schlesischen Friedrich–Wilhelms–Universität zu Breslau* 3 (1958): 111–135, here 131 and Stein, *Der Rat*, 199 (no. 1).

167 Ibid., 62.

168 Glesel, who owed money to a creditor from Buda (APWr., Lib. exc. sign., XXII, 93 [1418]), became a councilor in 1422 (Stein, *Der Rat*, 92). Reichel, who had contacts with Kremnica (see APWr., Lib. exc. sign., LVI, 37 [1478]) later became a councilor of Wrocław (1483–1489). See Stein, *Der Rat*, 128.

169 There were two of them: Thomas Saffran, who held the councilor's office in 1473, and Thomas Saffran Jr., a Wrocław merchant, see Stein, *Der Rat*, 193–194; Oskar Pusch, *Die Breslauer Rats-und Stadtgeschlechter in der Zeit von 1241 bis 1741*, IV (Dortmund: Forschungsstelle Ostmitteleuropa, 1990), 30, and Myśliwski, *Wrocław*, 146–148.

170 About Hildebrands in the early fourteenth century, see Stein, *Der Rat*, 72. Margaretha had commercial contacts with Buda in 1420 (Stobbe, "Mittheilungen [1866]," 189–90 [no 93]).

171 APWr., Lib. exc. sign., XL, 156 (1455).

172 Beside the already mentioned Glesel, Margaretha Hildebrand, Rymer, Hesse, Kunze and Zebrecht, as well as Hieronimus Rindfleisch, Sebald Sauermann, and Paul Hornig,

others need to be added: Hans Fleischer (*Fleisschir*) called Kennerdorff (*kennirdorff*), Frantzke Botener, Johann Lilgenstein (Hans Hesse's factor), Hans Lettner, and, after 1469, Hans Negersdorff, Valter Romer and Hans Hartenberg.

173 In 1492 the Wrocław authorities requested that their new ruler Wladislas II, king of Bohemia, guarantee them safe passage to the capital of Hungary. The king approved their petition (Klose, *Von Breslau*, III/2, 425).

174 Beside the already mentioned Mumeler, Geil, Neckil, Jentsch, and Reichel, two others need to be added: Henselin Kotvel and Johann Rohweide.

175 Beside Baltazar Hornig and Hieronimus Rindfleisch there was also Johannes Sindram.

176 These contacts were maintained by Lorenz Schultheis, Niklas Roseler, the mentioned Jorge Saffran, Johann Heinzendorff, Hans Schebek, Nicolaus Zornberg, Gregor Kammelbitz, and Georg Hirsch.

177 Friedrich Reichard kept contacts with Spišská Sobota, Otto Münzmeister with Smolník, Niklas Beutler with Svätý Jur, Hans Fleischer (*Fleisschir*) called on Kennerdorff (*kennirdorff*) with Sebeş.

178 In Bratislava: Hesse, Kunze, and Zebrecht, in Levoča: Niklas Banke (councilor) and Paul Wiener.

179 16 people came from Buda: Nickil Mendel, Jakub Hocheimer, Niklas Lange, Heyko, Mikołaj Unger, Dierżko von Domswald, Hans Hirsch, Markus Leitgeben, Michał Wachsmut, Jorg Krebs, Hans Scharz, Thomas, Peter Edlasberger, Ambrosius Hedan, Bartłomiej Kannengisser, and Lorenz Spore–Sporus. The last may or may not be identical with another inhabitant of Wrocław bore the same first name and a rather similar surname: Sporn (see Heinrich Wendt, "Breslau und Görlitz am Ende des Mittelalters," *Zeitschrift des Vereins für Geschichte und Alterthum Schlesiens*, 63 [1929]: 96 and 99; see note 116). In the case of Nickil Mendel alone (the note of 1413) can it be presumed that he was a member of the renowned Jewish Mendel family that lived in Buda (see Engel, *The Realm*, 173). From other towns only particular individuals are known: three from Levoča (Peter Lange, Hieronim Selin, and Mathias Weining), three from Košice (Donusch, Jorgen Melka, and an unspecified *Kaschawer*), two from Bratislava (Paul Kratzer and Hans Gleibitz), and two from Smolník (Bartłomiej, Niklas Behme) and Hans Confleischer from Spišská Sobota, Johann from Svätý Jur as well as an anonymous treasurer of the archbishop of Esztergom.

180 APWr., Lib. exc. sign., LX, 130 (1492). *Tricesimatores* were in fact the associates of special customs-collecting officials (Engel, *The Realm*, 226). About the collectors of *tricesima*, see Dąbrowski, "Kraków," 212.

181 APWr., Lib. exc. sign., XXII, 18 (1418).

182 Ibid., XIX, 86 (1413).

183 APKr., DmKr., no 245 (1438/1452). The repayment was guaranteed with his house with arable lands and with a 1/16 of share in the forges of Smolník.

184 APWr., Lib. exc. sign., XIX, 83 (1413).

185 Ibid., XXXIII, 83 (1440), XX, 121 (1416).

186 APWr., DmWr., no 1716 (year 1426).

187 Wim Blockmans, "Voracious States and Obstructing Cities. An Aspect of State Formation in Preindustrial Europe," in *Czas*, 399–416, here 406 and 409–413.

15

TRANSIT TRADE AND INTERCONTINENTAL TRADE DURING THE LATE MIDDLE AGES

Textiles and Spices in the Customs Accounts of Braşov and Sibiu

Mária Pakucs-Willcocks

Hungarian kings invited Western European colonists to settle in Transylvania from the twelfth century onwards. Eventually they became the privileged nation of the 'Saxons', active and successful economic middlemen in the region. This article examines a question that has a long history in the "forgotten region" of East Central Europe but is little known outside: the role of Saxon towns in the long-distance trade on the southern border of Transylvania during the Late Middle Ages. Since historians began to carry out research on this topic, beginning in the 1950s in Romania and then the 1970s in Hungary, no new or crucial documentary evidence has come to light.[1] A little used source material, however, notably the customs registers of Sibiu from 1500 and Braşov from 1503, has good potential for new conclusions.

The medieval Kingdom of Hungary became a serious player in Central European commercial exchange in the fourteenth century owing to the impressive output of gold and silver from its mines.[2] A strong network of trade routes began to criss-cross the kingdom to the benefit of its rapidly emerging political center in Buda. The Angevin kings in the fourteenth century and then the fifteenth-century Hungarian rulers created an institutional framework that supported and encouraged the trading towns, especially those on the borders. Extensive trading privileges, such as customs duties, exemptions for certain groups of merchants, and, more importantly perhaps, the granting of staple and depositing rights to certain towns on the border of the kingdom and to Buda were measures which stimulated economic growth and prosperity. Among the few towns that were affected by the royal policy of encouraging international trade, two were situated in Transylvania: Braşov and Sibiu. Furthermore, Braşov had a privileged position in neighboring Wallachia as well, where local princes granted the Saxon merchants exclusive privileges and invited them to do business in their realm. This was not an uncommon feature of the institutional organization of foreign trade; Sheilagh Ogilvie has noted that: "a ruler … granted it [a merchant association] an exclusive privilege for its members to trade in particular wares, transaction types, routes, or destinations."[3] In 1358, King Louis I granted the first privilege in favor of Brașov merchants who traveled through Wallachia to the Danube, exempting them from paying any customs duties along the way.[4] The terms of this privilege were renegotiated ten years later, when the Saxon merchants received clear customs exemptions in Wallachia and on the road to the mouth of the Danube (*per viam Braylam*).[5] Anca Popescu has stated that this direct route between Brașov and Brăila remained the only continental European road towards the Black Sea outside Ottoman control up to the middle of the sixteenth century.[6]

Șerban Papacostea has argued that in the fourteenth century there was a concentrated effort from all the local polities (the Genoese colonies on the Black Sea, Poland, Wallachia, and Moldavia) to shrink and push back the Mongol supremacy north of the Black Sea. Papacostea suggested further that the ultimate aim of their efforts was to open several intercontinental trade routes connecting the Black Sea to Central Europe,[7] while Louis of Anjou's plans were to create "a network of international trade routes within Hungarian territory" as well.[8] Sigismund of Luxemburg continued to act along the same lines of encouraging the use of the trade routes via his kingdom. In 1412, he sent a letter to Caffa urging the town to send common envoys to the Tatar khan in order to convince merchants traveling from Asia to come to Caffa and Chilia and then further west to territories under Hungarian control.[9]

Sibiu, the political capital of the Transylvanian Saxons (Germans), was the beneficiary of different trading privileges granted to its merchants who took their ventures towards Vienna and were systematically offered exemptions from paying customs duties on their way there. In 1372, merchants from Sibiu also obtained the right to trade freely in Poland on a par with local merchants from Cracow, Košice, and Levoča.[10] At the same time, merchants from Košice were fighting to obtain a similar standing as the Saxons for trading in Transylvania. In fact, the staple right of Sibiu began as a reaction to stop merchants from Poland from selling their cloth freely in Saxon areas.[11] Zsuzsa Teke has found records of Košice merchants buying Wallachian products in Sibiu in 1385 and 1397.[12]

King Louis I encouraged merchants from Brașov and Sibiu to become involved in direct trade with the Adriatic towns, especially Zadar, in 1367. To what extent Saxon merchants traveled to Zadar for business is not clear, although it seems plausible that these charters reflect more the intentions of the king to counter Venetian control in the region than the actual undertakings of his subjects.[13] This can be emphasized by the fact that the merchants of Bratislava received a similar privilege of customs duties' exemption on their route to Zadar.[14] Brașov merchants, however, were definitely conducting trade in territories south of the Danube, as shown by the free trade privilege granted by Tzar Stratzimir of Vidin in 1369.[15]

Merchants from Brașov and Sibiu received further privileges that gave them indisputable advantages in doing business. Besides customs duties' exemptions and the staple right in their hometowns, they were granted protection against reprisals.

In 1393, Sibiu merchants obtained a guarantee against arrest and liability for the debts of other Saxon merchants within the Kingdom of Hungary.[16] Braşov traders had a similar status in Wallachia granted with a 1368 privilege.[17]

Louis's and Sigismund's ambitious plans to attract foreign merchants and divert international trade routes onto their territory were part of the ongoing conflict with Venice, and these commercial measures were doubled by various political actions.[18] While a serious contender to La Serenissima's trade in the Eastern Mediterranean was unlikely to arise, the policy of the Hungarian kings was nonetheless beneficial to their towns in the long run. Braşov and Sibiu became attractive destinations for foreign merchants, especially of Italian and southern German extraction, to do business and to settle down.[19] Merchants and entrepreneurs dominated the political life of both towns at the end of the Middle Ages. Konrad Gündisch has shown that the leaders of Braşov's polity in the second half of the fourteenth century played an active role in negotiating privileges and customs' exemptions for the town.[20]

Creating these strategic trading centers on the southeastern border of the Kingdom of Hungary coincided with opening border customs in the vicinity of Braşov and Sibiu. There is no factual data to pinpoint the chronology of this institutional development, but Zsigmond Pál Pach has argued that these customs points on the Transylvanian border with Wallachia and Moldavia were set up around the same time as the commercial connections with these medieval Romanian states are first documented, that is, around the middle of the fourteenth century.[21] From the beginning the duties were imposed as duties on foreign trade at a rate of 3.33% (*tricesima* or thirtieth), but King Matthias Corvinus elevated them to 5% (*vigesima* or twentieth) in 1467.[22] At the end of the fifteenth century, the Saxon towns leased out the customs from the royal treasury and thus customs accounts were preserved in the local archives.[23]

Can the traffic that transited through the Transylvanian customs be qualified as "transcontinental" and "international"? A closer investigation of the structure of trade provides a definite positive answer to this question. Moreover, comparisons with other Hungarian and Ottoman border customs places reveals that Braşov and Sibiu were major trading centers in the region.

The early privileges and charters documenting the commercial activity of the Transylvanian Saxon merchants also give details on the goods they carried. For instance, the 1412 customs tariff issued by the Transylvanian voivode Stibor for the benefit of the Braşov traders opens with listing the duties to be levied on cloth: cloth of Ypres, cloth of Leuven, Italian cloth (*gallicali*), cloth of Cologne, and that of Polish origin (i.e., Moravian cloth).[24] Next follows the instruction that the thirtieth had to be paid on spices (pepper, saffron, ginger, and cloves), mohair (goat hair), cotton, and "all goods brought by the Saracens" (Turks):[25]

> De pipere, croco, sinsibero, cariofolis et de crinibus caprarum, bombasio et de omnibus rebus mercimonialibus quae per Saracenos asportantur, habetur tricesimum.[26]

The tariff details further the duties to be paid on wax and fish brought from Wallachia. This document is mirrored by the customs' tariff issued by the Wallachian Prince Mircea in 1413, in which goods "coming from the sea or across the Danube" are mentioned generically.[27] Customs tariffs with similar wording were issued to benefit the Transylvanian Saxons in Moldavia as well, showing thereby that spices and oriental textiles were traded for Western cloth and manufactured goods in a typical medieval East–West exchange pattern.[28] These early customs' tariffs capture the composition of commercial traffic as it is revealed in the later customs accounts of Braşov and Sibiu: fish, cattle, wax, and wool were also recorded besides the oriental goods.[29]

Spices came from across the Black Sea but also over the land routes of the Balkans, which brought in goods from Ottoman markets or those shipped across the Adriatic from Venice via Dubrovnik.[30] Oriental goods, spices, and textiles came via the Black Sea to the western ports of the sea. Registers from Caffa (1492) and Akkerman (1505) record the cargos of Ottoman ships coming from the southern ports of the Black Sea such as Balaklava and Trapezunt.[31] Another land route that continued the sea trade was the Moldavian road which linked the Black Sea ports with Lviv through Iaşi and Suceava. The main trading agents along the north-western shores of the Black Sea were undoubtedly the Genoese from Caffa, and to a lesser extent merchants from Tana (a Venetian colony), who also conducted a profitable slave trade, but their activity does not fall within the scope of this paper.[32] The institutional innovations and developments in the Hungarian administration and economic policy during the second half of the fourteenth and the beginning of the fifteenth century offered Saxon merchants many advantages on their home markets and also along the official roads leading to the supply of goods, whether that was Vienna or towards the Lower Danube.

Complete customs registers have survived in local archives, from 1500 in Sibiu and from 1503 in Braşov, and their unique data is invaluable for understanding commercial exchanges at the turn of the sixteenth century.[33] By this time, Southeast Europe and the Black Sea were under Ottoman control and both Wallachia and Moldavia were tributary states of the Porte. This new geo-political configuration stimulated commercial exchange with Central Europe on the sea routes, land routes via the Balkans, and along the Lower Danube. Ottoman products became a stronger feature of the commercial traffic, especially cotton textiles and leather goods (hides and finished products).

The customs accounts of both Braşov and Sibiu have similar concepts: they record the date the merchant(s) arrived, the place they had come from, and the amount of goods and duties paid in money or in kind. It is significant to highlight that merchants paid 5% customs duties, and these were paid in kind on oriental goods (especially spices and textiles). Town officials thus secured for themselves a reliable source for the highly sought-after spices and prized oriental fabrics which they sold on. After 1500, the Sibiu customs registers record in detail only the oriental trade, while in Braşov separate accounts were kept for these so-called Turkish wares.[34] Oriental trade, as a generic term, covers the commerce in highly specific goods, which can be unmistakably recognized in similar records from that period. The same products listed in the Transylvanian customs registers can be found in various accounts of merchandise transported from the Ottoman Empire into Central Europe as far as Poland and Lithuania, as well as in the records from the Ottoman customs points at the Black Sea and on the Lower Danube.[35]

Before a more detailed discussion of textiles and spices per se, a few notes on terminology and on the magnitude of commercial exchange at the customs of Braşov and Sibiu at the beginning of the sixteenth century are necessary. The terms used in the customs accounts for the direction of the trade were mostly concerned with Wallachia and Moldavia as places of departure or as destinations. For the transport of fish, cattle, or wax, the origins of these goods were obvious (to them), therefore not written down in the registers. Historians, however, especially Radu Manolescu, have chosen to analyze the data using the categories of "imports of Western and manufactured goods," "Wallachian exports of natural products," and the "transit of oriental goods" while acknowledging that Western products were sent further into the Ottoman lands. Hungarian historians also operate with the idea of "imports" of Western cloth and industrial products when it comes to the foreign trade of medieval Hungary.[36] It is clear however, that these "imports" of Western cloth and millions of knives were mostly intended for re-export and thus should be considered as transit trade in the cases of Bratislava and the Transylvanian trading towns alike.[37]

One third of commercial traffic recorded at the Braşov and Sibiu stations consisted of transports of fish and other natural products from Wallachia (cattle, sheep, and wax).[38] The customs accounts of Bratislava from 1457 to 1458 reveal a less balanced distribution of recorded types of goods: two-thirds of the total trade consisted of the transit of Western and Central European cloth, with few spices and other manufactured products (metal wares).[39] The overall values of transit trade at both customs places are shown in Table 15.1.

The differences in the values and volumes of transited goods between Braşov and Sibiu is salient, with Braşov having a turnover of merchandise eight times that of Sibiu. While Braşov was undeniably the most significant trading center in Transylvania, I argue that the figures for 1503 are exceptional. There are no similar customs records for subsequent years that could provide a basis for comparison and assessment. The figures on the collected customs duties between 1504 and 1508

TABLE 15.1 The values of recorded transit trade in gold florins[40]

	Sibiu 1500	Braşov 1503
Oriental trade	7500	85,000
Western products	6350	60,310
Overall value of recorded trade (transit and regional)	20,800	167,300

FIG. 15.1 Revenues (in florins) of the Brașov customs[41]

show that the traffic of 1503 was outstanding. In 1501 and 1502, the incomes of the Brașov customs were around 3000 florins, which reflect a value of trade of 60,000 florins, while in 1504 and 1505 the customs revenues moved to around 5000 florins, which means that the actual traffic was worth around 100,000 florins (see Fig. 15.1).

Radu Manolescu calculated that at the end of the fifteenth century the traffic through Brașov's customs amounted to 64,000 florins, which is consistent with the annual values for all the other years except 1503.[42] I have put forward the idea that Brașov was a temporary outlet for goods that Venice could not reach because of the war from 1499 to 1502, although this hypothesis does not explain why trading levels were not similarly high in 1501 and 1502.[43] The sharp rise in the value of overall traffic happened because of the transit trade; the transport of fish and other Wallachian direct exports remained remarkably stable throughout the first half of the sixteenth century.[44]

Breaking the general numbers of the overall values into further categories, Tabs. 15.2 and 15.3 show the composition of the transit trade in both Western and Eastern goods. Miscellaneous goods in the transit of manufactured goods are often recorded merely as *parvalia* (miscellaneous goods), even though they make up a large share in the value of the Western imports. According to Manolescu, these included items such as padlocks, clothing, small pieces of furniture, and glassware.[45] Besides cloth, knives (manufactured mostly in Steyr; *Stewer* in the customs accounts) were prized items in the transit trade to Ottoman markets. In 1503, over 2,400,000 knives were recorded in the Brașov customs accounts, for a total value of 29,000 gold florins. Known on the Ottoman market as "Wallachian" knives, they have been found as far away as Egypt.[46]

The counter flow to the transit of cloth and manufactured metal products was the trade with *res turcales*, Turkish goods: specific cotton or silk textiles, raw silk, cotton yarns, mohair, leather goods, dyestuffs (alum, indigo), and spices coming from Asia via the Ottoman Empire. The discrepancies shown above between the traffic at Brașov and Sibiu for the trade in cloth and knives are evident in the oriental trade as well. Textiles and spices were the largest parts of this segment of commercial traffic.

TABLE 15.2 The values of traded cloth and other manufactured goods in gold florins with the percentages of Western goods in transit[47]

	Sibiu 1500		Braşov 1503	
	Value in fl. Au.	Share (%)	Value in fl. Au.	Share (%)
Cloth	1450	22.8	12,260	20.3
Knives and metal wares	2300	36.2	29,150	48.3
Miscellaneous goods	2600	41	18,900	31.4
Total	6350	100	60,310	100

TABLE 15.3 The values of oriental goods in gold florins with the percentage of oriental goods in transit[48]

	Sibiu 1500		Braşov 1503	
	Value in fl. Au.	Share (%)	Value in fl. Au.	Share (%)
Textiles, silk, and yarns	745	23.3	28,000	33
Spices	4654	62.4	34,750	40.8
Miscellaneous goods	2058	14.3	22,250	26.2
Total	7457	100	85,000	100

Examining the transit of cloth (Table 15.4) shows the types, amounts, and values of cloth registered in both towns. Erik Fügedi stated that grey cloth, a cheap coarse textile, was in fact woven in Hungary.[49] The small quantities recorded did not have an effect on the overall values of trade. A piece (*pecia*) was a unit for measuring textiles, 20 or 28 meters in length.[50]

Textiles coming to Sibiu from the Ottoman Empire in 1500 were not very diverse: *bogasia*, a cotton twill, *domoslia* (probably damask), mohair, and taffeta. A wider variety of expensive fabrics was recorded at the Braşov customs, as shown in Table 15.5. Consignments of raw silk, cotton, and silk and cotton thread were also recorded for both towns.[51]

A full analysis of the transit of spices in the customs records of Sibiu and Braşov was carried out by Zsigmond Pál Pach in his seminal study from 1978.[52] For 1500, there are slight and irrelevant differences in his figures from my own. For both towns, pepper was brought in the largest quantities, making up 92% of the total spice transports. At the customs of Braşov, around 40 tons of pepper (719 *kanthner*, approx. 56.3 kilograms) were cleared in 1503, mostly by merchants coming from Wallachia, for a total value of 32,500 florins.[53] Other spices, such as ginger, cloves, cinnamon, incense, and saffron were recorded in much smaller quantities (see Table 15.6).

TABLE 15.4 Quantities of textiles from Western and Central Europe, in pieces (*peciae*)[54]

	Sibiu 1500	*Braşov 1503*
Görlitz	68 pc.	
Nuremberg	48 pc.	134 pc.
Werden[55] (near Essen)	32 pc.	111 pc.
Mechelen	30.5 pc.	182 pc.
Maastricht	10 pc.	414 pc.
Grey cloth	5 pc.	17 pc.
Speyer	3 pc.	8 pc.
Cologne	1 pc.	98 pc.
Zhorelec		151 pc.
Verona	2 pc.	114 pc.
Brugge		5 pc.
Wrocław (Breslau)		1 pc.
Italian cloth (*velestucher*)		3 pc.
Total	226.5 pc.	1238 pc.

TABLE 15.5 Quantities of textiles from the Ottoman Empire, in pieces (*peciae*)

	Sibiu 1500	*Braşov 1503*
Bogasia	792 pc.	24,320 pc.
Domoslia	3 pc.	2712 pc.
Mohair and camelot	44 pc.	737 pc.
Taffeta	9.75 pc.	167 pc.
Istar (cotton for lining)	–	54 pc.
Camucas	–	584 pc.
Halbatlas	–	91 pc.
Nassyncz (brocade?)	–	54 pc.
Purpura aurea (velvet?)	–	24 pc.
Total	848.75 pc.	28,783 pc.

TABLE 15.6 Distribution of spices in pounds (*librae*)[56]

	Sibiu 1500	*Braşov 1503*
Pepper	8460 lb.	43,155 lb.
Saffron	10 lb.	6 lb.
Ginger	240 lb.	2541 lb.
Cloves	160 lb.	546 lb.
Incense	360 lb.	1,755 lb.
Cinnamon		22 lb.
Caraway		1367 lb.

The distances merchants traveled to convey these goods cannot be assessed with the current source material. Sibiu traders traveled all the way to Vienna, as is documented by several fifteenth-century letters, but they also found a good market for Western goods in Oradea, where they definitely bought their Polish and Moravian cloth.[57] Most of the oriental goods coming from the Ottoman territories by sea or land were carried to the Transylvanian border by Wallachians or Balkan traders, but the Saxon merchants went to Wallachia for supplies as well. Around 1517, the Wallachian Prince Neagoe Basarab informed the Braşov city council about opportunities for good deals:

> I sent a man of my lordship to you, my friends, because a Turkish merchant has arrived with good and plentiful merchandise … And any of you who has merchandise should send his man to bargain and make a deal with the Turk here in the citadel of Bucharest.[58]

In 1503, the goods transported by the rich Saxon merchants were recorded under the heading of *mercatores grandi seu prima societas, videlicet Lucas Rener, Lucas Czeresch, Johannes Groman et Georgius Hyrscher.* On January 7, 1503, Peter Schram brought 1815 pounds of pepper into Transylvania; on May 12, three of these merchants carried in 25 pieces of Cologne cloth and 25 pieces of Werden cloth; and on June 12, Lucas Rener and Georg Hyrscher took 102,600 knives from Braşov into Wallachia. Between January and October 1503, these four merchants transited goods worth 6800 florins in eight transport trips, a remarkable feat.[59]

Pach has calculated that the volume of spices transited through southern Transylvania was almost 9% of Venice's import of spices from Alexandria and between 5.84% and 7.38% of Venetian imports of spices from all Mediterranean ports (such as Beirut). He agreed that in this wider perspective, the Transylvanian contribution to international spice distribution was small, but underlined that in a regional context, compared to the records from the Bratislava imports of spices in the middle of the fifteenth century, for instance, Braşov was a major player in supplying Hungary and Poland with spices.[60] These two Transylvanian towns stand out for their ability to attract the spice trade. No spices at all were recorded in other customs accounts from the region, such as the customs on the Hungarian-Ottoman border from Baric and Kulpin, today in Serbia, or the Ottoman accounts from Tulcea (1517).[61] Nor can spices be found in the shipments recorded in the Ottoman customs account from Akkerman.[62] Cloth and knives taken into the Ottoman Empire from Hungary feature in the registers from Baric and Kulpin, although in small amounts; Zsolt Simon has noted that the traffic at these two customs points was quite different from the traffic recorded in Braşov and Sibiu.[63] The fifteenth-century customs' tariffs from Wallachia, as cited above, list spices among the merchandise on which duties were levied, while the customs tariff from Oradea from the last quarter of the fifteenth century does not mention spices in association with the Western cloth.[64]

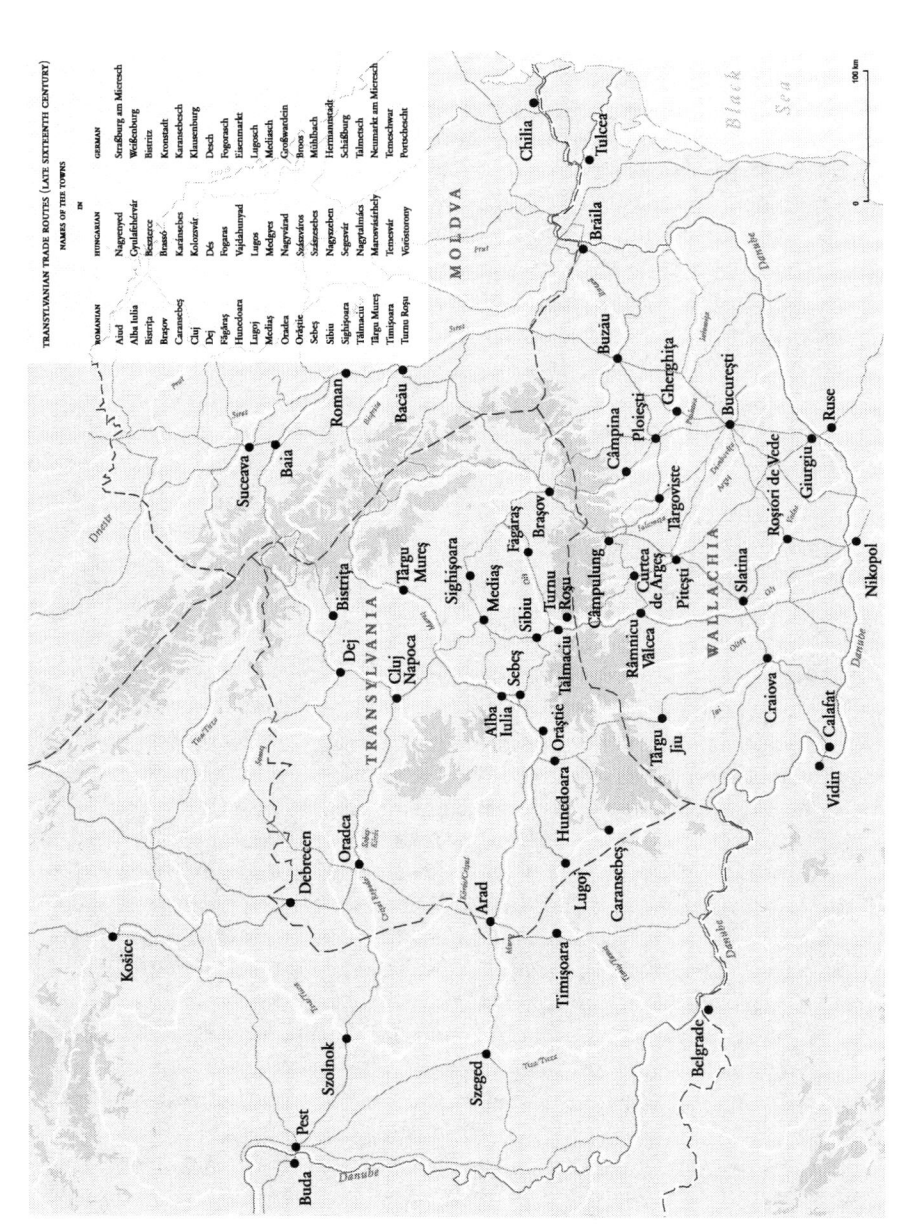

TRANSLYVANIAN TRADE ROUTES (LATE SIXTEENTH CENTURY)

NAMES OF THE TOWNS

ROMANIAN	HUNGARIAN	GERMAN
Arad	Nagyenyed	Straßburg am Mieresch
Alba Iulia	Gyulafehérvár	Weißenburg
Bistrița	Beszterce	Bistritz
Brașov	Brassó	Kronstadt
Caransebeș	Karánsebes	Karansebesch
Cluj	Kolozsvár	Klausenburg
Dej	Dés	Desch
Făgăraș	Fogaras	Fogarasch
Hunedoara	Vajdahunyad	Eisenmarkt
Lugoj	Lugos	Lugosch
Mediaș	Medgyes	Mediasch
Oradea	Nagyvárad	Großwardein
Orăștie	Szászváros	Broos
Sebeș	Szászsebes	Mühlbach
Sibiu	Nagyszeben	Hermannstadt
Sighișoara	Segesvár	Schäßburg
Tălmaciu	Nagytalmács	Talmesch
Târgu Mureș	Marosvásárhely	Neumarkt am Mieresch
Timișoara	Temesvár	Temeschwar
Turnu Roșu	Vöröstorony	Rotenturm

MAP 15.1 Trade routes in Transylvania in the sixteenth century

The traffic at the Ottoman customs in Giurgiu, however, was very similar to the Transylvanian trade, with spices present in the recorded stock of merchants.[65] It is safe to state that Braşov and Sibiu were the origins and also the destination of the goods crossing the Danube at Giurgiu (see Map 15.1).

This transit trade through Transylvania supplied mostly the regional markets and Poland; it functioned along the same routes for centuries. Spices continued to come into Transylvania from the Ottoman Empire throughout the sixteenth and most of the seventeenth century, albeit in increasingly smaller amounts.[66] Recent scholarship credits the Ottoman administration with maintaining a strong spice trade along the routes crossing its empire in the sixteenth century and the first quarter of the seventeenth century.[67]

Notes

1 Radu Manolescu, "Relaţiile comerciale ale Ţării Româneşti cu Sibiul la începutul veacului al XVI-lea" [The commercial relations of Wallachia with Sibiu at the beginning of the 16th century], *Analele Universităţii C. I. Parhon Bucureşti* 7 (1956): 207–259; idem, *Comerţul Ţării Româneşti şi Moldovei cu Braşovul (secolele XIV–XVI)* [The trade of Wallachia and Moldavia with Braşov, 14th–16th centuries] (Bucharest: Editura Ştiinţifică şi Enciclopedică, 1965); Zsigmond Pál Pach, "Die Verkehrsroute des Levantehandels nach Siebenbürgen und Ungarn zur Zeit der Könige Ludwig von Anjou und Sigismund von Luxemburg," in *Europäische Städtegeschichte in Mittelalter und früher Neuzeit*, ed. Werner Mägdefrau (Weimar: Böhlau, 1979), 60–91 and Zsigmond Pál Pach, "Levantine Trade Routes to Hungary, 15th–17th centuries," *Acta Historica Academiae Scientiarum Hungaricae* 33 (1987): 57–65.
2 Balázs Nagy, "Magyarország külkereskedelme a középkorban" [The foreign trade of Hungary in the Middle Ages], in *Gazdaság és gazdálkodás a középkori Magyarországon: ga zdaságtörténet, anyagi kultúra, régészet* [Economy and faming in medieval Hungary: economic history, material culture, archaeology], ed. András Kubinyi, József Laszlovszky, and Péter Szabó (Budapest: Martin Opitz, 2008), 253–276, esp. 268.
3 Sheilagh Ogilvie, *Institutions and European Trade. Merchant guilds, 1000–1800* (Cambridge: Cambridge University Press, 2011), 162.
4 *Urkundenbuch zur Geschichte der Deutschen in Siebenbürgen*, I–VII, ed. Franz Zimmermann, Carl Werner, and Gustav Gündisch (Sibiu and Cologne: Michaelis and Ausschuß des Vereins für Siebenbürgische Landeskunde, 1892–1991), II, 152–153. For a more extensive discussion of the trading privileges granted to Transylvanian towns, see, more recently, Boglárka Weisz, *Vásárok és lerakatok a középkori Magyar Királyságban* [Markets and staples in the medieval Kingdom of Hungary] (Budapest: MTA Bölcsészettudományi Központ Történettudományi Intézete, 2012), 61–63.
5 *Urkundenbuch zur Geschichte der Deutschen*, II, 306–307. See also Laurenţiu Rădvan, *At Europe's Borders: Medieval Towns in the Romanian Principalities* (East Central and Eastern Europe in the Middle Ages, 450–1450, 7) (Leiden: Brill, 2010), 223–224.
6 Anca Popescu, "Un centre commercial du Bas-Danube ottoman au XVIe siècle: Brăila (Bra'il)," *Il Mar Nero: Annali di archeologia e storia* 3 (1997–1998): 209–237, esp. 215.
7 Şerban Papacostea, "Un tournant de la politique génoise en Mer Noire au XIVe siècle: l'ouverture des routes continentales en direction de l'Europe centrale," in *Oriente e Occidente tra medioevo ed età moderna: Studi in onore di Geo Pistarino*, II, ed. Laura Baletto (Genoa: Glauco Brigatti, 1997), 939–947, esp. 942–944.

8 Şerban Papacostea, "Începuturile politicii comerciale ale Țării Românești și Moldovei (secolele XIV–XVI). Drum și stat" [The beginnings of the commercial policy of Wallachia and Moldavia (14th–16th centuries. Road and state], *Studii și Materiale de Istorie Medie* 10 (1983): 10–25, esp. 12.

9 *Zsigmondkori oklevéltár*, III, (1411–1412) [Sigismundian cartulary] (Magyar Országos Levéltár kiadványai, II. Forráskiadványok, 22), ed. Elemér Mályusz (Budapest: Akadémiai, 1993), 716; Zsigmond Pál Pach, "A Levante-kereskedelem erdélyi útvonala I. Lajos és Zsigmond korában" [The Transylvanian route of Levantine trade in the age of Louis I and Sigismund], *Századok* 109 (1975): 3–32, esp. 21 with a good summary of the document.

10 Mária Pakucs-Willcocks, *Sibiu-Hermannstadt. Oriental Trade in Sixteenth Century Transylvania* (Städteforschung, A 73) (Cologne: Böhlau, 2007), 9.

11 *Urkundenbuch zur Geschichte der Deutschen*, II, 491–492. See also my recent discussion of the staple right of Sibiu: eadem, "Dreptul de etapă al Sibiului în secolele XIV–XVII: parcursul secular al unei instituții medievale" [The staple right of Sibiu from the fourteenth to seventeenth century: the historical course of a medieval institution], in *Aut viam inveniam aut faciam. In honorem Stefan Andreescu*, ed. Ovidiu Cristea, Petronel Zahariuc, and Gheorghe Lazăr (Iași: Editura Universității Iași, 2012), 131–143.

12 Zsuzsa Teke, "Kassa külkereskedelme az 1393–1405. évi kassai bírói könyv bejegyzései alapján" [The foreign trade of Košice based on the entries in the judicial register from 1393 to 1405], *Századok* 137 (2003): 381–404, esp. 404.

13 Nicolae Iorga, *Istoria comerțului românesc* [History of Romanian trade] (Bucharest: Editura Științifică și Enciclopedică, 1982), 458, and Pach, "A Levante-kereskedelem," 10.

14 Zsuzsa Teke, "Adalékok Zsigmond várospolitikájához (1387–1405)" [Contributions to the town policy of Sigismund], in *Változatok a történelemre. Tanulmányok Székely György tiszteletére* [Versions of history. Studies in honor of György Székely] (Monumenta historica Budapestinensia, 14), ed. Gyöngyi Erdei and Balázs Nagy (Budapest: Budapesti Történeti Múzeum, 2004), 225–233, esp. 226.

15 Grigore G. Tocilescu, *534 documente istorice slavo-române din Țara Românească și Moldova privitoare la legăturile cu Ardealul, 1346–1603* [534 Slavic-Romanian historical documents from Wallachia and Moldavia concerning the connections with Transylvania, 1346–1603] (Bucharest: Libr. "Cartea Românească," 1931), 3.

16 *Urkundenbuch zur Geschichte der Deutschen*, III, 53–54.

17 Papacostea, "Începuturile," 15.

18 Ovidiu Cristea, "Venice: The Balkan Policy of Hungary and the Rise of the Ottoman Empire," *Revue des Etudes Sud-est Européennes* 40 (2002): 179–194.

19 Gustav Gündisch, "Die Oberschicht Hermannstadts im Mittelalter," in *Aus Geschichte und Kultur der Siebenbürger Sachsen* (Schriften zur Landeskunde Siebenbürgens, 14), ed. idem (Cologne: Böhlau, 1987), 182–200, esp. 188–192.

20 Konrad Gündisch, *Das Patriziat siebenbürgischer Städte* (Cologne: Böhlau, 1993), 185–188.

21 Zsigmond Pál Pach, *A harmincadvám eredete* [The origins of the thirtieth customs] (Budapest: Akadémiai, 1990), 36.

22 Pakucs-Willcocks, *Sibiu-Hermannstadt*, 18.

23 Samuel Goldenberg, "Despre vama (*vigesima*) Sibiului în secolul al XVI-lea" [On the (twentieth) customs of Sibiu in the 16th century], *Acta Musei Napocensis* 2 (1965): 673–677, esp. 673, and Pakucs-Willcocks, *Sibiu-Hermannstadt*, 20–22.

24 *Urkundenbuch zur Geschichte der Deutschen*, III, 545, and Pach, "A Levante-kereskedelem I. Lajos korában," 16. "Polish" cloth is translated in the Slavonic version of the document as "Czech."

25 Pach, "A Levante-kereskedelem I. Lajos korában," 17, note 76 explaining that in contemporary usage Saracens did not refer to Arabs but to Muslims generically.

26 *Urkundenbuch zur Geschichte der Deutschen*, III, 544–577.

27 Ibid., IV, 426.

28 Customs tariff of the same voivode Stibor from 1412: *Urkundenbuch zur Geschichte der Deutschen*, III, 528.

29 Manolescu, *Comerţul*, 104 sqq.

30 Pach, "A Levante-kereskedelem I. Lajos korában," 17–18.

31 Halil Inalcik, *Sources and Studies on the Ottoman Black Sea. I. The Customs Register of Caffa 1487–1490* (Cambridge: Harvard University Press, 1995), 189 sqq; Nagy Pienaru, "Cetatea Albă / Ak Kerman la începutul veacului al XVI-lea. Traficul portului în anul 1505" [Akkerman at the beginning of the 16th century. The port traffic in 1505], in *Aut viam inveniam*, 181–190.

32 Ştefan Andreescu, "Genovezi pe 'drumul moldovenesc' la mijlocul secolului al XV-lea" [The Genoese on the 'Moldavian road' in the middle of the 15th century], *Revista istorică* 10 (1999): 111–127. See also Eugene Khvalkov, "The Slave Trade in Tana: Marketing Manpower from the Black Sea to the Mediterranean in the 1430s," *Annual of Medieval Studies at CEU* 18 (2012): 104–118.

33 The 1500 Sibiu register is published in *Quellen zur Geschchte Siebenbürgens aus sächsischen Archiven: Rechnungen aus dem Archiv der Stadt Hermannstadt und der sächsischen Nation*, I (Sibiu: Buchdruckerei der Von Closius'schen Erbin, 1880), 270–327. The 1503 Braşov customs register is published in *Quellen zur Geschichte der Stadt Kronstadt in Siebenbürgen: Rechnungen aus dem Archiv der Stadt Kronstadt*, I (Braşov: Zeidner, 1886), 1–81.

34 Pakucs-Willcocks, *Sibiu-Hermannstadt*, 28–29 and 41–42.

35 Gilles Veinstein, "Marchands ottomans en Pologne-Lituanie et en Moscovie sous le règne de Soliman le Magnifique," *Cahiers du monde russe* 35 (1994): 713–738, esp. 729–730.

36 Most recently, Balázs Nagy, "Old Interpretations and New Approaches: The 1457–1458 Thirthieth Customs Register of Bratislava," in *Money and Finance in Central Europe during the Later Middle Ages*, ed. Roman Zaoral (London: Palgrave Macmillan, 2016), 192–201, esp. 192–198, and Erik Fügedi, "Der Aussenhandel Ungarns am Anfang des 16. Jahrhunderts," in *Der Aussenhandel Ostmitteleuropas 1450–1650: Die ostmitteleuropäischen Volkswirtschaften in ihren Beziehungen zu Mitteleuropa*, ed. Ingomar Bog (Cologne: Böhlau, 1971), 56–85.

37 Erik Fügedi did acknowledge that cloth and knives were mostly destined for resale and not for local consumption, and yet he continued to view trade in the import/export paradigm. Idem, "Der Aussenhandel," 64.

38 Manolescu, *Comerţul*, 110–112, and Manolescu, "Relaţiile," 234.

39 Nagy, "Old Interpretations," 194, tables 12.1 and 12.2.

40 Manolescu, *Comerţul*, 177, and Pakucs-Willcocks, *Sibiu-Hermannstadt*, 60.

41 Manolescu, *Comerţul*, 179.

42 Ibid.

43 Pakucs-Willcocks, *Sibiu-Hermannstadt*, 68–69.

44 Manolescu, *Comerţul*, 110–112.

45 Ibid., 152.

46 Halil Inalcik, "Bursa and the commerce of the Levant," *Journal of the Economic and Social History of the Orient* 3 (1960): 131–147, esp. 146.

47 Manolescu, *Comerţul*, 152.

48 Pach, "A Levante-kereskedelem a 15–16. század," 1026 table 12 and Pakucs-Willcocks, *Sibiu-Hermannstadt*, 75 and 163.

49 Fügedi, "Der Aussenhandel," 66.

50 István Bogdán, *Régi magyar mértékek* [Old Hungarian measures] (Budapest: Gondolat, 1987), 60.
51 Pakucs-Willcocks, *Sibiu-Hermannstadt*, 83, 85 and 163.
52 Zsigmond Pál Pach, "A Levante-kereskedelem erdélyi útvonala a 15–16. század fordulóján" [The Transylvanian route of the Levantine trade at the turn of the 15th and in the 16th century], *Századok* 112 (1978): 1005–1038, esp. 1026 with tables 4–12.
53 The figures at Pach, "A Levante-kereskedelem a 15–16. század," 1017, note 42 for the weights and equivalents and ibid., 1026 for the total figures.
54 Manolescu, *Comerțul*, 152; *Quellen zur Geschchte Siebenbürgens*, 271–327, and *Quellen zur Geschichte der Stadt Kronstadt*, 36–75.
55 Today part of Essen, Germany.
56 Ibid., 1026, tables 11 and 12 and Pakucs-Willcocks, *Sibiu-Hermannstadt*, 87.
57 Otto Fritz Jickeli, "Der Handel der siebenbürger Sachsen in seiner geschichtlichen Entwicklung," *Archiv des Vereins für siebenbürgische Landeskunde* [NF] 39 (1913): 33–184, esp. 69–70 and Fügedi, "Der Aussenhandel," 67. The long conflict between the Sibiu and the Polish merchants over free access on their mutual local markets ended after 1413, as Pach argued, when Oradea became the exchange centre for these traders. Pach, "A Levante-kereskedelem I. Lajos korában," 12, note 30. See also on the well-known trial of several towns in Hungary against the customs duties levied in Oradea in András Kubinyi, "A városi rend kialakulásának gazdasági feltételei és a főváros kereskedelme a XV. század végén" [The economic prerequisites for the formation of the urban system and the trade of the capital city at the end of the fifteenth century], *Tanulmányok Budapest Múltjából* 15 (1963): 189–224, esp. 190–193.
58 Ioan Bogdan, *Documente și regeste privitoare la relațiile Țării Românești cu Brașovul și cu Ungaria în secolele XV–XVI* [Documents and abstracts concerning the relations of Wallachia with Brasov and Hungary in the 15th and 16th centuries] (Bucharest: Socecu, 1902), 153–154.
59 *Quellen zur Geschichte der Stadt Kronstadt*, I, 36–37.
60 Pach, "A Levante-kereskedelem a 15–16. század," 1020.
61 János Hóvári, "Customs registers of Tulça (Tulcea) 1515–1517," *Acta Orientalia Academiae Scientiae Hungaricae* 38 (1984): 115–141, esp. 133, and Zsolt Simon, "A baricsi és kölpényi harmincadok a 16. század elején" [The customs of Baric and Kulpin at the beginning of the16[th] century], *Századok* 140 (2006): 815–882, esp. 836 sqq.
62 Pienaru, "Cetatea Albă / Ak Kerman," 187–189 provides details of the cargos of registered ships.
63 Simon, "A Baricsi és kölpényi harmincadok," 844.
64 Kubinyi, "Városi rend," 211.
65 János Hóvári, "Az oszmán gazdasági-struktúra az Al-Dunánál: 1496–1517" [Ottoman economic structure on the Lower Danube, 1496–1517] (Diss., Hungarian Academy of Sciences, 1996–1997), 41.
66 For the sixteenth century see Pakucs-Willcocks, *Sibiu-Hermannstadt*, 87.
67 Giancarlo Casale, "The Ottoman Administration of the Spice Trade in the Sixteenth-Century Red Sea and Persian Gulf," *Journal of the Economic and Social History of the Orient* 49 (2006): 170–198.

16

REFLECTED IN A DISTORTED MIRROR

Trade Contacts of Medieval East Central Europe in Recent Historiography

Balázs Nagy

Is it relevant to study the medieval commerce of East Central Europe in a regional framework?[1] Studying the history of trade relations and the exchange of goods is certainly an applicable approach if someone wishes to reconstruct the role of a particular region in the medieval world. The sources available to a research community affect both the quantity and quality of data and the choice of a suitable research framework. How has the basic information on medieval East Central Europe filtered into the forums of the Anglo-Saxon and German scholarship?

An overview of the information available to external scholars about the commercial contacts of a region reveals possible avenues of research.[2] Medieval East Central Europe is a region understood as the medieval territories of Poland, Bohemia, and Hungary. It is necessary to emphasize at the outset that the medieval lands of these states were not identical with their modern counterparts; the territories of medieval Poland and Hungary, especially, differed drastically from their modern equivalents. This paper will survey how East Central Europe is reflected in basic handbooks and encyclopedias and explore the accessibility of information from the point of view of a reader who comes from a different region and cannot use the local languages.[3] Collecting information on these questions might be difficult for interested external scholars, since most of the relevant publications are available almost exclusively in the languages of the region – Polish, Czech, Slovak, and Hungarian – and the selection of English- and German-language publications is even more restricted.

The basic sources of information are not very helpful for starting an investigation. The *Dictionary of the Middle Ages* is one of the most significant English-language encyclopedias on the European Middle Ages; its long general article on medieval trade includes specialized subchapters on trade in Armenian, Byzantine, Islamic, and Western European territories, but virtually no information on the commercial contacts of East Central Europe.[4] Neither the countries nor the commercial centers are mentioned in the *Dictionary*. The only exceptions are two short references to Poland, but that is only because of its Hanseatic connections.[5] The articles on the individual countries of the region give better insight into the history of commercial contacts. The specific articles were written by well-known experts on these countries; Paul W. Knoll authored the section on Poland, John Klassen wrote on Bohemia and Moravia, János M. Bak on Hungary.[6] The chapters have short overviews of the economic, financial, and commercial characteristics of each country, but are necessarily concise and short. It is clear from the entries in the *Dictionary of the Middle Ages* that although the specialist authors were certainly the right persons to write the individual sections, the editors of this publication did not consider the commercial aspects of the medieval history of the East Central European region worth further discussion.

The interested reader has better chances for orientation in the commercial contacts of East Central Europe based on the articles in the leading German-language lexicon. The expert authors of the *Lexikon des Mittelalters* clearly have wide knowledge of the medieval history of the region, including medieval commerce.[7] František Graus wrote the article on Bohemia, Aleksander Gieysztor on Poland and János M. Bak on Hungary.[8] Each entry on the individual country includes a subchapter on the medieval economy or even more detailed coverage of individual economic sectors. Since the volumes of the *Lexikon des Mittelalters* were published between 1977 and 1999, however, the articles do not reflect the results of the last two decades of research. The lexicon entries can serve as a useful first orientation, but cannot really support a more extensive study.

Medieval bibliographical databases are also useful resources. To take but one example, one can turn to the distribution of the bibliographic entries in the on-line database of the *International Medieval Bibliography* to find available references on medieval trade in East Central Europe.[9] The online version of *IMB* currently includes approximately 500,000 records, out of which 6851 (1.4%) are indexed as "Economics – Trade."[10] Out of this group only a few are connected to East Central Europe. The bibliography lists 171 records for Poland, 170 for Hungary, 63 for Bohemia, and 44 for Moravia;[11] these 448 records are an insignificant part of the whole *IMB* database. Comparing them with the entries on the trade of medieval Spain (504 records), Scandinavia (535 records), and Italy (1494 records) shows that East Central Europe is treated as a peripheral region. Although one can find entries in the IMB in all relevant languages, almost half of the records of the whole database are in English (30%) and German (18%), and the numbers of Polish, Czech, Slovak, and Hungarian references altogether do not make up more than 6.5% of the whole IMB. This data in itself demonstrates plausibly the (in)accessibility of information on this region.

Besides encyclopedias and bibliographies, textbooks, and general handbooks can be expected to have information about the position of a particular region in a comparative perspective. Just as examples, one might select two influential English language textbooks from the 1970s. Carlo M. Cipolla edited the small-format volumes of the series *Fontana Economic History of Europe*; the first volume on the medieval period is a widely circulated collection of concise essays on various aspects of medieval European economy and economic policy.[12] The most prominent authorities on medieval European economic and social history are among the authors, such as J. C. Russell, Jacques Le Goff, Lynn White, Georges Duby, and Sylvia Thrupp. The chapter on trade and finance was written by Jacques Bernard, a specialist in medieval maritime trade and monetary history.[13] This inspiring short summary discusses mainly the traffic of Italy and Flanders with some references to Eastern Mediterranean commerce, but excludes almost all hints of East Central Europe. This work basically reflects the conception that medieval commercial history is relevant only for Western Europe and that East Central and Eastern Europe can safely be excluded. The references to South German commercial metropolises like Nuremberg and Regensburg[14] are the nearest locations to East Central Europe. The medieval volume of the *Fontana Economic History* was published in several paperback and hardback editions after the first printing in 1972 and was even translated into German and Chinese.[15] Its neglect of East Central Europe certainly reflects not only the expertise of the author, but also that the publisher and editor of the volume did not expect that the readers would have a deeper interest in this region. Scholars from Western Europe have very limited access to the works published in East Central Europe, partly, but not exclusively, because of the language barriers. The existence of the Iron Curtain from the post WWII years until 1989 determined drastically the access to the scholarly literature and information for scholars on both sides of the political division lines.

Besides the encyclopedias, textbooks, and synthesizing works there are many more publications on trade in East Central Europe in the Middle Ages, even in the non-regional languages. In one of the pioneering publications on the medieval interactions of Eastern and Western Europe, Michael M. Postan wrote a chapter on the economic relations of the two regions. In *Eastern and Western Europe in the Middle Ages*, edited by Geoffrey Barraclough and published in 1970, Postan focused mainly on the Northern, i.e., Hanseatic contacts, the area where he had the most expertise.[16]

In the next year, 1971, another important volume of collected essays came out, the German-language volume entitled *Der Aussenhandel Ostmitteleuropas, 1450–1650*.[17] The most prominent experts from basically all the countries of the region contributed to this book, discussing many aspects of foreign trade. Here there are chapters about the trade of Poland by Antoni Mączak, Henryk Samsonowicz, and Benedykt Zientara, about Bohemia by Hans Schenk and Josef Janáček, and about Hungary by Erik Fügedi, Győző Ember, András Kubinyi, Oszkár Paulinyi, and László Makkai. The eminence of these authors makes this volume still an indispensable item on all reading lists on medieval economic history.

The prolific researcher Norman Pounds has authored several books on the economic history and historical geography of Europe. His one volume summarizing the medieval economic history of Europe was one of the most influential of his books. The first edition was published in 1974 and the second revised version in 1994.[18] A quick search of the Google Scholar database shows that it was among the most often cited textbooks on this theme for a long time, and the union catalogue of Worldcat registers many libraries worldwide holding copies of this book.[19] Pounds' book includes two chapters on medieval trade, one giving a chronological overview and a detailed section on individual commodities, and another on the concept of the "commercial revolution" of the Middle Ages with an overview of finances and banking in the later Middle Ages. This account, about a hundred pages long, cites hardly any information on trade in East Central Europe except for some references to the tenth-century commercial links of the Western territories with Prague and Cracow and, in a later period, the impact of the Hanseatic league. Thus, this influential textbook might have strengthened the preconception of readers that East Central Europe is irrelevant from the point of view of the network of medieval commerce and that this region was not integrated into the medieval commercial network of Europe.

Covering basically the same period as the book by Ingomar Bog (*Der Aussenhandel Ostmitteleuropas*),[20] another volume of collected essays was published by Cambridge University Press and the Maison des Sciences de l'Homme in 1985. In *East-Central Europe in Transition*, the editors, Antoni Mączak, Henryk Samsonowicz, and Peter Burke, assembled a set of papers from Polish and Hungarian historians that reflected the Late Middle Ages and the Early Modern period.[21] The essay by Marian Małowist, for instance, discusses one of the most relevant questions of the economic history of the period, the interactions of mining activity and the circulation of financial assets in Lesser Poland, Bohemia, and Upper Hungary (present-day Slovakia).[22]

The volumes of the *Cambridge Economic History of Europe* have a key position among the standard scholarly publications. These volumes are usually taken as the classic compendia of the economic history of Europe. The first volume of the series was published in 1941, thus the history of this publication itself embraces more than seven decades.[23] The first edition of the volume on medieval commercial history was published in 1952 and thirty-five years later – in 1987 – a second, revised and extended, version came out.[24] The second edition added four new chapters, and three out of this four expanded the territory covered by the volume. Besides the chapter by David Abulafia, who wrote about European trade contacts with Asia and Africa, two other chapters represent a shift towards Eastern Europe in the focus of the volume. Two acknowledged representatives of Polish historiography, Aleksander Gieysztor and Marian Małowist, authored chapters on "Trade and Industry in Eastern Europe before 1200" and "The Trade of Eastern Europe in the Later Middle Ages," respectively.[25]

Although both Gieysztor and Małowist were preeminent scholars of Polish and also East Central European history, their chapters, published three decades ago, concentrate mainly on the northern area of the region and also on the Russian territories.[26] Their argumentation is necessarily based on older, partly outdated, literature and omitted more recent approaches usually applied in the study of medieval trade, e.g., the use of archaeological material and reconstructions. It is also a revealing characteristic of this volume of the *Cambridge Economic History of Europe* that here all the countries of East Central Europe are grouped as Eastern Europe. This handbook, published before the political changes of the late 1980s, does not identify East Central or Central Europe as regions in their own right, just as a smaller fraction of Eastern Europe, an issue discussed in the introduction to this volume.

Synthesizing studies on the long-term development of larger regions unavoidably generalize many aspects and even include minor lapses.[27] The sections of Gieysztor and Małowist in *Cambridge Economic History of Europe* could not avoid some errors and misunderstandings, but, looking back to the main achievement of their chapters, one should conclude that these were the earliest comprehensive English-language overviews on the trade contacts of East Central Europe.

In almost the same years as this volume of the *Cambridge Economic History of Europe*, a German-language survey was published in the *Handbuch der europäischen Wirtschafts- und Sozialgeschichte* series. The volumes of the *Handbuch* cover European economic and social history from the late Roman Empire to the post-World War II period. The discussion of the Middle Ages is arranged in two volumes, the first covering the changes from the Great Migrations (of the fifth to sixth centuries) to the mid-fourteenth century, and the second from that time to the mid-seventeenth century.[28] The key importance of this publication is that the relevant chapters were written by experts from the individual countries. For the earlier period the sections were authored by György Györffy for Hungary and Aleksander Gieysztor for Poland, for the later Middle Ages by Miroslav Hroch and Josef Petrán for Bohemia, László Makkai for Hungary, and Marian Małowist and Adelheid Simsch for Poland.[29] These chapters survey diverse branches of economic life, including historical demography, social structures, and the ethnic characteristics of the individual countries as well as the various fields of production from agriculture to mining and crafts, and also external and internal trade, transport, and monetary history. Thus, these chapters represent formative contributions to the study of these issues. In addition to the text, the bibliographies are also useful tools for orientation. It is characteristic of the approach of the historiography of the 1980s, the period when these volumes were published, however, that the domestic and mainly Western-oriented trade is discussed in the relevant chapters while regional commerce, i.e., the traffic in commercial goods among the countries of the region, remains underrepresented.

The summarizing work of Jean W. Sedlar represents a later phase of historiography; his voluminous book, *East Central Europe in the Middle Ages, 1000–1500*, was published in 1994.[30] This work has an important role in the literature. As Piotr Górecki notes in his review, Sedlar's work reflects a "historiographic consensus" of the two decades preceding its publication, mainly using secondary literature in Western languages.[31] In the almost-thirty-page long chapter on "Commerce and Money" Sedlar gives a well-balanced outline of various branches of the topic from transport and navigation to mining and trade regulations covering different regions of Eastern and Central Europe from Albania to the territory of the Teutonic knights.[32] Despite several minor mistakes in Sedlar's work, this was the first concise modern English-language synthesis of the commercial conditions in medieval East Central Europe.

The most recent summary of the (early) history of East Central Europe, by Nora Berend, Przemysław Urbańczyk, and Przemysław Wiszewski, was published by Cambridge University Press in 2013.[33] This volume summarizes the history of the region until c. 1300, which means that the period of the intensive late medieval commercial contacts of the region is beyond its chronological limits. It was not the intention of this book to give a thorough overview of the commercial characteristics of the region; the focus is much more on political and social history; therefore, one cannot blame the authors for dedicating only ten pages out of a five-hundred-page book to crafts, trade, and urbanization. The conclusions thus inevitably reflect only the earliest phase of the medieval transformations of the countries in East Central Europe.

Browsing through recent publications on the commercial contacts of medieval East Central Europe, it is surprising that the overwhelming majority of publications discuss the trade links connecting this region to Western Europe and hardly any studies address the commerce between East Central Europe and Byzantine or Muslim territories. A historiographic overview demonstrates plausibly that the representation of medieval East Central Europe in English and German scholarly publications depended on a few expert historians active in the 1970s through the 1990s. In a list of authors cited, some names are repeated frequently. Aleksander Gieysztor and Marian Małowist had a special position in foreign language publications on Polish history, János M. Bak and András Kubinyi on Hungarian history, and František Graus on Bohemian history.

Concluding remarks

This short historiographic survey raises some further questions. What research tradition discusses the commercial history of East Central Europe as such?[34] How significant was East Central Europe in medieval commercial networks? The historiography and recent studies of these topics confirm that this region was relevant in the wider context of European commerce. East Central Europe supplied the European market with a broad selection of commercial goods in various periods of the Middle Ages and also served as a market for the products of other regions. To reconstruct the commercial characteristics of the area over a longer time span one would need more detailed specialized studies on the individual territories and products, although already at this stage of research one can form some general statements. Primary products have always had key importance among the exported goods of the region. The early phase of contacts was characterized by traffic in mineral goods (silver, salt), live animals and animal products, and slaves, all of which were in demand in Muslim and Byzantine territories, and in other regions of the continent.[35] At a later phase, agricultural products such as live animals (especially cattle and horses) were significant among the exported goods as well as grain and grain products. In the earlier phase luxury products, good quality high-priced textiles, were important among the imported goods. In the later Middle Ages, cheaper industrial products arrived on the market of East Central Europe in greater quantities; among them, various types of textiles as well as metal objects found their ways to markets in Poland, Bohemia, and Hungary.[36]

In the early 1980s, Jenő Szűcs, the prominent Hungarian medievalist, formulated his concept of the role of East Central Europe in his work on the three historical regions of Europe.[37] Although his primary research focus was not economic history, his model is still worth considering. Szűcs argued that the crisis of Western Europe in the fourteenth century contributed to the intensification of commercial contacts among the different regions of the continent:

> Ultimately the salient point in the West's recovery was the fact that even before 1300 the whole structure's center of gravity shifted once and for all to the urban economy. The urban economy was the first of the forces affected (and the crisis affected all strata) to recover from the crisis. This it managed to do chiefly by discovering East-Central Europe as the place where its market crisis could be solved and its demand for precious metals be fulfilled[38]

According to this concept, in the later Middle Ages East Central Europe served primarily as a market for the craft products of Western Europe and also as a region providing precious metals for the European financial system. It is certainly well documented that precious metal production expanded significantly in the four-teenth century, especially in Bohemia and Hungary. The growing yields of silver and gold contributed to an increase in purchasing power and thus created better market opportunities for industrial products from other regions. These circumstances cer-tainly cannot be disregarded in defining the role of East Central Europe from the point of view of medieval commercial networks.

Several papers in the current volume offer new perspectives on the trade contacts of the region and the authors have also published other essays and books in non-regional languages about East Central European trade in the Middle Ages. Many new aspects of the early trade after the tenth century are discussed using sources that have been under-utilized in recent scholarly literature. Dariusz Adamczyk,[39] Matthias Hardt,[40] and Bence Péterfi use numismatics, narrative sources, and archae-ology to reconstruct early trade contacts. Beata Możejko,[41] Grzegorz Myśliwski,[42] and Mária Pakucs-Willcocks[43] explore many characteristics of the transit and internal regional trade in the later Middle Ages, also usually underrepresented in the literature. The production, processing, and traffic in precious metals is clearly a predominant element, especially in essays by Dariusz Adamczyk, Matthias Hardt, Roman Zaoral,[44] and Grzegorz Myśliwski. Most aspects of the use of precious metals are comparatively well-documented and also paradigmatic for reconstructing commerce, thus it is an inevitable element of several papers in this volume. The studies of Beata Możejko and Mária Pakucs-Willcocks reveal the external contacts of the region differently from the traditional West-East Central Europe dichotomy and identify the significance of the transit trade.

The articles in this volume will contribute to assessing the foreign trade of East Central Europe as more complex than previously thought and present its compound character. Trade contacts connected the countries of the region in various directions and comprised traffic in very different commercial goods. More than thirty-five years after the publication of Jenő Szűcs's illuminating essay it is apparent that our understanding of the commerce of the region has been modified by several more recent studies.

Medieval commerce in East Central Europe should not be a *terra incognita* for interested readers now, since despite the traditional indifference in the scholarly literature one can find related and appropriate literature for further studies. But the mirror is still somewhat distorted. The specific research issues of East Central Europe are not fully integrated into the general European historiographic tradition and the particular role of East Central Europe in the wider European economy and commerce needs to be revisited as new research questions and proposals develop.

Notes

1 For the concept and the medieval role of East Central Europe, see the recent *Medieval East Central Europe in a Comparative Perspective. From Frontier Zones to Lands in Focus*, ed. Gerhard Jaritz and Katalin Szende (New York: Routledge, 2016).

2 The questions raised in this paper were inspired by the essay of Béla Zsolt Szakács, "The Place of East Central Europe on the Map of Romanesque Architecture," in *Medieval East Central Europe*, 205–224.

3 See the earlier works of the author of this chapter: Balázs Nagy, "The Study of Medieval Foreign Trade of Hungary: A Historiographical Overview," in *Cities – Coins – Commerce. Essays presented to Ian Blanchard on the Occasion of his 70th Birthday*, ed. Philipp Robinson Rössner (Stuttgart: Franz Steiner, 2012), 65–75.

4 *Dictionary of the Middle Ages*, 13 vols, ed. Joseph R. Strayer (Charles Scribner's Sons: New York, 1982–1989); see the entries in vol. 12 by Nina G. Garsoïan, "Trade, Armenian," 96–99; Angelike E. Laiou, "Trade, Byzantine," 100–104; A. L. Udovitch, "Trade, Islamic," i, 105–108, and John E. Dotson, "Trade, Western European," 108–116.

5 Ibid., 113.

6 Paul W. Knoll, "Poland," in ibid., IX, 716–731; John Klassen, "Bohemia–Moravia," in ibid., II, 297–315, and János M. Bak, "Hungary," in ibid., VI, 337–351.

7 *Lexikon des Mittelalters*, I–IX (Stuttgart and Weimar: Metzler, 1977–1999).

8 František Graus, "Böhmen," in ibid., II, col. 335–344; Aleksander Gieysztor, "Polen," in ibid., VII, col. 52–58, and János M. Bak, "Ungarn," in ibid., VIII, col. 1224–1234.

9 *International Medieval Bibliography*, ed. Alan V. Murray (Turnhout and Leeds: Brepols and University of Leeds, 1967–). See also its on-line version at www.brepolis.net (last accessed: 24 October 2017).

10 The indexing system of the IMB makes it possible to limit the search according to a field of study and combine it with a particular country, thus this database is particularly suitable for drawing the conclusions below. The numbers below reflect the data of September 2017.

11 In some cases the indexing of the bibliography entries can be misleading, but one has no reason to suppose that this distortion might significantly modify the representation of a particular discipline or territory in the bibliography.

12 *The Fontana Economic History of Europe. The Middle Ages*, ed. Carlo M. Cipolla (London: Collins, 1972).

13 Jacques Bernard, "Trade and Finance in the Middle Ages," in *The Fontana Economic History of Europe,* 274–338.

14 Ibid., 285.

15 *Europäische Wirtschaftsgeschichte: Mittelalter,* ed. Carlo M. Cipolla and Knut Borchardt (Stuttgart: G. Fischer, 1983), and Carlo Cipolla, *Ouzhou Jingjishi, Zhongshiji Shiqi,* trans. XU Xuan (Beijing: Shangwu Yinshuguan, 1988).

16 M. M. Postan, "Economic Relations between Eastern and Western Europe," in *Eastern and Western Europe in the Middle Ages,* ed. Geoffrey Barraclough (London: Thames and Hudson, 1970), 125–174.

17 *Der Aussenhandel Ostmitteleuropas*: Die ostmitteleuropäischen Volkswirtschaften in ihren Beziehungen zu Mitteleuropa ed. Ingomar Bog (Cologne: Böhlau, 1971).

18 N. J. G. Pounds, *An Economic History of Medieval Europe* (London: Longman, 1974; 2nd ed. London: Longman, 1994).

19 www.worldcat.org/title/economic-history-of-medieval-europe/oclc/600910594?refer er=br&ht=edition (last accessed: 16 September 2017).

20 *Der Aussenhandel Ostmitteleuropas.*

21 *East-Central Europe in Transition: From the Fourteenth to the Seventeenth Century,* ed. Antoni Mączak, Henryk Samsonowicz, and Peter Burke (Cambridge: Cambridge Univresity Press, 1985).

22 Marian Małowist, "Comments on the Circulation of Capital in East-Central Europe," in *East-Central Europe in Transition,* 109–127.

23 *The Cambridge Economic History of Europe from the Decline of the Roman Empire.* ed. J. H. Clapham and Eileen Power (Cambridge: The University Press. New York: Macmillan, 1941).

24 *The Cambridge Economic History of Europe. vol. 2. Trade and Industry in the Middle Ages.* ed. M. M. Postan (2nd ed. Cambridge: Cambridge University Press, 1987).

25 Aleksander Gieysztor, "Trade and Industry in Eastern Europe before 1200," in ibid., 474–524, and Marian Małowist, "The Trade of Eastern Europe in the Later Middle Ages," in ibid., 525–612.

26 On the life and work of Gieysztor, see Jacques Le Goff, "In memoriam. Aleksander Gieysztor (1916–1999)," *Cahiers de civilisation médiévale* 45, no. 180 (2002): 419–424. On Małowist, see *Western Europe, Eastern Europe and World Development, 13th–18th Centuries. Collection of Essays of Marian Małowist.* ed. Jean Batou and Henryk Szlajfer (Leiden and Boston: Brill, 2010).

27 See my earlier review article: Balázs Nagy, "Complaints from the Periphery," *BOOKS – Budapest Review of Books* 6 (1996): 73–78.

28 *Europäische Wirtschafts- und Sozialgeschichte im Mittelalter. (Handbuch der europäischen Wirtschafts- und Sozialgeschichte; Bd. 2),* ed. J. A. van Houtte (Stuttgart: Klett-Cotta, 1980); *Europäische Wirtschafts- und Sozialgeschichte vom ausgehenden Mittelalter bis zur Mitte des 17. Jahrhunderts* (Handbuch der europäischen Wirtschafts- und Sozialgeschichte, 3), ed. Hermann Kellenbenz (Stuttgart: Klett-Cotta, 1986).

29 György Györffy, "Ungarn von 895 bis 1400," in *Europäische Wirtschafts- und Sozialgeschichte im Mittelalter,* 625–655; Aleksander Gieysztor, "Polen zur Zeit der Piasten," in ibid., 703–727; Miroslav Hroch and Josef Petrán, "Die Länder der böhmischen Krone 1350–1650," in *Europäische Wirtschafts- und Sozialgeschichte vom ausgehenden Mittelalter bis zur Mitte des 17. Jahrhunderts,* 968–1005; László Makkai, "Ungarn 1382–1650," in ibid., 1006–1033; Marian Małowist and Adelheid Simsch, "Polen 1450–1650," in ibid., 1074–1096.

30 Jean W. Sedlar, *East Central Europe in the Middle Ages, 1000–1500* (Seattle: University of Washington Press, 1993).

31 Piotr Górecki, *Central European History* 28 (1995): 88–93. See also, János M. Bak, *Speculum*, 71 (1996), 1019–1021.

32 Sedlar, "Commerce and money," in *East Central Europe in the Middle Ages*, 334–361.

33 Nora Berend, Przemysław Urbańczyk and Przemysław Wiszewski, *Central Europe in the High Middle Ages: Bohemia, Hungary and Poland c. 900–c. 1300* (Cambridge: Cambridge University Press, 2013).

34 Szakács, "The Place of East Central Europe," 207.

35 Ahmad Nazmi, *Commercial Relations between Arabs and Slavs, 9th–11th centuries* (Warsaw: Wydawn. Akademickie Dialog, 1998).

36 Balázs Nagy, "Transcontinental Trade from East-Central Europe to Western Europe (Fourteenth and Fifteenth Centuries)," in … *The Man of Many Devices, Who Wandered Full Many Ways. Festschrift in Honor of János M. Bak*, eds. idem and Marcell Sebők (Budapest: Central European University Press, 1999), 347–356.

37 Jenő Szűcs, "The Three Historical Regions of Europe. An Outline," *Acta Historica Academiae Scientiarum Hungaricae* 29 (1983): 131–184. Szűcs's essay was published first in Hungarian in 1981. See idem, "Vázlat Európa három történeti régiójáról," *Történelmi Szemle* 24 (1981): 313–359.

38 Szűcs, "The three historical," 158.

39 Here and below I refer some works of the authors of the present volume which were especially important from the point of view of this essay. Dariusz Adamczyk, *Silber und Macht. Fernhandel, Tribute und die piastische Herrschaftsbildung in nordosteuropaischer Perspektive (800–1100)* (Wiesbaden: Harrassowitz, 2014).

40 Matthias Hardt, *Gold und Herrschaft. Die Schätze europäischer Könige und Fürsten im ersten Jahrtausend.* (Europa im Mittelalter. Abhandlungen und Beiträge zur historischen Komparatistik 6) (Berlin: Akademie, 2004).

41 *New Studies in Medieval and Renaissance Poland and Prussia*, ed. Beata Możejko (London: Routledge, 2017). Idem, "Financial Obligations of the City of Gdansk to King Casimir IV Jagiellon and His Successors in the Light of the 1468–1516 Ledger Book," in *Money and Finance in Central Europe during the Later Middle Ages*, ed. Roman Zaoral (New York: Palgrave Macmillan, 2015) 181–191.

42 Grzegorz Myśliwski, *Wrocław w przestrzeni gospodarczej Europy (XIII – XV wiek): centrum czy peryferie?* [Wrocław in Europe's economic space (13th–15th centuries): Center or periphery?] (Wrocław: Wydawnictwo Uniwersytetu Wrocławskiego, 2009) and idem, "Central Europe," in *Agrarian Change and Crisis in Europe, 1200–1500*, ed. Harry Kitsikopoulos (Routledge Research in Medieval Studies, 1) (New York: Routledge, 2012) 250–291.

43 Mária Pakucs-Willcocks, *Sibiu – Hermannstadt. Oriental Trade in Sixteenth Century Transylvania* (Städteforschung, A 73) (Cologne: Böhlau, 2007).

44 *Money and Finance in Central Europe during the Later Middle Ages*, ed. Roman Zaoral (New York: Palgrave Macmillan, 2015); idem: "Wirtschaftsbeziehungen zwischen Bayern und Böhmen: Die Handelskontakte Prags mit Eger, Regensburg, Nürnberg und Venedig im 13. Jahrhundert," in *Bayern und Böhmen: Kontakt, Konflikt, Kultur*, ed. Robert R. Luft and Ludwig Eiber (Munich: Veröffentlichungen des Collegium Carolinum, 2007), 13–34.

INDEX